CREATING CONTENT MANAGEMENT SYSTEMS IN JAVA

Teaches the architecture, design, code, and creation of a complete CMS in Java

Covers critical design issues, including interface design, multi-tiered architectures, and OOAD

The CD-ROM contains many examples in Java, XML, XHTML, CSS and XSLT, and a Java-based CMS with features such as a search engine, forum manager, skinnable Web site look-and-feel, and a Java administration applet for managing the CMS

Programming Series

ARRON FERGUSON

CREATING CONTENT MANAGEMENT SYSTEMS IN JAVA

CREATING CONTENT MANAGEMENT SYSTEMS IN JAVA

ARRON FERGUSON

CHARLES RIVER MEDIA
Boston, Massachusetts

Cover Design: Tyler Creative

CHARLES RIVER MEDIA
25 Thomson Place
Boston, Massachusetts 02210
617-757-7900
617-757-7969 (FAX)
crm.info@thomson.com
www.charlesriver.com

This book is printed on acid-free paper.

Arron Ferguson. *Creating Content Management Systems in Java.*
ISBN: 1-58450-466-8

Library of Congress Cataloging-in-Publication Data
Ferguson, Arron.
  Creating content management systems in Java / Arron Ferguson.
     p. cm.
  Includes index.
  ISBN 1-58450-466-8 (pbk. with cd : alk. paper) 1. Digital media--Management. 2. Multimedia systems--Management. 3. Java (Computer program language) I. Title.
  TK6680.5.M38 2004
  006.7'6--dc22
                          2006012903

Printed in the United States of America
06 7 6 5 4 3 2 First Edition

To my Lord Jesus Christ my Savior,
and to whom I owe my life.

Contents

Preface

There are many Content Management Systems (CMSs) in existence. There are open source CMS projects that offer limited functionality, all the way to CMS enterprise software (that can cost in the hundreds of thousands), which offer support for an entire organizational entity. What we can learn from all of this is the importance in being able to manage content of all kinds—not just text. There are many different technologies that are used as the foundation for the CMS software. For starters, a programming language is required to articulate the functionality of the CMS. Some of the choices we have are Java™, C#®, PHP, and Ruby to name a few.

Next we need to consider storage technology for persistence. Most CMSs default to a relational database, although many are now starting to (at the very least) support the eXtensible Markup Language (XML) as a transitional data transfer mechanism while some CMSs are actually using XML as the default storage technology. We also need to choose presentation formats for delivering the content to the user. Most CMS solutions will use the Hypertext Markup Language (HTML) and thus require some sort of Web server support—either by running on a Web server, or the CMS itself becomes a Web server. With all of these choices, we can create a solution based on our technology needs and our familiarity of particular technologies.

This book takes the approach that Java offers a powerful programming language and environment (via its virtual machine) and also takes advantage of the Web framework that Java has become famous for: servlet technology running within a Web server. Additionally, that XML can and is able to handle content needs as a native storage mechanism. Using XML as the native storage mechanism automatically simplifies the middleware solutions because much of the Web content delivered today is XML based. If the storage is XML then there is a natural progression in presenting the content to the user as Web content. Thus, much of the talk in this book focuses on XML and XML-related technologies for storing and transforming XML within the rich Java environment. As well, this book walks the reader through a complete working example of a CMS, starting from conceptual ideas in content management, then diving into a pragmatic approach by offering design solutions, to final implementations in each of the tiers of the software that becomes the CMS. In the end, an implemented CMS is offered as an example of what is possible, instead of merely suggesting what may (or may not) be possible.

Target Audience

This book is intended for software developers (specifically Java software developers) who wish to learn more about the field of content management and about CMSs by applying technologies presented in this book to an actual working system. This book leans more toward an applied perspective, giving demonstrations using code to offer the reader a solution on how a feature can be implemented, versus simply talking on a theoretical level about what may or may not be possible.

Even by having narrowed our focus to CMS development in Java, there are still many choices that could be made in presentation technology, although this book focuses on using XML and Extensible Stylesheet Language Transformation (XSLT) for performing transforms. The administration interaction feature offered in this book focuses on using Java applet technology although several other options do exist such as Asynchronous JavaScript and XML (AJAX) and Java Server Faces (JSFes), to name a couple. Readers should already know the Java programming language and have a basic understanding of the Web in order to appreciate many of the topics covered in this book. Readers need not know XML, XSLT, CSS, or XHTML because these topics are covered, although a basic understanding will be helpful.

Summary of Chapters

This book consists of 11 chapters which cover:

> **Chapter 1:** Covers content management in general, including defining goals, type of content, target audience, and the look-and-feel of what your Web site should include. Also covered are how to define content granularity, metadata, the separation of presentation formatting from content, and user interface (UI) design heuristics and choices.

> **Chapter 2:** Looks at some of the finer points of what make up a content management system and then delves into implementation issues such as multi-tiered architectures, scalability issues, security, and performance issues. A design is used to model the content management system that is built through the rest of the book, and finally a look into some of the tools that are used to build the content management system which is offered in this book.

Chapter 3: Investigates some of the important details concerning software licenses including the differences in copyright and copyleft, different perspectives of what open source is, and some of the more commonly used open source licenses in use today including GPL, LGPL, MPL, and the Apache license. Lastly, this chapter looks at some of the complexities in mixing licenses up from different software libraries and applications that are considered as part of a system as a whole.

Chapter 4: Introduces the topic of XML including what XML is and what XML is not. The chapter walks the user through examples of well-formed XML, valid XML, how to use name spaces, entities, and the topic of validation using XML DTD schemas.

Chapter 5: Applies XML knowledge from Chapter 4 to the process of data modeling using XML. The XML data model is compared and contrasted to the relational model and the object model. Other topics covered are document-centric data versus data-centric data, when to use elements versus attributes, granularity, and how to deal with formatting issues in XML. The chapter also looks at how to model many-to-many relationships with XML. The last part of the chapter walks the user through the data model that will be used to define the content management system used throughout the rest of the book.

Chapter 6: Offers a detailed look into using Java APIs for the manipulation of XML content. Topics covered include model driven parsers, event driven parsers, push versus pull parsers, and the benefits and shortcoming of each. The reader is shown a custom document object model for the CMS used throughout the book. Source code is referenced from the CD-ROM.

Chapter 7: Presents the reader with knowledge about how to create a Web application using Java servlets and how to apply this knowledge to the content management system that is developed throughout the book. Topics include servlet technology, multithreading issues, configuring Web applications using deployment descriptors, and how to handle serialized access to shared resources. The last half of the chapter walks the reader through setting up the build project using Apache's Ant build tool and the server side logic which includes source code from several different Java classes that make up the server side logic for the content management system built for the book.

Chapter 8: Discusses protocol topics including some of the finer points of HTTP, the application protocol used for the Web. Actual status codes and HTTP headers for requests and responses are presented and then Java code examples of how to manipulate this data are shown. The reader is then shown the source code for the CMS from the book, which covers how to tunnel object serialization through HTTP so that the client applet can communicate with the server side logic.

Chapter 9: Presents the reader with the admin applet for the CMS and shows how to create layouts and build event handling for complex components that make up the UI that is used with the book's CMS.

Chapter 10: Discusses the differences in HTML versions, focusing on XHTML with an eye for XHTML strict being the emphasized version of HTML that the W3C is directing users toward. Cascading style sheets are investigated, showing how to format and create certain types of style formatting. It also shows the creation of an XHTML template that can be used to style the CMS presentation.

Chapter 11: Introduces the reader to XSLT style sheets and how to refactor XHTML templates. The reader is shown examples of XSLT style sheets from the book's CMS, which allows the Web content to be completely skinnable so that the Web presentation can be changed with the click of a button.

About the CD-ROM: Discusses how to install and build the content management system provided (which is called Kucing CMS—pronounced Kooching) with the book, requirements for building the CMS, and how to use the admin applet that allows the user to manage content for the book's CMS.

Acknowledgments

I feel honored to have been given this opportunity to write this book and I would like to thank a few people who helped me either directly or indirectly. First I would like to thank Jim Walsh, David Pallai, and Jenifer Niles for their help and guidance in answering all of my questions when I had them (there were many!). I would also like to thank my colleagues at the British Columbia Institute of Technology, Burnaby, British Columbia, Canada who have always been supportive when coming to furthering one's knowledge and experience, Ken Takagaki, our Dean, who encourages us to inspire, Paul Harris and the rest of the Super PD Committee for granting me time for this endeavor, Keith Tang for his expertise in SQL and database technology, D'Arcy Smith for his advice in code refactoring, Stephen Meyles for his suggestions with XML data structures, Jim Parry for being more than just an office mate, but also a partner in crime, a great inspiration, my mentor, and a good friend—you have taught me about guinea pigs and chaos ("has learned to *embrace* guinea pigs and chaos!"). I would also like to thank my parents for their encouragement, and most of all I would like to thank my wife June for her love, encouragement, and patience in being a computer-geek widow for a good portion of a year—you are my greatest support of all!

1 Content Management

The information age has helped us to rapidly disseminate information of many differing kinds. One of the biggest strides in advancing the spread of information has been the World Wide Web, better known as the *Web*. Everybody seems to have a Web site these days. There are Web sites for promoting companies and businesses, displaying research content, and sharing software projects. There are Web sites dedicated to individuals who wish to share with the world their personal experiences on a daily basis. Clearly, there is an unprecedented abundance of information in the world today. We have the world at our fingertips. Or do we? The source code listings referenced in this chapter are located on the CD-ROM in the *Chapter 1* folder.

ON THE CD

DEFINING A METHODOLOGY

In the early 1990s, the Web was in its infancy. The number of Web sites was counted in the hundreds or less! Information on the Web was scarce and so finding information was difficult. But by the late 1990s, the Web had taken a whole different characteristic. The problem was no longer trying to find the information, but rather, how to sort through the millions of documents on the Web to find relevant information. The needle in a haystack analogy is an accurate depiction of what the Web is today.

As we find ourselves sorting through the ocean of documents containing irrelevant information, we come to a new milestone in the Web's history: how to better manage information. This is where *content management* becomes essential. From a Web perspective, managing content is more than just creating some content and organizing files into appropriate directories. Content management is all about how to define, categorize, store, and manipulate information. Thus, we need to formalize a process, a *methodology*. The first step is to express what processes or tasks make up this methodology, listed here:

- Defining content
- Categorizing and organizing content
- Storing content
- Manipulating and maintaining content

These tasks are iterative. Without the acceptance of an iterative methodology, we would be committing a non-editable, unchangeable *information design* to an ever-changing piece of work. This contradicts everything we know about Web site content and Web sites in general. At most steps in the methodology, there is the possibility that the process may go forward or that it may go backward and be repeated.

Figure 1.1 shows the *iterative lifecycle* of content management based on our list. Once content is defined, it must be slotted into categories and then organized. Content is then ready to be stored in the appropriate format and chunked to the ap-

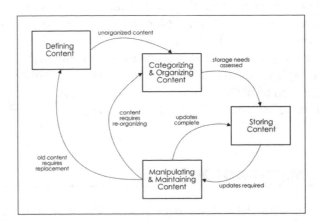

FIGURE 1.1   The iterative lifecycle of the content management methodology.

propriate granularity. A Web site is clearly not a finished work and is in continual need of updating and re-organizing. Once updates are complete, content can then be chunked and stored once again. Sometimes content needs to be re-categorized and re-organized. And finally old content is eventually replaced by new content and the cycle repeats. This methodology is worth formalizing so that this process can be repeated in a timely and consistent manner.

TIP

Choosing a methodology is more important than choosing which particular methodology. If you have already experienced a different methodology and you feel that it serves your purposes of helping to define, categorize, store, and manipulate your content, then you should stick with it. However, the fields of content management and information design are both relatively new, so you may want to read this section regardless of how successful you feel your current methodology is.

DEFINING CONTENT

Before we delve into the features required of a Content Management System (CMS) and how it works, it helps to determine a methodology for defining content first. While defining the content for a small Web site can be trivial, doing so for a large corporation or organization can be quite difficult. The following steps can help alleviate the complexities and reduce the amount of time taken defining content:

- Determining the goal of your site
- What type of content do you require?
- Who is the target audience?
- What technology requirements does the target audience need?

Determining the Goal of Your Site

So you have an idea for a Web site. Now you need to define some of the particulars as to what exactly you are trying to accomplish. Here are some categories of goals that you might want to consider:

Selling a product or a service: Be concise, make information easy to find, don't stretch the truth

Sharing knowledge: Categorize your information into clearly defined topics, have an introduction, topic description, and summary at the end

Creating an online diary: Be creative, try to be exciting, share inspiration

Supporting an online forum: Be clear about what is supported, decide the rules for the forum

Promoting a product, service or idea: Be descriptive, give features and benefits, say why it's good

Making a statement: Don't generalize, don't insult, use facts

Sharing creative works: Categorize with clearly defined types, don't be afraid to discuss your work

Selling a Product or a Service

When you are trying to sell a product or a service, the information should be concise and crystal clear. A potential customer will not spend a lot of time at your site if you make the information hard to find or if the information is overly verbose. For example, read the advertisement in Figure 1.2, and then read the advertisement in Figure 1.3.

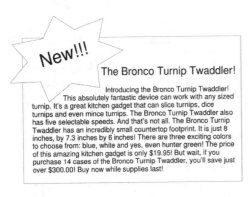

FIGURE 1.2 Advertisement using long description.

FIGURE 1.3 Advertisement using bulleted list.

Aside from the advertisement in Figure 1.3 taking up less space, it is still the clear winner simply because it is concise in making the information easy to gather. What can be easy to forget is that the Web is a different medium than television. The advertisement in Figure 1.2 sounds very much like an (annoying) infomercial. That format works quite well on television, but it doesn't work well within the medium of the Web. Readers of Web pages want their content to the point and they want it now. This is even more important when readers are attempting to purchase something.

It should also be clear to the reader that the information that you have posted is meant to sell a product or a service. A reader should not be confusing your motives of selling with promoting or making a statement. Readers looking for a sale have most likely already decided if they will purchase the product—they don't need to see any more promotional information.

Sharing Knowledge

While selling a product or a service was an example of brevity, sharing of knowledge is broader in nature. While there are times when it's necessary to be brief, sometimes you need to be quite descriptive. It all depends on the knowledge that you are sharing. For example, are you sharing instructions or a recipe? Are you sharing lessons on a particular technology? Are you sharing a review or an article on a product?

When writing information about instructions it is important to remember all details. Do not assume the reader knows what you are talking about. Let's take a look at three different approaches to delivering a set of instructions.

Change the Web look-and-feel:

1. Click "Get List"
2. Choose a look and feel from the list
3. Click "Apply LnF"
4. Done!

That is one example. Another, more detailed example would be:

Once at the form titled "Manage Look and Feel" of the Admin applet, you have the ability to change the Web site's look-and-feel. To do so, follow these steps:

1. Left-click (single-click) Get List. After performing this operation you should see the look-and-feel List Box populated with a list of selectable look-and-feels that can be applied to the Web site. You should see the look-and-feel List Box on the left side of the Form. If instead you encounter a dialog with the message LnF List Request Denied!, then your session may have already timed out. You need to log in again.
2. From the look-and-feel List Box, left-click (single-click) one of the named look-and-feels found in the List component (e.g., Zowie). Notice that the current look-and-feel that the Web site is using is by default selected in the List component.
3. Once you have chosen a different look-and-feel from the List component, left-click Apply LnF. A pop-up dialog box should appear and state: Look and Feel successfully changed. Click your browser's Refresh button to see changes. If you see this dialog, you can press OK, which brings you back to Manage Look and Feel. If instead you encounter a dialog with the message LnF List Request Denied!, then your session may have already timed out. You need to log in again.

And finally the third example is found in Figure 1.4. Looking at all three examples (two lists and a picture in Figure 1.4), the first version of the instructions on how to change the look-and-feel of the Web site gives a low level of detail without much description. For instructions, this is not the best solution. Most people

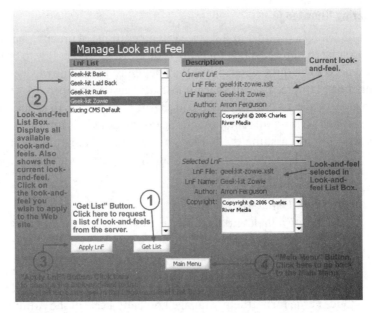

FIGURE 1.4 Instructions using screen capture of application.

become confused and probably even frustrated. In the second example, although the instructions are clear, a reader could still find it easy to get lost if one of the details is misread or ignored. The third version (Figure 1.4) emphasizes the power of images. After all, an image is worth a thousand words. A *screen capture* with annotations is provided giving the reader a very clear idea about the process. Instructions with visualizations and screen captures help immensely.

If you are sharing lessons on a technology or reviewing a product, you should follow the golden rule of teaching: tell them what you'll tell them, tell them, and finally tell them what you told them. That is, start off with an introduction that clearly states what you will talk about, provide your information in detail, and finally summarize what you've covered. This format helps the audience (in this case, your reader) remember the details of what you've covered.

Creating an Online Diary

This is a relatively new use of the Web medium. A site that is created as an online diary is known as a *blog*. The user who creates the blog is referred to as a *blogger*. If you belong to a community of *bloggers,* then you'll be known as a fellow *bloggarian* within that community. Blogs are a form of expression and are used to report daily activities in one's life. It is a modern day version of a diary except with the added characteristic that the diary is open for all to read.

TIP

If you haven't been living in a cave for the last four years, you've no doubt come across the expression blog or blogger. The word originates as a slang term taken from the two words "Web" and "log." Journaling or logging content on the Web is therefore Web logging, or if you pronounce the expression quickly enough the "b" from the word "Web" becomes fused with the word "log" making it sound like "We-blog" or simply "blog."

Information in this form is usually considered to be freeform and does not usually follow the standard rules of conciseness or description. In fact, blogs usually contain *online lingo* rather than proper English or proper grammar. Although freeform is the norm with online diaries, a few rules can still be followed. First, you should try to inform the reader in a way that captivates him. Droning on about how long it took to paint the fence is about as much fun as actually being there and watching it dry. Try to excite the readers. Make them laugh. Offer analogies that may help them understand what you were feeling. Tell a story that makes the reader want to come back tomorrow and read more about your life.

Second, you can use your ability to write your experiences to help others. In this way, an online diary can become therapeutic for both the author as well as for the reader. Sometimes a story of courage can help inspire readers to be more courageous in their own life too. Remember also that if you begin to tell a story just remember that there needs to be a closing to the story. Don't leave the reader hanging—unless of course you intend to bring them back later for a conclusion of your story.

Supporting an Online Forum

Online forums allow for, well, support. There are many different types of support forums ranging from self-improvement and self-help to how to program 3D graphics. But they all share a consistent goal with their information. Provide the user (the user being both the reader as well as the person posting information) a way for discussing a particular topic. As a provider of such a site, you need to consider some of the issues associated with online forums. For example, is this forum going to be moderated? Moderated forums require someone (a *moderator*) to read through the postings on the forum to ensure that: (1) users of this forum are staying on topic, (2) users are not being abusive to others within the forum and, (3) all irrelevant material is removed from the forum. Another issue worth contemplating is whether to allow *anonymous posting*, which means the users do not have to have an account in order to post messages to the forum. This provision may require more of a need for a moderator because there is a good chance that posters may become abusive or simply post *spam*[1]. Although these questions sound more like the types of questions you would ask at the development stage, it is important to state them up front because they are part of your goals.

Online forums can also offer a range of forum topics. For example, you could create a Web site forum for developers programming in *Java*, developers programming in *C++*, and developers programming in *C#*. It is important to decide the scope of your forum at the beginning.

Promoting a Product, Service, or Idea

Sometimes a Web site is geared towards promotion. Salesmen usually talk about features and benefits. These are the two main selling points of any product, service, or even idea. Features should be clearly spelled out for the reader to see. They should usually be in point form and presented as a list. Let's look at The Bronco Turnip Twaddler again.

Features:

- Five selectable speeds
- Dices turnips
- Slices turnips
- Minces turnips
- Works with turnips of all shapes and sizes
- Small countertop footprint ($8" \times 7.3" \times 6"$)
- Comes in three colors: blue, white, hunter green

Whereas features are fairly easy to find, benefits are a little more subjective. What you may think is clear winner of a benefit, the next person may find as only a mild benefit, which may not be enough to entice the reader to "buy in" to your product, service, or idea. It helps to try and think like the target audience for your promotion.

For example, if the promoting item is a product (The Bronco Turnip Twaddler), we can assume the target audience is interested in cooking and has an interest in comparing certain key features. Looking at Table 1.1, we see the relationship between features and benefits.

TABLE 1.1 Features to Benefits

Feature	Benefit
Five selectable speeds	Ability to slice turnips quickly
Small countertop footprint	Product is compact
Small countertop footprint	Stored easily in a cupboard

Selling an idea is a little more difficult because they are less tangible. While the idea is usually either something new or a new way of using an old idea, it's usually a new approach to solve an old problem. For example you could be promoting the idea of using the Bronco Turnip Twaddler to dice carrots instead of turnips. Sure, it probably works with carrots, but it doesn't mention carrots. Justification would be required as to why it can work with carrots. Do carrots fit? Do carrots get cut up properly? Do all size carrots work?

Sometimes promotion is for some form of entertainment. A Web site that is put together to promote a form of entertainment needs to be exciting, attractive, or humorous—or all of the above. For example, many movies that are released from Hollywood have their Web sites set up well in advance. What types of information do they put in to these sites to make them exciting, attractive, or humorous?

Interest can be piqued by offering the reader information that might be considered new or never before seen. Again, using Hollywood movies as examples, behind the scenes secrets can be revealed showing some information about how certain scenes in the movie were made. The reader is then given the impression that they have been allowed to see secret information or information that is not common. This interest can be emphasized by showing images from the movie. Some images can be promotional posters, others publicity shots of the actors. These images can be labeled *wallpaper* for the reader's computer desktop. Previews and sound clips of the movie can also be found and can bring excitement to the reader.

Making a Statement

Making a statement is similar to an online diary because it is usually based on user experience and opinion. If this is your goal, then you want to be clear what it is you are making a statement about. You should usually avoid ranting and making blanket statements. Statements are accepted more if they have firsthand facts or experiences to back them up. Generalizations like Polka Music Sucks usually don't get much attention and are rarely taken seriously. Also, be careful not to offend people. Making fun of race, sex, or religion can easily turn off your readers and depending on the severity of what you say, could get you into legal trouble.

Also consider whether you are expecting debate or feedback on your statement. If others disagree with your statement, then you should expect responses that offer alternative opinions. If you are unwilling to accept debate on an issue that you've raised on the Web, then you may wish to reconsider posting the material.

Sometimes making a statement is not based in words but based instead on art—a great medium for making statements. As the saying goes "A picture is worth a thousand words." Again, it is important to remember that artwork should not be placing you into legal trouble. If the artwork offends race, sex, or religion, then you may face legal action.

Sharing Artwork

The Web is a great medium for exchanging ideas, opinions and even self-promotion. Creating a *virtual gallery* can help promote your abilities. If this is your goal, then you should try to group your artwork into categories. For example, you could lay out your categories like the page shown in Figure 1.5.

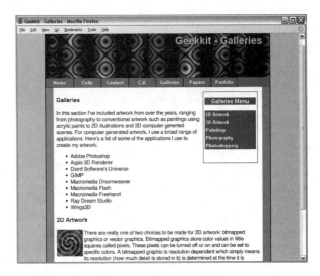

FIGURE 1.5   Web page with artwork categories.

Although the graphics and colors shown on the site in Figure 1.5 can be pleasing to the eye, it's the appropriate method of categorizing the artwork using concise labels for the categories (2D Artwork, 3D Artwork, Paintings, etc.). Another thing to keep in mind is to discuss your artwork as well. Readers are usually more intrigued by your work if you provide possible sources of inspirations, influences, and what you were trying saying with your artwork. You can also talk about the methods you used to reach the end result. This can inspire other artists to use the same techniques you used.

Whenever sharing content, you must ensure that you have the legal right to copy the material you are posting. Always remember to get the artists permission to do so if the artwork is not yours. Licenses and copyright are covered in Chapter 3.

What Type of Content Do You Require?

The Web allows for a rich mixture of content including, but not limited to, text, audio, video, interactive animation, and games. Based on your goal from the previous section, you should be carefully thinking about what types of content help support your goals. Does a video clip help to promote a product? Does interactive animation give a clear step-by-step set of instructions on how to perform a certain task? Multimedia content can help add clarity and style to your content.

Figure 1.6 shows an example of using images and text together to present the content. A recipe accompanied with images showing at least some of the steps of the process can offer an invaluable insight into the cooking process. The reader does not have to make very many guesses about what their dish should look like.

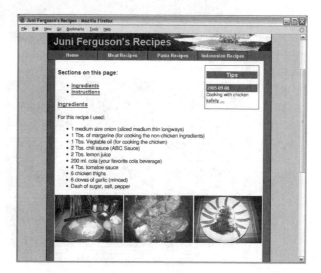

FIGURE 1.6   Multimedia content can help add clarity and style to your content.

Audio and video can also be used but should be used sparingly for several reasons:

- The bandwidth can severely limit users with slower Internet connections from viewing the content
- Audio and video can limit the navigability of the site if too much of the information is found within the audio and video
- Users may not have the multimedia software and hardware on their computer in order to view certain types of video and audio

Any sort of high bandwidth audio and video should be displayed to the user in the form of a text link, an image thumbnail, or both. If it is a video, a screen capture thumbnail of the video can be provided, rather than loading the video into the Web page. In Figure 1.7 thumbnail images in a gallery are hyperlinked to the actual video clips for download. The user can then either save the video (usually by right-clicking on the *hyperlink*) or open a new *Web browser* window to view the video clip. If all videos were embedded in the Web page, the Web browser would attempt to load all of the videos at once. This would most likely take a very long time since the videos could be several dozen megabytes long.

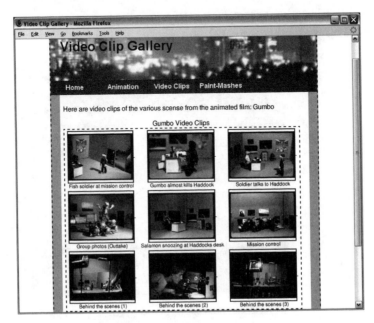

FIGURE 1.7   Video gallery with thumbnails.

Audio should be linked to as well. Typically, audio should never be directly embedded into the Web page itself because the Web browser and the audio plug-in on the reader's computer may automatically start to play the audio, which could be startling to the user.

Much debate rages on about the use of interactive animated graphics for both content and navigation. Although there are no absolute design laws dictating what is good and bad, Table 1.2 lists some heuristics to help you avoid misusing interactive animated graphics.

However, it is all too easy to use multimedia content simply for the sake of using multimedia content (example in Figure 1.8). The Web page looks cluttered, information is hard to read, and if any of the images are flashing or animated, it is nothing more than a distraction for the reader.

TABLE 1.2   Heuristics for Using Interactive Animated Graphics

Reason for Use	Use	Don't Use
Navigation		x
Interactive diagrams	x	
Promotional animation	x	
Instructions	x	
Custom user interfaces		x

FIGURE 1.8   Too much multimedia is embedded within this Web page.

Who Is the Target Audience?

Understanding your target audience is almost as important as specifying your goal for the Web site. You need to address the concerns and interests of your audience. For a small Web site project this can be done by asking a few simple questions.

Why Is the Audience Going to Come to Your Web Site?

Again, this relates to your goal. If you find that the audience is coming to your Web site for a reason that conflicts with your Web site goal, then you need to rethink your goal. If you're promoting material, your audience should be seeking promotional material.

What Level of Knowledge Does the Target Audience Possess?

This is an important question to be able to answer. This helps determine the types of information that you display to the audience. For example, a Web site where the target audience is *Unix* programmers can make several assumptions about the terminology used on the Web site. Anytime the target audience has a high level of knowledge or expertise, you can make assumptions about the language that you use. If the audience is more varied, then you may have to offer alternative terms to the same topics based on the levels of understanding. This can be challenging to keep each section of information consistent.

What Is the Demographic of Your Audience?

Another important consideration is who the audience actually is. Young children, for example, need information that is easy to understand. Simple words should be used and complex concepts should be avoided. Pictures should be used in place of long sentences and paragraphs. A demographic consisting of university students can allow for more complex concepts and explanations. If the language that the content is posted in is not the target audience's primary spoken language, then you need to use wording that is easy to understand—don't use slang.

What Technology Requirements Does the Target Audience Need?

Simple text requires no extra technologies. However, with video or sound, certain Web browser plugins are expected, as is the requirement of having appropriate supporting hardware. You should also consider the demographic of your target audience. For example, if the target audience is children under the age of 12, then they may not have the ability (or authority) to download certain plugins in order for certain types of media to be displayed.

CATEGORIZING AND ORGANIZING CONTENT

Categorizing is the process of placing information items into groups. Organizing is the process of arranging those items by some specified rule. It is important to group items of information in a way that provides an association with those items within the group. Once the items of information have been grouped, the arrangement of items can be chosen. Arrangement allows for items to be ordered based on some set principle. This process of grouping and arranging can be difficult for the following reasons:

- Categories are usually context sensitive
- Importance of categories is often subjective
- Granularity of categories can sometimes be difficult to define

- Items may sometimes cross several different categories
- Arrangement may not always be important or significant

To test these reasons, let's look at an example of some items that need to be categorized and organized:

Unordered, ungrouped list: apple, pear, banana, orange, grape, kiwi, peach, watermelon, cantaloupe, plum, cherry, cranberry, lime, lemon, papaya, pineapple

Based on the previous ungrouped, unordered list of fruit, let's create some groups and arrange them:

TABLE 1.3   Fruit Categories One

Category 1	Category 2	Category 3
Apple	Kiwi	Banana
Cantaloupe	Lemon	Pear
Cherry	Lime	Pineapple
Cranberry	Papaya	
Grape	Watermelon	
Orange		
Peach		
Plum		

TABLE 1.4   Fruit Categories Two

Category 1	Category 2
Apple	Banana
Cherry	Cantaloupe
Cranberry	Kiwi
Grape	Lemon
Peach	Lime
Pear	Orange
Plum	Papaya
	Pineapple
	Watermelon

TABLE 1.5 Fruit Categories Three

Category 1	Category 2	Category 3
Apple	Cherry	Banana
Grape	Peach	Orange
Orange	Plum	Grape
Papaya		Watermelon
Pear		Cantaloupe
Watermelon		Cranberry
		Lime
		Lemon
		Pineapple

Because categories are context sensitive, it may be difficult for readers to understand the reasoning for choosing the defined categories. For example, what categories have been used in Table 1.3? It's not apparently obvious. Only when you are told that the categories are based on shape (spherical shaped in Category 1, oval shaped in Category 2, and miscellaneous shape in Category 3) does this categorization make any sense[2]. Context-sensitive categories are usually problematic unless the context can be clearly defined. If categories are used as menu items or links, there should be no need for explanation as to what the categories are, other than a label for the category name (e.g., spherical). It should be apparent. Another or additional way to ensure that the reader has a clear understanding of categories is to use symbols— a powerful method for providing clear category types. In fact, if chosen appropriately, symbols can be used on their own and can even be used across languages and cultures. Labels and symbols are discussed in more detail in Chapter 9.

Often the actual choice of categories is subjective. One person may feel that a particular category choice is quite important, yet others may not see the significance. By looking at Table 1.4, can you see what the categories are? They are categorized by whether the skin on the fruit can be eaten (Category 1) or not (Category 2). This choice of categorizing fruit by edible skin may be unimportant to most people. Others may prefer that fruits be categorized by which part of the world the fruit comes from, or the types of sugar that are found in a particular fruit. Even more subjective can be the choice for which particular category an item should be placed. Most people agree that a banana's skin is inedible; however, some may decide that apple skin is inedible and therefore may disagree with it in the eat skin category. Because of the subjective nature of these chosen categories, the end result may not be as obvious.

Granularity is challenging too because it requires a degree of subjective opinion. Look again at Table 1.3 and the choice made for shape categories. Is it sufficient to create only a spherical category, oval shape category, and lastly a miscellaneous category? Should there be other categories? Elongated or tube shaped (like bananas)? How about a shape category with a large amount of surface area (i.e., bumpy) such as pineapples? The answer to the granularity question can usually be better answered by deciding which is more important: (1) the categories themselves, or (2) the fact that each category has at least two or more items in it. In Table 1.3 the emphasis was placed on each category having two or more items in it. A more scientific approach to creating categories would probably be to choose a finer granularity even if it meant that each group could have only one item in it.

Another problem is when an item can be placed in two or more categories. Take a look at Table 1.5. The categories are based on whether the fruit has objectionable seeds in it (Category 1), the fruit has pits in it (Category 2), and the fruit has no objectionable seeds or pits in it at all (Category 3). Watermelon is found in two categories because it comes either with or without seeds. Likewise, we find oranges and grapes in both the objectionable seed category and the no objectionable seed category. This problem may be pointing to the fact that the categories chosen are not appropriate because they do not concisely separate items into different categories.

Lastly, when categories are created, organizing (arranging) is then performed on the items within each category. Most of the time it is important to chose a particular arrangement. In the very least, the arrangement can be made by sorting the items alphabetically in ascending order. Other choices may be to arrange the items lexicographically or by size, location, or color. However, there may be times when the arrangement is simply not needed. An example would be a multiple choice exam. The order of the questions within the exam would be insignificant and, in fact, may be unwanted. Arrangement in this case would be meaningless.

STORING CONTENT

Defining a methodology for content management requires a commitment to a particular storage procedure and format. Although this sounds more like an implementation issue that should only be considered at the implementation phase, the decisions about storage greatly affect the management of content.

Granularity of Content

As we saw in the categorizing and organizing process of the previous section, defining granularity can be difficult. This is especially true when storing content. The question becomes to what granularity level do we choose to break down the content?

Is a transaction record a sufficient level of granularity? Or do we need to break that down further? This process of breaking down items is called *chunking*. Chunking allows us to choose a level of granularity that meets the needs of content management. Each chunk of content becomes a unit of measure within the content management application. An example would be a date value. Is it sufficient to chunk the date down to the value April 1, 2006? Or do we need to perform more chunking so that the date is broken down into three separate values of month, date, and year? A useful way to guide this chunking process is to use the following heuristics:

- Chunk atomicity
- Chunk scope is searchable
- Chunk is meaningful

Chunk Atomicity

When content is chunked, it is important to ensure that an individual chunk is one indivisible element rather than a composite chunk made of up several elements. A chunk of content that cannot be broken down any more is said to be *atomic*. Figure 1.9 shows a content structure describing a record. The record element itself is composed of three child elements (customer, purchase and comment). The customer element contains several of its own child elements as well, including a name element. The name element that belongs to the customer element has two child elements: first and last, which describe the customer's first and last name respectively. This level of granularity makes sense since a name (in this example) requires both a first and last name. Without going this far, the customer element's child element name would not be atomic. Usually it is important to ensure that all chunks of content are atomic for accurate organizing, categorizing, searching, and indexing.

Chunk Scope Is Searchable

Another heuristic that is useful is determining whether or not the chunk is at a level of scope that is searchable. That is, will the chunk of content be used by some sort of search process in the application using this content? Referring to Figure 1.9, the record element contains a comment child element (last element). The textual data found within that chunk of content is made up of two sentences. Should the comment element be chunked again into a group of two child elements of type sentence elements? Or how about going even further to word elements? If we assume that comment elements will be searched for only particular words, then it is appropriate to simply leave the content element at that level of granularity and not perform any more chunking. If, however, we were interested in sentence structure and the rules of English language grammar (e.g., if we were writing grammar-checker software), then we would probably want to perform chunking to a finer level of granularity.

Chunk Is Meaningful

When we say that a chunk is meaningful, we are stating that its value contains a decipherable piece of content. The chunk can hold meaning without being grouped with other chunks. In Figure 1.9, there is an `address` element (child element of the `customer` element). The value given for the address element is "3700 Willingdon Avenue." Is this chunk of data meaningful? Could we break this down into three subelements (number, street name, and street type)? The answer to this is not so clear. It would depend on the business rules of the software managing the content. If, for example, the software was a *Geographic Information System (GIS)*[3], then it would probably make sense to break the element down into the three subelements in case there is a Willingdon Avenue and a Willingdon Street. A transaction recording system may not need this level of granularity for the addresses and would most likely find the current address granularity sufficient.

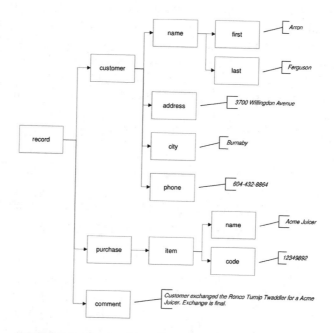

FIGURE 1.9   Content describing a record.

NOTE

Although we have so far only talked about granularity and chunking textual content, the same rules can be applied to other types of content such as images, video clips, sound clips, and interactive multimedia animation. The process does become a little more difficult though because file formats for images, sound, and video require complex codec (coder/decoder) software that has the ability to extract the content from the files. Because of this, it may be difficult to chunk, for example, video content into pieces rather than one whole clip. However, given the right codecs, video could be chunked into scenes or shots (or even individual frames) and stored as a series of individual files. This would be a useful feature for an application that allows users to perform video editing where raw video footage is given to the application and then chunked into shots.

The Need for Metadata

As the content management needs grow in complexity, so do the needs to store information about the management of content itself. An application that contains many different types of content (text, images, video, audio, interactive animation), that has many different categories of content (e.g., reviews, research documents, news items, etc.), and that has many different authors needs to store information about the type of content, ownership, author, category, and update permissions within that application. Therefore, we need *metadata*—data about data. Metadata makes it easier for applications to differentiate between different chunks of data. For example, looking at Figure 1.10, we see some content about a GUI component called a List Box. Using the rules we discussed previously about granularity, we can chunk the content into a title, two paragraphs, a figure that contains an image, and an important note about the List Box. Listing 1.1 shows the chunked textual content that is used to represent the finished content from Figure 1.10.

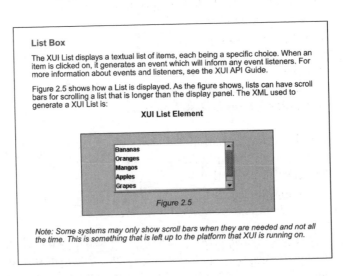

FIGURE 1.10   Example chunk of content.

In Listing 1.1 it may not be too easy to interpret the textual content as a title, two paragraphs, a figure, and a note. This is because the content has been separated from its formatting. It is even more difficult for software to interpret the structure that we've just described.

LISTING 1.1   Chunked Textual Content without Metadata

```
__List Box__
The XUI List displays a textual list of items, each being a
specific choice. When an item is clicked on, it generates an
event which will inform any event listeners. For more
information about events and listeners, see the XUI API Guide.

Figure 2.5 shows how a List is displayed. As the figure shows,
lists can have scroll bars for scrolling a list that is longer
than the display panel. The XML used to generate a XUI List is:

XUI List Element
** "./images/figure-2.5.png" **
Figure 2.5

Note: Some systems may only show scroll bars when they are
needed and not all the time. This is something that is left up
to the platform that XUI is running on.
```

Throughout this book the terms content, information, and data are used. It is important to make the distinction between them. Content is the general description for all types of media (text, images, sound clips, video clips, and interactive animation). Information refers to the actual knowledge which is made up of (sometimes) many pieces of data. Factual statements are called data. Data is used in the construction and composition of information, and information that is stored in various different media formats is collected as content.

To address this limitation, we might decide to interpret two underscore characters before and after a phrase to mean a title, and we may also interpret two new line characters to mean that we've begun a new paragraph. However, what if the user typing the content (or the application acting on the user's behalf) decides to place only one underscore character before and after the phrase that constitutes the title? What if the user stops (or forgets) to place two new line characters after what is considered a paragraph? Any application performing content management quickly loses its ability to search, categorize, or update content. Listing 1.2 displays the same raw textual data with the addition of metadata. The metadata is in the form of tags (shown in bold). There are `title` begin and end tags wrapped around the title data, `paragraph` begin and end tags wrapped around paragraph data, a figure tag that contains information inside of it for constructing a figure, and finally there are note begin and end tags for note data.

LISTING 1.2   Chunked Textual Content with Metadata

```
<title>List Box</title>
<paragraph>The XUI List displays a textual list of items, each
  being a specific choice. When an item is clicked on, it
  generates an event which will inform any event listeners. For
  more information about events and listeners, see the XUI API
  Guide.</paragraph>
<paragraph>Figure 2.5 shows how a List is displayed. As the
  figure shows, lists can have scroll bars for scrolling a list
  that is longer than the display panel. The XML used to
  generate a XUI List is:</paragraph>
<figure title="XUI List Element" url="./images/figure-2.5.png"
  caption="Figure 2.5"/>
<note>Some systems may only show scroll bars when they are
  needed and not all the time. This is something that is left up
  to the platform that XUI is running on.</note>
```

Based on the metadata within our content, we have allowed any software application the ability to not only search words, but search for a word found only within a paragraph, search for a title based on a particular name, search for important notes, search for all references to a particular image, and count paragraphs. Not only do we open up our ability to search, but we also add the benefit of being efficient in doing so because we can choose to search only one type of content chunk.

Metadata isn't only for textual data. It is also found in other types of content such as images. Let's look at the *Portable Network Graphics (PNG)* image file format for examples of metadata. Figure 1.11 depicts the file format structure for the PNG image file format [Adler03]. It contains a signature at the beginning that denotes that the file is of type PNG. Following the signature is a series of chunks (formally called chunks in the PNG specification). The first chunk is of type IHDR (header) which contains information such as the image's width, height, bit depth (pixel depth), etc. The second chunk is of type PLTE (palette) which contains red, green, and blue triples. The third and subsequent chunks are of type IDAT and contain the actual image data. Figure 1.11 also gives further detail into subchunks (called fields in the PNG specification). The last chunk is of type IEND (image trailer) which denotes that the end of file has been reached.

A software application providing content management could use this information to then search through all PNG files in a filesystem and possibly categorize images based on width and height, or sort images based on bit depth. We could even take this further. Because we can search for chunks that contain image data, we could have our software application decode the image data into a format-independent

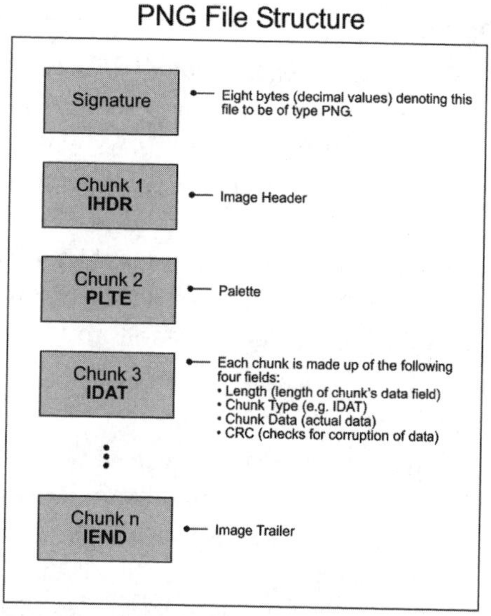

PNG File Structure

Signature — Eight bytes (decimal values) denoting this file to be of type PNG.

Chunk 1
IHDR — Image Header

Chunk 2
PLTE — Palette

Chunk 3
IDAT — Each chunk is made up of the following four fields:
• Length (length of chunk's data field)
• Chunk Type (e.g. IDAT)
• Chunk Data (actual data)
• CRC (checks for corruption of data)

⋮

Chunk n
IEND — Image Trailer

FIGURE 1.11   The PNG file structure.

manner and pass this data to another program with the ability to scan the image data and recognize certain types of shapes, for example, people. A search could be performed on a large number of PNG images for a certain person. This type of content management would be an invaluable tool for law enforcement.

NOTE

The need for metadata is becoming more and more important for content management and the Web in general. Many different initiatives are involved in formalizing metadata. One such initiative is the Dublin Core Metadata Initiative (DCMI), which has created a metadata format that can be used to provide information about content. Some of the types of information found in the DCMI's metadata element set include title, contributor, author, publisher, and rights. By creating such a standard, Internet applications can use this metadata for searching, cataloging, and organizing content. For more information about the DCMI, visit their Web site at: http://dublincore.org/.

Storage Container Considerations

After content has been chunked to the appropriate level of granularity and metadata has been created, the focus then shifts to storage requirements. Because there can be so many different types of content, choosing a storage container can be quite difficult. Even if all of the content is textual, the choice can still be confusing.

Relational Databases

A *relational database management system (RDBMS)* is a practical choice if most of the textual information consists of *records,* such as in a *transaction processing system.* An RDBMS stores all information into *tables* with records being *rows* (also called *tuples*) in each table. Records can then have key data values to uniquely identify that particular record. References to those unique keys can help make searching for complex relationships easier. Another advantage is that the textual content can be broken down to a very fine level of granularity. Since RDBMS technology is mature (over twenty years), it is considered a stable and efficient choice.

Flat File

Flat file storage simply means that the textual content is stored in files within a file-system. There is no consideration given to granularity of the textual content, although the textual content can be broken up into separate files. This choice can be useful if the textual content being stored does not require a lot (or any) referencing or indexing and just requires simple word searches. Another reason for choosing flat file storage is that the amount of textual content is enormous. For example, a search engine for the Web would be fast if all it had to do was search for key words found in one or two text files.

XML

Using the *Extensible Markup Language (XML)* as a storage container is still considered a relatively new concept. One of XML's greatest strengths is its extensibility (that's the 'X' in XML). New *data structures* can be created as the need arises, so complex *data modeling* can be supported. Since XML is text based, XML documents can easily be read by applications existing on multiple computer platforms and operating systems. XML documents can also be easily read and edited by users since the XML is currently stored in text files and not binary files.

Multimedia Storage Needs

Support for the storage of image data, sound data, video data and interactive animation is still considered sparse, at best. Because of a few issues, few applications can actually store and manipulate multiple types of media.

Codec Complexity

Codecs are usually complex to implement (especially for video data). Because of this, it is often expensive to pay software developers to create software that is able to read and write all of the various different video and sound formats. Even if price is overlooked, the development of codec software can take a long time (months). It can be quite frustrating to spend several months completing a codec for a particular video format only to find that there is a newer version available. And lastly, complexity increases the probability of software bugs.

Media Type Variety

Not only is there a large amount of different types of content (image, sound, video, and interactive animation content) there is also a large number of different formats that are used to store these different types of creative works. For example, some of the more common image file formats to choose from are *JPEG, GIF, BMP, TIFF, PNG,* and *TGA.* Although they are all image file formats, they do indeed store information differently. Although they all support some form of compression, JPEG supports a variety of compression techniques, whereas TGA and BMP support rudimentary compression. JPEG offers the most compression but at the expense of quality because it throws out some information in order to deflate file sizes considerably. TIFF, TGA, and PNG all offer extra channels, although TIFF allows for more than just one extra channel. GIF offers animation (multiple images stored as one image), whereas none of the other file formats offer this. And although GIF does not throw out information in order to reduce file size, it does throw out color information which can cause images to appear grainy. Reflecting upon this, it is apparent that it would take several months to develop support within a storage container that was able to read and write (decode and encode) all of these image file formats.

Legal Issues With Codecs

Content types such as video are usually accompanied by proprietary codecs that require strict licensing and fees for use. For example, the Microsoft® *Audio-Video Interleave (AVI)* format can use the *DivX®* codec. A storage container supporting AVI with the DivX codec would require a storage container administrator to download (and pay for) the DivX codec. A company releasing multimedia storage container software would not be able to bundle their application with the DivX unless they worked out a licensing agreement with DivX, Inc., which is assuming such an agreement could be reached. Because there are many different codecs (just for the AVI format), the licensing issues would become complex and potentially costly.

Large Size of Content

Image content, video content, audio content, and interactive animation content are all usually considered to be quite large in file size (compared to simple text files). Any storage container maintaining this type of content would have to find an efficient way to store as well as retrieve the content. For example, if a user is attempting to view 30 seconds of video starting after the first five minutes, the storage container has to read through to that point in the video file. For a video with dimensions of 640-pixels wide by 480-pixels tall, 24-bit color (eight bits for each of the red, green, and blue channels respectively), with a frame rate of 30 frames per second (fps), then the storage container has to start reading at byte 8,294,400,000—roughly 8.3 gigabytes worth before arriving at the right point. We calculate this by:

$$640\ pixels\ wide \times 480\ pixels\ tall \times \frac{(24\ bits\ per\ pixel)}{(8\ bits\ per\ channel)} \times 30\ fps \times 60\ sec.\ per\ min. \times 5\ min \approx 8.3\ GB$$

Because most programming languages give us the ability to access random files by simply providing a *file pointer* value (the value being the byte number to start reading from), things aren't too difficult if we can remember our formula. However, if video is compressed, our formula won't work because compression changes the position of video we are looking for, and we'll be at the mercy of the codec to help us determine where to start reading. References to particular chunks of content (in this case second's worth of video) may cause unacceptable wait times for users searching for content.

Granularity Complexities

Choosing granularity for chunking for any type of content other than textual content can be extremely challenging. Even with image content there are a few different ways to chunk content. Figure 1.12 shows three different ways that the original image data can be chunked. The first option shows each color channel (red, green, and blue) being used to chunk the image data. This would be an appropriate method for an image processing application that required fine tuning of each of the separate color channels in order to perform *color correction*. The second option shows the image data being chunked into smaller blocks of data. This method might prove useful for an application that displays only certain parts of an image. An example might be a *facial compositing* program where each block contains only a portion of the face. This would allow the software to construct a person's face based on blocks chosen by the user. The third option shows the image data being chunked based on layers. Each layer has transparent pixels so that layers underneath are visible. This method could offer applications the ability to create new composite images with different backgrounds and different foregrounds such as an animation program.

Because of the specialized needs of a particular software application, the choice made for chunking image data would be have to be thought out and done so well in advance. Video is even more difficult because it contains multiple images. A video could be chunked based on channels, blocks, layers, frames, shots, or even scenes. The chunking could get quite complex if, for example, the video was both chunked in shots as well as in layers. However, doing so would allow a content management application to build up a store of video clips of background shots that could be used over and over again for different videos such as interviews. The audio could also be separated and stored in separate left and right channels.

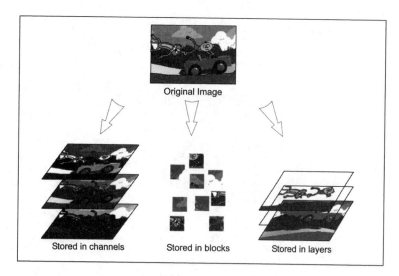

Original Image

Stored in channels   Stored in blocks   Stored in layers

FIGURE 1.12 Different ways of chunking the image data.

Separating Content from Presentation Formatting

One of the reasons for cost and time getting in the way of revamping Web content is due to the amount of time spent on changing the presentation of the content. A company that wishes to update its Web site will spend quite a bit of time waiting for designers to apply a new look-and-feel to the company Web site. This process can be simplified greatly by doing what's called separating the content from the presentation information. When content is separated from the presentation information, the content is removed and stored in a separate file, files or content container than where the presentation information is stored. Figure 1.13 displays how content can be separated from presentation formatting. On the left side, we see the textual data from Listing 1.2. On the right side, we see the data describing formatting. Both are stored in separate files. A program that manages content would contain program code with the ability to use the presentation formatting information to format the content and render what we saw in Figure 1.10 (also visible at the bottom of Figure 1.13).

This separation of content from the presentation formatting may seem like an extra unwanted amount of complexity in our content management application. However this separation buys us several advantages:

- Presentation changes independent of content
- Separation of duties
- Presentation consistencies easily achieved
- Multiple presentation formats easily attained

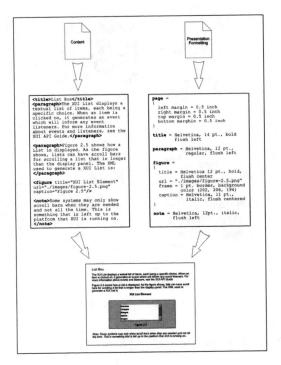

FIGURE 1.13 Content separated from presentation formatting.

Presentation Changes Independent of Content

With a large Web site, the amount of content and the amount of types of content can be large. Because of this, it may be difficult and time consuming to be able to sort through the vast pages of information and attempt to remove any presentation formatting from the content. It can be all too easy to accidentally remove content instead of just removing or changing the presentation formatting. With the content separate from the presentation formatting, it can be guaranteed that none of the content will be edited or deleted during the process of editing or replacing the presentation formatting information.

Separation of Duties

The duty or job of creating, editing, and maintaining content is not the same as presentation formatting. If we think about a newspaper for example, would it make sense for the columnists and reporters to be responsible for how their articles are laid out on the page? Should we ask them to pick a font, pick a type size? The answer of course is no. Then why should (do) we expect a content provider for a Web site to be responsible for presentation formatting as well? By separating the content from the presentation formatting, content providers are removed from the design task of creating a Web look-and-feel (via the presentation formatting).

Presentation Consistencies Easily Achieved

Maintaining a large Web site poses the challenge of keeping the presentation formatting consistent. It is all too easy to forget to bold a heading or correctly choose a particular color for hyperlinks. By separating the content from the presentation formatting, we can develop templates (rule sets) that are used by our application software. The software can use our templates to format the entire Web site based on the rules within that template. Because of this, the formatting is consistent (either consistently what we want or consistently not what we want).

Multiple Presentation Formats Easily Attained

Because presentation formatting has been removed from the content, we can create several presentation formatting rule sets. For example, we can decide that we're going to create one presentation formatting rule set that uses small layouts for devices that cannot display a lot of content at once (e.g., cell phones or *personal digital assistants (PDAs)*). We can create another presentation formatting rule set that displays a lot of color and a rich layout for computers with feature-capable Web browsers. An additional, presentation formatting rule set could be created that feeds the textual data into a *voice synthesis engine* that can read out the content for viewers who are visually impaired. Because the content is separated from the presentation formatting, when we want to create a new rule set, we don't have to worry about updating the content, we just create a new rule set.

We have simply touched the surface in terms of removing the content from the presentation formatting. There are many implementation details concerning how to attain a complete separation. These details are in Chapter 9.

MANIPULATING AND MAINTAINING CONTENT

The beginning of this chapter showed that a Web site is an ever-changing piece of work. Web sites that don't change rarely exist on the Web for more than a couple of years. This dynamic nature requires our content management methodology to allow for manipulation and maintenance of our content.

Granularity and Manipulation

As we discovered when we talked about storing content, we realized that granularity of content and chunking both become issues. This issue is revisited at the manipulation and maintaining phase or simply editing. Content that is scheduled for updating needs to be presented to a user so that the user can make the required changes. What level of granularity do we present to the user concerning the content (assuming for now we're just discussing textual content)? Do we present a word, a sentence, a paragraph, or a whole document to the user? These questions cannot be answered without knowing some of the details of the content. Again, we can use a set of heuristics to determine what level of granularity is desirable by looking at Table 1.6. In this table, all of the listed types of textual content suggest multiple levels of granularity.

In the least, it helps if the user has options for editing. For example, in editing an article it would be a useful feature to have the ability to only see one particular paragraph or to be able to change the whole article based on the document level. It would be useful to be able to edit individual fields in a contact list as well as delete individual records. Another reason why there are several granularity levels is because content may be different in size. If an article is quite large, the choice for editing may only be at the paragraph level. However, if the article is quite small, then a document level of granularity might make more sense.

TABLE 1.6   Heuristics for Granularity of Textual Content

Type	Field	Record	Sentence	Paragraph	Document
Advertisement			x	x	
Article				x	x
Contact List	x	x			
Forum		x	x	x	
Presentation				x	x
Research Paper				x	x
User Profile	x	x	x		

Remember, these are the rules for editing the content, not describing it. We need to be careful about the granularity of the content that we present to the user. If we choose too large of a chunk of content to the user, there will be extra processing overhead for sending and receiving large amounts of content data. Not only that, but it may present a situation where a user accidentally edits something they are not supposed to change. If we choose a chunk that is too small, the user can grow frustrated with the content management application because he will be spending much time in the user interface requesting content. If bandwidth is limited, this further compounds the frustration.

Metadata Requirements

As we saw in the section about storing content, metadata is important in allowing a content management enabled application to perform useful operations on the content, such as searching. When we present the feature of editing, we find even more need for metadata. The metadata tags shown in Listing 1.2 (which represented the raw textual data of Figure 1.10) provided granularity chunking that was appropriate for searching and storage, but there is no way of knowing who created the content or when it was created or edited. Listing 1.3 provides some additional metadata (shown in bold) that can help address this need.

LISTING 1.3   Chunked Textual Content with Author/Date Metadata

```
<title authorID="A32-094" created="1105955589625"
 edited="1114743888431">List Box</title>
<paragraph authorID="A32-094" created="1105955589625"
 edited="1114743888431">The XUI List displays a textual list of
 items, each being a specific choice. When an item is clicked
 on, it generates an event which will inform any event
 listeners. For more information about events and listeners,
 see the XUI API
 Guide.</paragraph>
<paragraph authorID="A32-094" created="1105955589625"
 edited="1114743888431">Figure 2.5 shows how a List is
 displayed. As the figure shows, lists can have scroll bars for
 scrolling a list that is longer than the display panel. The
 XML used to generate a XUI List is:
 </paragraph>
<figure authorID="A32-094" created="1105955589625"
 edited="1114743888431" title="XUI List Element"
 url="./images/figure-2.5.png" caption="Figure 2.5"/>
<note authorID="A32-094" created="1105955589625"
 edited="1114743888431">Some systems may only show scroll bars
 when they are needed and not all the time. This is something
 that is left up to the platform that XUI is running on.</note>
```

Because of the additional metadata found in Listing 1.3, a content management application can present users with information about who created the content (based on an author ID), when the content was created, and when the content was edited last. The application could use this metadata to determine who has editing and viewing rights, and to provide logs concerning updates done on the site.

Multiuser Issues

Having talked about both granularity and additional metadata requirements for editing, we can now address the issue of multiuser applications. Most (if not all) content management applications provide support for many different users and even several different types of users. After all, content rarely comes from just one source. Because of this, the granularity and metadata requirements can help shape multiuser requirements. When a user is about to edit a particular chunk of content, it is assumed that the content the user is editing is locked. By locking that particular chunk of content, we mean that no other user can edit or change that content. Not only that, but if that chunk of content contains other subchunks of content, then those subchunks should also be locked. This would be very important in the case where a user was deleting a chunk of content at the same time another user was attempting to edit a subchunk of the first user's chunk of content. This would cause inconsistencies in the content and would probably cause many errors in the software application. Listing 1.4 offers one additional piece of information.

LISTING 1.4   Chunked Textual Content with Locking Metadata

```
<title authorID="A32-094" created="1105955589625"
edited="1114743888431" locked="true">List Box</title>
<paragraph authorID="A32-094" created="1105955589625"
edited="1114743888431" locked="true">The XUI List displays a
textual list of items, each being a specific choice. When an
item is clicked on, it generates an event which will inform
any event listeners. For more information about events and
listeners, see the XUI API Guide.</paragraph>
<paragraph authorID="A32-094" created="1105955589625"
edited="1114743888431" locked="true">Figure 2.5 shows how a
List is displayed. As the figure shows, lists can have scroll
bars for scrolling a list that is longer than the display
panel. The XML used to generate a XUI List is:</paragraph>
<figure authorID="A32-094" created="1105955589625"
edited="1114743888431" locked="true" title="XUI List Element"
url="./images/figure-2.5.png" caption="Figure 2.5"/>
<note authorID="A32-094" created="1105955589625"
edited="1114743888431" locked="true">Some systems may only
show scroll bars when they are needed and not all the time.
This is something that is left up to the platform that XUI is
running on.</note>
```

By placing metadata in our chunked textual content that holds state about whether or not it's locked, the content management application can use this information to determine whether any user is allowed to edit (or even read) this chunk of content. Lastly, we could take this one step further and allow for different permissions based on the type of account that the user has. Table 1.7 shows the permissions and types of accounts for consideration.

TABLE 1.7   Permissions and Account Type Matrix

Account Type	Read	Write	Edit	Delete	Create
Author	x	x	x	x	x
Editor	x		x		
Proof Reader	x		x		

PRESENTING CONTENT

After defining content, categorizing and organizing it, dealing with the storage of content, and the manipulation and maintaining of content, we finally need to work out the details of presenting content. For a CMS there are two areas of content presentation: end user content presentation, and administration user content presentation. Both areas require careful consideration as to the look-and-feel, layout, composition, fonts used, and interactive components offered. We can use the same technology to present the content (e.g., Web documents and supporting scripts), or we can use a combination of Web documents (for the end user content), as well as a full-fledged programming language (for the administration user content).

The administration content is the content presented to users who are administrating the CMS site and performing procedures such as adding and deleting users, adding new pages to the CMS, and deleting old news items from the news section of the CMS. This is in sharp contrast to the end user who is simply viewing content and not necessarily manipulating content.

In the case of end user content, a particular format needs to be chosen for presentation delivery. Many free and commercial CMSs in circulation today use HTML (or XHTML) as the presentation format for delivery of content. This is useful because the Web is a standard that many can use to display content, not to mention there are many supporting technologies that can be used to deliver the Web documents [CMSMatrix06]. Large corporate CMS solutions may use a choice of formats including Web documents (HTML) and other content formats.

In the case of content that is being presented to an administration user, our choices become a little more complex because the user needs for interactivity increase based on maintenance and manipulation (adding, editing, and deleting content) requirements. Because of the need for higher interactivity, there is a need for user interface components (also known as widgets or controls) that allow the user to carry out certain operations such as pressing buttons, choosing items from lists, and typing text.

What Look-and-Feel Do You Require?

You shouldn't judge a book by its cover, but the truth is most people do. For this reason, choosing an appropriate look-and-feel is quite important. Look-and-feel can be described as the visual qualities and interactive behavior of a *user interface* (*UI*) that distinguishes it from other user interfaces. Some of the visual characteristics that can be differentiated are:

- Color
- Color scheme
- Typeface
- Layout
- Groupings
- Shading
- Shape

Behavioral characteristics can include (but not limited to):

- Types of UI components
- Which mouse buttons are recognized
- How UI component selection is handled
- Defined mnemonics and keyboard shortcuts
- How the help system responds to the user
- The types of sounds that are associated with certain UI interactions

NOTE

Although the previous two lists define a rich set of characteristics, many are unavailable to Web page designers. This is because of the limited features of Web browsers and their representation of Web content. This lacking is however being addressed with AJaX (which is a re-bundling of current Web technologies) in the hopes that rich graphical user interfaces can be provided within a Web page without the need for additional plugin support. Because AJaX is still new, there are few completed AJaX solutions that address all UI needs consistently across all browsers and browser versions.

For now, we only want to define (on a high level) what the look-and-feel should, well, look and feel like. Table 1.8 can be used as a set of heuristics for choosing the characteristics for a look-and-feel. Remember that a heuristic is more of a rule of thumb and not necessarily an unbreakable rule.

TABLE 1.8 Look-and-Feel Matrix

Characteristic	Business Oriented	Artistic	Playful	Dark/ Ominous	Ceremonial
Highly saturated colors	X	X	X	X	
Low saturated colors		X			X
Color schemes < 3 colors	X	X		X	X
Color schemes >= 3 colors		X	X		
Dark colors				X	
Light colors	X	X	X		X
Menus with >= 5 items	X				
Menus with < 5 items		X	X	X	X
Serif typeface	X			X	X
Sans serif typeface	X	X	X	X	
Script typeface		X			X
Thick borders	X	X	X	X	X
Lots of white space		X	X		X

We can quickly take a look at a few of these characteristics. For example, high saturation is attention grabbing and is considered loud (color-wise). Although a ceremonial look-and-feel has the goal of being an attention grabber, most ceremonial Web sites aren't meant to be loud (think of a wedding Web site). Color schemes that use more than three colors are well suited to artistic Web sites but not for ceremonial or business Web sites because more than three colors can be confusing to the eye. Dark colors are only really suited to dark or ominous Web sites. Large numbers of menus can also cause confusion and are usually limited to large corporate Web sites which contain large numbers of choices for information.

Serif typefaces such as *Times* or *Times Roman* have fine lines or *feet* at the tops and bottoms of characters. A *sans serif* typeface such as *Helvetica* does not have feet. A *script* typeface looks more like a person wrote the type instead of being printed by a computer. Although serif typefaces can be difficult to read at small sizes, they usually convey elegance, professionalism, or class. This is why most business or legal documents are found to be printed using serif typefaces. Sans serif typefaces project more of a clean or modern look. Because sans serif typefaces are easier to read, they usually appear much more in television and film. Script typefaces should only be used for ceremonial Web sites and still only sparingly. Script typefaces suggest formality and ceremony, such as a wedding or funeral.

Thick borders can help define containment and can really be used for any type of Web site but should be used sparingly; otherwise, the layout seems fragmented. *Whitespace,* which is the space between letters, images, menus, backgrounds, is usually welcome in generous amounts. The more whitespace there is on a Web page, the easier the content is to read and view. If there is not enough whitespace on a page, the audience has a difficult time reading and viewing the content.

Whitespace gets its name from the print industry. It refers to the places on the printed page where ink has not been laid down. This term has been carried over to the computer world since most Web documents still use white as the background color. Many graphics artists and Web designers agree that more whitespace is better. Unfortunately, this is often ignored, especially on corporate Web sites where advertisement space is rented on the Web page. The company can earn more money if it fills up the whitespace with advertisements.

Required Content for a Web Page Layout

Sitting down and drawing up what the layout should look like is important because it gives us a starting point for our coding when we create the actual Web pages for the CMS. Although we won't be doing the coding for HTML until Chapter 10, we can proceed with a rough layout of how we want content to be displayed within a page. Although Chapter 5 covers the specific types of content within our data model, we can still identify three different ways in which we'll produce content: explicit data model content, implicit data model content, and non-data model content.

When we talk about a data model, we're talking about a logical structure where we've gathered chunks of data together consistently with organization. The data model allows us to determine relationships of data with other data within the model as well. One representation may consist of records within a table. Another representation may consist of nodes within a tree. As well, data can also be labeled and grouped so that it is referred to in a consistent manner.

Explicit data model content comes in the form of labeled chunks of data that we wish to be able to refer to later on as being a particular type or representing a particular structure. This content has been chunked and grouped in a specific manner within our data model. Examples of explicit data model content may be paragraphs, pages, and sections within our CMS.

Implicit data model content is content that may exist in the data model but hasn't been structured as static data structures. Implicit data model content examples can be such things as menus within a Web page that are generated by CMS software which determined which pages should be displayed within the menu based on an attribute (e.g., isInMenu = true). Another example may be a list of forum post within the form where only the title of each top-level post is displayed in the list. The list is generated by the CMS software, which iterated through a list of forum post data structures to find and display the title of each in this dynamically generated list displayed to the end user. Both of these examples exhibit the need for dynamic content generation in order to realize the data structure. Implicit data model content can be considered a different perspective of the same content but one that requires programmatic manipulation in order to realize it.

Non-data model content is content that is not found within the data stores at all. Usually this type of content is used as control or interactive support within a Web document. Some examples within the context of a CMS can be things such as a search form within a page, or a login form within a page, or a post a message form found within a forum page. While these types of content do not actually exist within our data model, they are supportive content structures that assist in the interactivity of the CMS.

Design Choices

There are some basic rules of design that we can follow to help aid us in creating Web pages that are not only functional, but also fun to look at, fun to use, and that attract the user.

Choosing a Theme or Style

It is important to choose an appropriate style for a Web site. Failing to do so may result in users having little interest in visiting it. It would be inappropriate, for example, to choose a style that was considered for young children but used instead for a corporate Web site. Unless, of course, the company sells young children's toys. As we discussed earlier, there were certain types of fonts and colors that were appropriate for different types of Web sites. Themes can also be added to add flavor. For example, if a Web site was in the business of selling custom made solid wood furniture, graphics used for backgrounds, borders, and menu items could be images of wood texture patterns. Wood color and other natural colors (low in saturation) could be used within the Web site's look-and-feel.

Choosing the Right Colors

Choosing the right colors is also important because it helps to establish the style and the mood of a Web site. In the previous chapter we looked at color models and how to represent color in terms of color channels. We referred to the RGB color model which used the channels red, green, and blue. We can, however, use the

Hue, Saturation, Luminance (HLS) color model, as well. In HLS, hue represents the color (e.g., red). Saturation represents the intensity of a color. For example, a red apple has a high saturation color—it is deep in intensity. The color of pinewood is very low in saturation—the wood color does not appear too brown. Luminance is the brightness of the color. White is considered high in luminance, while black is not.

Understanding these concepts helps to pick the right colors. When we deal with colors that are bright and highly saturated we are displaying contrast. This may be appropriate for attention-getting where the Web site colors are meant to lure users to read and see more. Other times, the colors chosen are meant to be subtle so that the user does not so much focus on the look but rather the textual content being provided. There are different ways to create contrast with color. Allowing a particular color to take up a larger amount of area has the effect of insinuating that color as the background. This is called the dominant color. On the other hand, a color that contrasts the background (either brighter on darker or darker on brighter), but that only exists within a small area, will create what is called an accent.

Creating Pleasing Composition

With XHTML and CSS offering features for layout, we can make use of these features to create rich layouts that help complement the content and make the delivery of content easier. Understanding flow and composition helps ensure that users will know where to look and when. When we refer to flow, we are referring to the direction of attraction that the user follows when viewing content. We want to control where the users first look, where they look next, and so forth. Flow should not be discontinuous, nor should it suddenly change direction. The concept is not unlike film or television where the camera leads the viewer to look at a specific point of action.

Figure 1.14 shows a Web page layout and an arrow that has been traced over the page to show the general flow. The eye is first drawn to the stack of menu items on the left side of the page at which point the user can't help but trace up to see the monitor with the name of the site. The eye is trained to scan across the page and then finally look toward the content within the page itself. Although this happens within fractions of a second, it still helps settle the user to a certain spot within the page. Without flow the user would not know where to look. This can cause a feeling of confusion for the user if he does not know where to look on the page.

Another important consideration is balance. Web pages must demonstrate balance within the content that is presented; otherwise, the user feels somewhat uncomfortable viewing the page or pages of the site. Figure 1.15 shows a Web page with a banner (top), a news section (right), and main content section (bottom left).

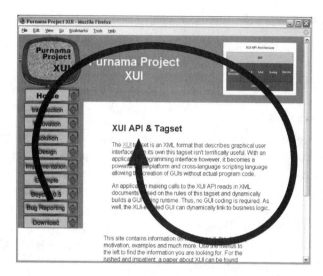

FIGURE 1.14   Web page showing compositional flow.

Each of these items has been placed within an area that appears to hold the general shape of a rectangle in the middle of the page. If this content were not centered, or if the main content section was narrower, the layout would appear to be unbalanced. It is important to always attempt to create a layout that displays balance to the user.

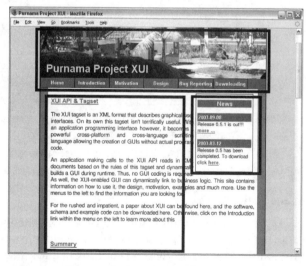

FIGURE 1.15   Web page showing compositional balance.

Design Pitfalls

The Web provides many examples of good design as well as bad design. Searching through personal sites, corporate sites, and organization sites can be a source of inspiration—even if what you see teaches you what *not* to do.

Too Much Clutter

It is tempting to fit as much information as possible within a Web page. Many companies do this because they are attempting to provide as much information to the user in the hopes that the user will see the information before moving on. A general rule of thumb is to provide lots of whitespace. The less whitespace there is on a Web page the more cluttered a Web page looks to the user and the harder content is to read and view. Figure 1.16 shows a Web page that contains very little whitespace. Although the text is small on the page, even if we were to increase the font size the text would still be difficult to read. It is important to remember to include plenty of whitespace on a page.

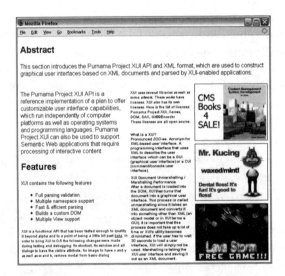

FIGURE 1.16   Web page with very little whitespace.

Bad Text and Font Choices

Although the Web does not allow for hundreds of fonts, the number of fonts supported does not suggest that they should all be included within a single page or Web site. Three fonts are plenty. Body text should all be the same font unless some of the content is referring to code or possibly hyperlinks. It usually makes sense to place text displays of some sort of program code as a mono-spaced font such as Courier.

Font sizes should be consistently chosen. Large fonts should be used for headings and titles, whereas medium-sized fonts should be used for body text. Small fonts can be used for representing information that is not part of the main body, such as legal notices or references.

Sometimes designers attempt to get around the problem of having so little choices when it comes to fonts that they create images that display titles in them. These images contain fonts that would normally not be found in a Web page. Although this idea looks appealing (because it does show different fonts), it is not text and, therefore, search engines cannot allow the page to be searched based on titles. Text should not be displayed as images for this reason.

Too Many Colors

When creating a layout for the Web, the number of colors chosen should be limited. Usually three or four colors are plenty. Sometimes it is difficult to find a set of colors that make your Web page look good. A rule of thumb is to choose complementary colors. That is, colors that are on the opposite end of the color scale. When we say they complement each other, we are referring to the values found in the color channels. If we chose a blue color with the values 69 (red), 97 (green), 228 (blue), and an orange color with the values 255 (red), 123 (green), 60 (blue), we notice that the channel values are almost inverse. That is where red and green are high in value in one color, those same channel values in the other color are low. Sometimes it is hard to think of which color schemes will look appealing. Common household items can be a source of inspiration for color. For example, a favorite tie, a tablecloth, a favorite chair or dress, can all provide color combinations that look appealing.

Nonintuitive Navigation System

The navigation system of any site should be easy to use and not cause the user to become confused with how the navigation system works. If a navigation system requires a tutorial, then it's a good sign that the navigation system is not intuitive. With plugin support from technologies such as the Macromedia™ Flash tool, there is the temptation to make use of the animation features to animate a sophisticated looking user interface. Unfortunately many designers place more of an importance on aesthetics rather than on usability. Figure 1.17 shows a user interface that is interesting to look at and could even be mesmerizing if animated. Unfortunately, if this is used as a menu system, it may not be apparent what the user is supposed to do with the graphic.

UI Design Heuristics

Creating a successful user interface requires that (in the least) certain heuristics are followed, although one can follow a strict set of rules and guidelines for a particular

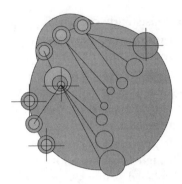

FIGURE 1.17   Graphically interesting, nonintuitive user interface.

operating system platform such as Microsoft Windows [Microsoft04] or the Apple Macintosh [Apple06], both of which have strict guidelines as to how a user interface should look and function. The following list provides the most fundamental of heuristics that should be followed in order to provide a user interface that provides the end user with utility:

- Simplicity
- Consistency
- Be forgiving
- Prevent errors
- Always provide feedback
- Offer help as a last resort

Simplicity

One of the keys to creating an elegant user interface is the characteristic of being simple. Simple doesn't necessarily mean that the user interface has little or no functionality. It means that the interface is elegant in design. It provides the functionality required and yet does not confuse the user with too much at any one given time. Functionality should be broken up into sections and chunks just like content is chunked.

For example, in Figure 1.18, we see a user interface with a large number of features for managing user accounts all placed in the same panel. This interface appears cluttered even though it provides all the required functionality. Figure 1.19 breaks the functionality up into three separate tabbed panes: one for adding new user accounts, one for editing the existing open account, and another for deleting user accounts. By breaking up the functionality, the user does not have to visually sort out all of the individual functions that are found.

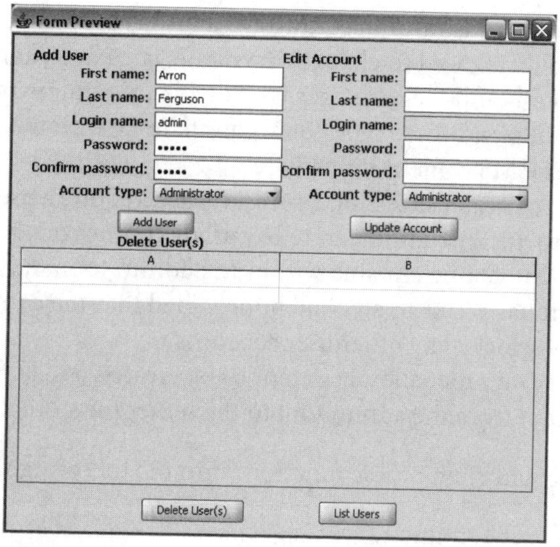

FIGURE 1.18   Cluttered user interface.

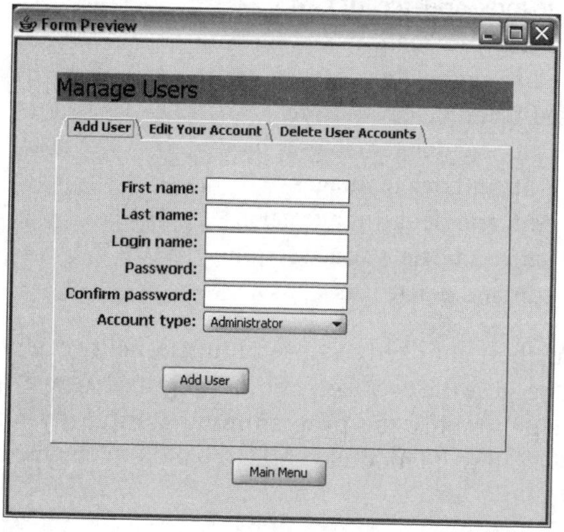

FIGURE 1.19   User interface with simplified layout.

This is something to keep a mind for when functionality requirements are being realized as user interface design components. For example, based on the following functional requirements (from Chapter 2):

■ CMS administrators are allowed via the User Interface (UI) to add, edit, and delete user accounts

- Only administrator accounts are allowed to change their account attributes and only allowed to change first name, last name, and password
- The look-and-feel manager is available to administrator accounts and author accounts and these types of accounts to change the look-and-feel of all published CMS content immediately
- The CMS can use session certificates and require a username and login name to be provided to administrate or author content on the site
- Content can be editable within the admin tool and any author or admin account has access to all content provided that the content being accessed is not already locked by other user accounts
- The admin tool allows content to be created and added via sending the added content from the admin tool to the server for storage into its XML format

We could chunk these functions into the following UI areas:

- Add user accounts
- Edit current user account information
- Delete user accounts
- Change look-and-feel of CMS
- Edit footer information
- Add, edit, and delete pages
- Add, edit, and delete sections
- Add, edit, and delete paragraphs
- Add, edit, and delete images
- Add, edit, and delete image galleries
- Add, edit, and delete code sections
- Add, edit and delete lists

Seeing these chunked sections of functionality can help us build a much easier to use UI because the user won't be looking at a barrage of information and option. It also helps simplify the programming complexity for the admin tool as well because we can write modular code to handle each type of functional requirement separately.

Consistency

Being consistent is just as important as keeping the design simple. Consistency should be applied to both functionality features of the UI as well as visual elements.

Functional Consistency

Functional consistency refers to like UI components behaving in similar or identical ways as others. Application programmers don't usually have control over functional consistency unless they are developing their own custom components. Most UI APIs provide a consistent behavior between components. For example, a simple press button and a menu item respond the same way in that if they are clicked on with a single-click, they generate an event. It would be an inconsistent behavior if the simple press button required one click but menu items required two clicks. Another example would be between combo boxes and lists. Both represent lists of components. Users expect that by clicking on an item in the list that the item is considered selected. This functional behavior should be consistent between both components.

There are some areas of functional consistency that can be controllable by application programmers. For instance, high-level functionality that requires a more complex action where the event is not necessarily mapped to one particular UI component. A specific example would be when the user is confronted with a dialog box. Some dialog boxes require a *modal* behavior which do not allow the user to carry on to the previous window until he has responded to the modal dialog that has taken focus. A situation where the user is about to close the application without saving changes to any open files would warrant using a modal dialog because it prevents the user from accidentally choosing to close without saving files. However, the application may contain another dialog box that simply provides tools for operation within the program. In this case, the dialog box should not be modal. In most programming environments, dialog boxes can either be modal or non-modal. The action dictating modality would however need to follow consistent conventions. That is, any action taken that requires a dialog box and that is non-reversible in nature (e.g., closing a file without saving changes) would require the dialog box to be modal. Otherwise dialog boxes could be non-modal.

Another example where application programmers may control functionality would be with text field selection. Text fields allow a user to type in a single line of text. It may be warranted in some circumstances to automatically select all the text within a text field if that particular text field gains focus. If the text field is a field for typing a username and password, then the application programmer could enable the behavior of those fields to automatically select the text so that when the user starts typing, the old text values are replaced by new text. In this case the functionality provided (selection of all text within the field) would have to be consistent throughout the UI because the user would expect it to happen for the rest of the text fields that were encountered.

Color Consistency

Current operating system GUI APIs provide chosen color schemes. However, developers can usually programmatically override the color schemes. In either case, color choices should be consistent throughout the interface. All dialog boxes should contain the same border, font, and background colors. Changing the colors on each dialog would cause confusion for the user. Furthermore, the user may get the impression that a certain color is to mean something. While this may seem like a good idea, it flies in the face of our first heuristic, which is simplicity.

Size Consistency

Size consistency is especially important since size can imply importance. Looking at Figure 1.20, we see three buttons displayed. Although each button in the UI is the same size, the first button's font size is larger than the second two. This seems to imply that the first button carries more importance or more meaning or possibly represents more functionality. Size should not carry this meaning in our UI. In this case, the font was not chosen as larger but rather the other two button's text would not fit inside of the button so their font sizes were changed to fit the word into the button. Alternative solutions for this would be to either choose shorter action words for the button functionality, decrease or increase the font for all buttons, and make the buttons wider.

FIGURE 1.20   UI showing size inconsistencies.

Style Consistency

Choosing different styles can be equally as confusing as size differences. Figure 1.21 shows a UI that contains two inset areas which both contain functionality provided by UI components. However, they both contain different styles for font, border, and colors. The user quickly can become confused or at least question the significance of the differences.

Be Forgiving

It is inevitable that users will make mistakes using the software no matter their level of expertise. Even experienced users or users considered to be experts with the software. It is therefore important to offer users the ability to step back from a particular action or state that may cause damage or unwanted changes to be made either

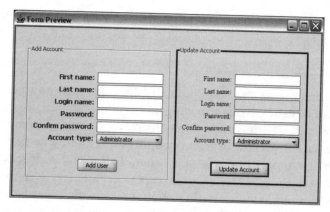

FIGURE 1.21   UI showing style inconsistencies.

within the environment or with files or data that the software is allowing the user to manipulate. Adhering to this heuristic allows users to feel confident when they need to use the software because they have the security of being able to undo certain actions. Being forgiving can be applied to several different types of situations.

User Forgets to Perform Something

Everybody makes mistakes, from novices to expert users. It is easy to forget to perform a certain operation or to simply not know how to perform an operation. Users will inevitably make mistakes. For this reason it is important to handle all situations that may arise. In fact one of the best ways to test software is to allow users to "test drive" the software and record the mistakes made and how the software responded. Some of the more common mistakes users make are forgetting to:

- Save a file before attempting to exit the application
- Log out before shutting down a client application that is connected to the server
- Enter a subject line for an email before attempting to send the email
- Ensure that an image to be printed to a page fits within the dimensions of the page

There are several ways of handling these situations. As we discussed earlier, if a user forgets to save, a dialog box can prompt the user to cancel the operation or continue. A modal dialog box takes care of the problem. We can handle the logging out situation the same way by presenting the user with a modal dialog that reminds the user that he is about to close the application without logging out with the server. In fact, modal dialog boxes can help out with most situations by simply providing the user with feedback that reminds them that they may be forgetting to perform an operation.

User Chooses an Option by Mistake

Sometimes users choose options that they didn't mean to choose (e.g., bold text instead of italic). Being forgiving means allowing users to unroll or undo certain operations. Offering undo functionality is not easy and requires programmers to store data structures in memory and possibly to cache files in the filesystem in order to support undoing operations. This extra work makes a UI easy to use because of its ability to allow the user to explore and even make mistakes. By not allowing users to undo certain operations, your application may take on a minefield atmosphere where the user is afraid to do anything.

User Chooses an Option Just to See What Its Result Is

There are times when it helps to actually see the change made in order to determine whether or not the operation should be performed. An example may be an image manipulation program that offers image filters that distort the image somehow. The user may not exactly know what the effect will be. Offering some form of temporary snapshot of the completed operation can help the user choose whether or not he wants to apply the changes. Although providing this feature can be done using undo operations, it may not always be feasible to perform the entire operation. For example, if the application is a 3D animation program that offers particle effects that generate water, it may be too time consuming to apply these effects to the currently open project. The computations may take minutes—even hours. Instead, a dialog box could provide a quick sample window with a scaled down version or approximation of the operation that is sought. This would give the user immediate feedback. Without this, the user may feel hesitant about exploring or experimenting with features that may make him wait long periods of time.

Prevent Errors

An apple a day keeps the doctor away. Stay healthy in the first place and keep from needing a doctor in the first place. This works in real life, so why shouldn't it work within the world of interface design. The previous topic suggests being forgiving and helping the user to get out of a situation that may cause a loss of data or some sort of unwanted changes to data. Of course there won't be any problems to deal with if we can eliminate most of the scenarios that allow the user to become stranded in the first place. Prevention can go a long way. For example, we may wish for the user to type in a date for a transaction, as in Figure 1.22. This, however, is going to lead to errors. First, we have not specified to the user which format the date should be in. We can catch the errors that the user types in and give feedback in a dialog stating the correct format. But this solution is not very elegant because there may still be chances that the user will forget the exact format and type it in wrong again. This will cause some frustration.

We can help alleviate the problem by providing some feedback right next to the field where the date should be type into, as in Figure 1.23. The user now has some idea as to what the correct format for entering the date but could still type the date incorrectly.

FIGURE 1.22   Text field for entering in a date.

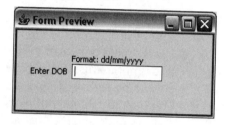

FIGURE 1.23   Text field with instructions for entering a date.

An even better solution would be to prevent the typing errors in the first place and simply offer the choice using different components. One possible solution is to offer combo boxes for choosing the year, month, and date, as shown in Figure 1.24. This allows the user to select choices that are presented so there are no typing errors. By doing this we prevent the errors from ever happening in the first place.

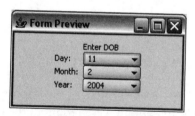

FIGURE 1.24   Combo boxes allowing for entering a date.

Always Provide Feedback

There are many ways to offer the user feedback as to what exactly is happening. This is a common practice and it helps greatly. Feedback can be quite subtle such as a word processor displaying which column and line the cursor is at when the user is typing a document. Or it can be as direct as a modal dialog box that is informing the user that the printer is out of paper. Feedback can be like a coach directing new users how to perform a certain action, such as user interface wizards that walk a user step-by-step through a process for the first time. Feedback can also be an occasional reminder such as a red highlight denoting a spelling mistake within a paragraph. We can also provide hints such as pop-up boxes that appear over user interface components that briefly describe what action the component is responsible for performing. We can provide implicit feedback by enabling and disabling components based on a specific context (e.g., a save menu item being disabled because no changes to any open files have been made).

Offer Help as a Last Resort

Users should only turn to the manual or instructions as a last resort. A user interface is not useful if every time the user wishes to perform some task that he has to go reading several paragraphs that describe the set of steps to accomplish a task. A user interface should not require a lot of reading in order to use it. This pertains not just to simple applications such as word processors or spreadsheets. It is also quite relevant to other types of software, such as 2D animation applications as well as Computer Aided Design (CAD) applications.

Having said that, help files should be as descriptive as possible and accompanied with pictures (e.g., screen shots) that clearly demonstrate how to carry out a particular task within the user interface. Describing all details, options, combinations and all output solutions is important so that the user does not become frustrated and give up using the software.

SUMMARY

In this chapter we looked at the importance of defining a methodology for managing content. The methodology we used defined an iterative model where content is defined, categorized and organized, then stored and manipulated, and maintained. For defining the content we recognized the importance of determining the goals of the site, what types of content were required, the target audience, and technology requirements the target audience would need. We looked at useful practices for grouping and arranging content.

We also looked at how granularity, chunking of content, and metadata needs are important for storing content as well as storage container considerations and separating content from presentation formatting. We looked at manipulating and maintaining content, which requires consideration for granularity and metadata requirements. We also looked at presentation issues such as choosing an appropriate look-and-feel, choosing content for a layout, good design choices and design choice pitfalls to be avoided, and UI design heuristics.

Having addressed general concepts in defining, organizing, storing, and manipulating content, we can look forward to the next chapter which shows us how this is applied within the context of a content management system.

ENDNOTES

1. Spam is a term to describe unwanted, unsolicited, and usually inappropriate email which is sent in bulk (thousands or even millions at a time). Spam is also known as junk mail.
2. Apparently in Japan, consumers can now purchase square watermelon. This new variation could totally change the category structure in Table 1.3. This square watermelon is called designer fruit since it is usually double or even triple the price of a typical oval-shaped watermelon.
3. A Geographical Information System (GIS) is a computer application that stores information into a database. A GIS may contain information in it such as population distribution, landscape attributes, city planning data, and species distribution. GIS applications usually present the data graphically in maps and often have the ability to display multiple layers of information within a map.

2   Introduction to Content Management Systems

In This Chapter

- What makes up a Content Management System (CMS)
- Common CMS features
- Designing a CMS by identifying functional requirements, creating entity-relationship diagrams, creating dataflow diagrams, and creating class diagrams

ON THE CD

Before we can start building our own CMS, we must first find out just what exactly a CMS is. The term CMS is much like the term multimedia: vague and open to interpretation. If you ask 20 people what a content management system is, you will likely get 20 different answers. Of course the witty individual will respond quickly that it is a system that manages content. The source code listings referenced in this chapter are located on the CD-ROM in the *Chapter 2* folder.

WHAT IS A CONTENT MANAGEMENT SYSTEM?

We can look at a CMS as a publishing tool that allows users to create, edit, delete, and present content in various forms including text, imagery, video, sound, and animation. But there's much more to a CMS than this. A better way to come up with a definition of CMS technology is by pointing to a set of features that are associated with CMS technology:

- Allow users to easily search for information using well-defined categories
- Present content to users quickly
- Offer users the choice of different presentation views

- Offer users the choice of different content views
- Allow administrators of the CMS to monitor and manage content and users
- Allow authors to manipulate content
- Provide facilities that allow users to communicate with others in a forum format
- Provide an open architecture to support pluggable components
- Allow for future expansion of metadata

This list is by no means all encompassing, although we can say that it represents a core set of features that should be present within a standard CMS. We also have to be clear that (for now) we're only defining features—not implementation decisions.

Search for Information

The ability to search for content is one of the most important features of a CMS, being only second to publishing content. The ability to search at varying levels of granularity for certain types and chunks of information is imperative. A basic search will allow for a simple shotgun approach, which is to search the entire CMS for various words, returning a result of the searches. However, this would not be efficient and searches could take too long if the CMS contains thousands of pages of content. Therefore, there is a need to differentiate between various types of content on the site. We may wish, for example, to restrict our searches to:

- Paragraphs that contain a certain word or phrase
- Content based on a particular author
- Images not found in an image gallery
- Images found in an image gallery
- Images with a certain caption or file name
- Code that contains a certain word or phrase
- Content based on a date/time stamp

This list may seem excessive. But by providing this amount of granularity, we make our searches more efficient, more succinct, and more useful. Figure 2.1 shows a search form that allows users to narrow their searches to specific types of content.

Present Content Quickly

Everyone has experienced visiting a Web site only to find that it takes forever to complete certain operations, such as a simple search or possibly visiting a message board. When this happens, it becomes difficult to enjoy the visit to that Web site no matter how important it may be to view the content on the site. A CMS must have the ability to present the information in a timely manner. Searches should only take seconds not minutes, and a page refresh should not take more than a second, as-

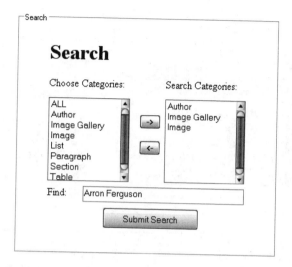

FIGURE 2.1   Search form based on content types.

suming high-speed Internet. At this point, we are not interested in defining what technology that we're looking for to make this happen quickly, but we are interested in defining this feature as one of great importance and one that should be in the back of the mind of every developer as the CMS is built.

Multiple Presentation Views

The ability to offer multiple presentation views is really just a fancy way of saying that the CMS can change its look-and-feel. This feature is akin to a desktop application being *skinnable*. An application is skinnable if its user interface can change the colors, layout, and style of user interface components such as buttons and menus. For a CMS to be able to do the same thing, it must be able to change the look-and-feel dynamically. That is, if the look-and-feel is changed for a certain amount of content on the CMS, then the next visit to a particular piece of content must also be different. It is an automatic effect. Figures 2.2(a) and (b) show the same content from a page of content, but represented with two look-and-feels. A CMS may be able to change the look-and-feel for the entire site or may be able to differentiate between certain sections of a Web site and present them differently, depending on who the viewer is. If users are allowed to log into the site, then the CMS may give them the ability to customize their look and feel when they visit. Additionally, when pages are rendered, there may be multiple ways to render the pages (e.g., HTML, PDF, Postscript). If this is the case, then each format of rendered page will need to have this feature.

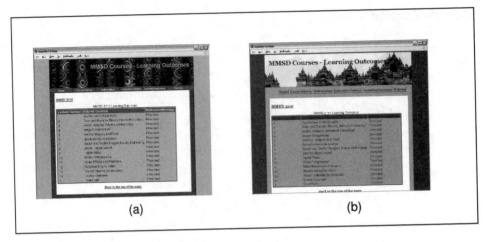

(a)   (b)

FIGURE 2.2   Multiple presentation views of a course.

It is expected that a CMS will also have the ability to present multi-types of content (e.g., images, video, sound, animation). Multiple presentation views affect these other types of content too, but in different ways. For example, images may need to be dynamically changed to add borders around them or change their size. Video clips may require different formats and different sized clips (e.g., high bandwidth and lower bandwidth).

When we refer to changing content dynamically, we are referring to the ability to perform dynamic content generation (DCG). This type of feature is usually associated most with Web servers and Web content. It is the ability for a Web server to deliver content that is not prepared for consumption until the time of a request. Once this request is made, the server pieces together all of the bits from varying sources and presents the content to the user. This is very much different than static content presentation which is simply a Web server retrieving files from the file-system and sending them to the end user.

An analogy is eating a hot meal made at a restaurant versus going to a convenience store and picking out a cold sandwich in the refrigeration unit. The hot meal at a restaurant is akin to the DCG in that both must be prepared before end user consumption can take place. Additionally, the cold sandwich in the refrigeration unit in the convenience store is like the static content presentation—both are ready for consumption and no preparation is required.

Multiple Content Views

Whereas multiple presentation views deal with the look-and-feel of content, multiple content views offer slightly different perspectives of the same content. This refers not to how the content looks, but to the content itself and what portions of that content are presented. Figure 2.3 shows an example of slightly different material but based on the same content. Figure 2.3(a) contains the learning outcomes for a list of courses, whereas Figure 2.3(b) contains the deliverables for the same list of courses. Although they are both based on the same larger chunk of content (a list of courses), both Figure 2.3(a) and Figure 2.3(b) contain different subchunked content (learning outcomes and deliverables respectively).

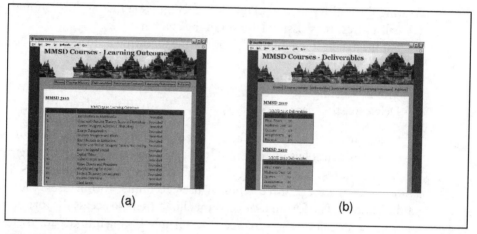

(a)   (b)

FIGURE 2.3   Multiple content views for a course.

Administrators Manage Content and Users

In order to perform tasks in a CMS, there is a need to both manage content and users. In the case of content, the ability to manage content is only as good as the UI that provides this feature. Without a proper user interface, content management can become cumbersome at best. Some content management systems will require users to dive deep into configuration files and scripts, leaving the content manager (CM) to learn a new configuration format and possibly a new scripting or programming language. If the UI that is provided is intuitive, then all management of content can take place within the administration tool and will likely take very little time. Content management UIs should allow for the:

- Creation of content (e.g., stories, articles)
- Modifying of content (e.g., changing the number of columns in an image gallery and changing the thumbnail size of the preview images)
- Deletion of content (e.g., removal of references to a video clip as well as the option to remove the video clip itself)

An extra feature that is coveted once it's been introduced is the ability to change content views (discussed earlier). Again, this should be provided in an easy-to-use UI, such as the one shown in Figure 1.4. It is important to address many of the content management questions. For example, what levels of content can be managed by administrators? Are administrators allowed to author (create) content as well, or do they simply create blank pages for authors? Are administrators responsible for creating the entire page template, or is that an issue that authors should address? We will address these issues later on in the chapter.

For the management of user accounts, the following features should be available:

- Add new user accounts
- Modify existing user accounts
- Delete existing user accounts

The ability to manage users and content presents quite a few challenges. There are questions that if left unanswered, will cause severe problems during runtime if we do not address them during design and development of the CMS. First, let's assume that there are three types of user accounts: forum users, authors, and administrators. The forum user account allows users to access the forum only. The author account allows users to access the forum plus log into the admin tool where they can create, edit, and delete content and change the CMS look-and-feel. The administrator account allows users to do everything that the author account allows plus create new user accounts and delete existing user accounts.

In the case of forum user accounts, questions arise pertaining to granted permissions. Should a forum user account be able to delete forum posts? If we allow this, it may solve moderating issues within the forum. Can a forum user delete replies even if the replies are not their own? By saying yes, we may help alleviate most of the moderating tasks within the forum, especially if there are replies that are abusive.

With author accounts, it makes sense to allow the author of the content to edit or delete his own work, but should another author be allowed to edit or delete the content as well? If we allow authors to delete each other's content, then we must ensure that this is a business rule that is stated clearly to all users of the CMS. If we only allow authors to edit or delete their own content, then we must address the case where the author account is deleted. Without addressing this event, there is the possibility that content remains within the CMS that cannot be deleted. A possible solution is to allow administrator accounts to delete any content from any author (or administrator).

Another possibility to consider is creating different types of author accounts for the different types of content. For example, we may wish to have photography-author accounts that only allow users to import photos into the CMS. Another type of account may be writer-author. This type of an account would only allow the user to create textual content, such as articles and stories.

With administrator accounts, can an administrator delete an account that is logged in? For a forum user account, the repercussions are not severe because all that is lost is either a forum post or a reply. The issue is a more difficult if the logged in account is an author. What if the author is in the middle of creating an article and has typed four or five paragraphs of content already? Then we have partial content that will either have to be deleted or continued by another author. A more practical solution is to disallow author accounts from being deleted. Administrator accounts should never be deleted while they are currently logged in. Not only could the administrator be authoring content, but he could also be adding new accounts.

Role Based Access Control (RBAC) is a formal methodology of defining roles (account types) and access control (permissions) to various resources of a system. It makes sense to use RBAC if a CMS is quite complex and has more than the three different types of accounts that we've given in our simple example and the permissions of accounts are numerous and varied.

Authors Create Content

We can define author accounts as being responsible for authoring content, which also includes the creations of pages and the content within those pages. Content can be in the form of words, sentences, paragraphs, stories, and articles, and it can also include content such as video, sound, and animation. Authors, therefore, have to have the ability to bring this type of content into the CMS. Again, this issue rests on the shoulders of the CMS's UI.

When dealing with textual content, an extremely useful feature that the CMS can provide is the ability to log into an admin tool and author content directly. As a software developer, this can cause a lot of extra work if the different types of content require different UI options. For example, a UI component for writing paragraphs would need the ability to format the words within the paragraph (e.g., bold, italic, underline) as well as provide the ability to insert hyperlinks into the paragraph itself. This can be problematic. If the tools used to build the user interface do not allow symbols (that represent links) to be inserted into the text, then the author may be required to remember certain script or XML tags to represent hyperlinks. This exposes the author to the underlying technology and this is usually considered a bad thing. With UI technology being where it is today, authors may be expecting some advanced features as well such as searching, undo, and redo of text.

There is much more variance to the degree of support a CMS offers when dealing with multimedia content such as images, sound, video, and animation. A simple and inexpensive CMS will probably only provide a way for authors to log into the CMS and import content. The content is then placed in the appropriate place on the server for the CMS to find and present to viewers of the CMS content. If this feature is not provided within the CMS UI, then the user will be required to upload all files to the filesystem where the CMS exists, which exposes the author to the inner workings of the CMS. This may not even be possible if there are security restrictions on the computer acting as a server. A more complete and expensive CMS (such as Stellent Content Management Suite) will offer the ability to import, convert from one format to another (e.g., BMP to TIFF), offer viewers multiple format options of the same file (e.g., AVI or MPEG), create thumbnail image representations of the files (useful for videos), create storyboards, and many other choices.

A more extensive CMS may offer the ability to import multiple file format types from various applications. If an author has a previously created story or article stored in a word processor document, it would save the author considerable time if he can simply import it to the CMS instead of having to copy and paste the content into the custom UI of the CMS.

Forum Communication

Offering forum communication allows users to usually sign on (although this is not necessary) and communicate with others. There are a number of features that can be provided, but some of the more important (and basic) features are the ability to:

- Add, modify, and delete messages
- Search the forum for a word or phrase by searching topic title or posting
- Record and display information of each post in the forum such as the author, time, and date of the post, the contents of the post, and any links to replies to the post

A more comprehensive CMS will allow for scheduling of meetings, contacts, and posting of multimedia within the forum content.

Open Architecture

When we refer to a CMS having an open architecture, what we're really referring to is the ability to add new components to the CMS itself. For example, third-party software developers should be able to create some components or modules that add more functionality to the CMS, such as a new forum that supports video conferencing or the ability to directly manipulate images by cropping them or changing their size. A CMS does not have to expose its source code in order to do this, but it does have to offer the ability to link modules to the main core of the CMS so that these modules will be loaded and executed when it is executed and running. More importantly, there should be plenty of documentation to third-party software developers on how to achieve this. By providing this ability, the CMS gains exposure and popularity within the software industry and will tend to be more commonly used if third-party developers can add their own specialized modules to it.

Metadata Extensibility

The ability to expand the metadata is not a trivial feature to implement. What this really means is that the underlying metadata structures that describe the content can be expanded on by third-party developers and authors (or the original developers). Expanding should not hamper the CMS's ability to use and manipulate existing metadata, nor should the expansion metadata cause problems to the CMS. Although this feature sounds great to offer, practically speaking, it can be difficult to implement. For example, Figure 2.4 shows an entity-relationship diagram (ERD) with data types and their relationship to one another.

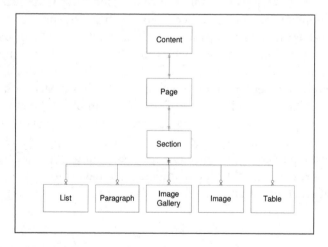

FIGURE 2.4   Entity-relationship diagram showing metadata format.

Within Figure 2.4, we see that section entities can have paragraph entities, list entities, table entities, image entities, and image gallery entities. These are the metadata types that are found within this CMS metadata format. However, what if we wish to provide a new type of content (e.g., a metadata type that represents a chunk of program code)? The implications of supporting this stretch into many areas of the CMS design. Any parsing engine that reads in the content will have to have the ability to look for new types of metadata within the format. The rendering engine and supporting framework will require the ability to recognize new types and offer authors and administrators the ability to provide formatting for these types. The most difficult question will be whether the CMS administration and authoring UIs will allow customization to support properties of these new types. A small inexpensive or free CMS will most likely not provide this ability.

CMS ARCHITECTURE

When creating a CMS (or even choosing a CMS to use), it is important to look at the architecture that is used within the CMS. One big advantage to building CMSs with current technology is that there are many different frameworks, many different types of data storage, many different platforms, and many different languages available to meet the needs for building a sturdy CMS. For programming languages, there a few that are popular choices for building CMSs including Java, PHP, C# and Ruby. Each of these languages requires a runtime environment that offers a rich set of API calls that offer developers the ability to create innovative CMS features. These runtime environments can then be called from a Web server, and therefore take advantage of the Web framework using the Hyper Text Transfer Protocol (HTTP), multithreading (for handling multiple requests and Web document serving).

Many of the popular small to mid-size CMSs fit within this framework (such as Mambo and OpenCMS). By allowing a CMS to piggyback with Web server technology, presentation and delivery of content is simplified because file formats already exist and middleware technology is already in place that allows for the manipulation and integration and dynamic delivery of content to the end user. Furthermore, because middleware is already in place, accessing other types of server technology (such as databases) is simplified, in comparison to having to write supporting software to tie different servers and server types together.

Different Tiers

A *tier* (sometimes referred to as a layer) is a distinct and independent component that offers a specific service within a greater system of running software. Tiers usually run on separate computers and communicate with each other using various protocols. For example, a Web server is a tier, a database server is a tier. A Web browser is a tier. Any particular tier can be a consumer, a producer, or both a consumer and a producer. There can be any number of tiers within an architecture. To start off with a basic example, Figure 2.5 shows the classic three-tiered architecture as applied to a CMS architecture. Starting at the bottom, the database is considered the *data tier* (or *data layer*), sometimes referred simply as the *back-end*. The data tier is responsible for storing and retrieving data for other tiers' consumption. Most data tiers are not consumers of anything, but they are producers. The *business logic tier* (sometimes referred to in the three-tiered architecture as the *middle-tier*) is shown as the CMS server. The business logic tier is appropriately named because it offers the functionality and services based on the business rules of the system. For instance, in our example the business logic is a CMS. Other solutions could possibly be a multiuser animation storyboarding tool, an accounts payable system, or anything else. The business logic tier is both a consumer and a producer, as it consumes content from the data tier and produces content for the *presentation tier*. The presentation tier simply consumes and produces nothing other than a rendering of the material sent to it from the business logic tier. The presentation tier is usually lightweight, meaning that it doesn't contain much logic for processing user requests—the requests are sent to the business logic tier.

The term tier can and often is used synonymously with the word layer. You may see documentation that uses the term layers instead of tiers.

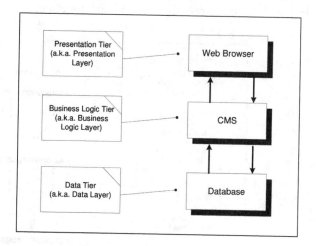

FIGURE 2.5   Three-tiered CMS.

Each tier usually runs on a separate computer (or even a set of computers if required). But one computer could be sufficient if the computer is fast enough, has enough main memory to support all the applications in memory all at the same time, and the computer and supporting network can cope with the client requests in a timely manner. Therefore, one of the first questions that comes to mind is why bother going through all of this trouble? Why not just create one executable application and be done with it? The answer is *scalability*. Any Web-based service (such as a CMS) needs to be *scalable*. Although this term is constantly over-used in industry (especially in many computer server television advertisements), it is a technical feature that can make or break a CMS. When we say scalable, we mean that the software (CMS in this case) can support a wide range of users, requests from users, services, requests for services, or even more tiers. When a CMS is scalable, it means that when we've outgrown the current configuration and architecture, like outgrowing a house, we can perform some renovations to either the configuration or the architecture or both in order to answer the demands being placed on the CMS.

For example, we may realize that the numbers of users that are connecting to the CMS are causing the CMS to make a higher frequency of requests for data from the database. This may in turn be causing the database to perform slowly, thus slowing down the CMS as a whole. This now removes the feature (discussed earlier) to present content to users quickly. A solution to the problem is to add another database within that tier—basically changing the cardinality of the architecture. Figure 2.6 shows the updated CMS. We now have a *cluster* of databases (for now just two, but we could grow it to three or more). A cluster is the term we use to describe a series of the same type of piece of software for that particular tier. They work in parallel and are coordinated to work together.

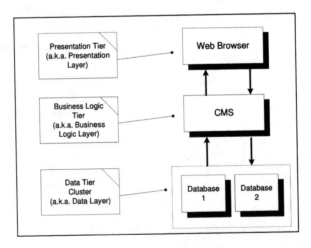

FIGURE 2.6   Three-tiered CMS architecture with clustering.

Although we've solved the solution to the database slowdown, we've inadvertently added a new problem: which database does the CMS request and post data to and from and when? Clearly this is something that the CMS will have to address. Assuming the CMS doesn't currently support this feature, some remodeling will be required. If we are to address this issue with a mind for the future, we will approach the problem in a slightly different manner. Instead, we will add another tier. Figure 2.7 shows the additional tier. We've added a data access tier (also called the data access layer). The data access tier (shown as a *data access object*) offers the feature of an abstraction between the business logic tier and the data tier. This abstraction is useful because it hides from the business logic tier any implementation details of what type of database is being accessed or if there are multiple databases being accessed. This last point about multiple databases is something that we can take advantage of because we've already created a cluster of databases. This data access tier will allow us to load balance access to multiple databases. The data access tier is both a consumer and a producer, as it produces data for the business logic tier (by collecting data) and consumes data from the data tier. The data access tier can respond to changes in load demands and will help ensure data is received and updated in a timely manner by not overloading one particular database with too many requests.

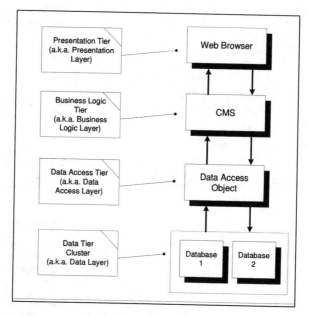

FIGURE 2.7 Four-tiered CMS architecture with data load balancing.

To make our example well-rounded, we can add one last change to the architecture we've created. Let's assume that the new bottleneck has become the CMS itself. That is, no matter how many more databases we add at the data tier level (in the cluster), the CMS is still causing a delay in requests by users. A quick solution may be to put the CMS software on a computer with more memory, faster CPU, and higher bandwidth connection; but this short gain will quickly be overshadowed with a lack of response from the server. This will not be enough. The solution (if you haven't guessed it already) is to add another tier.

Looking at Figure 2.8, we see our new architecture now with a new tier called business logic access tier. This tier acts much like the data access tier in that its job is to balance the load between CMSs. This makes the business logic access tier both a producer (it produces for the presentation tier) and a consumer (it consumes from the business logic tier). The business logic access tier must ensure that no one CMS is being overloaded with requests otherwise the speed at which requests can be answered will diminish. It is important to recognize that if we've built a system this large, we're answering a large volume of requests from users; therefore, each of these tiers is assumed to be found on a separate computer.

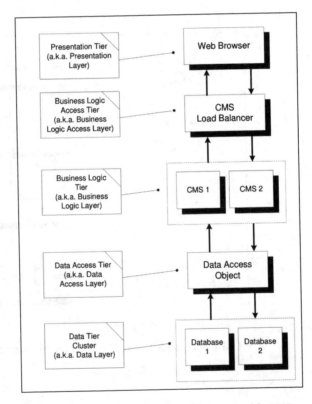

FIGURE 2.8 Five-tiered CMS architecture with CMS load balancing.

Scalability Issues

Having just looked at multitiered architectures, we can now look at some of the issues concerning scalability. Recall that scaling a system is meant to address a shortcoming. In our previous example, we addressed data tier access limitations. Although this looks easy to answer, further analysis needs to be performed in order to determine what exactly is causing the slowdown. In general (and in our previous example), there are two issues that scalability needs to address: (1) lack of processing power, and (2) lack of data bandwidth.

The lack of processing power can be dealt with in two ways. First, the computer hardware that is running the CMS tier can be replaced by computer hardware that is newer and thus faster (along with more memory). However, this is usually only a temporary fix because processing needs can quickly increase as the number of users grows. Because of this, hardware replacement is usually considered only a bruteforce solution, which doesn't necessarily address the real problem. Thus a different strategy is required. The second choice is that the CMS itself can be partitioned into several components allowing the possibility of each component to run as a separate process on separate computer hardware (servers). Going back to our CMS example, Figure 2.9 shows the breakdown of the CMS into separate components.

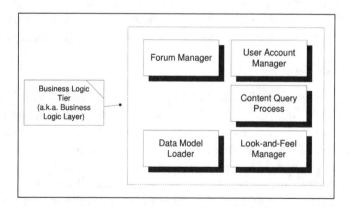

FIGURE 2.9   CMS business logic tier, exploded view.

By designing each part of the CMS as a component, we have the liberty to decide which components need to be detached from the main program and modified to run as separate programs (a point for the "design now, code later" camp). Some easy logical divisions may be to remove the account manager and the look-and-feel manager because both of these components are not directly dealing with content— only users who deal with the content and the presentation tier that transforms the content, respectively. That leaves the forum manager, the content query process, and the data model loader. At this point, it would be hard to use intuition to answer this question quantitatively without having some concrete evidence as to which of these components is the bottleneck. The answer could be solved by running a *code analyzer* on the software, which would generate statistics about which parts of the program are running the most. If we were to assume that the code analyzer reported that the content query process was using the CPU the most, then we would redesign the CMS by extracting this component and running it as a separate program. However, doing so would require creating a data protocol that would allow other components (such as the forum manager) to communicate with the content query process. This may cause data bandwidth problems.

Bandwidth problems are much more difficult to analyze because there are so many variables in the bandwidth equation. We must ask ourselves if the bandwidth shortcoming is a hardware problem or a software problem. Can the bandwidth problem be addressed by upgrading the server and network card(s)? Replacing the computer hardware (specifically the network card) can solve the problem, although it may not solve the entire problem. If the frequency of access increases, then the answer may be have to be found in software. This may mean making protocols more efficient by sending binary streams instead of text-based streams, compressing sent data, or using a caching mechanism that sends requests in groups rather than individual requests. Another useful strategy is to ensure that all data input by the user is validated on the client side so that invalid data is not sent to the server from the client, only to have the server reject the data because it is not valid (e.g., a date is in the wrong format).

Security Issues

Security issues can be addressed by supplying sufficient checks within each part of the CMS. This means that messages and content that are passed from tier to tier must be authenticated first. Authentication can be done using a combination of methods. First, usernames and passwords can be used on more than one tier. Second, session tracking can be used by using session certificates. A particular tier will assign consumers of that tier a session certificate which is simply like a limited-time pass card. When a consumer attempts to access the service on that tier, the consumer is required to give the session certificate. In order to make session certificates secure, it helps to put certain key pieces of information into the session certificate:

- Date and time (using a granularity of milliseconds or better) of the original requested session
- Username and user password
- Internet Protocol (IP) address of the consumer
- A randomly generated unique ID value

Figure 2.10 shows (in the form of a sequence diagram) how authentication can be achieved using session certificates. In this case, the consumer is an administration client application (AdminTool) that connects to the user account manager (AccountManager). The administration client application sends the username and password (which the user provides), to the account manager. The account manager then checks with the data store (DataStoreObject) to authenticate the user. Assuming the user is authenticated, an authentication response is sent back to the account manager which creates a session certificate and sends the session certificate to the administration client application.

Figure 2.10 shows the values that are contained within the session certificate. The administration application contains a copy of the session certificate and matches the original session certificate on the server (business logic tier). These values exist until the certificate expires. A session certificate usually expires due to inactivity of the consumer. When this happens, the consumer must request another certificate based on a username and password. To further protect against unwanted requests and consumers, the tier that authenticates could have a list of accepted IP addresses that are allowed to connect. If any request is made by a potential consumer that is not connecting from one of the allowed IP addresses, the request for a session certificate or content would be refused—even if the username and password do check out. A third layer of security is to encrypt all requests and content. Most breaches of security can be avoided by doing this along with the authentication of username and password, using session certificates and only allowing consumers from certain IP addresses.

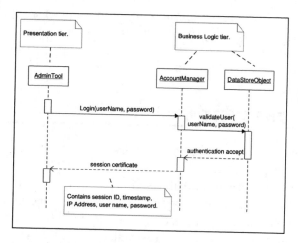

FIGURE 2.10   Authentication between tiers using session certificates.

Another point to note is that more than one tier can provide authentication. In fact, several tiers can provide different authentication and authentication identities. Looking back at Figure 2.8, we could require that the presentation tier (the Web browser in this case) authenticate by using a username and password. The username and password given would be an end user name and password. These values would be forwarded to the business logic tier. Since the business logic access tier is acting more as a traffic cop, there's no need to authenticate on that tier. Instead it simply forwards the username and password onto the business logic tier.

The business logic tier would have to authenticate against the data access tier. This authentication would be different (i.e., different account). By making this authentication based on a different account (different from the end user account), we eliminate the possibility of a cascading breach. Another advantage of having different accounts is that the type of authentication may be different. The end user accounts, for example, may be account names that are eight characters long, whereas the accounts that the business logic tier uses to authenticate into the data access tier may have to be 15 or 20 characters long or may be based on numbers only.

Lastly, the data access tier would have to authenticate against the data tier. Having separate authentication between the data access tier and the data tier means that if a cluster of data stores is being used (i.e., different types of databases), then the business logic tier won't have to contain multiple accounts. That can be managed by the data access tier.

Although this is a lot of extra work, it provides several levels of security that may be necessary if each of these tiers exists publicly on the Internet. Without all of this, unwanted requests by unauthorized hosts could make use of the CMS. For the business logic access tier this may not be much of an issue. However, if the data tier contains sensitive and private content that should not be publicly accessible, then this could have dire consequences for any company using this system, should an unwanted and unauthorized access be made.

DESIGNING THE SYSTEM

We now turn to the process of designing the CMS. We've covered some of the characteristics that we expect CMSs to possess, and we've looked at the different ways to categorize and organize content. Now it's time to start the development process. It is important to remember to start the design process before coding. A small application, may be hacked out in several days without requiring much (or any) design. However, with a large system (like a CMS), we need to carefully think through and plan what we're going to build. We'll tackle this project using the following:

- Requirements analysis (specifically functional requirements)
- Entity Relationship Diagrams (ERDs)
- Data Flow Diagrams (DFDs)
- Class diagrams

TIP

It is tempting to immediately start coding. However, more time will be spent building such a system without design because inevitably mistakes will be made. Why should building software be any different than any other discipline? After all, you don't build a house without first creating and using the blueprints to guide the implementation of the house.

Chosen Technology

For the purpose of our CMS (and the book), we'll be using Java as the programming language (that is part of the title of the book after all). Additionally, like many of the small to mid-size CMSs currently available, we'll be making use of Web server technology. That is, we'll build a Java Web application that will run within a Web server environment—specifically Apache's Tomcat Web server. This allows us to take advantage of many of the Web server features such as multithreading for supporting multiple requests, the HTTP, configuration support, logging, and session tracking capabilities to name a few. Because of the context (Web server), the chosen presentation format will be HTML (specifically XHTML). XML will be our storage format for data storage and persistence. This choice will allow our CMS Web app to require no other tiers (e.g., a relational database) and will greatly simplify the application development process.

We'll also be making use of XSLT, which will allow us to perform what are called transformations on our XML, which is a fancy way of saying that we'll convert the XML to another format—in our case XHTML. We will need to also offer administration support for the CMS because content needs to be maintained. We'll be using Java applet technology which will connect to the Web server, and thus our CMS server side, by using the HTTP protocol. Our choices here are defensible because each of these technologies have been proven to work and offer the types of features that we're looking to offer within our CMS.

Capturing Requirements

For the sake of keeping this book focused on CMS development (and not a software design methodology book), we'll limit our requirements capturing to functional (behavioral) requirements. Functional requirements deal with inputs, outputs, process, and data. They are important since they address the features that are required of the system. Additionally, functional requirements are very narrow in focus. This is important because each functional requirement needs to address one and only one requirement. Each requirement should be concise and contain no ambiguities so that there are no misunderstandings.

CMS Requirements

We can divide the functional requirements of our CMS into the following categories:

Metadata Requirements: Metadata must allow content to be broken down to fine enough levels of granularity to record information about the author, date created, date changed, author, and whether the content is published (on the site).

System Security: All data must be kept secure from unauthorized access attempts and must include logging of all suspicious activity.

Content Consistency, Reliability, and Access: Any accesses to the data model must ensure that updates and reads are done in a consistent and reliable manner.

Content Search Granularity: Content searches should be performed on sub-chunks of content such as paragraphs, code sections, lists, images, image galleries, and tables and be cross-referenced from other areas of the site that the CMS encompasses.

User Management: Administrators can add, delete, and modify user accounts.

Look-and-feel Management: Administrators can change the look-and-feel of the site that the CMS manages and ensure that the entire site remains one consistent look-and-feel.

Forum Requirements: Forum accounts as well as administrator accounts and author accounts can log into and use the forum feature which will allow them to post to, reply to, and create new topics.

Technology Requirements: The CMS is a Web application running within a Web container.

Data Store Requirements: The data store uses XML along with a fast pull parser API that allows quick loading of documents and that does not build its own data model. The data model will be part of the CMS design.

Protocol Requirements: The protocol for the system is HTTP because the CMS will be written as a Web application running within a Web container.

Metadata Requirements

The metadata format created should have page chunks, content chunks, section chunks, paragraph chunks, list chunks, image chunks, image gallery chunks, table chunks, code block chunks, and forum post chunks. The following metadata will be recorded for each of these chunks of data[1]:

- Date created (including year, month, day, hour, minute, and second)
- Date modified (including year, month, day, hour, minute, and second)
- Author of the created content
- Unique ID value in order to uniquely identify that particular chunk of data

The metadata format should contain a hierarchy of varying levels of granularity with the following characteristics:

- At the top of the hierarchy are pages.
- Each page has exactly one section container that holds section chunks.
- Each section container contains any number (zero or more) section elements.
- Each section element contains any number (zero or more) of paragraphs, lists, images, image galleries, tables and code blocks and any combination of these subchunks.
- There is a many-to-many relationship between the pages and the sections. That is, a section can belong to many pages and a page can contain many sections.
- There is a many-to-many relationship between each subchunk of a section (i.e., paragraphs, lists, etc.) and section chunks. So, a subchunk (e.g., paragraph) can be placed in many sections, and each section can have many subchunks.
- The many-to-many relationships require that metadata structures be used within the data store, be referenced rather than copied. For example, a paragraph will be referenced (not copied) to each section that has a relationship with that paragraph.
- The special case of the forum post metadata allows for a recursive referencing structure. Each forum post can contain another forum post. The relationship however is a one-to-many relationship between the parent and the child forum posts (i.e., the parent thread has many children, but each child only belongs to one parent).

System Security

The CMS should use session certificates and require a username and login name to be provided to administrate or author content on the site. The username and the password must be at least six characters long. All usernames and passwords can contain uppercase and lowercase letters as well as numerical values and special characters. Both are case sensitive. When a user (administrator or author) logs into the administration tool, the CMS will create a session certificate for that user. This session certificate will contain the following pieces of information:

- The username and password.
- The account type (e.g., administrator, author, or forum user).
- Timestamp which contains the date and time down to the millisecond containing the last access to the CMS.

■ A session ID which will be generated by the underlying servlet container and will be platform dependent. It will be assumed that the servlet container has the ability to generate unique random values for each session that is requested, making it highly improbable for session ID values to be duplicated by a third party for the purpose of breaching security.

Each time a user requests information or attempts to submit updates to the CMS, the administration tool will submit the username and password to the server. The server will authenticate and honor the request if and only if:

■ The username and password are of a valid user
■ The username and password are based on an already existing session certificate
■ The session certificate has not timed out

Each time a successful request is made, the timestamp will be updated with a new date time stamp value. The session certificate will time out after a default time period of 10 minutes of inactivity, at which point the user will have to log in again. Any suspicious activity such as attempts to log in with the same username and password but a different IP address will result in the activity being logged to a log file. Additionally, any attempts to connect to the administration service but using an incorrect protocol will result in the activity being logged to a log file. The log file will record the date, time, username, password, and IP address of the attempt.

Content Consistency, Reliability, and Access

When the server starts up it unlocks all user accounts and all content chunks that may have been locked during a previous execution. When a user session times out, any and all resources that were locked (content chunk), will be freed by the CMS in a timely manner (e.g., no more than a few seconds after the system detects the user is timed out. Content is editable within the admin tool and any author or admin account has access to all content provided that the content being accessed is not already locked by other user accounts. In edition to providing edit functionality, the admin tool should also allow content to be created and added via sending the added content from the admin tool to the server for storage into its XML format. All changes made to the data model on the server side takes place in a timely manner.

Content Search Granularity

Content searches allow a search to be performed on paragraphs, lists, images, image galleries, tables, code blocks, or any combination of any of these. Searches are based on one ore more words (e.g., phrases).

User Management

CMS administrators are allowed (via the UI) to add, edit, and delete user accounts. Administrator accounts are the only accounts allowed to alter other accounts (including other administrator accounts). Administrator accounts are allowed to delete other accounts that are not currently logged in. Administrator accounts should not be allowed to delete themselves—this will eliminate the accidental removal of all administrator accounts from the CMS. Only administrator accounts are allowed to change their account attributes and only allowed to change first name, last name, and password. Administrator accounts cannot change their login name because this may cause account name collisions.

Look-and-feel Management

The look-and-feel manager is available to administrator accounts and author accounts and allow these types of accounts to change the look-and-feel of all published CMS content immediately. The update happens instantly for all content (pages) of the CMS. The technology used to power the look-and-feel manager is the Extensible Stylesheet Language Transformations (XSLT) technology. Each XSLT contains Extensible HyperText Markup Language (XHTML) documents that will use Cascading Style Sheets (CSS) formatting. Administrator account and author accounts can choose any of the available premade templates. The look-and-feel manager allows these accounts to change between existing templates. This version does not support the ability to create a new look-and-feel. Each premade template is displayed to the administrator account user showing the following information:

- The name of the actual XSLT file
- The template name
- A copyright notice

Forum Requirements

The forum allows reading and forum posts by any of the three types of accounts available (administrator, author, forum user). The forum should not be publicly viewable. This version does not support the deletion of forum posts or replies (that can be an exercise for the reader). Administrator accounts, author accounts, and forum user accounts should be able to post new threads as well as reply to current threads. When a user posts a new topic, the following information will be displayed and stored:

- The username
- The user's account type
- The date and time that the post was made (based on date/time of the CMS locale)
- The subject line
- The comment of the post

The comment only supports plaintext (no HTML in this version). For each forum post, it must contain comment. This is mandatory although the forum post's comment content can be a zero-length string.

Technology Requirements

The CMS consists of a Web application written in the Java programming language using standard edition 5.0. The CMS will use JavaServer Page (JSP™) technology requiring the JavaServer Pages Standard Tag Library (JSTL) specification 1.2 as well as using Java Servlets conforming to the 2.2 Servlet specification. The administration program is a Java applet requiring the Java Runtime Environment (JRE) standard edition 5.0 or better to be installed and available to any Web browser as a plugin. The Web browser is required to support this runtime in order to use the administration applet. All pages served up by the CMS should be based on the XHTML 1.0 Transitional recommendation and CSS level 2.0 revision 1.0. The data stores are based on XML 1.0 recommendation. The look-and-feel support requires the XSLT recommendation 1.0 to transform the XML to the appropriate look-and-feel. Although any Web container suffices (that supports all of the above), the Web container that is used is Tomcat version 5.0 or better. The Web container used must support the ability for the Web application to be expanded from its compressed archive file.

The Web browsers supported for Web pages found within the CMS will be Internet Explorer 5.0 or better, Firefox 1.0 or better, Netscape 8.0 or better, Opera 8.51 or better and Safari 1.2 or better. Any Web browser that supports the Java runtime 1.5 or better is capable of running the administration applet.

Data Store Requirements

The data store uses the XML 1.0 recommendation to build the XML metadata format. XML parser used is the XML Pull Parser (XPP) API version 3.0 using the reference implementation parser MXP. The CMS builds its own unique and specialized Document Object Model (DOM) based on the narrow and specialized needs of the CMS data model. The data model is able to marshal[2] itself out as XML when the content needs to be made persistent. Every time the content has been modified (edited, something deleted, added), the CMS model component immediately save changes to the XML metadata documents. The process of saving of XML metadata documents is atomic and is not be delayed.

Don't worry if you're not familiar with some of the specific terms used (e.g., XML pull parser) as these topics are covered in depth in Chapter 6.

TIP

Protocol Requirements

The CMS is a Web application running within a Web container and, therefore, uses the HTTP application-level protocol. Content from the Web site is delivered through HTTP and is presented as XHTML 1.0 Transitional recommendation CSS level 2.0 revision 1.0. All forum material is delivered as XHTML 1.0 Transitional recommendation CSS level 2.0 revision 1.0. The administration applet uses HTTP as the protocol, but it tunnels responses back and forth within the HTTP protocol with Java's object serialization feature. This tunneling approach requires the administration applet to contain the Java classes of the data model within the packaged applet.

Entity Relationship Diagrams

In order for the CMS to manage, modify, and publish content, a design of the metadata that defines the data model should be created. By defining the data model here, we can save ourselves time in redesigning the CMS. Working from the functional requirements we can identify the following separate sub-data models that need to be created:

- Look-and-feel data model
- Users data model
- Forum data model
- Page content data model

In order to properly describe these data models, we need to apply the modeling technology known as entity-relationship diagrams (ERDs) to our design. ERDs allow for the modeling of data as well as the modeling of the relationships between data. We create entities and draw lines between entities to display relationships. Entities are anything that we decide to throw into our data model. For example, with our page content data model, we know there is a page entity (to represent pages), a section entity to represent sections and so on. There are a few different variations of symbols used for ERDs (called notations). Figure 2.11 shows the symbols for the *Crow's Feet* notation (appropriately called because some of the symbols look like crow's feet).

TIP

When doing design work using ERDs, notice that things are called entities. Later, when we create objects in class diagrams, we call those same things classes, or if we refer to an instance of a class, we call it an object. It is helpful to remember which design perspective we are taking in order to ensure we use the appropriate terminology.

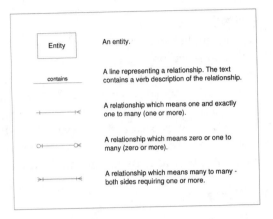

FIGURE 2.11   Crowsfeet ERD notation.

Look-and-feel Data Model

The look-and-feel data model is a nice way to ease ourselves (back) into entity relationship diagramming. The look-and-feel data model does not have to show any relationships with the other types of data simply because there are none—the look-and-feel entity is an island unto itself. Figure 2.12

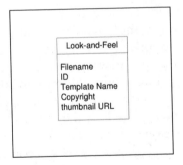

FIGURE 2.12   The look-and-feel ERD.

Forum Data Model

The forum data model is fairly simple except for the recursive nature of forum posts. A forum post can have one or more child forum posts underneath it, and so on. Each forum post contains a comment. Although the comment can contain a zero-length string, the Comment entity must still exist. The forum can have zero or more forum posts. The forum data model is represented in Figure 2.13.

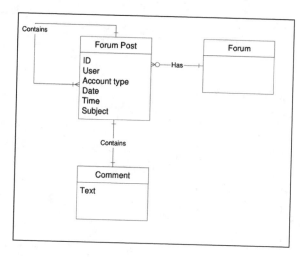

FIGURE 2.13   The forum ERD.

Page Content Data Model

Because most of the functionality evolves around the page content data model, it is the most complex of the data models. Figure 2.14 shows the ERD for the page content data model. There are several many-to-many relationships in this model. For example, each page can contain many sections, and each section can be placed in many pages. Additionally, each section can contain many subchunks (paragraphs, lists, images, tables, image galleries, and code blocks) and each subchunk can belong to many different sections. These many-to-many relationships may seem superfluous and simply there to create confusion. But by creating these as separate entities that are referenced, it allows a code block, for example, to exist in two different places within the CMS content. This gives us two benefits. First, searches are faster because subchunks are referenced allowing the data access layer to look up references (e.g., a code block). Second, because the code block is one chunk of data, there are no duplicates of it. This reduces the size of the content in our data store and eliminates inconsistencies caused by duplication.

Looking at Figure 2.14, we note several important aspects about this data model:

- Because of the relationship between sections and pages and sections and sub-chunks (which is many-to-many), we have to support the functionality and ability for the user to create sections without actually having a page to link to. Additionally, a subchunk (a paragraph, for example) can be created without assigning it to a section or a page. Because of this we have to keep this in thought for later when we develop the user interface. The user interface can

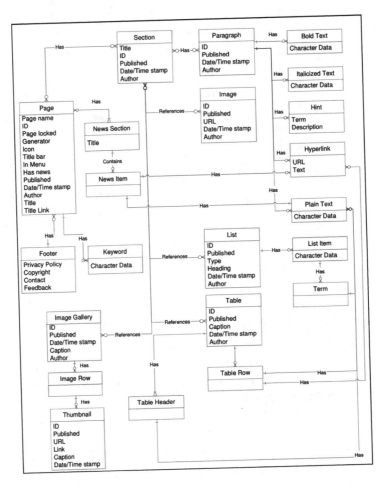

FIGURE 2.14 The page ERD.

support the feature of creating these chunks of content without assigning them to sections.

- Pages must have exactly one footer. The footer is shared between all pages, but pages can only have one and only one footer.
- Pages can contain (many) keywords. The keywords are assigned to only one page therefore it is a one-to-many relationship. The key words are used as metadata for Web pages for search engines to use to categorize the Web page.
- Paragraphs contain plain text, bold text, italicized text, hyperlinks, and hints. The relationship with these entities and the paragraph is a one-to-many. The paragraph is the only one that refers to these entities. Therefore, the relationship is unlike the section-to-page relationship. This is a design decision to keep

paragraphs as the finest granularity level for individual entities within the data model.

- Lists can have zero or more list items. Each item belongs to only one list.
- A table has either zero or one table header. The table header can only belong to one table. Each table header can have one or more Plain Text entities (character data). A table can have zero or more rows, but each row belongs to only one table. Each table row can have zero or more Plain Text entities (character data).
- Image galleries have zero or more image rows. Each Image Row entity belongs to only one image gallery. Image Row entities can have zero or more Thumbnail entities. Each Thumbnail entity belongs to only one image row.
- Each page has either one or zero news sections. The news section can belong to one or more pages. Each news section has zero or more news items. Each news item belongs to only one news section.
- There is a common set of attributes that the subchunks for sections all seem to contain: an ID, Published (whether or not the content is associated with a page—therefore publicly viewable), a Date/Time stamp and Author. Because the entities (the subchunks) are used in searches, they need these key pieces of metadata.

Users Data Model

The users data model does not require very much complexity because it does not need to be referred to by any of the other entities. Figure 2.15 shows the ERD for the users data model.

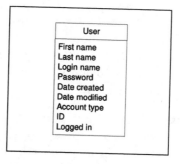

FIGURE 2.15   The users ERD.

Data Flow Diagrams

So far we've addressed functional requirements (what the system must do as far as technical features); we've also designed the data model so that we understand the relationships. Now it's time to design the flow of data and control within the system. Data Flow Diagrams (DFDs) are a natural means of communicating flow (both data and control). For example, when we're creating the protocol between the client applet and the admin service, the DFDs help guide us in the correct direction—hopefully eliminating any duplication or omissions of flow. Creating DFDs also gives us the ability to see the inputs and outputs of the system. If you're not familiar with DFDs. Figure 2.16 shows the DFD notation (using Yourdon/DeMarco notation[3]).

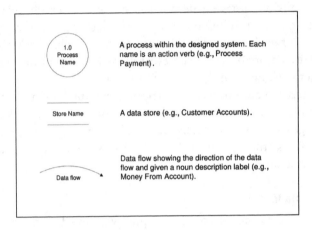

FIGURE 2.16   DFD notation.

DFDs are started by showing a context diagram. The context diagram is an overview diagram showing how the system being modeled interacts with external agents (also called entities, but not the same as ERD entities). External agents are outside of the scope of the system but must be shown if they interact with the system. DFDs do have some rules that need to be followed to correctly model data and control flow within the system:

- A process must both have inputs as well as outputs
- Data must come from data stores and (eventually) go into data stores
- Flow between external agents is not relevant to the modeled system—those flows are outside of the scope of the system
- Direct flow between data stores is not correct—there must always be a process that sends and/or receives the flow
- Direct flow between a data store and an external agent is incorrect—there must always be a process that does this as we do not want to expose data stores to external agents

- A process should not have one or more data flows coming out of it but nothing going into it (sometimes called a miracle)
- A process should not have a whole bunch of data flows going into it but with nothing coming out of it (sometimes called a black hole)

Having gone over the rules (a crash course) of DFDs, we are now ready to start modeling our CMS. The initial context diagram (shown in Figure 2.17) displays the four external agents that interact with the system: author, administrator, forum user, and finally the general viewer. We don't show the data stores at this point because they are within the system, which should not be shown at this high level in the design. What we do have to remember is that all of the data flows within the context diagram must be found below in the exploded views.

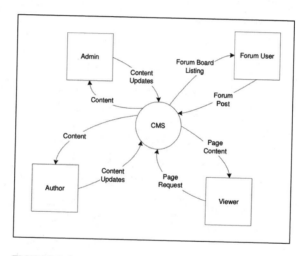

FIGURE 2.17   Context DFD.

Level 0 is the next level down. Level 0 is actually a decomposed (or zoomed in) look at the context diagram. This is what is called *functional decomposition*. Functional decomposition is incredibly helpful because it allows us to take a large unwieldy process and break it up into several smaller but manageable processes. Level 0 is where we can finally start showing data stores (although in ours we don't). Depending on the system being modeled there may be several levels down of functional decomposition. There is no set rule that dictates how many levels down one must go (or any limit for that matter) although there is a rule of thumb that states that a certain diagram should not have less than two processes and no more than seven. Less than two, and it should belong back at a level above; more than seven, and there's probably several levels down that the system should be decomposed.

Figure 2.18 looks complex, but it displays all what the system is supposed to do (based on our functional requirements). If we trace, for example, the process of an administrator changing the look-and-feel of the CMS, we start off with the admin logging in with username and password as well as a request for the template list (not shown explicitly, but rather as a general request). This request is sent to process 1.0 (Authenticate User). Process 1.0 checks the username and password against the data store "User Accounts" where it receives the status. If the username and password are not valid, a denied response is sent to the administrator. If, however, there is success, then the request portion of the data that was sent is forwarded on to process 2.0 (Manage Look-and-Feel), which retrieves the template list (each template represents a different look-and-feel) and forwards the list back to the administrator. At this point the administrator now has the list of current templates but has not yet changed the look-and-feel—a user must have a list to choose from before a choice can be made.

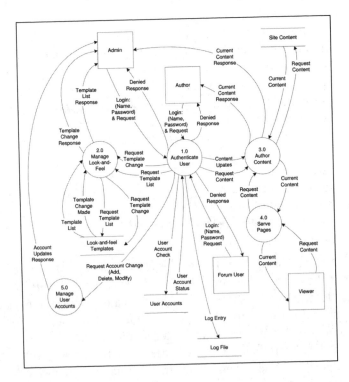

FIGURE 2.18   Level 0 DFD.

So the administrator makes another request by sending the name of the template to set as the new current look-and-feel, which is accompanied by the username and password. It may seem funny to be required to resend the username and password again. However, as we've mentioned in our capturing requirements phase, we mentioned that we are using HTTP as the application protocol. Although we've not yet covered protocols (that's not covered until Chapter 8), suffice it to say for now that HTTP is a stateless protocol that requires the resending of state (such as username and password).

Again, authentication is performed by process 1.0, and if the username and password combination are not found in the user accounts data store, the request is denied and the denial is sent as a message back to the administrator external agent. It also should be noted that in the case of an attempted request based on a username and password where the IP address is different, not only will the request be denied, but the system also records the attempt to a log file (shown in the log file data store). As mentioned earlier, it is not usual (but not wrong) to have a data store that does not have both an in flow and an out flow. However a log file is different in that it is a simple text file that can be viewed by a system administrator at a later time and collection of the data within the log file data store is outside of the scope of the system (at least this system). With the correct username and password being sent, the request is sent to process 2.0 where the template change request is performed. Process 2.0 checks the look-and-feel templates data store for the correct name of the template and changes the CMS look-and-feel. The last step is to send a template change response to the administrator as an acknowledgement of what action just took place.

Another walk through worth noting is to see what needs to happen when a general viewer attempts to look at content from the CMS. A viewer external agent sends data as a request for content. This request goes to process 4.0 (serve pages) which forwards the request to process 3.0 (author content). Process 3.0 must be a conduit to the data store for content since it is responsible for putting together all content from the CMS. Process 3.0 then retrieves the content from the site content data store and returns it to process 4.0 which forwards it to the viewer. All content updates happen by either an administrator or an author making changes by first sending username and password and then making content requests and then sending content updates—again with username and password. Like the changing of the look-and-feel, the same set of procedures is used to manage user accounts.

Although this looks like an incredible amount of work (it is!), the benefits of drawing this out and explaining it help to catch errors in logic and in design. It would be all too easy to start programming all of this and find out that something as important as the authentication process is not checking the user account data store or that a response back to the administrator has not been sent. None of these details are necessarily difficult to solve. Rather it's the composition of them that can cause confusion and result in bugs in the code.

Depending on whom you talk with, you will inevitably get debate as to whether the context diagram is level 0 or whether the context diagram and level 0 are two different levels. There are actually many different text books that show both ways. To add to the confusion, there are DFD purists who insist that control flow should not be shown in a DFD ("that's what Control Flow Diagrams (CFDs) are for"), while others may argue that control flow is fine in a DFD, so long as it is used sparingly.

One last issue is whether to show data stores in the context diagram. Most users of DFDs shy away from showing this because it's within the system and shouldn't be shown in the context diagram. While it is important to note the differences of opinion with DFD design, you should pick the variation that works best for you and solves data flow issues. After all, it's only a diagram!

Class Diagrams

Class diagrams come from the world of Object Oriented Programming (OOP) and help us to partition our design into Java classes. For example, the functional decomposition that we just did with the DFDs can help guide us as we split the functionality up into separate classes. Each diagramming language that we use allows us to look at our project in a slightly different perspective. It's similar to a potter slightly turning the pottery wheel to view the lump of clay from a different angle. Software developers need to see all sides of the project so as to better understand what to design and how to design it. Another crash course in diagrams, Figure 2.19 shows class diagram notation.

As information can be chunked into reasonable and manageable pieces, so too can program code. That is what class diagrams help us to do: split up the functionality into separate logical partitions called classes. Each class defines a separate entity of grouped, alike operations and attributes. For the CMS we are embarking on, we need three main areas of functionality:

1. The data model
2. The server-side code that manipulates the data model and sends the content from the data model for presentation as Web pages
3. The client-side application that allows users to make changes to the content within the data model

Since we are committing our project to using XML as our data store implementation technology, we'll be using XML-speak. In the database world, a chunk of data is referred to as a record. In XML, we'll be referring to those same chunks of data as nodes. This is very much an XML-specific term. However, within the context of what we're designing in this chapter, you can synonymously interchange the term node with record.

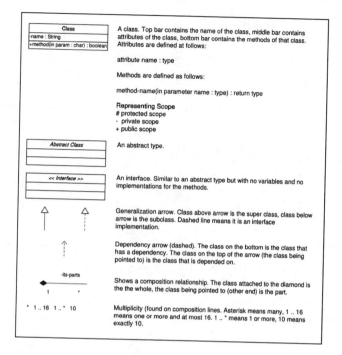

FIGURE 2.19   Class diagram notation.

The Data Model Class Diagrams

Based on the ERD that we created earlier, we can derive some classes from the entities in the ERD. Although classes and entities are different, they do share the similarity of storing attributes (state information). Figure 2.20 contains the class diagram of the data model. We see most of the entities from the ERD in this class diagram except for plain text, table header, term (from the List Item entity) and keyword. These entities (or classes in our new class diagram) can be contained as collections within their owning parent containers, which is why we don't need them as classes. Because these classes have a strict relationship with only one parent (not multiple parents), they can be contained within their lone parent.

We've also created a few interfaces: `Lockable`, `ModelNode`, `Publishable`, and `Searchable`. All of these interfaces are inherited by the abstract class `AbstractNode`. In order to better understand the relationship between these interfaces and the `AbstractNode` class, it helps to see what proposed methods and states are to be found within abstract classes. Figure 2.21 gives us just that level of detail.

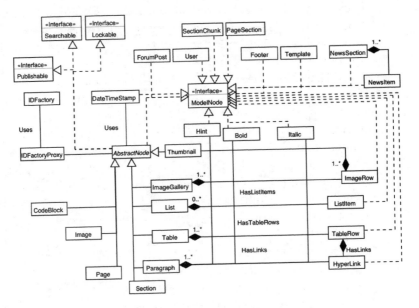

FIGURE 2.20 CMS data model class diagram.

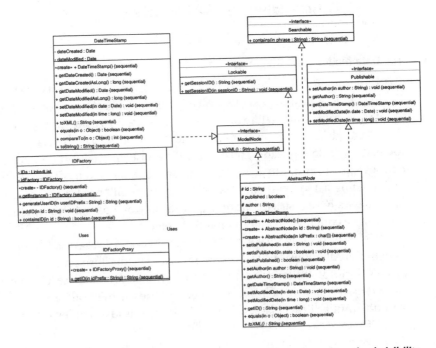

FIGURE 2.21 CMS data model class diagram with state and method visibility.

Looking at Figure 2.21, we can start with the simple interface ModelNode. ModelNode only has one method called toXML. Implementing classes provides specific behavior for what is called marshalling the object out as XML. Marshalling means that the object will be saved out as an XML document. XML and marshalling objects in XML will be covered in detail in Chapter 4 and Chapter 5. The Publishable interface contains several methods for getting data values, as well as setting data values. In OOP, these are often called getters and setters, or accessors and mutators, respectively. The Publishable interface encapsulates pertinent information about any content that is to be published within the CMS, such as the author name, a timestamp (date time) indicating when the content chunk was created, as well as a timestamp indicating when the content chunk was modified. It is important to note that there is no mutator for setting the timestamp for creation date. The creation timestamp should not be changed—only the modified timestamp should be changed.

The Lockable interface gives content chunks the ability to be locked. This is important when we consider that more than one user may attempt to log in at the same time and modify or even delete a content chunk. The accessor and mutator for the Lockable interface accept a string value that belongs to the session certificate. The Searchable interface allows content chunks to accept a search string and return a string result. The string result displays the textual content that contains the actual search string. If the content chunk does not contain the search string, the contains method returns a null value.

We've also created a class called DateTimeStamp, which holds both a dateCreated data value and a dateModified data value. Both of these are assumed to be java. util.Date. This class may seem to be superfluous, but it does buy us the following:

- Consistency and a guarantee that all classes contain both date values.
- Convenience methods for getting and setting the date value either as a Date object or as a long scalar type.
- It is required that these date values can be marshaled along with the classes that are contained within them. It makes much more sense to have the marshalling support in one class, rather than scattered across several other classes. This ensures consistency, as well as cuts down on the amount of coding needed later on.

The AbstractNode class implements Lockable, ModelNode, Publishable, and Searchable and implements the functionality of the Lockable interface and Publishable interface. Since the functionality for the ModelNode toXML method and the Searchable contains method are both specific to the subclasses of AbstractNode, neither of these methods are implemented by the AbstractNode class. The AbstractNode class uses the IDFactoryProxy class to create ID values for each instance of the class. The IDFactoryProxy gets the id values from the IDFactory class. It may look confusing as to why there should be a proxy between the `AbstractNode` class and the `IDFactory` class. The reasoning for this separation is that the model classes can be bundled up and given to the client side, for example, and not be required to expose the `IDFactory` implementation to the client. The `IDFactory` class ensures that only one instance of itself is ever created (using a static variable of itself—shown underlined). Because of this, we say that the `IDFactory` is using the *Singleton* design pattern. The implementation (programming) of the model is covered in Chapter 5.

The Server-Side Class Diagrams

With the data model taking shape, we can now focus on the server-side of the CMS. Figure 2.22 shows the server-side class diagram. The `ConnectionManager` class handles requests to list, add, edit, and delete user accounts. It also is responsible for listing and setting the default look-and-feel for the CMS. If the `ConnectionManager` encounters any requests to list, add, edit, or delete content, it forwards the request to the `CMSDefaultModel`. The `CMSDefaultModel` is responsible for handling all requests that deal with content manipulation (i.e., list, add, edit, or delete). The `CMSDefaultModel` updates the appropriate data store based on the type of content that the user is requesting to manipulate.

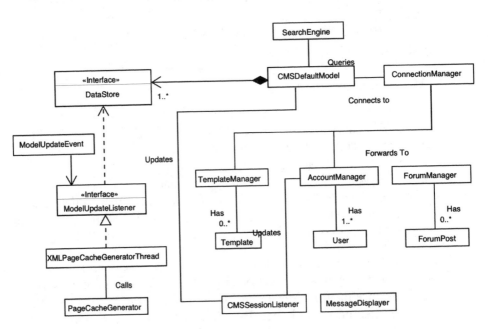

FIGURE 2.22   CMS server-side class diagram.

The SearchEngine takes requests for searches. When it accepts a request to perform a search, the SearchEngine contacts the CMSDefaultModel and retrieves a list of all content. Once the SearchEngine has a content listing, it then performs an (exhaustive) search by doing the following:

- Checking if there are any pages.
- If there are sections that belong to pages, a check is performed to see if there are content chunks that belong to each section
- If content chunks are found in each section, then the SearchEngine calls each content chunk's contains method.
- For each content chunk whose contains method returns a result (other than null), the result is added to a temporary (in-memory) page and converted into a Web page which contains a listing of all results that matched the search phrase.

The ForumManager class handles forum posts and replies as well, it lists all forum topics. The AccountManager is responsible for adding, deleting, and modifying accounts. The AccountManager is able to perform a check whether or not a particular user in logged on thus ensuring that users who are logged in don't get their accounts deleted.

The MessageDisplayer is responsible for responding to an invalid request for content (Web page) and delivering an error message (usually an HTTP 404 error message or "Page Not Found" message). Within the diagram (Figure 2.22), the MessageDisplayer is not tied to anything. This is because it is called up directly by the server and, therefore, does not need to interact with the content model. The CMSSessionListener listens to the server when sessions are started and ended. This allows the CMSSessionListener to unlock content chunks, as well as user accounts when sessions expire. Normally this operation is instigated when a user logs out. However, a user may forget to explicitly log out or may inadvertently allow the session to time out. In either case, the server informs our CMS that this has taken place (by calling the CMSSessionListener). The CMSSessionListener can then unlock any content chunks, as well as accounts that have been locked with a certain session. The Template manager is responsible for looking after our look-and-feel content. The ConnectionManager forwards both the list look-and-feel request and the apply look-and-feel request to the TemplateManager.

As mentioned, the CMSDefaultModel handles all content requests. It informs ModelUpdateListeners of changes that have taken place within the model. A concrete implementation of the ModelUpdateListener is the XMLPageCacheGeneratorThread. This class is a separate line of execution (thread) which wakes up every 10 seconds and checks to see if any changes have happened within the model. If changes have taken place, the XMLPageCacheGeneratorThread makes a call to the PageCacheGenerator, which generates temporary XML documents that represent each page of content within the CMS. We need to perform this operation because the content in the CMS is separated into different data stores based on the type. For example, all paragraph chunks are stored in the `ParagraphDataStore`, all image content chunks are stored in the `ImageDataStore`, all page content chunks are stored in the `PageDataStore`, and so forth. The particular data store classes are shown in Figure 2.23.

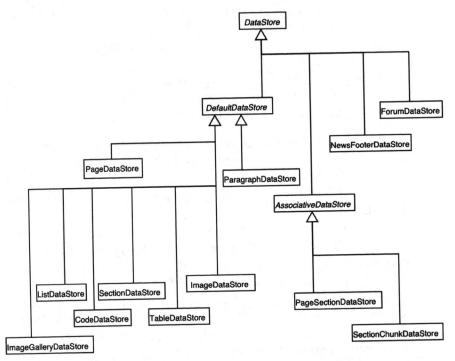

FIGURE 2.23   CMS server-side class diagram showing data store inheritance hierarchy.

Figure 2.23 gives us a detailed look at the specific data store classes that handle the various types of content. All data store classes derive from the abstract class `DataStore`. `DataStore` only provides a limited implementation of functionality that includes adding and removing `ModelUpdateListeners` and calling the XML parser, although loading of XML documents is completed by subclasses because each subclass deals differently with each type of XML content type. The `DefaultDataStore` class is the jumping-off point for all data stores that deal with model nodes that must have their `id` values referenced by other model nodes (many-to-many relationships).

The `AssociativeDataStore` class is the jumping-off point for all associate data stores. Associative data stores contain model nodes that reference other model nodes thus allowing for many-to-many relationships. In this case, we have `PageSectionData-`

Store and SectionChunkDataStore which offer model nodes that form relationships to pages and sections and sections and subchunk types (e.g., paragraph, code, etc.), respectively. Lastly the ForumDataStore and NewsFooterDataStore manage the common content for the CMS as a whole. Forum content is not referenced and the news section and footer content exist for all of the CMS; so no attempt is made to tie these content types in (via id references) with the rest of the content data stores.

Looking at Figure 2.24, we're given a more detailed view of the CMSDefaultModel class, as well as the ConnectionManager both with attributes and methods. Looking from a top-level of the design, the ConnectionManager contains references to the TemplateManager, UserManager, CMSDefaultModel, and a Logger. The Logger is a class that allows the ConnectionManager to log any unexpected or odd behavior to file. The ConnectionManager hides most of the methods it uses because most of them are protected (represented by the pound symbol). Of interest in the ConnectionManager is the fact that there is no particular reference to any particular type of content chunk (e.g., list or table). This is intentional since the ConnectionManager should not be exposed to a model-specific implementation detail. The ConnectionManager simply forwards the request to the CMSDefaultModel.

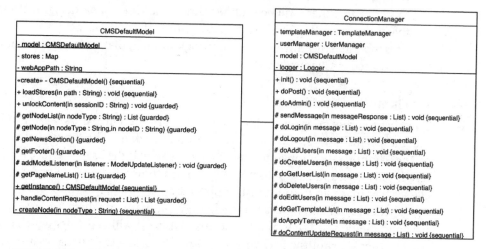

FIGURE 2.24 Data model and connection manager class diagram.

Looking at the CMSDefaultModel in Figure 2.24, we see the following methods:

addModelListener: Adds a ModelUpdateListener. ModelUpdateListeners are any classes that are interested in being informed if something within the model changed (i.e., model node(s) added, edited, or deleted).

createNode: Creates a node based on a particular type (e.g., paragraph).

getFooter: Returns the footer content chunk.

getInstance: Returns the one instance (singleton) object of this class.

getNewsSection: Returns the news section content chunk.

getNodeList: A protected method that returns a collection of nodes based on a particular data store (e.g., all paragraph content chunks).

getNode: Returns a node (from one of the data stores) based on the node id value and the node type. Returns nothing if no node is found by that id and type.

getPageNameList: Returns a list of page names.

handledContentRequest: Accepts a list (based on a protocol) and processes the content request. The protocol for this CMS is covered in Chapter 8.

loadStores: Loads all data stores into memory.

unlockContent: Unlocks all content (i.e., removes session id values from each of the content chunks). This operation may take time, depending on the amount of content within the CMS. Within the diagram in Figure 2.24, we can see the keyword guarded used at the end of each of the methods for the CMSDefaultModel. In object oriented programming and object oriented design, we use this keyword to signify that there will be multiple threads accessing a particular method, and that we're restricting access to only one thread at a time (using synchronization). This topic and the implementation (programming) of the server side of our CMS is covered in Chapter 7.

The Client-Side Class Diagrams

The client administration tool contains several different panels—each one handling a specific task for the user. It is important to divide the functionality offered by the administration tool into separate panels so that the user interface is not cluttered. This would make the user interface hard to use. Figure 2.25 presents the UI classes that make up the administration tool.

There are quite a few classes in Figure 2.25, many of which are part of an inheritance hierarchy. For example, there is a CMSPanel which defines which colors to use in order to paint the background color. The ContentChunkPanel is a subclass of the CMSPanel and offers more specialized behavior for creating, adding and editing content. The subclasses of the ContentChunkPanel class are responsible for interaction for the subchunk types of content for our CMS (e.g., paragraph, list, code, etc.). We also have containment in our class diagram, such as with the UsersPanel, which contains three other panels: AddUserPanel, EditUserPanel, and DeleteUserPanel. The ManageContentPanel contains all of the panels that deal with content management. The AdminTool class contains all of the high-level panels: UsersPanel, MainMenuPanel,

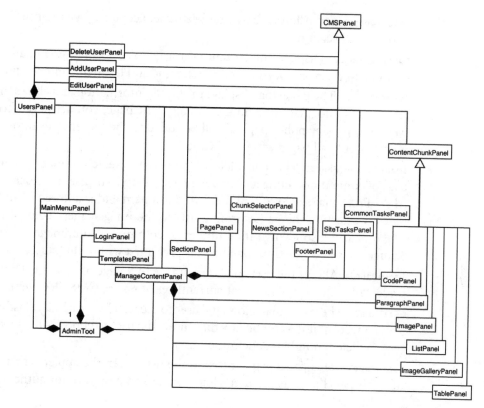

FIGURE 2.25   Client-side class diagram.

LoginPanel, TemplatesPanel, and the ManageContentPanel. Our panels offer the following functionality:

AddUserPanel: Allows for user accounts to be created and added to the CMS.

AdminTool: The administration applet itself.

ChunkSelectorPanel: A panel that presents the user with a selection of subchunk types (e.g., paragraph, code, list, etc.). This panel displays a list of the content subchunks as a list. The user can then choose which type of subchunk type to add to a section.

CMSPanel: An abstract class defining base functionality for all panel subclasses.

CodePanel: The panel that allows the user to add and or edit a code chunk.

CommonTasksPanel: This panel displays a short menu that allows the user to choose between editing the footer and editing the news section.

ContentChunkPanel: The abstract class for all content chunk types of content.

DeleteUserPanel: Allows the user to delete user accounts, by presenting a list of current user accounts.

EditUserPanel: Displays the current user account information and allows the user to edit their password or their first name and last name information.

FooterPanel: The panel that displays the footer information and allows the user to edit this information. A link to a copyright page, contact page, feedback page, and privacy policy page can all be added to the footer. This information is common to all pages within the CMS.

ImageGalleryPanel: This panel allows the user to create an image gallery in a page of content or editing an existing image gallery. The user is presented with a list of files that are found on the CMS filesystem and is allowed to add these files (by selecting the names from a list) to the image gallery content chunk. The user can also change the number of columns of the image gallery and change the size of the thumbnail that is presented within the gallery.

ImagePanel: Allows the user to add an image to a page of content. The user is presented with a list of files that currently exist on the CMS filesystem.

ListPanel: The panel that allows the user to create a list or edit an existing one. This panel contains a combo box that allows the user to choose what type of list (e.g., bulleted, numbered, definition list).

LoginPanel: This panel is presented to the user when the applet is first started up. This panel accepts the user's login name and password for authentication into the CMS.

MainMenuPanel: Displays three menu options to the user: manage users, manage look-and-feel, and manage content. The manage users button allows the user to view the manage users panel (assuming they have the correct account). The manage look-and-feel button allows the user to view the look-and-feel panel, and the manage content allows the user to view the manage content panel.

ManageContentPanel: A larger container for displaying several different other panels.

NewsSectionPanel: The panel that displays the news section and allows the user to add, edit, and delete items from the news section.

PagePanel: Displays page information within the form and allows the user to add and edit pages.

ParagraphPanel: Allows the user to add or edit existing paragraph content chunks. Offers rich text formatting.

SectionPanel: This panel allows the user to add or edit existing section content chunks.

SiteTasksPanel: Displays a menu to the user allowing them to choose to: add, edit, or delete pages; add, edit, or delete sections; and add, edit, or delete sub-chunk content types (e.g., paragraph, list, table, etc.).

TablePanel: Offers the user the ability to add or edit existing tables. Provides the user the ability to specify how many rows or columns of information the table has, in addition to allowing the user to individually edit each cell within the table.

TemplatesPanel: Allows the user to select a look-and-feel from a list of currently existing look-and-feels. No editing is offered in this panel.

UsersPanel: The users panel that offers the user with the ability to add, edit, and delete user accounts. This panel contains the add users panel, edit users panel, and the delete users panel.

REQUIRED SOFTWARE

ON THE CD

In order to build our CMS, we'll need certain software applications as well as libraries. The applications and libraries that are required for the designing, developing, building, and running of the CMS are included on the CD-ROM that accompanies this book. All applications used in this book for the creation of our CMS can be found on the CD-ROM in the *software* directory. All libraries that are used in this book for the creation of our CMS can be found on the CD-ROM in the *CMS-project\thirdparty\lib* directory.

NOTE

The CMS software referenced in this book is found on the accompanying CD-ROM and is called Kucing CMS 1.0, and is called such throughout the remainder of the book.

Java Development Kit

In order to compile and run the examples as well as Kucing CMS, you need to install the Java 2 Platform Standard Edition Development Kit 5.0. Previous versions of the Java 2 Platform Standard Edition Development Kit will not work. This is because Kucing CMS 1.0 uses one of the new features found in the Java platform: generics. Generics is a useful feature because it helps us to enforce type safety. For example, in our CMS, we may create an ImageGallery object:

```
ImageGallery imageGallery = new ImageGallery("Arron Ferguson");
imageGallery.setCaption("Camping Trip");
ImageRow imageRow = new ImageRow();
imageRow.addThumbnail(new Thumbnail("Arron Ferguson", "./thumb1.png",
    "./image1.png", "caption 1"));
imageRow.addThumbnail(new Thumbnail("Arron Ferguson", "./thumb2.png",
    "./image2.png", "caption 2"));
```

```
imageRow.addThumbnail(new Thumbnail("Arron Ferguson", "./thumb3.png",
    "./image3.png", "caption 3"));
imageGallery.addRow(imageRow);
```

Later on in our program (and in a different part of the software), we may wish to retrieve the thumbnail objects from the ImageGallery object:

```
List<Thumbnail> thumbnailReferences;
thumbnailReferences = imageGallery.getAllImageReferences();
```

The list that we've declared only accepts objects of type Thumbnail. We say that this list is a *generic* list that only accepts the type Thumbnail. This ensures that we'll only ever put Thumbnail objects into that list. In fact, by declaring the list using generics, we get compile-time errors if we attempt to put a different type in (other than objects of type Thumbnail). We've only scratched the surface with generics, but this should give a good impression on the importance of committing to Java 2 Platform Standard Edition Development Kit 5.0[4].

The latest Java 2 Platform Standard Edition Development Kit 5.0 can be obtained from Sun by visiting their Web site at *http://java.sun.com/j2se/1.5.0/download.jsp*. Be sure to select the J2SE Development Kit (JDK), not the J2SE Runtime Environment (JRE).

CAUTION

If you have a previous version of the Java 2 Platform Standard Edition Development Kit, be sure to uninstall it first before installing version 5.

jEdit

It is important to have efficient development tools that help us to be more productive in our software developing activities. Having an IDE or in the very least a source code text editor is considered core. At a bare minimum, we come to expect having the ability to display line count in our source code file, as well as color coding for keywords such as programming language reserved words, and standard library methods and classes. Without line count and color coding, we cannot be efficient. Other features that are considered essential are:

- Check-style—A feature that checks that syntactical rules of the programming language are being followed (e.g., code does not extend past 80 columns).
- Code folding—The ability to collapse a particular code block, method, or class in order to temporarily hide that particular portion of code from the viewer.
- Code completion—A feature that helps the programmer by completing code expressions. This helps alleviate the need by the programmer to remember all methods and variables within a class.
- Search—Not just searching a particular word, but also supporting regular expressions.

■ Line markers—The ability to flag a particular line of code and use quick keys to jump to any particular marked line.

■ Column markers—A feature that allows columns to be marked by a vertical line. This is useful for source code that may be printed in a document because the source code text may not wrap the page or may cause inconsistent formatting.

■ Split screen—offer multiple panes, which allows the programmer to simultaneously view different lines of code within the same source code file.

■ Compile call—Calling up the compiler to compile all code.

■ Runtime call—Calling up the runtime to run the program.

■ Project Management—The ability to manage a group of source code files together as a project (manage can mean add and delete files from the project—not necessarily from the filesystem).

Other features that are not necessarily considered essential but are definitely welcome:

■ Subversion support—Access to a subversion system so that version management and control can be performed on the source code.

■ Documentation support—Ability to generate documentation based on code comments found in the source code.

■ GUI Builder—The ability of being able to perform drag-and-drop GUI development.

■ Debugging—Allowing for the step-through of program code one line at a time, as well as tracking things like objects in memory, being able to see their values, and even stopping at break points.

About jEdit

While jEdit does not offer us all of these features, it does offer the essentials. Figure 2.26 shows jEdit in action. From this figure we can see the code folding, color coding (may not be completely visible in the grayscale image), column markers, line markers and line numbers. What's not available in the direct downloaded executable jEdit can most likely be found in a plugin that can be installed into jEdit. jEdit offers a handy feature that allows for the direct and up-to-date downloading of available plugins. By going to the Plugins menu of jEdit and selecting Plugin Manager, the set of plugin options becomes visible, as shown in Figure 2.27.

The plugin manager contacts the jEdit Web site (at *http://plugins.jedit.org*) and retrieves a list of available plugins, although you may not see this list retrieval operation if you have a fast connection to the Internet because it happens instantaneously. Figure 2.27 shows the list of plugins that are available within the Plugin Manager's Install tab.Installing jEdit.

FIGURE 2.26 Screenshot of jEdit.

FIGURE 2.27 jEdit Plugin Manager.

ON THE CD

The CD-ROM that came with this book contains a copy of jEdit. However, you can always obtain the most recent copy of jEdit; it is actually written in Java and requires the Java 2 Platform Standard Edition Runtime Environment. Therefore, it is cross-platform. In addition to a platform-independent Java Archive (JAR) installer, there are platform-specific install packages for the Microsoft Windows XP operating system, Apple Mac OS X, and the Linux Slackware. There are also installation instructions for each of these platforms, as well as a downloadable PDF document. The jEdit installers are easy to use and should not require any extra configuration choices other than following the directions found within the jEdit installer.

Apache Ant

Managing the compilation of software is greatly simplified with the use of a build tool. The Apache Software Foundation's Ant gives us much more than just building. Apache's Ant divides the functionality up into what are called tasks. A list of some of the types of tasks that can be performed by Ant are:

- Archiving (e.g., creating Java Archives (JARs), Gzip, and ZIP archives, Tape Archives (TARs), Web Archives (WARs), and Enterprise Archives (EARs). It can also extract GZip and ZIP archives, JARs and TARs
- Perform auditing which requires auditing types of tools such as Jdepend, which generates design quality metrics for each Java package in your build
- Compiling which includes, but is not limited to, the Java compiler `javac`
- Server deployment (for "hot" deployment on vendor specific Java 2 Platform, Enterprise Edition 1.4 servers)
- Generating documentation (e.g., `javadoc`)
- Developing Enterprise Java Beans (EJBs) which are vendor specific
- Execution tasks such as, but not limited to, calling the Java Virtual Machine (JVM)
- File tasks for checking/verifying, touching (updating timestamp), moving, copying, renaming, and deleting files
- Logging
- Sending mail to alert developers that a certain task has been performed (calls up a SMTP server)
- Remote tasks such as reading and writing files using FTP or perform filesystem tasks with Telnet
- Version control tasks

Testing tasks, which includes running JUnit for unit testing. All of these types of tasks make Apache Ant a powerful build and management tool because of Ant's extensibility. Ant can even be used to build Microsoft .NET applications. Although we'll be going through how to create and run build files for Ant in Chapter 7, we can look at how to install Ant in this chapter so as to be ready for building later on. Ant is under the Apache Software License Version 2.0. Based on this license, Ant is free to use, distribute, and also comes with the source code.

Installing Ant

ON THE CD

A copy of Apache's Ant comes on the CD-ROM that accompanies this book. However you can always check Apache's Web site (*http://ant.apache.org/*) for the most recent version. If you do decide to check for the most recent version of Ant, it is acquired by going to the download page for the Ant Web site at Apache (*http://ant. apache.org/bindownload.cgi*). Make sure to download the binary version instead of the source (unless you want to compile Ant on your own). Since Ant is written in Java, it does require the Java 2 Platform Standard Edition Development Kit to run and build applications. However, by using the Java 2 Platform Standard Edition Development Kit, it means that we can use Ant in multiple operating systems (OSs). Apache's Ant Web site states that Ant runs in Solaris, HP-UX, Windows 95 OS, Windows NT OS (although any NT-based OS works as well such as Windows 2000 OS, Windows Server 2003 OS, and Windows XP OS), OS/2 WARP®, Novell® NetWare® 6.x, and Apple Mac OS X. Ant comes as a zipped or gzipped archive and has no installer but that is okay because it is quite easy to install. Simply unzip (extract) the archive and choose a spot in your filesystem to place the Ant directory into. Figure 2.28 shows a possible choice for the Ant directory.

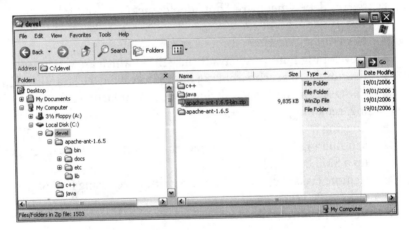

FIGURE 2.28 Ant download unzipped to filesystem.

The next step is to set up an Ant environment variable so that the command line (also called console or prompt) recognizes Ant at the command line. The Ant `bin` directory (see Figure 2.28) contains the appropriate batch and shell scripts in order to correctly run at the command line. All you need to do is create two environment variables and append to your path environment variable. To do this in the Windows OS, you need the following:

```
set ANT_HOME=c:\devel\apache-ant-1.6.5
set JAVA_HOME= c:\Program Files\Java\jdk1.5.0
set PATH=%PATH%;%ANT_HOME%\bin
```

The ANT_HOME environment variable simply points to the directory that you've installed Ant. The Java home environment variable (if you don't already have this set up for another application) simply points to the root directory of your Java 2 Platform Standard Edition Development Kit and the last statement simply appends the ANT_HOME environment variable to the path which makes the batch files and shell scripts visible to the command line. Doing the same thing in Unix using the bash shell:

```
export ANT_HOME=/usr/local/apache-ant-1.6.5
export JAVA_HOME=/usr/local/jdk-1.5.0
export PATH=${PATH}:${ANT_HOME}/bin
```

Or Unix using the csh shell:

```
setenv ANT_HOME /usr/local/apache-ant-1.6.5
setenv JAVA_HOME /usr/local/jdk-1.5.0
set path=( $path $ANT_HOME/bin )
```

The complete Ant manual can be viewed at Apache's Web site (*http://ant.apache.org/manual/index.html*). Chapter 7 covers creating Ant build files and running them.

ArgoUML

Designing a software system using Unified Modeling Language (UML) helps speed up the development process. However, there is a shortage of free (or in the very least inexpensive UML tools). ArgoUML is an open source UML design tool, which means it is free to download (*http://argouml.tigris.org/*), use, and redistribute. The ArgoUML manual (which is found on the Web site at: *http://argouml.tigris.org/documentation/defaulthtml/manual/*) points out that ArgoUML tries to make the design process more intuitive by taking into account cognitive psychology theories. Application of these theories in ArgoUML offer:

Checklists: Suggestions given by the software (e.g., naming associations, method naming, design pattern choices, whether or not classes may be subclassed, etc.) that assist the designer through the design process.

Design Critics: An interesting feature that keeps threads running in the background which check your design choices to determine if there are possible ways to improve the design.

To-do Lists: A feature that allows design critics to offer suggestions which encourage collaboration and feedback to the design.

Figure 2.29 shows an example of the ArgoUML UI and a design that is opened. Projects can be created and developers can import existing source code and packages, as well as output source code stubs. ArgoUML can build class diagrams, use case diagrams, collaboration diagrams, state chart diagrams, activity diagrams and deployment diagrams. At the current version (0.18.1) ArgoUML, does not allow the developer to create sequence diagrams. However, for the price paid, ArgoUML offers some excellent features—including outputting diagrams as Scalable Vector Graphics (SVG) files, Postscript (PS) files, and Encapsulated Postscript (EPS) files.

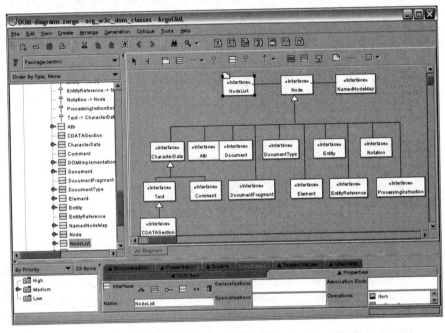

FIGURE 2.29 Screenshot of an ArgoUML class diagram.

Installing ArgoUML

ON THE CD
A version of ArgoUML is found on the CD-ROM that came with this book, but you can always check the Web site for the most recent version (*http://argouml.tigris. org/servlets/ProjectDocumentList*). ArgoUML is written in Java and so it requires the Java 2 Platform Standard Edition Runtime Environment. The software is archived inside of a zip file, so you'll need Zip extraction software to unzip the file. Simply unzip the archive and place the extracted directory into a directory of your choosing. If the graphical environment you're working in associates JAR files with the Java runtime, then it's simply a matter of double-clicking the argouml.jar file

icon. If this doesn't work, then you'll have to invoke the software yourself. First, navigate to the directory that you installed the archive into (for example):

```
cd c:\apps\ArgoUML-0.18.1
```

Then invoke the Java runtime using the `-jar` option:

```
java -jar argouml.jar
```

You may wish to create a batch file or shell script in place of invoking the program at the command prompt.

Abeille Forms Designer

Abeille Forms Designer is a GUI Builder for Java's Swing API. The application itself is licensed under the Lesser General Public License (LGPL); so it is free for download, distribution, and using (home page at: *https://abeille.dev.java.net/*). However, for greater flexibility, some of the libraries that Abeille Forms Designer uses are under the Berkeley Software Distribution (BSD) license, so any software application's GUI built using Abeille Forms Designer can be incorporated into free software or commercial (proprietary) software.

Software licenses, software license issues, and open source licenses are covered in Chapter 3.

NOTE

Abeille Forms Designer uses a layout manager called the Forms Layout, which is a library found under the JGoodies Project (home page: *https://jgoodies.dev. java.net/*). Figure 2.30 displays one of the GUIs build for Kucing CMS 1.0. The design view displays the layout by using a grid where each row and column can be widened or narrowed. The Toolbar (left side) offers a choice of components that can be dropped into the layout and modified. Drag-and-drop is supported and the Control Panel (right side, under Form Properties label) displays all attributes of a particular GUI component, making it quite easy to change, for example, the color or font used for a component.

Having a rich set of components to choose from within an API means that the application programmer will not have to write GUI components from scratch. Having to write custom components, such as graphical tree components or table components, means that the time spent writing the software increases, which increases the cost of the software development process. Java's Swing API offers a rich set of GUI components that prevent the application programmer from having to reinvent the wheel. Abeille Forms Designer supports the Swing GUI components by displaying them graphically and allowing the user to simply drag and drop the components

NOTE

into the form in design view. Additionally custom components can also be brought into the design view.

In addition to a rich set of components, most GUI designers and programmers expect WYSIWYG tools or GUI builders, as they're sometimes called. These tools allow the developer to visually create UIs by using drag-and-drop technology. Creating UIs this way can drastically reduce the amount of time spent writing GUI frontend code. Finding a GUI builder in the Java world can be a challenge because it is hard to find a GUI builder that manages to support the complex layout model that is part of the GUI building process.

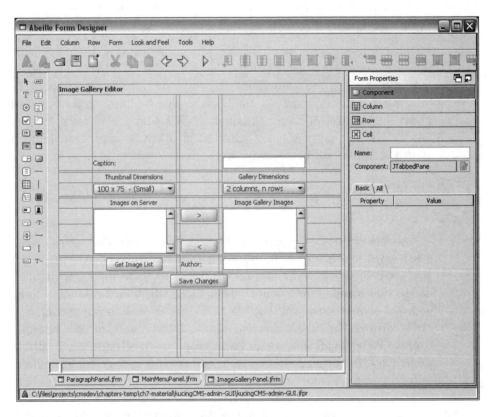

FIGURE 2.30 Screenshot of an Abeille Forms Designer form.

To keep in line with the notion of modular design, Abeille Forms Designer allows for forms to be linked into other forms. This is extremely useful, especially for complex layouts that may have different justification and fill characteristics. Figure 2.31 shows an example of five different forms. The Site Tasks (top left), Page Tasks (mid-

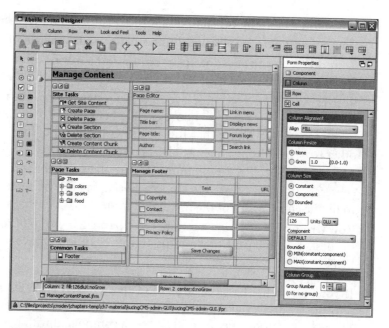

FIGURE 2.31   Design view showing a form within a form.

dle left), the Common Tasks (bottom left), Page Editor (top right), and Manage Footer (bottom right) forms are all shown linked within the Manage Content form.

The three icon group that represents a linked form is found in Figure 2.32. The minus icon collapses the linked form making it invisible in the design view. Clicking the diagonal arrow jumps to that form and opens it up in a separate tab. The grid icon toggles between showing the grid in the linked form or hiding it. When changes are made to the linked forms, the update is shown in the containing form. This is useful in situations that have a different number of rows and columns for certain parts of a layout. As well, the developer can concentrate on specific portions of the UI.

FIGURE 2.32   Linked form icon group.

Creating layouts is accomplished by first specifying a grid and then assigning row and column weights to them. Components can span more than row or column. Row and column widths can be defined using the following characteristics:

Constant: Choosing constant disallows a row or columns to be resized.

Component: Sets the row or columns to the width or height of the component.

Bounded: Sets the lower or upper bounds for a row or column's start size before it has been resized.

Resize: Allows for a resizable layout. If you feel that your GUI needs to support resizing, then you need to choose a value between 0.0 and 1.0. The value is a percentage of weighting that the row or column should be given relative to other rows or columns that are also attempting to resize.

Alignment: Specifies how components are aligned in the row or column. Top, center, bottom, or fill are the choices. Specifying fill will force the component to fill the entire width of the row or column.

Row Group: By applying a number to a particular group of rows or columns, the designer can ensure that groups of rows or columns have the same width or height.

If you've ever used Web design tools that offer WYSIWYG design features, then Abeille Forms Designer may seem quite familiar. This is because components are dragged into cells within the grid and each component within a cell can have independent alignment attributes given to it, including how many rows or columns a particular component spans. Abeille Forms Designer does allow for specifying layout using absolute coordinates (using pixels as the unit of measure, for example). Normally specifying absolute coordinates is considered to be a bad thing. This is because the look-and-feel in Swing may change, and specifying absolute coordinates will be dependent on the width and height that each component from the previous look-and-feel was defined in. However, Abeille Forms Designer offers several different units of measure, including one unit called DLU, which is a unit of measure that scales with the font. So if the look-and-feel changes the size and type of the font, the layout adjusts, based on the new font size used. This approach takes the best of both worlds, allowing quasi-absolute positioning while at the same time offering freedom to be specific about coordinates.

Code Generation

Abeille Forms Designer outputs clean code (as compared to some GUI builders) although this is only a one-way procedure—code cannot be imported, only exported. As mentioned earlier, Abeille Forms Designer is offered under the LGPL license, whereas the runtime is offered under the BSD license. This difference allows for outputted GUIs to be included in proprietary applications without causing license breaches (LGPL would not allow for this). By outputting to code, however, the developer loses some of the features found in the runtime:

- Fill effects (e.g., gradient fills, texture fills)
- The horizontal and vertical line components
- Some of the line borders
- JList items
- JComboBox item icons

Losing these features is not too much of an inconvenience, and it offers the simplicity of being decoupled from the runtime leaving the only dependency on the JGoodies Forms library and the JGoodies Looks look-and-feel library (assuming you want to use a different look-and-feel). It is also easy enough to add, for example, your own gradient effects or anti-aliased labels or images.

Installing Abeille Forms Designer

Abeille Forms Designer is written in Java and so it requires the Java 2 Platform Standard Edition Runtime Environment in order to run. This, however, is a perk because it means that it is cross-platform. Installing Abeille Forms Designer is quite simple, and like ArgoUML, it comes as a compressed archive (zip format). Therefore, installing Abeille Forms Designer is simply a matter of extracting the archive and placing the extracted directory (usually called `abeilleforms`) into a directory of your choosing. You can run Abeille Forms Designer from the command line by navigating to the extracted directory and typing:

```
java -jar designer.jar
```

Or you can create a batch file or shell script depending on the operating system you're running in.

Tomcat

Tomcat is another Apache Software Foundation offering. It is a reference implementation servlet container that supports the Java Servlet and JavaServer Pages™ technologies. Tomcat is an open source project developed under the Apache License 2.0; so it is free to download, use, and redistribute under different needs (e.g., commercial). When Tomcat was first released, it was considered only for presenting dynamic content (content generated by piecing together data from various sources including databases, text, XML, or Web documents) and not static Web pages. However with version 5.5, Tomcat can handle static content as well as dynamic content for small to mid-size Web sites. As always, it can be used solely for the generation of dynamic content. Chapter 7 covers configuring Tomcat to use with Kucing CMS 1.0.

Installing Tomcat

Because Tomcat is written in Java, it is cross platform. Although it can run with Java 2 Platform Standard Edition Runtime Environment 1.4 or 1.3, it takes an extra step in downloading an extra library. Using the Java 2 Platform Standard Edition Runtime Environment 5.0 platform requires no extra downloading or configuring; so it is best to use the 5.0 runtime environment. A copy of Tomcat is on the CD-ROM that came with this book. If however you wish to, you can go to the Tomcat Web site (*http://tomcat.apache.org/*) and check for the newest version. Tomcat is open source; therefore you can choose to download the source code if you wish. Most will want to simply download the binary version.

ON THE CD

NOTE

Older versions of Tomcat prior to 5.5, required the Java 2 Platform Standard Edition Development Kit rather than the Java Platform Standard Edition Runtime Environment. This was because the JSP compiler required the Java compiler. However, with the arrival of 5.5, you do not need the development kit: only the Java runtime. Tomcat 5.5 now uses the Eclipse JDT Java compiler. There are several download choices that can be made for Tomcat 5.5. Apache has conveniently split the functionality up so that developers only download what they need (e.g., only the Web application deployer or the embedded version of Tomcat, which assumes that Tomcat will only be used as a servlet container and not a Web server). All but one download is in the form of a compressed archive (zip format). This makes it easy for developers on any platform to simply extract the archive into the directory of choosing and run Tomcat. The noncompressed archive is for the Microsoft Windows platform and comes in the form of a self-extracting and self-installing executable which installs itself as a service.

Required Libraries

Our CMS application requires some extra libraries in order to run within the Apache Software Foundation's Tomcat. The libraries are free to download and distribute, are included on the CD-ROM that comes with this book, and are found in the *CMS-project\thirdparty\libdirectory.JSTL.*

The JavaServer Pages Standard Tag Library (JSTL) is tag library that supports functionality for basic scripting, doing XML processing, internationalization, formatting, and support for databases that support the SQL. JSTL is fairly easy to understand and use because it is more of a functional language which focuses on the evaluation of expressions. A simple example using the JSTL is found in Listing 2.1.

LISTING 2.1   Hello World With JSTL

```
<%@ page contentType="text/html; charset=ISO-8859-1" %>
<%@ taglib uri="http://java.sun.com/jstl/core" prefix="c" %>

<html><head><title>Hello World JSTL!</title></head>
  <body>
    <p>
      <c:set var="greeting" value="Hello World!"/>
      <c:out value="${greeting}"/>
    </p>
  </body>
</html>
```

 Although the finished implementation of our CMS (that we are creating in this book) actually uses JSP technology and the JSTL, we don't cover it because we are making little use of its functionality.

XPP/MXP

XML Pull Parser (XPP) is a pull parser that offers an interface written in Java that allows implementing classes to offer pull parsing functionality. The Maximum Performance (MXP) parser is one of the implementing parsers of XPP. In order to keep the CMS memory footprint down to a minimum as well as make an attempt at making the parsing process fast, this library is used to read and write all XML documents within Kucing CMS. The topic of XML parsing is covered in Chapter 6.

JGoodies Forms and JGoodies Looks

The JGoodies Forms and Looks libraries have been used specifically in the Kucing CMS applet's GUI. First, the Forms library offers a powerful yet simple way to use layout manager, which allows for extremely complex GUI layouts with a minimal amount of work. The Looks library offers different look-and-feels to be applied to a Java GUI. Both of these libraries are required for the Kucing CMS applet.

Apache's Xalan

Xalan is Apache's library for transforming XML using XSLT style sheets. Xalan has been around for a few years; so it has the advantage of being quite stable and rich in features. And because it is made by the same developers as the Tomcat Web server, it works flawlessly with Tomcat.

SUMMARY

In this chapter we looked at what a CMS is by studying some of the core features we expect from a CMS. We also looked at CMS architecture and explored scalable designs using multitiers for constructing the CMS, as well as potential solutions to load balancing. We finally started the process of designing a CMS where we first addressed the functional requirements, created ERDs, DFDs, and class diagrams for each tier of our CMS project. The designs that we produced in this chapter can help guide us through the rest of the book and help us in the development process. Finally, we looked at some of the applications and libraries available to us for creating our software.

The next chapter looks at some of the issues software developers (specifically CMS developers) face when attempting to build a CMS from pre-existing libraries that may contain restrictive software licenses and how problems can be avoided.

ENDNOTES

1. Forum posts only contain the date created and not a date modified. This is because once a post is created, users are not allowed to modify a post.
2. Marshal is a term that means that the objects and data structures in memory (based on whatever programming language is being used) can be saved out as XML as per the W3C's XML recommendation.
3. Yourdon/DeMarco notation, named after Ed Yourdon and Tom DeMarco, is a DFD style where the processes are represented as circles. Because this notation allows for both data as well as control flow (within the diagram), it can be used to model real-time systems.
4. For a thorough introduction to generics in Java, Sun has provided a document for Java programmers wishing to get up to speed on this topic at *http://java.sun.com/j2se/1.5/pdf/generics-tutorial.pdf.*

3 | Licensing Issues

In This Chapter

- What types of information are covered in a software license?
- What is copyright?
- What is open source software?
- Popular software licenses
- Popular documentation licenses
- The issues in using multiple licenses

Most software developers don't want to have to deal with licensing issues when they develop software. They often put off addressing licensing and suggest that it's more of an issue for lawyers or individuals with legal experience. Current times, however, dictate that software developers be part lawyer as well. This is because of the multitude of licenses and software components that are available to the typical software developer. A software developer rarely builds an entire piece of software from scratch. Many tools and code libraries are available, and many are even free. The astute software developer embraces the topic of licensing so as to be careful not to infringe on copyright or break licensing terms. Today's software developer must sidestep the licensing landmine landscape that exists today.

LICENSES IN GENERAL

Licensing can be an issue of contention if it is not understood. Many licensing rules get broken simply out of confusion or a lack of understanding of the terms of the license. Therefore, it helps to fully understand the world of software licensing before producing and delivering our content management system. By being informed, we can avoid litigation and other annoyances.

Unlike other industries, the software industry does not deal with physical products or services. Software is abstract by its very nature (hence the word soft in software). For this reason, it must be treated differently than products from other industries. When you purchase a car, you purchase that particular car. You are not licensing the car (unless you have explicitly done so), you own it or the bank owns it, depending on whether you borrowed the money to make the purchase. Additionally, the car is physical. You can walk around it, touch it, drive it, and show it off in your driveway on Saturday morning as you wash it. When you purchase a suit, you are purchasing the actual articles of clothing that make up that suit (coat, slacks, vest). There is no need to restrict how or where you use the suit, or even if you lend it to a friend. The suit is yours.

Both the car and the suit are physical and are made of substance. It would be quite costly for an individual to plan and actually make a copy of either. The time involved and the parts or the material for duplicating the car or suit respectively would be costly at best, not to mention the expertise that would be required in doing so. Software, on the other hand, is much more abstract. It exists only within a computer's memory and storage devices. And unlike a nice car (or suit), software can easily be duplicated by transferring the data from one storage device to another. The storage media is cheap, the time taken to perform the duplication process is measured in minutes not days or months, and the expertise required to perform the duplication could be obtained by a trained monkey[1]. Because of this, the rules for selling and distributing software have to be much more complex than the rules for selling and distributing cars and suits. In order to start understanding software licensing, it first helps to understand the following terms[2]:

License: A document or form that contains rules for usage, distributability and ownership of a piece of software.

Licensee: The person, company, or organization to which a license is applied.

Licensor: The person, company, or organization that is granting the license.

Exclusive License: A license that restricts the software to only one licensee.

Non-exclusive License: A license that pertains to more than one person, company, or organization.

Third Party: Refers to a person, company, or organization that is neither the licensee nor the licensor. Refers to anyone outside of the license agreement.

End user: An individual who uses the software to which the license is made for.

EULA: An acronym which stands for End User License Agreement. It refers to a software license.

Software: Usually means the executable binary program that an end user runs, but can also mean all other accompanying files including (but not limited to) documentation, example files, templates, multimedia files, the license itself, and any other accompanying files.

Intellectual Property: Also known by its acronym (IP). Material including (but not limited to) software, files, documentation that has been created by a person, company, or organization. It is referred to in licenses, copyright material, patents, and trademarks to specify ownership and rights.

Commercial Version: A particular version of software that allows the software to be used in a commercial setting. This means that the software can be used to make profit from.

Educational Version: A particular version of software that restricts the software from being used commercially. This means it is restricted to students and faculty of educational institutes, such as grade schools, universities, and colleges.

TBYB: The acronym for Try Before You Buy. It refers to software that can be acquired (usually by downloading) and used first in order to see if the software's features live up to user expectations, at which point the licensee is expected to purchase the software.

Trial Version: A TBYB version of the software that is to be used only for demonstration, testing, and evaluation purposes only. Trial software usually has a usage limit that is imposed on either the number of uses or the number of days that the software can be used—after which the software may stop working. Alternatively, trial versions may run indefinitely, but have certain key features disabled, such as saving files.

NFR: The acronym for Not For Resale. This term is usually applied to software that is being used for demonstrational, testing, and evaluation purposes. It means that the software cannot be sold.

Serial Number Validation: A step required by the user in order to enable the software. The licensee acquires the serial number at the time of purchase and is expected to enter the serial number, usually on the first time the software is executed.

Decompile: Converting the binary executable software into source code. Requires a high level of understanding and a software application that can change the binary executable into source code of a particular programming language.

Reverse Engineer: Decompiling the software so as to make changes to it, which changes the software's original behavior. This can mean changing the software so that it does not require registration, serial number validation, or enabling features that require further licensing.

Work: Usually referring to the finished product, which is the software, although it can also mean the source code that was used to generate the software, as well. Usually the term work is used to describe noncommercial software.

Product: The software. This term is used when referring to commercial software that was purchased. It usually means the binary executable, documentation, and any other accompanying files. More often than not, there is no source code included.

Derivative Work: A work that is based on the original software.

Distribution: The process of disseminating the software to the licensees. This is done by either the licensor or by a third party that is acting on the licensor's behalf, based on some prearranged agreement.

Redistribution: Refers to the dissemination of software (usually but not always) by a third party, but can also be the licensee.

Transferable: Used within the context of a license (e.g., transferable license). Means that a license can change licensees. Most software licenses are non-transferable.

Mindshare: The ability to make the general public think of a particular brand name or company when there is desire for a type of service or product.

Copyright: Legal protection that is given to a work such as intellectual property. It restricts all but the copyright holder from the ability to copy, distribute, redistribute, and make changes to, produce, or publish a work. A copyright may or may not be required to be registered with a country's government. A copyright usually lasts at least the lifetime of the creator of the copyright and can usually be extended some additional years.

Trademark: A name, word, symbol, or logo that is used to identify a company, organization, or product. It is a way of ensuring that a company, organization, or product maintains public visibility for the purposes of doing business or keeping mindshare. Trademarks must be registered by a country's government. A trademark does not usually have a limited lifetime.

Patent: Legal protection of an invention that is applied to a work, such as intellectual property. Patents are either given to the inventors of the work or the company or organization that the inventor works for, depending on contractual obligations between the inventor and the company or organization. Patents must be registered by a country's government. A patent has a limited lifetime which is based on the rules given by the particular country's government that the patent is registered with.

The terms copyright, trademark, and patent often get confused and misused by interchanging them. Copyrights are applied to original works, such as written material like books, artwork (e.g., painting), and software. Patents are quite specific and can only be applied to inventions. An invention can be quite concrete, such as a mechanical device like a combustible engine. An invention can also be quite abstract, such as the process for determining which genes in the human body can cause lung cancer. A trademark is only applicable to a name, word, symbol, or logo. For example, you cannot trademark a book, nor can you trademark an invention (but you can trademark a name or logo that you assign to that invention). One characteristic all three share is legal protection—they all provide legal protection to the holder.

Many countries offer copyright, patent, and trademark protection and even honor the same from other countries. However, not all of the rules may be the same. For example, the lifetime of a copyright in one country may be different than the lifetime of the same copyright found within a different country. For developing software, you will probably only use copyright protection. Putting copyright protection on your software will help to ensure (at the least) that you are given credit for being the original author.

One last point to note is that all three (trademark, patent, and copyright) are transferable. This means that you can give, sell, or trade your trademark, patent, or copyright to another party. For example, when an author of a book wishes to sell the book, he will sign a contract, which legally transfers the copyright over to a book publisher. This must be done because the publisher must have copyright in order to mass-produce and distribute copies of the book.

With all of these legal terms thrown around, it's easy to get discouraged and wonder why a software developer should even be considering the whole licensing issue. The answer is clear. Understanding licensing offers us the ability to reduce or hopefully eliminate confusion concerning:

- Ownership of the software
- Usage rights and restrictions of the software
- Distribution rights and restrictions of the software
- Transfer rights and restrictions of the software
- Copyrights and restrictions of the software
- Publishing rights and restrictions of the software
- Editing rights and restrictions of the software
- Output rights and restrictions of the software

Ownership Rights

It helps to understand ownership when talking about software. When you purchase (or acquire) a software copy, you are not actually the owner of that software. This may sound confusing, as it is clearly in your possession. The truth is, you don't own the software. We can go so far as to say that you have not even purchased the software—you've only purchased a license for (or of) that software. This may sound like splitting hairs, but it is important to make this distinction because whoever owns the software controls the rights to that software. An example of what you may find in a typical EULA:

```
This software is protected by copyright and is the intellectual
property of Arron Ferguson. Arron Ferguson retains all rights and
permissions to the software. This software is licensed, not sold.
```

This means that you do not own the software; you have simply purchased the right to adhere to the license of the software. If you do not agree to the terms of the license, you are expected to abandon both the license and the software that the license binds to.

Exclusivity

The term exclusive has been misused in many industries—especially by the media. It is quite common to hear a news report starting off with "We bring you this exclusive interview . . ." Clearly the news report looses its exclusivity once it is broadcast. To be exclusive is to offer something that is not offered to others. Software that is given exclusively to a licensee is software that cannot be licensed to anyone else. For this reason, most software falls under a *non-exclusive* license. All software that you purchase, such as operating systems, productivity applications such as office programs, image manipulation programs, animation programs, and all other software programs refer to the license as being non-exclusive. A typical EULA contains something like:

```
This software license is non-exclusive.
```

If the license were exclusive, only one person would be able to purchase and use this product under the license. Being non-exclusive is not just for commercial software. Free software also must be non-exclusive. For example, the Apache License Version 2.0 in Section 2 contains the following:

```
2. Grant of Copyright License. Subject to the terms and conditions
   of this License, each Contributor hereby grants to You a
   perpetual, worldwide, non-exclusive, no-charge, royalty-free,
   irrevocable copyright license to reproduce, prepare Derivative
   Works of, publicly display, publicly perform, sublicense, and
```

```
distribute the Work and such Derivative Works in Source or Object
form.
```

Usage Rights

A good software license makes explicit the usage rights of the software. This becomes especially important if there are different versions or editions of the software. Having different versions of a piece of software can help increase the marketability and interest in the software. With different versions, come different usage rights. Looking at the different versions helps us to identify the differences in usage rights. Typically there are four different types of usage rights for a piece of software:

- Commercial
- Educational
- Trial
- Free

Commercial Version

A commercial version of the software offers the greatest amount of flexibility for usage to the licensee. Most importantly, it allows the licensee to use the software to make profit. Profit can be money, recognition, market share, digital resources, or anything else that is considered profit. The licensee can be a corporation, partnership, or proprietorship. If the software is an imaging program, then the outputted images from the software can be sold. If the software is a 3D animation package, then the outputted 3D animation can be sold (e.g., TV or motion picture films). If the software is a compiler, then the outputted binaries can be sold as software products. However, compiler software is not usually as straightforward because there are usually dependencies on code libraries requiring further investigation into distribution and redistribution rights.

Educational Version

An educational version is more restrictive with usage rights. A software version that is considered educational restricts the usage to a formal classroom setting or, in the least, to a registered student of a course or program and to the faculty teaching that course or program. Most educational licenses make it clear that a user cannot simply acquire a copy of the software and decide to use it for the sake of learning how it works. The usage restriction most likely states that the software is not to be used in a commercial setting (i.e., for profit). An example may of educational restrictions within an EULA may look like:

```
This software is for educational use only. You may only use this
software either as a student, instructor, or faculty of a public or
private education institution and you are directly involved with
the course(s) that the software is licensed for. You may not use
this software for commercial use, within any business setting or
government setting other than the course(s) stated above.
```

The above statement makes it clear that the software may not be used for the purpose of profit (i.e., in a commercial setting) and also goes on to ensure that there is no confusion about whether the software can be used for individual training—it must be a course. It is important to remember that the more detail the license contains, the less chance there is for misinterpretation and misuse. Sometimes the software license is intended to be distributed with several different versions of the software (e.g., commercial, educational, trial). Although this practice helps to eliminate accidentally distributing the wrong license with the software, it increases the need to list all rules for every licensing scenario and to ensure that the rules are all compatible with each version of the software[3].

Trial Version

A trial version only allows the licensee to use the software for the purposes of determining whether the software is acceptable and worth purchasing a license on. The licensee is expected to use the software to see if the features live up to expectations and nothing more. This type of usage restriction is useful because it doesn't require a potential customer to commit to the purchase before feeling comfortable with the software. The licensee can download the software and simply start using it. This is important because most software licenses clearly state that once the software has been opened from its packaging, the software license is considered purchased and nonrefundable.

Software that is licensed under a trial version has a usage limit imposed on it. This limit may be either a time limit or a specified number of times that the software may be used. Some software simply informs the licensee that the usage limit has expired, but this is usually avoided because it is all too easy for a licensee to continue using the software past the usage limit. More often than not, the software simply refuses to execute past the limit. Another mechanism for limiting usage is by turning off key features. For example, the software can allow all features to be used with the exception of saving files. A 3D animation software program that is a trial version may allow potential animators to use the software to see how the interface feels, the quality of the renderer, but not allow the files that contain the 3D objects to be saved.

Free Version

A free version of the software allows users free access to the software. The term free usually applies to more than just the usage (i.e., distribution, copy, transfer, etc.). Software that comes as a free version may have certain limitations placed on it, such as requiring any output generated by the software to bear a logo, company, organization name, or copyright notice. More often than not, free software does not contain very many restrictions or limitations. Free version software can be quite a successful vehicle for getting exposure to the software out to the public. Unlike trial version software, free version software can be used indefinitely and usually doesn't contain any limitations imposed on features that exist in the software. A company or organization may release two versions of the software: (1) a full commercial version with all features, and (2) a limited feature set free version that anybody can use for any reason. This allows licensees to make use of the software without paying for it, while at the same time helping the company or organization gain mindshare of the product. If licensees consider the software useful and want to upgrade, they can then move to the full commercial version and pay for the extra features.

Distribution Rights

A distribution right is the right to make copies of the software and share those copies with others, whether privately or publicly. Most (if not all) commercial versions of software completely restrict licensees from all distribution rights. Educational versions of the software also restrict from distributing the software. Only trial versions and free versions of software allow distribution and redistribution. An example of the wording that restricts distribution rights might look something like this:

```
License Restrictions
By accepting this license, the licensee agrees:
A. Not to distribute, redistribute, publish in any form of
electronic or printed communication, the software that falls under
this license.
```

If a software license allows distribution, it most likely disallows modifying the software[4]. If the license allows for redistribution, there may be restrictions imposed on the licensed software, such as:

- Not attempting to decompile, reverse engineer, replace, or add to any of the existing software.
- You do not attempt to remove or change any of the notices or rules stated in the software.
- You do not attempt to place the software in another license agreement that contradicts what the license has already stated.

By placing all of these restrictions clearly and concisely into the license, this eliminates misunderstandings as to what the software is allowed to be used for. Any breaches of a license of this kind are most likely be the fault of the licensee, not the licensor.

Transfer Rights

A transfer right within the context of the software license is the ability to transfer the license from one licensee to another (second) licensee (sometimes referred to as a sublicense). Most commercial versions of software do not allow transfer rights and instead restrict them. Recall that software can easily be copied, unlike a car or suit. Because of this, it would be easy for the licensee to make a copy and pass along the original to another person.

Transfers can be applied to the following scenarios:

- Consignment
- Rentals
- Leases
- Lending
- Selling

In other words, a license can completely restrict all transfer situations. Again, stating these rules in a license is beneficial because it clears up any misunderstandings between the licensor and the licensee.

Copying Rights

Unless software is free and all other rules allow for unlimited distribution and unlimited transferability, copying most likely is restricted, as well. Copy restrictions are in place for the same reason that transfer restrictions are in place: to stop anyone other than the licensee from obtaining a copy of the software. Sometimes a license may allow for a second copy to be made, by and for the licensee. Usually when a license allows for a second copy to be made, there is a restriction placed on the purpose of the second copy:

- Second copy is a backup copy
- Second copy is on a secondary computer

Backup Copy

A backup copy is made so that if the primary copy of the software becomes damaged or corrupted, then the licensee has another copy to use. Licenses that allow this make it clear that this is the only reason for making a backup. We may see something like:

You are allowed to create one copy of the licensed software that is
to be used solely for the purposes of creating a backup copy. All
copyright notices, all trademarks, and all patent notices must be
copied along with the licensed software.

Copy on Secondary Computer

Sometimes a license may allow for the licensee to have a second copy actually installed on another computer. When a license allows for this, it's usually made explicit that the computer is an auxiliary computer. An example of this situation may be when a person has a primary desktop computer that is in the office, but also has a laptop computer that he takes with him. It would be inconvenient to have to uninstall and then reinstall the software on each computer each time the licensee wished to use the software. Therefore, a provision such as this helps accommodate this situation, as well as keep the licensee honest. Setting up such a license needs to address the following issues:

- Does the software run from a network server?
- Does the software require connection to a server application that validates the licensee and the software?
- Do software upgrades affect the version (i.e., do the upgrades need to be of the same version of the software as was originally obtained by the license)?
- Does the need to install on an auxiliary computer require a different type of license?

CAUTION

It is important to make the distinction between copying rights and a copyright. Copying rights are the rights and/or restrictions placed on duplicating the software. A copyright is usually a formal registration (with government) that is made not only to restrict copying but also to publicize the author.

Publishing Rights

Publishing is really a specific form of distribution. It is usually applicable only to book publishers who release computer media with a book. This is a common desire when the license is based on software that is a software development kit (SDK). Common restrictions and requirements that must be adhered to include (but are not limited to):

- Disallowing modification of the licensed software.
- Restricting a publisher from simply distributing the software only—it is expected that the licensed software is included with published material.

■ Prominently placed logos of the company, its trademarked name, and copyright notice.

■ No monies should be charged for publishing the licensed software unless the license allows for this.

Editing Rights

The editing or modifying issue can be applied to the executable binaries as well as other files that are included with the software including templates, example files, and artwork. Most licenses make it clear that editing or modifying is not allowed. An example of such a restriction may be:

```
License Restrictions
C. You may not edit, modify, decompile, reverse engineer, or change
in any way the licensed software.
```

It is important to remember that the clearer you make the license, the less chance there is of misunderstanding. This provides legal protection if there is ever a dispute.

Output Rights

Output rights and restrictions can be difficult issues to deal with. This is because the output can contain content from the original licensed software. Content can be in the form of:

■ Executable binaries

■ Artwork from the original software licensed

Executable Binaries Output

Unless a separate license exists for output, software that is licensed to include part of itself with the end result output can cause immense difficulties if the licensing for the original software contains restrictions with distribution, copying, and usage. This is especially true if output relies on the executable binaries from the original software licensed. An example would be a runtime environment, such as interpreter software, or prebuilt code libraries that perform some sort of function, such as socket connections to Web servers. It is best to include all details when the licensed software includes part of itself with the output that the licensee generates.

Original Artwork Output

If original artwork (artwork that is part of the original software license) is included with the output, the rights and restrictions should be clearly defined. An example of this may be a computer game. With current operating system software and video software, it is quite easy to either create screen captures or record to digital video a game in progress. On its own, this action sounds rather harmless, assuming the licensee is viewing this content privately. But it may not be clear if the screen capture or video clip is presented in any other medium (e.g., film, television, the Web). To ensure that this is adhered to, it makes sense to insert a restriction into the license:

```
Publicly displaying either the game, gameplay, or artwork from the game
in any medium be it television, film, or World Wide Web is strictly
prohibited.
```

Alternatively, to loosen the restriction by permission from the licensor:

```
Publicly displaying either the game, gameplay, or artwork from the game
in any medium be it television, film, or World Wide Web is strictly
prohibited without written permission from the licensor.
```

The goal is to remove all ambiguities from the license so that no rules of the license are broken—intentionally or unintentionally.

Source Code Visibility

A fairly new issue, now part of software licenses, is the issue of whether the source code is visible to the licensee. Historically, software was not included because it exposed the inner workings of the licensed software to all who purchase it. The fear was that others would copy the source code for their own use, and they would no longer require the original licensed software. Current software trends have dictated that some or sometimes all of the source code should be visible to the licensee. Although there is a danger that the source code will be duplicated, there are several advantages in including the source code:

- Knowledgeable licensees can help debug the licensed software if they encounter bugs and are able to trace the source code.
- It forces developers to write neater and more efficient code because their customers can see how they've written the software. If the licensed software source code is written poorly and the customer can compare it to other source code, it may cause licensees to turn to a different source for the software.
- Current software is usually so large in size that it is difficult (if not impossible) to commercially copy software source code in its entirety and get away with claiming the copy is not the same as the original.
- If the licensed software contains a plugin architecture (i.e., the ability for third party software developers to write components that work with the original software package), then it is easier for third party developers to create plugin software components—the interface and its implementation are easy to trace through.

■ Licensee trust can be increased. This is important if the software requires the ability to connect to central servers. A licensee can see exactly what the licensor's software source code is doing and not have to suspect anything strange.

The term source code visibility should not be confused with the term open source. Although there is some overlap with both definitions, they do not mean the same thing. Open source is covered later in this chapter.

When source code is visible, there is the need to stipulate what exactly is (not) allowed:

```
License Restrictions: Source Code
The licensed software contains source code which is provided as is
and is strictly for reference purposes only. The source code falls
under the same license as the software.
```

By providing source code, licensees can use it as an example of how to build components and how to write efficient and tidy code (assuming the licensed source code is efficient and tidy). Some of the restrictions that can be placed on source code are:

■ Use for reference purposes only
■ Interfacing to the licensed software only
■ Used for educational purposes only
■ Nondistributable, nonpublishable
■ Not to be built with any other software other than the original licensed software

General Structure

Like a good book, a good license follows a particular structure. In fact, most licenses follow the same format, regardless of what they stipulate. Although this may appear overly fussy, it contributes to the license being easier to read. If it's easier to read, it's easier to understand. If it's easier to understand, then there is less chance of any misunderstandings arising, and again the utmost protection can be achieved with the license. A typical license is comprised of:

■ The license title
■ The preamble
■ Definitions used in the license
■ Core restrictions and rights
■ Supplementary or special restrictions and rights
■ Contact information

License Title

The license title is short and sweet. It contains the name of the company and the name of the software that is being licensed. If the license is well written, it makes clear which version (e.g., version 2.6.1) the software is and what edition of the software (e.g., professional, educational, limited edition, etc.). It is important to include all of this information, especially if there are multiple editions and versions of the software. Sometimes there are restrictions and rights that differ from version to version or from edition to edition.

Preamble

The preamble may or may not contain a title (e.g., Preamble). The job of the preamble is to inform the licensee that what he is reading is in fact a license, and that he (the licensee) must read carefully all that follows. If there is a clause that states the licensee can reject the license, it makes it clear that the licensee must remove all parts of the licensed software from their computer. If the license is meant to be displayed in an installation utility, then the license may contain instructions for how to decline (within the UI) the license:

```
PREAMBLE
THIS LICENSE PERTAINS TO THE ZIBBLEFRITZ SOFTWARE PACKAGE AND IS
OFFERED BY ARRON FERGUSON. YOU SHOULD READ THE FOLLOWING TERMS,
RESTRICTIONS, AND ALL OTHER STATEMENTS MADE IN THIS LICENSE
CAREFULLY AND UNDERSTAND THE TERMS AND CONDITIONS BEFORE PROCEEDING
TO INSTALL AND USE THE LICENSED SOFTWARE. IF YOU DO NOT AGREE WITH
THE TERMS OF THE LICENSE THEN YOU MUST REMOVE THE LICENSED SOFTWARE
FROM ANY AND ALL COMPUTERS.
```

A concise preamble makes it clear that the license agreement is between the licensor and licensee.

License Definitions

Although most of the terminology used within a license is straightforward, a section may contain terms followed by definitions of what those terms mean. It is a way of making the license easier to read and to reduce the amount of ambiguity. A software license with terms and definitions usually labels that section *Definitions*:

```
Definitions
A. "Software" means machine readable executables which contain any
and all executable files, binary libraries, header files, source
files, data files, documentation files.
B. "Educational Software" means software that falls under an
educational license which restricts the software from being used
for commercial use and requires the licensee to be either a
student, instructor, or faculty of a private or public educational
college, university, or school and taking a course where the
software license has been directly purchased for that course.
```

The definitions should be listed with alphabetic characters or letters next to each term and definition so that each term can be explicitly referred to later on in the license. This is useful because the alphabetic letter can be referenced, instead of the term making for a concise license document.

Core Restrictions and Rights

This section is where most of the important details are. All restrictions placed on the software should be found here. Restrictions should cover the usage of the software, the number of copies that can be made of the original licensed software, whether editing is allowed, what distribution and publishing restrictions are placed on the software and any of its output. Additionally, included is information about transferability, ownership rights, and any other details concerning what the licensee is allowed to do.

If there are any warranties, there should be an explanation as to what is covered. If a warranty is stated, it should have all details and limitations of the warranty clearly spelled out. For example, many warranties cover a limited time period (e.g., 90 days). Usually, software is said to be delivered "As is," which means that there are no promises as to the consistency or reliability of the software's functionality. A well-written license makes it clear that the software that is licensed is not guaranteed to work and that the licensor is not responsible for any damages or problems that occur while using the software for any use, whether it be for personal or business use. This is important because without this clause a licensee may have legal ground to sue the licensor.

If there is a certain set of procedures that need to be taken to remove the licensed software from the licensee's computer, then there should be information on how to do this and what exactly needs to be removed. There may also be the need to restrict exports of the licensed software due to what it can be used for. For example, if the licensed software contains a feature that allows for automatic upgrading where the software itself contacts a server, this may infringe on privacy laws in certain countries. If there are any limitations that need to be stated, such as how many host connections the software is expected to be able to process per second, this should be stated.

Supplementary Restrictions and Rights

A supplementary section contains information that may only apply to certain licensees. A license may need a supplementary section if the license applies to certain editions or versions of a particular software package. For example, the same license may be used for a full commercial license, a trial version, and an educational version. There may be certain limitations of use in certain situations, such as the licensee is an educator or the licensee works for government. There may be certain restrictions placed on distributors of the software or on publishers who wish to include the software in other packages or other mediums such as printed material.

Contact Information

The last section is considered optional, although it makes sense to include it. The full address, both electronic and regular, should be included so that if there are any questions, problems, or issues with the license, a licensee can contact the licensor. Again, the whole purpose of the license is to eliminate misunderstandings.

OPEN SOURCE

Unless you've been living in a cave up in Alaska, you likely have heard about open source. Open source is another area of controversy and confusion. This is mainly because of the different perspectives of what open source is.

What Is It?

Although the notion of including source code for a software package is not entirely new, the formalization of restrictions and rights of source code inclusion is relatively new. The Open Source Initiative (OSI) is an organization that was founded in 1998 by Chris Peterson, John Hall, Larry Augustin, Sam Ockman, and Eric Raymond. The OSI is now a well-established, well-respected organization because of its strong influence in the software industry, as well as acceptance in the free software development community. The OSI has detailed clearly what constitutes open-source software. The OSI has created a document, *The Open Source Definition* [Perens97], currently at version 1.9, which contains 10 rules that must be adhered to in order for software to be considered open source.

Free Redistribution

The first rule deals with distribution and fees:

```
The license shall not restrict any party from selling or giving
away the software as a component of an aggregate software
distribution containing programs from several different sources.
The license shall not require a royalty or other fee for such sale.
```

This statement is actually saying two things. First, the license that is attached to the software must not restrict anybody from giving or selling the software. As well, the software can even be included with other software that comes from another source (e.g., licensor and license). So if you wish, you can charge money for distributing the software or you can charge no money for the distribution—it's up to you. The second part is making it clear that any redistributors are allowed to give the software away for free if they choose to.

Source Code

The second rule deals with the requirements of the software being accompanied with the source code:

```
The program must include source code, and must allow distribution
in source code as well as compiled form. Where some form of a
product is not distributed with source code, there must be a
well-publicized means of obtaining the source code for no more than
a reasonable reproduction cost—preferably, downloading via the
Internet without charge. The source code must be the preferred form
in which a programmer would modify the program. Deliberately
obfuscated source code is not allowed. Intermediate forms such as
the output of a preprocessor or translator are not allowed.
```

The software must be accompanied with the source code that made the software, or there must be a place that is easily accessible on the Internet for downloading the source code for the software. Again, there must be no fee for accessing the source code. Additionally, no attempt should be made to hide the details of the source code (via obfuscating).

Derived Works

The third rule deals with works that are derived from the original work:

```
The license must allow modifications and derived works, and must
allow them to be distributed under the same terms as the license of
the original software.
```

Any license that is attached to the software must allow for the original work to be used in new derived works. As well, the software must follow the same terms as the original license that is adhering to the opens source rules. This stops any attempts to steal the work or parts of the work.

Integrity of the Author's Source Code

The fourth rule describes the way in which the original author can protect his name and reputation:

```
The license may restrict source code from being distributed in
modified form only if the license allows the distribution of
"patch files" with the source code for the purpose of modifying the
program at build time. The license must explicitly permit
distribution of software built from modified source code. The
license may require derived works to carry a different name or
version number from the original software.
```

Any license attached to the work may restrict the distribution of modified source code, only if the license allows for the distribution of what are called patch files. However the patch files must include the source code as well, the license must allow the modified (patched) software to be distributed, although it may need to be distributed under a different version name. This is placing importance on an author's right to protect his name and reputation because he may wish to control what source code gets added to the work and control the quality of the changes that are made.

No Discrimination Against Persons or Groups

The fifth rule lists the requirement that no restrictions of persons are allowed to be attached to any license considered to be open source:

```
The license must not discriminate against any person or group of
persons.
```

There must be no restrictions placed on who is allowed to use and distribute the software. Although this sounds petty, it is in place so that a person, organization, company, or even a country is not excluded from using the software.

No Discrimination Against Fields of Endeavor

The sixth rule states that no restrictions may be placed on what the software can be used for:

```
The license must not restrict anyone from making use of the program
in a specific field of endeavor. For example, it may not restrict
the program from being used in a business, or from being used for
genetic research.
```

There must be no restrictions placed on what the software is allowed to be used for. Any company, organization, or person is free to use the software.

Distribution of License

The seventh rule states that no other license is needed to anyone who receives the distributed software:

```
The rights attached to the program must apply to all to whom the
program is redistributed without the need for execution of an
additional license by those parties.
```

This helps to ensure that no other stipulations or licenses or agreements can be attached after the fact.

License Must Not Be Specific To a Product

The eighth rule deals with needs of the software to be attached to other software products:

```
The rights attached to the program must not depend on the program's
being part of a particular software distribution. If the program is
extracted from that distribution and used or distributed within the
terms of the program's license, all parties to whom the program is
redistributed should have the same rights as those that are granted
in conjunction with the original software distribution.
```

So if the software came with one distribution or product, it can easily be included into another distribution or product and the exact same license is applied to it (same rights).

License Must Not Restrict Other Software

The ninth rule deals with other software and restrictions:

```
The license must not place restrictions on other software that is
distributed along with the licensed software. For example, the
license must not insist that all other programs distributed on the
same medium must be open-source software.
```

Any license with the software that is to be open source must not require all other software to conform to the same rules. All other software, meaning any and all other software that may work in conjunction with or be distributed with the original software.

License Must Be Technology Neutral

The tenth and last rule deals with the technology that is used to distribute the software:

```
No provision of the license may be predicated on any individual
technology or style of interface.
```

This rule sounds confusing by its name. It means that no matter how a licensee comes into possession of the licensed software (i.e., no matter what technology is used to acquire the software), the same rules apply. The licensee may explicitly purchase the software in the store requiring a shrink-wrap agreement, the licensee may download the software from a Web site or FTP server, or the licensee may install the software through a Web form, which requires a click-wrap agreement.

TIP

The term shrink-wrap agreement refers to the way in which a licensee may agree to the rights and restrictions found within a software license. It refers to the procedure where a potential licensee purchases a software license and is confronted with a sealed package, which contains the software media (e.g., CD-ROM). The packaging contains a printed label, which cautions the potential licensee that by breaking the seal to the media, the individual is agreeing to the license terms (found separately as a printed document). If the individual does not agree with the license, he simply does not open the package and can still acquire a monetary refund.

Similar to the shrink-wrap agreement, the clip-wrap refers to the procedure where a potential licensee is given a choice within a user interface of a program running on the computer to either agree with the terms or disagree. If the potential licensee disagrees, the software installation and/or download process is aborted and no license agreement is bound; therefore no software is acquired or installed.

It is important to note that your software doesn't use the open source license. In fact, open source isn't even a license. It is a concept, a paradigm. It is a different way of thinking when releasing software. It allows a greater amount of transparency with the process of developing and creating software, it allows for others to add to the software and it also offers software to those who may not be able to purchase similar software that is not under the same types of rules. As long as you adhere to the previous set of rules listed, the OSI allows for a software licensor to release software and calls it OSI Certified.

It is important to note that Microsoft's shared source license program is different than the open source concept. Microsoft's shared source program is actually made up of several different licenses (e.g., academic, government security enterprise, etc.), each of which is meant to address a specific set of restrictions and needs based on the usage and the licensee.

Differences of Opinion

Unfortunately, the popularity of open source has also brought much confusion. The reason is that there are differing views as to what open source should mean. Many companies who wish to include source code with their product still wish to restrict distribution and modifications. This does not adhere to the OSI's specification of open source. Therefore, there is open source (OSI style) and there is open source (source code is included). What can be even more frustrating is that some developers will release open source (OSI style), but not follow the conditions that the OSI has specified. Legally there is little the OSI can do because the term open source cannot be trademarked—the name is too broad.

The OSI, in response to the rejection from the U.S. Patent and Trademark Office, registered a slightly different trademark—OSI Certified. The trademark and logo can be downloaded from the OSI site at: http://opensource.org/trademarks.

As a software developer, you can take measures to ensure that you do not add to the confusion, by carefully reading the OSI definition of open source. If you can ensure that your software and its accompanying source code can adhere to the rules found within the open source definition from OSI, then you should feel comfortable with using the logos (OSI Certified as well as open source) and branding your software as open source. Otherwise, you may wish to simply state that your software contains source code.

Free Software vs. Open Source

Another mistake made is assuming that free software and open source are one and the same—there is a distinction. Similar to the OSI, there exists an organization known as the Free Software Foundation (FSF). The FSF was founded in 1985 (considerably earlier than OSI) and prides itself in promoting the notion that software should be free for the general public. The FSF points out that the word free in "free software" means free as in freedom. Freedom as in a fundamental right. There is a stark contract between what the OSI promotes and what the FSF promotes. The OSI promotes software as open source in the hopes that transparency of source code will lead to better built software. They make it clear that they are neither for nor against software patents or copyright. Because of this, the OSI takes more of a pragmatic approach to their cause.

In contrast, the FSF is very much idealistic concerning free software. Their cause is much more political, and they strongly oppose copyrights and patents on software because they take away freedom. Whereas the OSI looks at their cause as being one to educate industry and work with the corporate software world, the FSF looks at proprietary software as the enemy. In order to be considered free software (as per the FSF "Free Software Definition"), software must grant the freedom to [FSF05]:

- Run the program for any purpose. The FSF calls this "Freedom 0."
- Be able to study how the program works (by seeing the source code) and to be able to modify it for any reason and as the user sees fit. The FSF calls this "Freedom 1."
- Redistribute the software (and source code) so that anyone can do the same (as per the first two points). The FSF calls this "Freedom 2."
- Make changes to the program (via the source code) and redistribute your changes (and source code) to the public so that there is a general benefit to the public at large. The FSF calls this "Freedom 3."

Although they look similar (they are), they are not entirely identical. First, the OSI definition of open source is very particular and worded with legalese terminology. The FSF free software definition only consists of four rules, and they are very broad and casually defined. Second, the OSI open source definition explicitly deals with the issue of charging money for distributions; the four definitions for the free software definition do not cover this, although later on in the document it is made clear that you may charge money for distribution.

Third, the OSI open source definition makes an attempt at protecting the author's name and reputation by allowing the author to require derived works to carry notices that state that the software is a different version. Thus, if an author creates a stable version of the software and a second author creates a derived unstable version, the original author will not lose his credibility because the second version has to carry a notice stating it is a separate version. There is nothing found in the free software definition to deal with this issue.

There is currently (still) much debate about which term a software developer should choose or which perspective one should take on why one should include the source code and allow for distribution. The one you choose depends on your perspective as to why you wish your software to be freely available as well as containing source code. Last, the FSF uses the analogy that free software uses the term free as in "free speech," not as in "free beer." The difference being that free speech is considered a right and not a privilege or gift (like free beer).

COPYRIGHT

The formalization of copyright has its roots going all the way back to 1886, when an agreement was made between sovereign nations to recognize and honor copyrighted works between those sovereign nations. The agreement was called the "Berne Convention for the Protection of Literary and Artistic Works" and was formalized, surprisingly enough, in Berne, Switzerland. Prior to this time, if a person created a work in England, for example, that copyright was not recognized in any other country. Thus, anybody in any other country could reproduce that work and not have to face any penalties for doing so.

Copyright is really the recognition by government that a work belongs to a creator and that the creator has full control of the selling, distributing, copying, and publicly displaying the work. All others (excluding the creator) are restricted from doing anything with or to the work unless they have written permission by the creator (usually in the form of a license agreement). Copyright covers many different types of work including music, recordings (both audio and video), artwork (including paintings, sculptures, photographs), films, literary works, and software.

It is important to note what exactly is covered when we say a work. For example, you can write a piece of software that allows artists to create images that appear to have been painted using oil paints. But you can't copyright the idea of a program that allows artists to create images that appear to have been painted using oil paints.

Anyone else is free to create a program that allows users to do the same thing—they just can't copy your software (unless you express otherwise).

Many countries state that copyright is automatic, which means that there is no formal registration process required by the country's government. This means that an unpublished work is still considered copyrighted. So, when you write a piece of software, it is automatically copyrighted. However it is a wise idea to formally register your work with your country's government so that you can easily defend your claim of being the author and creator of that work. In the least, it is wise to somehow record a copy of the work so that there is proof of the original date of creation.

The old-fashioned way was to send oneself a copy of the work through the postal system, which offered proof based on dated marks on the envelope by the postal service. With computer backup technology, it is easy enough to simply make backup copies onto optical storage media, such as CD-ROMs or DVD-ROMs.

Assuming the country you're in complied with the Berne Convention, copyright is usually covered for the duration of the life of the creator (you), plus 50 years. Copyright cannot be used for things such as methods or procedures for creating things (e.g., a method for mixing paint), names, slogans, titles, phrases, or factual information. Copyright is strictly for a work and is not to be confused with a trademark or a patent. So copyright is really protection for creators of works and can be registered. It is protection against use or misuse, and the creator is entirely in control of the work that is copyrighted.

Copyright vs. Copyleft

Copyleft is a relatively new term to be used; it is associated with the FSF. Whereas copyright is meant to keep ownership of the work to one person and restrict any others from viewing, copying, distributing, redistributing, modifying, publishing, and publicly displaying a work, copyleft is meant to allow the general public to view, copy, distribute, redistribute, modify, publish, and publicly display the work freely. You could say that copyleft is a restriction that restricts further restrictions. Unfortunately, copyleft goes against the norm of existing laws that have been constituted already, namely copyright law. Because of this, copyleft cannot be law because any copyleft law would nullify existing copyright law. Instead, copyleft becomes much like open source and free software: a set of rules that are followed.

In order to make a work copyleft the first step is to claim copyright of the work. Once this is in place, the creator of the work can then turn around and start adding details in a license that allows the work to be freely viewed, copied, distributed, redistributed, modified, published, and publicly displayed by anyone and everyone. One of the most important details added is that no other one person or entity (e.g., business or organization) can further restrict this work, and as long as they follow the rules of allowing anyone else to view, copy, distribute, redistribute, modify, publish, and publicly display the work, they are freely allowed to continue using it too. It's analogous to building a house, ripping out all of the locks from the doors, and insisting that anyone who wishes to come in and use the house must not attempt to place locks on any of the doors.

PUBLIC DOMAIN

Public domain is another term that is often misused and misunderstood which, surprisingly, hasn't caused tremendous amounts of litigation. It is not uncommon to see someone releasing a piece of software with the following statement:

```
This software is hereby released into the public domain.
```

While this seems harmless, it is ignoring current copyright laws. Remember from the previous section that there exists such a thing in most countries known as automatic copyright. Because of this, the work (whether the creator likes it or not) is copyrighted and, therefore, protected. Furthermore, government law usually states very specifically that public domain is the term used to describe a work whose copyright has expired (life of the creator plus 50 years or so depending on the country). For example, all the works of Shakespeare are in the public domain and are therefore legally available for copying, distributing, etc.

In the very least it is in err to simply state that your software is in the public domain based on current government laws and definitions of the definition for public domain. By doing this, two problems are added. First, if a work is stated to be in the public domain, and many others use it, the creator of the work could (at some later point in time) retract the desire to place the work in the public domain and instead attempt to enforce copyright. Doing so would cause all those who are using the work to be infringing on that copyright. This could cause thousands of dollars in legal wrangling to say the least—even if a court of law was to rule in favor of the body of defendants. Second, by releasing the work without any subsequent license containing disclaimers, the creator of the work could possibly be setting himself up for a massive amount of litigation if anyone was to attempt to sue him for damages incurred during use of the work. Clearly the better choice is to stay away from claiming your work is in the public domain and choose a license that states the rights and restrictions of your choosing.

SOURCE CODE AND BINARY LICENSES

So far we've been going over the structure and components that make up a good license. We have to remember that when we say "good license," we mean that the rights and restrictions are spelled out clearly in order to eliminate confusion and misunderstanding, as well as protect the ideals that the license stands for. In no way are we attempting to debate issues, such as proprietary versus non-proprietary, educational versus non-educational, open source versus closed source, or distributable versus non-distributable. Our goal for this chapter is to be able to understand the ingredients that go into a clear and concise license, and to be able to choose an appropriate license based on our needs.

Commercial Licenses

As we've seen, commercial licenses require certain restrictions that disallow the licensee from certain rights that only the licensor should have. Remember, software is easily copied, unlike a car or a suit, and requires certain restrictions that would normally be absent if the work was anything other than software.

If the software is under a commercial license, then the licensee has the freedom to use the software to make money from (profit in legalese). If the software is educational, then the licensee is only able to use the software in a classroom setting. If the software is trial software, then it is placed under a trial or demo license, which simply means that the licensee cannot use it for anything other than for purposes of determining whether the software is appropriate for their needs. Sometimes a software license lumps educational and trial together. This is okay, but the details must be spelled out clearly in order to avoid misunderstanding.

Commercial licenses restrict transferability. They disallow licensees to transfer the license to someone else (third party in legalese). This is in place to eliminate licensees from making a copy and selling the original (or selling the copy). Commercial licenses also restrict redistribution of the software. Again, this is to disallow licensees from making copies and giving them away because it is so easy to duplicate software (as apposed to cars and suits), the license needs to make this clear. Without this clause, a business entity would have difficulties making a profit from the investment of building the software in the first place. Publishing will also be restricted.

It is important to also disallow reverse engineering by restricting the ability to decompile and edit the software. And the license also makes it clear that the software is not sold, but is licensed instead. The owner of the software is always the licensor. And lastly, the output of the software may be restricted, especially if portions of the software (and works) are part of the output as in compilers and interpreters and, in general, software whose output is in binary form.

GNU General Public License Version 2.0

Of all the free software/open source licenses available today, the GNU General Public License (GPL) version 2.0 is one of the most common if not the most common free licenses available.

Although we are looking at some of the more popular open source licenses in use, the licenses covered in this chapter are by no means the complete set in existence. There are many more licenses. For more information, you can visit the FSF Web site for compatibility issues and you can visit the OSF Web site for listings of the actual licenses.

GPL Description

The GPL license is one of the few open source licenses that is *strong copyleft*. Being strong copyleft means that the license adheres to the strict description of free software that the FSF has created. Some of the other licenses are *copyleft compatible,* but are not considered strong copyleft. Being copyleft-compatible means that the license can be used with strong copyleft licenses but can also swing the other way and be used with copyright software (e.g., the software may be allowed to be bundled with non-GPL licensed software). For many developers in the free software community, the GPL is everything that copyleft purports to be.

GPL Rights and Restrictions

The GPL starts off with a statement with section 0 stating:

```
This License applies to any program or other work which contains a
notice placed by the copyright holder saying it may be distributed
under the terms of this General Public License.
```

It is important to note that only the copyright holder can place the work into the GPL license. The GPL is also a non-exclusive license (it is copyleft after all). All restrictions in the GPL are in place to disallow further restrictions such as copy restrictions modification restrictions and redistribution restrictions. The first part of the license is the preamble, which is more of a statement of ideals as to why the GPL exists (e.g., free as in freedom not free as in price). The GPL makes it clear that its focus is on copying, distributing and modifying. All other issues are outside of the scope of the GPL:

```
Activities other than copying, distribution, and modification are
not covered by this License; they are outside its scope.
```

The GPL is allowed to be freely copied but not changed in any way. Copying, modifying and distributing are allowed so long as you do not restrict others from the same (in legalese this is called reciprocity).

The GPL allows you to charge a fee for the act of physically transferring the software and even offer for a fee warranty protection. There is no lower limit nor is there any upper limit on the amount to be charged. Although it would be easy to pull a number out of the air for what you might consider an appropriate fee for physically transferring the software, it is the market that ultimately decides market value because the same software can be found elsewhere at a more reasonable rate.

A common misconception about the GPL is that any software that is bundled with GPL software must too become GPLed. This is not true. In section two, it states:

```
In addition, mere aggregation of another work not based on the
Program with the Program (or with a work based on the Program) on
a volume of a storage or distribution medium does not bring the
other work under the scope of this License.
```

This is why you'll find Linux distributions that contain GPL software and non-GPL/commercial software.

GPL Gotchas

Retractors of the GPL have often referred to the GPL as a "license virus," an "infectious license," and even in some circles (specifically the BSD community) referred to as the "GPL poison pill." Their rationale is based on the fact that if you create a derivative work it must fall under the GPL. Ten years ago, this issue would have been easy to solve. But today, with technology being where it is, this question is not easily answered. There are technologies that blur the lines such as interpreters, runtime environments, Remote Procedure Calls (RPCs), serialization of objects within runtimes, the list goes on. These grey areas in technology create gotchas.

GPLed Linking

One of the most contentious issues with GPL is the matter of software linking. For example, to write a plugin (an image filter) for a paint program that is GPLed, would require that image filter plugin be GPLed as well. This is because the work is based on the program. Or is it? Reading section 2:

```
If identifiable sections of that work are not derived from the
Program, and can be reasonably considered independent and separate
works in themselves, then this License, and its terms, do not apply
to those sections when you distribute them as separate works.
```

The question becomes: what is considered independent and separate works? If the image filter plugin was written only for that particular GPLed paint program, then it would be clear that the plugin was part of the work. If however the image filter plugin was written as a separate program that could be run on its own, as well as used with other paint programs, then we could call the plugin a separate, independent work. Or could we? At this point, we have to dive into the technical details of how the software is called.

The FSF makes clear in their FAQ that if a plugin is called as a separate process (e.g., fork or exec functions), then it is a separate work. If the program calls the plugin by calling dynamically linked libraries, then the plugin is considered to be a part of the work and, therefore, under the GPL. Their reasoning is that the close relationship of the linked library is requiring both pieces of software to share data structures which may include classes from an OOPL library. Lastly, they outline what they consider to be a grey area .which is if the plugin is a dynamically linked library and the GPLed work calls the plugin's "main" function.

Not mentioned but additionally intriguing is the RPC scenario. This scenario does not fit neatly into calling a main function, yet an RPC could be available to other programs—not just the GPLed software. In the case of Java, this scenario looks as if it is unanswerable. For example, using the RPC scenario, would the plugin be considered an independent work if the communicated data was both a serialized object and a Java class? The serialized object can be ignored in this scenario because it is just considered data for the interpreter. However, the Java class now requires us to dig further. Is the Java class (being sent from the plugin) a derived class of an existing class found within the paint program? If so, then the plugin appears to be a derived work. If however the plugin is sending a Java class that is not derived from anything found within the paint program, then the plugin appears to be an independent work.

But the FSF has dealt with this problem, thus saving a lot of headaches dealing with interpreted languages. The FSF has decided to treat the interpreted classes simply as data. Because of this, all class files are not considered program code to the interpreter: just data. So based on our discussion of RPC plugin architecture, the class files sent would not cause problems. If however the RPC call was sending true binaries (i.e., natively compiled executables from C++), then the sending of classes and libraries could violate the GPL if any of the binaries were derived classes.

GPL Breach

What's even more interesting in the GPL is what is considered to happen to you if you do not follow the rules set forth by the GPL in Section 5:

```
You are not required to accept this License, since you have not
signed it. However, nothing else grants you permission to modify or
distribute the Program or its derivative works. These actions are
prohibited by law if you do not accept this License.
```

This statement seems to allude that the rules revert back to the original copyright—which restricts all but the copyright holder the rights of copying, distributing, modifying, etc. This situation would be outside of the terms of the GPL and would require tort law to settle the dispute. This would require the copyright holder to take action.

GNU Lesser General Public License 2.1

The GNU Lesser General Public License (LGPL) is currently at version two and had its name changed from the GNU Library General Public License to the GNU Lesser General Public License. Although it may seem like such a trivial change, the FSF considered the change appropriate because the LGPL wasn't just for software libraries, although terminology in the document alludes to otherwise.

LGPL Description

The LGPL is basically a much more lax version of the GPL and does not enforce as many restrictions as the GPL. The FSF makes it clear that they are reluctant to endorse the use of the LGPL for everything—their intension is that it only be used in special circumstances. Like the GPL, the LGPL is formed when a copyright holder places the work into the LGPL:

```
This License Agreement applies to any software library or other
program which contains a notice placed by the copyright holder or
other authorized party saying it may be distributed under the terms
of this Lesser General Public License (also called "this License").
```

LGPL Rights and Restrictions

Like the GPL, the LGPL is meant to protect the user freedom to copy, modify, and distribute works under the license, and that the source code must accompany the work. It allows for copying, distributing, and modifying of the work and also requires that the same freedoms be given to the licensees. However the LGPL affords a special case that allows the LGPL to be linked and used with non-LGPL works thus the LGPL does not share the same requirement as the GPL. Section 5 of the LGPL states:

```
A program that contains no derivative of any portion of the
Library, but is designed to work with the Library by being compiled
or linked with it, is called a "work that uses the Library." Such a
work, in isolation, is not a derivative work of the Library, and
therefore falls outside the scope of this License.
```

This clause is different than the GPL; it doesn't require anything that is attached to the work to be part of the work and hence the LGPL. In the case of the GPL, a work using a GPLed library would thus have to be GPLed, as well. However, in order to be allowed to take advantage of this laxness, the non-LGPLed work must not be statically linked to the LGPLed work. Statically linking would create a derived rather than a separate work that uses the original work. Section 6 however allows for a non-LGPLed that uses the LGPLed work to be statically linked or combined as long as the following requirements are met:

- That non-LGPLed work allows for licensees to modify and reverse engineer both the LGPLed work as well as the non-LGPLed work.
- Make the non-LGPLed work that is created carry a prominent notice stating that it contains part LGPLed work.

One of the more confusing parts of the LGPL is Section 2. It first states that the software must be a software library (Section 2(a)), that any modified files contain notices stating changes made (Section 2(b)), and that the whole work must be under the same license at no charge (Section 2(c)). Section 2(d) attempts to address issues dealing with linking to non-LGPLed code:

```
If a facility in the modified Library refers to a function or a
table of data to be supplied by an application program that uses
the facility, other than as an argument passed when the facility is
invoked, then you must make a good faith effort to ensure that, in
the event an application does not supply such function or table,
the facility still operates, and performs whatever part of its
purpose remains meaningful.
```

This statement, albeit confusing, is an attempt to stop a loophole, which would otherwise allow a derived work to be altered in such a way that it would allow the work to tightly couple itself to non-LGPLed works. By requiring the LGPLed work to "still operate" without functions or tables requires the LGPLed code to contain the same functions, thereby putting a stop-plug in the ability to attach to non-LGPLed code.

Like the GPL, the LGPL allows for LGPLed works to be part of an aggregation of non-LGPLed works on a storage medium without requiring the other works to conform to the LGPL.

LGPL Gotchas

The LGPL appears to be a license that both the FSF and the proprietary camp seem to agree to dislike. The FSF doesn't necessarily approve of the LGPL because it doesn't completely protect the free software ideal (free speech, not free beer). The supporters of proprietary software licenses do not necessarily like the LGPL because it doesn't do enough to allow proprietary works to easily join to the LGPL. Needless to say, there are gotchas.

LGPL Conversion To GPL

There is a clause in the LGPL that allows for the work to be licensed under the GPL. This makes the LGPL much like a chameleon; able to change its color to suit its environment. While the free software supporters look at this as a happy invite to encourage licensors into the GPL realm, supporters of proprietary licenses look upon this as an uncontrollable fork, which removes the ability to keep the software closed if the need should arise. In theory, this could create two versions of the software: one that is GPLed and that disallows any restrictions on copying, distributing, and modifying, and another version that allows for certain restrictions to be placed on the software. When software splits like this, the production of the work is usually reduced because efforts become fragmented.

LGPL Is Vague

The LGPL contains terms and descriptions that do not offer enough description. For example, in Section 2(d) where it stated a "good faith effort" must be made to ensure that if the application does not supply the function or table, that the modified library must provide that same facility. Good faith effort is extremely difficult to define much less prove within the litigation process. Additionally, Section 2(d) also states that the work "performs whatever part of its purpose remains meaningful." This is another vague term and would be extremely hard to enforce in a lawsuit. It's not just terminology; even parts of the LGPL make it clear that in the case of linking to header files and other libraries, there is no cut and dried rule for determining whether the work that uses the library is a derivative work of the library or not and thus it is difficult to determine what is allowed and what is not. (Section 5):

```
When a "work that uses the Library" uses material from a header
file that is part of the Library, the object code for the work may
be a derivative work of the Library even though the source code is
not. Whether this is true is especially significant if the work can
be linked without the Library, or if the work is itself a library.
The threshold for this to be true is not precisely defined by law.
```

Mozilla Public License 1.1

The Mozilla Public License (MPL) 1.1 is a license used by and founded by the Mozilla Foundation™. It is a non-exclusive royalty-free open source license. Out of all of the open source licenses, the MPL is one of the (if not the most) well-put-together licenses. The MPL is clear, concise, and leaves no guessing as to the restrictions and rights of the licensee.

MPL Description

The MPL begins with the first section (section one) containing definitions—each one listed as a subsection (e.g., 1.1, 1.2, etc.). The next few sections deal with rights and restrictions until section seven, which covers the disclaimer. The next few sections cover issues not usually found in other licenses (e.g., multiple licensed code, U.S. government end users, termination of license). At the end of the license is a section (exhibit A), which is basically a form for putting down information in it such as the author, copyright notice, and any other contributors. The MPL feels like a license.

MPL Rights And Restrictions

The MPL offers clear definitions of, for example, what/who the initial developer is:

```
1.6. ''Initial Developer'' means the individual or entity
identified as the Initial Developer in the Source Code notice
required by Exhibit A.
```

And what/who a contributor is:

```
1.1. ''Contributor'' means each entity that creates or contributes
to the creation of Modifications.
```

Section 2 is specific enough that it differentiates between the "initial developer grant" (the copyright holder's permission) and the "contributor grant" (any others that add to the work), although the terms are the same. The fact that there are descriptions for both the initial developer and the contributor leaves no questions pertaining to rights. The MPL is similar to the LGPL in that it allows copying, modifying, and distributing of both the executable and the source code, as long as the same permissions are granted to others. However, the MPL uses a finer grain for its licensable material. It does this by giving a succinct definition of what a modification is (in terms of the license):

```
1.9. ''Modifications'' means any addition to or deletion from the
substance or structure of either the Original Code or any previous
Modifications. When Covered Code is released as a series of files,
a Modification is:
   A. Any addition to or deletion from the contents of a file
   containing Original Code or previous Modifications.

   B. Any new file that contains any part of the Original Code or
   previous Modifications.
```

The MPL makes it clear by its definition that a modification is on a per file basis, not a per work basis. This difference allows proprietary code to be attached to MPLed code and not have to follow the MPL (unlike the GPL and the LGPL).

One (quite valuable) detail that is found within the MPL is how to modify the MPL to create your own custom license. To do this, the requirement is to remove all references of Mozilla, MPL, NPL, and Netscape™. Because of this, the MPL becomes a great template for creating your open source license.

MPL Gotchas

Because the MPL is so well-defined (definitions, restrictions, etc.), the intentions of the MPL are made clear: allow both the open source world to interact with the closed source and proprietary world. If, however, one takes a strict copyleft stance, then the MPL suffers from not adhering to the spirit of copyleft. This is because of the finer granularity (licensing based on individual files versus the work as a whole). The GPL would require any and all files contributed to the work to become part of the GPLed work as well. The MPL does not require this. Because of this difference in perspective, it is difficult to fit works that are under the GPL and the MPL; however this can be dealt with by using multiple licenses (covered later).

Apache License, Version 2.0

The Apache license comes from the Apache Software Foundation (ASF) and is currently at version 2.0. It is a non-exclusive, royalty-free open source license. The Apache license is associated with many Java software applications, which include the Apache Web server, Tomcat the servlet and JSP container, ANT (the Java build tool), and many more.

Apache Description

The Apache license provides definitions at the beginning (in section one) of the license document so as to eliminate misunderstandings of terms. Most of these terms are well-described, leaving little or no ambiguities. Sections two and three both deal with grant of copyright and grant of patent, respectively. The rest of the license deals with distribution, contribution, warranty, disclaimer, and liability. The Appendix of this license offers a boilerplate notice that is to be used in all works that are part of the Apache license.

Apache Rights and Restrictions

In a nutshell, the Apache license allows for copying, distribution, and modifying, so long as the same is granted (again, remember reciprocity) the Apache license treats the work as a whole similar to how the LGPL does. However, the Apache license is more lax when it comes to the binding issue when non-Apache-licensed work is linked or bound to Apache-licensed work. Essentially, the Apache license is similar to how the MPL treats other works. For example, in section one the definition for derivative works, the Apache license states:

```
"Derivative Works" shall mean any work, whether in Source or Object
form, that is based on (or derived from) the Work and for which the
editorial revisions, annotations, elaborations, or other
modifications represent, as a whole, an original work of
authorship. For the purposes of this License, Derivative Works
shall not include works that remain separable from, or merely link
(or bind by name) to the interfaces of, the Work and Derivative
Works thereof.
```

The laxness comes from the fact that a derivative work must be based and inseparable from the original work. If you link to the bindings for the work, this does not constitute a derivative work. This allows proprietary and closed code to link to Apache-licensed code and not have to be part of the Apache license.

Apache Gotchas

The Apache license suffers from the same problem as the LGPL where some of the definitions are not well-defined. Referring back to the definition for derivative works, the term "works that remain separable from" is ambiguous. It requires litigation to determine whether a work is separate from the original work or not. Compare the Apache license definition of derivative work to the MPL description of modification and the definition modification.

Additionally, the Apache license does not conform to a strict copyleft ideal. The FSF has determined that the Apache license is incompatible with the GPL, whereas the ASF is unsure whether there is compatibility or incompatibility. Because of this, attaching multiple licenses is problematic at best and could terminate one or both licenses.

DOCUMENTATION LICENSES

Up until now all of the licenses that we've looked at have been for software. But this does little to address software that is accompanied with content such as a CMS. Because of this there are several licenses that have been created to address documents such as Web or printed. As well, there are even general licenses for general artistic work. It therefore helps to look at and understand these types of licenses.

GNU Free Documentation License Version 1.2

The GNU Free Documentation License (FDL) is another offering from GNU. The FDL covers works that are textual based such as manuals, textbooks, and other types of various documents. The FDL allows for the free copying, distributing, and modifying of any work placed within the FDL. While the author and/or publisher maintain credit for the work, others are still allowed to make modifications. By this nature, the FDL is geared more toward educational and reference material rather than novels (although a novel under this license would prove to be quite interesting because it would allow people to change things in the story).

The preamble comes with the usual GNU evangelism of copyleft and then continues with section one which states the definitions used in the license. The FDL is non-exclusive, royalty free, and unlimited in duration, although based on copyright law this would extend to the lifespan of the copyright holder plus 50 or so years, at which point the work under the license should enter into the public domain. The idea of a modified version of the licensed work is a situation where actual portions of the document have been changed, including translations into other languages. There are some well-thought out definitions such as invariant sections, which are sections of the document that don't necessarily deal with the main topic (e.g., Appendix).

The FDL also defines what transparent means and what opaque means in context of a document. You can think of a transparent document as a document that is formatted using an open or publicized standard (e.g., PDF, Postscript, HTML, or XML where the validation and encoding is openly publicized or standardized). A document is considered opaque if its format can only be read with proprietary software. Copying and distributing require all copies to contain the copyright notice, license notice (of the FDL), and that no other restrictions or limitations are added. Modifying requires keeping the copyright and FDL prominently in the document as well as displaying the modifiers copyright too. Like the GPL, the FDL allows for a FDLed work to be part of an aggregate of other works, including some that are non-FDLed.

Creative Commons Attribution 2.5 License

The Creative Commons Attribution 2.5 license is meant to address a broader range of artistic works. Artistic works can be anything from written material like manuals, stories, reference material, pictures, photographs, videos, music, animation, and other sorts of creative works, although the Creative Commons works best with media in the digital realm that can be copied verbatim with little effort. The Creative Commons Attribution license is a fairly compact license—it only contains six definitions. It provides a non-exclusive, royalty-free, and perpetual license. On a side note, they've acknowledged the fact that a license based on copyright law can only exist for the duration the copyright life, hence the mention of perpetual.

The Creative Commons Attribution license allows for copying, distributing, displaying, performing the work, and making derivatives of the work. As well, the work can be used for commercial purposes. The Creative Commons Attribution license is nice for work that is not documentation because it acknowledges that some work can be performed, as in the case of a play, script, or interactive media. As well, there is mention pertaining to performance royalties for musical compositions. What's not allowed is omission of the copyright notice, the Creative Commons Attribution license itself, or changing the current license. This is a good license to use for multimedia applications.

USING MULTIPLE LICENSES

As we've seen, there are several popular licenses. By no means is this list complete—there are many other open source licenses. The four (software licenses) covered here do represent a good sampling of the types of licenses and their differences of perspective on rights and restrictions. Because there are quite a few different licenses one of the biggest problems creating open source projects is ensuring that there is compatibility of licenses. Ironically this can sometimes be the biggest constraint placed on software projects (no longer do only language and platform issues cause compatibility problems). Software developers now have to be part lawyer in order to carefully weave software libraries, components, servers, and applications together.

To illustrate such an issue, let's look at a real-world example. Figure 3.1 shows a very possible scenario containing several software layers, each with its own separate license. There are several perspectives that we need to take with the software layers and licenses.

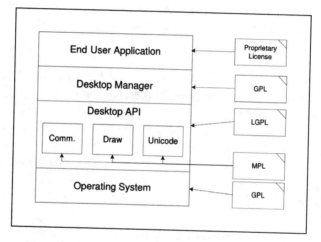

FIGURE 3.1   Software environment layers with licenses.

Copying and Distributing With Multiple Licenses

Since copying is followed by distributing, these two granted rights can be lumped together. Based on Figure 3.1, there are a few questions that we need to answer before we can put together the operating system, desktop API, desktop manager, and end user application all as one distribution. If we start from the bottom of the stack and work our way upwards, we are confident that there is compatibility with both the GPL as well as the LGPL. We can copy them together and put them as an aggregate on a copy medium. However, the components found within the desktop API contain components that are under the MPL. While the distribution of these components as an aggregation with other software (e.g., the operating system) does not cause issues, real problems becomes apparent when we realize that the LGPL has requirements for linking that contradict the MPL.

Thus, if the MPL components are called by a separate process (remember the fork call mentioned in the LGPL?), then all is well, and the aggregation is okay; we can ship. But if the MPL components are linked tightly with code (statically compiled for example), we're going to break the LGPL license, which in turn causes the MPL to fail too because it requires other code that's not MPLed to allow MPL to remain unmodified; thus, the whole pyramid comes crashing down like a deck of cards. Therefore, we have two options: (1) not distribute the MPLed components and require the users to download them or; (2) *license fork* the desktop API components. The first option is not necessarily appealing because it requires users to download components, possibly discouraging all but the most technically hip users to use this software. The second option requires the software components to be released under multiple licenses. Although the second option is better for business (and users), it becomes messy because some of the restrictions in one license may cancel out rights in another license.

TIP

The notion of license forking may sound like an undoable situation. However, remember that these open source licenses are based on copyright law. Therefore, if the holder of the copyright agrees to release the software under multiple licenses, then he is free to do so. Remember, the copyright holder is the one by default (based on copyright law) who is allowed to do anything they wish with their work. If the copyright holder wishes to include a clause in the license that states all licensees must wear fez caps while running the software, then licensees must adhere to the whims of the licensor.

Another layer up and we have to consider the desktop manager that works with the desktop API. The FSF have made sure that both the GPL and the LGPL are compatible. No problem there. The next layer up, however, can cause problems. The desktop manager has to interact with the end user application, which contains a proprietary license. For this example we can assume that the proprietary license is a closed source, but free-distributable and royalty-free license. This presents a grey area and therefore a problem. Recall in the GPL that:

```
If identifiable sections of that work are not derived from the
Program, and can be reasonably considered independent and separate
works in themselves, then this License, and its terms, do not apply
to those sections when you distribute them as separate works.
```

Although the end user application is not a plugin (like the first example we used), there still may be a crossover into the ugly grey area that winds up violating this license. If the work is heavily intertwined with the desktop manager (such as a calendar applet) or is statically linked with parts of the desktop manager included, then we've likely violated the GPL, and once again the whole pyramid of cards comes crashing down. If, however, the end user application is a standalone application, such as a Web server or a CMS or paint program (and the application is dynamically linked), then there won't likely be any problems. If this situation were to cause problems, then once again we could seek the license fork option, assuming that the desktop manager copyright holder would be willing to create a license fork.

Modifying With Multiple Licenses

In dealing with the modifying issue, we start at the bottom and check with the operating system with the desktop API. These are compatible because they are mere aggregations (assuming the desktop API is very much a separate work and is not tightly bound to the operating system). The real problem comes, however, with the desktop API and its components which are licensed under the MPL. The LGPL and the MPL are at odds because the LGPL requires all files to be part of the work as a whole and thus conform to the LGPL. The MPL refuses with its specific policy which allows individual files to exist under separate licensing terms. Again, the solution is either to release and distribute as separate distributions or to invoke the license fork option.

The desktop API and the desktop manager can easily link and bind to each other because the FSF has made them compatible. The desktop manager and the end user application, however, may cause problems if the binding is too tight. Additionally the end user application may not allow modifications because we're assuming it's a close source license. It's easy to see how this entire stack can come crashing down if there are issues with licensing. As a software developer in today's computer industry, it helps to be able to see software from this angle (the legal angle) because it can save you the headache of having to remove things that cannot be compiled, modified, or distributed with your current work.

SUMMARY

In this chapter, we looked at some of the terminology that is found in licenses. We also looked at the various different rights and restrictions that are likely to be found in a license, and we studied what the implications were of each. We looked at the open source movement, discussed the differences between open source and free software, and we looked at copyright and public domain. We also looked at and compared open source licenses as well as licenses made for written material and other artistic works. Lastly, we covered scenarios where multiple licenses were required. The next chapter walks through a detailed discussion on XML because XML is used in many of the different parts of building this CMS, including creating a data model, performing transformations, creating XHTML, and using Ant build files.

ENDNOTES

1. This may be a bit of an exaggeration, but then again monkeys have been used in experiments where brain-machine interfaces (BMI) were created so that the monkeys could move a cursor on the screen with their thoughts.
2. All of these terms are given within the context of software development.
3. Software that is anything other than commercial most likely contains, either in the title of the software product/work, in the documentation or in a splash screen (or all), a statement that clearly states the version (e.g., Educational Version).
4. The exception to this rule is open-source software—covered later in this chapter.
5. Patch files are upgrades to the software that allow the developer to fix inefficiencies and bugs that were released with the original software. Patch files can be manually downloaded by users or can be automatically downloaded from a server by the software itself (assuming there is a network connection).

4 Introduction to XML

Software development has been enhanced by the use and support of XML. New specifications and new APIs support innovative ways to use XML. Software developers are discovering uses for XML that don't always at first look feasible or useful. XML has been used to create protocols, file formats of various types, describing how other XML should look on a Web page, and even how executables should present a UI. Therefore, it helps to understand XML so that its power can be harnessed. For our CMS that we develop in this book, we use XML as the technology for storing our content, rather than using a relational database. The choice means that we need to write less integration code with other tiers. The source code listings referenced in this chapter are located on the CD-ROM in the *Chapter 4* folder.

ON THE CD

UNDERSTANDING XML

If you are familiar with XML and using Document Type Definitions (DTDs) to validate XML then you may wish to skip this chapter and go straight to Chapter 5. However, if you've never seen XML, if you are still new to XML, or you wish to brush up on your XML skills, then you may wish to continue reading.

XML is a recommendation from the W3C, and is currently at version 1.1[1]. You can think of the W3C's term recommendation as meaning a specification. That is, they create the documentation for how a particular technology should be used and present the documentation to the information technology public at large. XML is actually the successor (and really the descendant) of SGML.

There is often confusion around what XML is and what XML is not. To be as concise as possible, XML is a *markup syntax* that allows information and content designers to create metadata formats for describing data and information. The syntax of XML is easy to read and can be used to describe most anything that has to do with information and data. A simple example of some XML data:

```
<?xml version="1.0" encoding="UTF-8"?>
<record>
  <customer id="123456" firstName="Arron" lastName="Ferguson"/>
  <purchase>
    <item id="p-2390-b" productName="Zibblefritz CD-ROM"
      quantity="1"/>
  </purchase>
</record>
```

Looking at the simple example, it is easy to discern the different types of information that are being recorded in this data. It appears to contain a purchase and includes the name of the customer as well as the name of the item being purchased. Because the encoding of XML is character-based, we can simply read the document if we are willing to become accustomed to the formatting and use of symbols (such as the less than and greater than symbols). The following is a quick list of various different XML formats in use today:

Extensible Business Reporting Language (XBRL): For describing business and financial data for corporations and organizations.

DARPA Agent Markup Language (DAML): Describes inferences for Internet and Web intelligent agent programs.

Hypertext Markup Language (HTML): Used for the World Wide Web to describe documents with text, hyperlinks, and multimedia.

Math Markup Language (MathML): A format used to describe and present formatting for mathematical formulas and equations.

Simple Object Access Protocol (SOAP): A protocol used for sending messages on the Internet.

Scalable Vector Graphics (SVG): Stores vector graphic information for imagery.

Extensible Stylesheet Language Transformations (XSLT): An XML format that describes how to transform one type of XML format into another XML format (e.g., XML to HTML).

XML User Interface Language (XUL): Used to describe how GUIs should be displayed.

Based on the previous list of XML formats, it is easy to gain an appreciation for the extensibility of XML and how easy it is to find a use for it.

You may see the term tag set or language used in place of format in some documentation describing XML. The terms tag set, language, and format are all synonymous.

TIP

What XML Is

Because there is much hype surrounding XML, it is easy to become confused as to what exactly XML is and what it can do.

A Description of Metadata Structures

As mentioned previously, XML is a markup syntax for creating metadata formats. But what does this mean? First, markup syntax is really a set of characters used to carry a particular meaning. Markup syntax (at least in the case of XML) is hierarchical in nature. We can place markup syntax within markup syntax. This creates a tree-like structure. This does differ from straight text, which is simply linear in nature—text, after all, is read character after character in sequence [Dürst03]. Second, as shown in Chapter 1, metadata is data about data. Metadata allows us to describe and create data structures. For example, if we need to create a file format for a word processing program, we need to store the text that the user types, alignment, margins, as well as format which fonts are used, and their sizes and styles, etc. That information needs to be stored in a consistent and reproducible manner. We could do this in an XML format, as shown in Listing 4.1.

LISTING 4.1   Example Word Processing Format

```
<document author="Arron Ferguson" created="2005/05/10"
 modified="2005/06/22" font="Times" font-size="12pt"
 left-margin="1.0inch" right-margin="1.0inch" top-margin="1.0inch"
 bottom-margin="1.0inch">
  <section id="s12" title="Purnama XUI Project">
    <paragraph id="p23">An <i>XML tag set/specification</i> and
    accompanying <i>Java API</i> that allows developers to create
    GUI's by describing the interface via XML.
    <link uri="http://geekkit.bcit.ca/xui" font-style="italic"
    font-highlight="underlined">Purnama XUI </link> supports
    dynamic binding of business logic at runtime.</paragraph>
  </section>
</document>
```

Listing 4.1 gives a consistent manner in which to store various pieces of data and metadata. The actual content that is stored has been chunked into appropriate pieces of data. We can determine who the author is, what font size and style is being used at various different levels within the document, as well as distinguish between regular text within a paragraph, italic, and hyperlinks as well. This is important to an application developer who is writing a word processing application. Without saving all of this extra (metadata) information, there would be no way for the word processing application to reproduce the document after reopening the document at a later date.

Text Formatted

Currently, XML is stored in text files rather than in binary format (although there is a current effort to offer XML in binary as well). This means that any text editing or word processing application can easily open an XML file and allow the user to view, edit, and save the content. This makes XML easy to manipulate because any text editor can be used to view, edit, or save XML files.

Extensible

When we say that XML is extensible, we mean that it has the ability to be used in ways which may not have originally been intended or even anticipated for. This is because we can create our own metadata language. Looking back at Listing 4.1, there are several different chunks of metadata (e.g., section, paragraph, link). XML would not be as useful if these were the only metadata names that we could use. When creating an XML format, any metadata names can be used and any level of granularity can be chosen. This gives us extensibility.

What XML Is Not

There are a few important points to make, so as not to confuse XML for something that it is not.

A Tag Set

Many people compare XML to, for example, HTML. XML is not just another tag set. XML is a technology for creating tag sets. What we can really say is that HTML *is* a tag set and HTML *is* XML (assuming the HTML in question conforms to the rules of XML).

A Presentation Format

Software developers and information and content designers usually become confused when creating their first XML format. Their first question becomes "Great, now how do I view it?" Although XML can simply be viewed in a text editor, it does not carry any particular formatting information with it. Even with a format that is made for presentation formatting (such as Listing 4.1), the actual data does not display color, font, alignment, or font size. An XML format simply describes data. It is up to an application developer to choose what to do with that data and how to present it.

Syntax and Markup

Now it's time to understand the syntax and markup of XML. Although the syntax and markup of XML is simple to use and understand, there are still a few rules we need to follow.

Using Tags

When creating markup in XML we use what are called *tags*. Tags allow us to do a couple of things. First, tags allow us to partition data into chunks. Second, tags allow us to wrap metadata around the data and assign a label to that particular chunk of data. Thus, tags surround or encompass a particular chunk of data. Except as noted later, we always use a *begin tag* and an *end tag* to surround a particular chunk of data (the content). Listing 4.2 shows an extremely simple XML document. There is a begin tag (shown in bold), some content, and the end tag (also shown in bold). The three of these together form an *element*. In XML, an element is the smallest chunk of metadata that can be formed.

LISTING 4.2   Simple XML Document

```
<first-name>Arron</first-name>
```

Syntax of the Begin Tag

To create a begin tag, we use the less than symbol followed by the string literal, which gives the element its name, then followed by the greater than symbol. This constitutes the begin tag.

Element Names

As mentioned previously, XML is extensible. This means that we can create our own names for metadata. In the case of Listing 4.1, we created a metadata chunk (element) called `first-name`. There are a few rules, however, that we must adhere to when creating element names:

- All names must be one word (i.e., no spaces, tabs, or new line characters found within the name). If you require compound names use either dashes, underscore characters, or the period character to separate each word. Another alternative is to use initial caps.

- The name of the begin tag must be *exactly* the same as the name of the end tag. It is an error, for example, to give the begin tag the value `first-name` and the end tag the value `First-name`. This is because XML is case sensitive (like many programming languages are).
- All element names must begin with an alphabetic character (a–z, A–Z) including characters from other character sets (e.g., Ж) or the underscore character, and cannot contain non-alphanumeric characters, with the exception of these characters: dash, underscore, and period.
- After the first character of the name, any choice of alphanumeric, or dash, underscore, or period character is allowed.

Actually we've said that element names can only begin with these characters: alphanumeric, dash, or underscore. This is not entirely true, as there is one more character that can be used: the colon character (":"). However, you should not use this character because it is used with namespaces in XML.

Syntax of the End Tag

The end tag for an element denotes the end of the element. The end tag is slightly different than the begin tag. The end tag uses the less than symbol, followed by the forward slash character ("/"), followed by the element's name (the same name that was used in the begin element), followed by the greater than symbol.

Content

Content within an element can be any character data except for special characters that are used for markup. Within an element's content, we cannot use these symbols: greater than, less than, or ampersand. We see later in the chapter how to represent these characters within an element's content.

Empty Elements

Most of the time elements in XML have a begin tag, content, and then the end tag. The tags surround the content and the content is considered the message (the data). However, sometimes XML elements can themselves be considered the message. An example would be:

```
<break/>
```

The `break` element represents a command and, therefore, no content is required. This element could be used as a command for a printing device to start a new page. This type of element is considered an *empty* element because it does not have any content inside of it. An empty element starts with the less than symbol, the element name, then the forward slash ("/"), and finally the greater than symbol.

Element Attributes

Elements can also contain attributes. Attributes are small chunks of data that can be nested inside of an element[2]. Listing 4.3 contains two `record` elements each with three attributes (shown in bold). Attributes can be considered key value pairs. The name of the attribute is the key and the string surrounded in double quotes is the value. There are a few important things to remember when creating attributes within elements:

- Attribute names must start with alphabetic character (a–z, A–Z), and cannot contain non-alphanumeric characters with the exception of the dash, underscore, and period. After the first character of the name, any choice of alphabetic, numeric, or dash, underscore, or period character is allowed.
- All attribute names must be one word (i.e., no spaces, tabs, or new line characters found within the name). If you require compound names use either dashes, underscore characters, or the period character to separate each word. Another alternative is to capitalize the first letter of each word.
- The attribute name is followed by the equals sign. Although there can be whitespace (space characters, tab characters, or even new line characters), it is considered good practice not to place any whitespace between the attribute name and the equals sign (e.g., `id="13241234"` and not `id    ="13241234"`).
- After the equals sign, there should be either a single quote or double quote, followed by the actual attribute value and lastly the single quote or double quote. Again, it is good practice to not place spaces between the equals sign and the quotes (e.g., `id="13241234"` and not `id=  "13241234"`). If you use a double quote for the begin quote, you must ensure you use a double quote for the end quote. It is considered good practice to use the double quotes instead of the single quotes for attributes. This is because there are times in XML when you may have to place quotes within quotes. For this reason, you should train yourself to use double quotes for XML element attributes.
- The order of attributes within an XML element is not significant. Listing 4.3 shows how attributes can be placed in any order within that element.
- Both regular elements (with a start and end tag) and empty elements can contain attributes.
- Attribute values can contain any characters except for markup characters (less than, greater than, double quotes within double quotes, or single quotes within single quotes, and the ampersand character).

LISTING 4.3   Elements with Attributes

```
<?xml version="1.0" encoding="UTF-8"?>
<records>
```

```
      <record id="r23423" created="2005/05/10" sales-rep="JLP">
      </record>
      <record created="2005/05/10" id="r23424" sales-rep="JLP">
      </record>
   </records>
```

The Root Element

One of the rules with XML is that every document must contain one and only one element within the start of the document. We call this element the *root element*. Once the root element has been defined, child elements of the root element can be added. It is an error to create an XML document with more than one root element.

Element Nesting

So far we have only looked at single elements. One of XML's features is the ability to add elements to existing elements. Looking at Listing 4.4, we see a `record` element, which contains a `customer` element. Elements that are found within other elements are called *child elements*. We can nest child elements as many times as we see fit in order to create our metadata structures. Looking again at Listing 4.4, we see an element depth of three: (1) the `record` element, which contains (2) the `customer` (child) element, which contains (3) the `first-name` and `last-name` child elements.

LISTING 4.4 XML Element with Child Elements

```
      <?xml version="1.0" encoding="UTF-8"?>
      <record id="r23423" created="2005/05/10" sales-rep="JLP">
        <customer id="c238423">
          <first-name>Arron</first-name>
          <last-name>Ferguson</last-name>
        </customer>
      </record>
```

We can also look at the XML elements from a different perspective. The `customer` element is found within the `record` element. We say that the `record` element is the `customer` element's *parent element*. All child elements have one and only one parent element. For this reason, the data structure appears to look like a tree structure where each branch (child element) can itself contain more branches (child elements). Any element at any given level can contain as many child elements as is required.

One of the important things to remember with element nesting is the order. Since elements usually have a beginning and end tag the order for which the tags can be given is important. Element tags cannot overlap each other. The order is, therefore, *Last In, First Out* (*LIFO*). Thus, it is correct to say:

```
<record id="r23423" created="2005/05/10" sales-rep="JLP">
  <customer id="c238423">
  </customer>
</record>
```

but not correct to say:

```
<record id="r23423" created="2005/05/10" sales-rep="JLP">
  <customer id="c238423">
  </record>
</customer>
```

The `record` element has been started (with the begin tag) first and contains a `customer` element. Because of this, the `customer` element must end (with the end tag) before the `record` element ends because the `customer` element is a child element of the `record` element (and was the last in so should be the first out). Child elements must display their end tags before their parent elements do. In programming terms, you can think of it as a stack.

The use of terms such as parent element and child element helps to determine a relative position within an XML document. However, neither term (child element, parent element) helps determine absolute positioning. A common way to express the depth of an XML document is to state how many levels deep the element you are referring to is (e.g., the customer element is two levels deep). Additionally, you may also hear the XML document referred to as a hierarchy. This is also common because XML documents are hierarchical in nature.

XML Documents

When creating XML, it is assumed that the end result is an XML document. Although the term document implies a file that will be eventually saved and stored to a filesystem, this does not necessarily always have to be the case. Sometimes XML documents exist only for short periods of time. For example, an XML document could exist in memory within an application for the purpose of transferring the document to another application via the Internet or Web.

Processing Instructions

A *processing instruction* is a special type of markup in XML that allows information to be conveyed to applications that are going to read the XML document. For example, Listing 4.5 shows a processing instruction (in bold) at the beginning of the XML document. The information in the processing instruction could be used to request that a particular object in program code be the receiver of this content.

LISTING 4.5   XML Document with Processing Instruction

```
<?java class="CMS.model" id="c-234i2342s"?>
<record id="r23423" created="2005/05/10" sales-rep="JLP">
  <customer id="c238423">
    <first-name>Arron</first-name>
    <last-name>Ferguson</last-name>
  </customer>
</record>
```

Processing instructions can be placed anywhere within the XML document except within an element tag. Processing instructions must start with a less than sign followed immediately by a question mark, followed immediately (no whitespace) by a string value called the *target*. The target is the name of the application that is considered the reader of the processing instruction, and it is assumed the application that is processing this document knows just exactly what to do with the processing instruction. For this reason, processing instructions are usually specific to a particular application. After the target, pretty much any content and character sequence can be written (with the exception of the question mark followed by the greater than sign). To end the processing instruction, a question mark is immediately followed by a greater than sign. Processing instructions can also contain multiple lines of content. Listing 4.6 shows an entire Java class embedded within the processing instruction.

LISTING 4.6   Multiline Processing Instruction

```
<?java
  public class Record {
    private Customer purchaser;
    public Record() { purchaser = new Customer(); }
  }
?>
<record id="r23423" created="2005/05/10" sales-rep="JLP">
  <customer id="c238423">
    <first-name>Arron</first-name>
    <last-name>Ferguson</last-name>
  </customer>
</record>
```

XML Declaration

The *XML declaration* is found at the beginning of an XML document and looks suspiciously like a processing instruction (but it isn't). The XML declaration is there to inform any application that this document is, in fact, an XML document. Although it is not a requirement for every XML document to contain the XML declaration, it is good practice to include it. This is because an *XML parser* reading the document can read pertinent information about the XML document[3].

Like processing instructions, the XML declaration starts with a less than symbol, immediately followed by a question mark, immediately followed by the string literal xml. To end the XML declaration, the question mark is followed immediately by the greater than sign. In the middle of the XML declaration are attributes. Listing 4.7 shows the XML declaration (in bold), with two key pieces of information: (1) the version of the XML recommendation, and (2) the encoding type that is being used. Although XML is at version 1.1 as of this writing, it is recommended that you continue to use 1.0 as the version number because many XML parsers still only recognize version 1.0. Encoding is talked about later.

NOTE

XML Version 1.1 no longer depends on a specific Unicode® version (as does XML Version 1.0). Also, documents are expected to be fully normalized, which means that the text is in a Unicode encoding form (e.g., UTF-8) and doesn't contain any character escapes [Bray04].

Unlike processing instructions, the XML declaration must be placed at the exact beginning of an XML document: before the root element and even before any whitespace. It is an error to place even one space character or new line character before the XML declaration.

LISTING 4.7   XML Document with XML Declaration

```
<?xml version="1.0" encoding="UTF-8"?>
<record id="r23423" created="2005/05/10" sales-rep="JLP">
  <customer id="c238423">
    <first-name>Arron</first-name>
    <last-name>Ferguson</last-name>
  </customer>
</record>
```

Comments

Like many programming languages, XML allows for comments. And like comments in programming languages, XML comments help to document the structure of the XML. However, unlike processing instructions and elements, comments may or may not be passed to an application by the XML parser. For this reason, you should not rely on any pertinent information in comments. Comments in XML start with the less than symbol, followed by the exclamation point, followed by two dashes. Ending a comment is done with two dashes and a greater than symbol. Listing 4.8 contains several comments (in bold).

LISTING 4.8 XML Document with Comments

```
<?xml version="1.0" encoding="UTF-8"?>
<!- This record is used for test purposes only ->
<record id="r23423" created="2005/05/10" sales-rep="JLP">
  <!- customer ids must start with a c character
       in order to signify that the id is of type customer.
    ->
  <customer id="c238423">
    <!- the customer's first name must be the first element. ->
    <first-name>Arron<!- Empty default -></first-name>
    <!- the customer's last name must be the last element. ->
    <last-name><!- Remember to capitalize->Ferguson
    </last-name>
  </customer>
</record>
```

There are several observations that we can make about comments: Comments can

- extend multiple lines
- be placed at any level within the element hierarchy (even before the root element)
- be placed before element content
- be placed after element content

Comments cannot

- be placed inside of tags or processing instructions
- be placed within other comments
- be placed before the XML declaration

Marked Sections

Sometimes it is important to send content to an application that is not to be processed by an XML parser. For example, how do you represent an XML document within an XML document? The answer is to use a *marked section*. A marked section is a portion of the XML document that is ignored by the XML parser. Listing 4.9 gives an example of an XML document containing a marked section (shown in bold).

LISTING 4.9 XML Document with a Marked Section

```
<?xml version="1.0" encoding="UTF-8"?>
<record id="r23423" created="2005/05/10" sales-rep="JLP">
  <customer id="c238423">
    <first-name>Arron</first-name>
    <last-name>Ferguson</last-name>
    <![CDATA[
```

```
<?xml version="1.0" encoding="UTF-8"?>
<record id="r23423" created="2005/05/10" sales-rep="JLP">
  <customer id="c238423">
    <first-name>Arron</first-name>
    <last-name>Ferguson</last-name>
  </customer>
</record>
        ]]>
    </customer>
  </record>
```

Generally it is not considered good practice to use marked sections because doing so defeats the purpose of using XML. After all, XML is for creating metadata, which chunks data and content.

Encoding

Recall the XML declaration from Listing 4.8 that one of the attributes was labeled `encoding`. This specifies the method in which the characters within the XML document are encoded. In order to fully answer the question about what encoding to use, we need to address the topic of Unicode. The Unicode Standard is an effort to map all known written languages, currently being used, no longer being used, and even some imaginary (e.g., Klingon). It does this by offering a *codespace* that contains *code points*. The term codespace describes a range of values. Code points are simply unique numeric values, and each character required of each, and every printed language is assigned a code point.

There are empty areas within the Unicode codespace that have not yet been assigned to characters from written languages. There are also areas of codespace that are for private use (not part of the Unicode standard but reserved for whoever wants to use the space internally). For now, there are over a million code points, which should be more than enough and then some.

So Unicode is the mapping of all characters of all printed languages; we therefore need a mechanism to transfer these character sets (written languages)—preferably a mechanism that has been standardized. This is where encoding comes in. As there are different ways of encoding bitmap image data (discussed in Chapter 1), so, too, are there different ways to encode character data. Some encodings support the whole range of Unicode code points. Others only support a limited range of the most used. An encoding is simply a transport mechanism, a method of storing the values of the characters into a sequence of bytes so that they can be transferred from computer to computer. There are several different encodings that can be used with XML, as shown in Table 4.1.

TABLE 4.1   Encodings XML Parsers Need to Handle

Header	Header	Header
UTF-8	UTF-16	UTF-32
EUC-JP	Shift-JIS	USC-2
USC-4	ISO 8859-1	ISO 8859-2
ISO 8859-3	ISO 8859-4	ISO 8859-5
ISO 8859-6	ISO 8859-7	ISO 8859-8
ISO 8859-9	ISO 8859-10	ISO 8859-11
ISO 8859-12	ISO 8859-13	ISO 8859-14
ISO 8859-15		

NOTE

There are several different encodings. However, many of them are different versions of one particular encoding (e.g., ISO 8859).

UTF-8

One of the more commonly used encodings is UTF-8. This is because UTF-8 is backwards-compatible with regular ASCII text documents. It is also the assumed encoding if none is stated. This is important in North America, where many documents over the years have used ASCII as the encoding for text. UTF-8 can be used to encode any of the character sets found within the Unicode codespace because UTF-8 can be variable length. That is, characters in the lower range of the codespace may only take one byte, whereas characters in the higher range of the Unicode codespace may take four bytes to encode.

As well, UTF-8 places the basic Latin (Roman) alphabet characters in the same numeric position as where they are found in the ASCII encoding (0–127). If the ASCII characters are 7-bit, then the ASCII text can be treated directly as UTF-8 because the *Most Significant Bit* (MSB) is not set. If the ASCII characters are 8-bit, then the XML software can simply set the MSB to the value of zero, and once again there is UTF-8 compatibility. However, with this, the range of values from 128 to 256 are ignored, so only the English language characters will easily be re-encoded (other Latin-based languages take more effort).

ISO 8859-1 to ISO 8859-15

ISO 8859-1 (formally known as ISO/IEC 8859-1, less formally known as Latin-1) uses the full 8 bits to store characters, but only covers the range 0 to 191. Since the character set is only for Latin characters, only countries that use the Latin alphabet can benefit by this encoding. Japanese Hiragana and Katakana, and ideographs from Chinese Mandarin and Cantonese cannot be encoded because they take up much more than two hundred characters.

CAUTION

A common misconception is that Unicode is only 16 bit. It is easy to see why many software developers assume this because programming languages such as Java use the 16-bit char for their character type. Additionally, documentation states that the 16-bit char is used to support Unicode. While this is true, it is misleading because Unicode supports over one million code points. This would require at least 21 bits. However, most character sets can be found in Unicode's Basic Multilingual Plane (BMP), which are found in the range from 0 to 65,536.

We have still not answered the question about how an XML parser determines which encoding is being used. After all, the parser must read the XML declaration first before it can get to the encoding attribute and its value, and there are several different encoding choices to be made. Additionally, we also have the added complexity with *endian* issues (e.g., *big endian* or *little endian)*. Although this topic is well beyond the scope of this book, suffice it to say that XML parsers use a set of heuristics to determine which encoding is being used. Each encoding starts off with a certain sequence of bytes, and so an XML parser can usually guess (if computers are capable of doing this) which encoding is being used after the first four bytes. As well, XML parsers assume that bytes are stored in big-endian format, which helps to save time determining this.

Well-Formedness

So far we have been talking about all of the rules of the syntax concerning XML documents. We can say that if these rules have been followed, that the XML document in question is *well formed*. So, to recap, the following rules need to be followed in order for an XML document to be considered well formed:

- All elements have an end tag to complete a start tag or are defined as empty elements.
- Start tags and end tags start and begin with a less than sign and a greater than sign.
- Element names start with either an underscore character or an alphabetic character and only contain alphanumeric characters, or the dash, underscore, or period character.
- The name given in an end tag of an element is spelled exactly the same as the start tag (case sensitive).

■ All attributes contain either a single quotes or double quotes surrounding the value for the attribute.

■ All attribute names are followed by the equals sign (with optional spaces) followed by the double quotes or single quotes.

■ Attribute values that start with double quotes end with double quotes (or start with single quotes, then end with single quotes).

■ All attribute names start with either an underscore character or an alphabetic character and only contain alphanumeric characters or the dash, underscore, or period character.

■ All element tags are nested properly and do not overlap.

■ Any processing instructions start and end with the correct syntax and have not been placed within a tag.

■ If the XML declaration is declared, then it is the first thing in the XML document (even before comments or whitespace characters).

■ All comments use the correct begin and end syntax and are not placed within tags or within other comments.

■ All element content contains legal characters only (no ampersand, less than, or greater than symbol).

■ The XML document contains one and only one root element.

This is a long list and doesn't actually represent all of the rules that need to be followed (there are still more). However, the previous list covers most of the problems that you will encounter and, therefore, should be sufficient for a quick checklist in order to ensure that your document is accepted by an XML parser.

Entities

Previously we encountered the problem of not being able to insert certain characters within the content of an element. Without any solution to this problem, we are severely limited to the type of content that we can place inside of an element. For example, we would not be able to say

```
3 < 10 = true
```

We could type the phrase "less than" but this would not be an appropriate solution, especially if the content is describing mathematical formulas or program code. XML does have a solution to this problem. The solution is to use *entity references*. An entity reference does exactly what its name implies: references an entity. An entity in XML is like an alias or a macro: it represents a string of characters that are either defined somewhere else or that can't be directly inserted (such as the less than symbol).

The syntax for entity references is &name; for named entities or by providing the numeric value for the character in Unicode such as &nnn;. In XML there are five predefined entities that you can reference within your XML document:

- < which represents the less than symbol (<)
- > which represents the greater than symbol (>)
- & which represents the ampersand character (&)
- ' which represents the single quote or apostrophe character (')
- " which represents the double quote (")

Thus, the XML non-well-formed document

```
<?xml version="1.0" encoding="UTF-8"?>
<section>
  <code>3 < 10 = true</code>
</section>
```

can easily be fixed and, thus, well-formed by changing the content to

```
<?xml version="1.0" encoding="UTF-8"?>
<section>
  <code>3 &lt; 10 = true;</code>
</section>
```

Another example is when a character is required, but that character is not mapped to a key from the keyboard. We can solve this problem by giving the numeric value. Using the copyright symbol as our example, we can solve the problem with:

```
<paragraph>Copyright &#169; 2006 Charles River Media.</paragraph>
```

The character sequence '©' will be rendered as © when displayed.

We haven't yet covered what happens to entities, nor have we covered how to create entities instead of just referencing them. Both of these issues are covered later in this chapter.

Understanding XML Parsers

So far we have only been looking at XML documents. The XML parser is just as important to understand so that we can ensure we avoid any problems with the parsing process. As we discussed during the beginning of this chapter, XML is markup that allows for the defining of metadata.

The XML parser is the program that reads through the markup and content and is able to differentiate between the two. A parser is really a program that reads through a stream of characters and distinguishes between *tokens*. An XML parser simply reads the XML document and determines when it encounters the start of an element, the end of an element, character data, attributes of an element, and so forth. There are a few important points to note about XML parsers.

The Parsing Process

Once an XML parser is given an XML document, it either attempts to read the entire document into memory or passes the data to another program for further processing, depending on the type of parser. The first thing the parser does is attempt to figure out what encoding is being used. Recall we talked about this in the encoding section.

As the document is parsed, the XML parser reads elements and content, and if it encounters an error that breaks a rule of well-formedness, it stops and (hopefully) offers an error message that points to the offending syntax. At this point, parsing is stopped. This is why it is important to ensure that when you pass an XML document to a parser, that it is well-formed.

XML Document Source

Most XML parsers have the ability to accept XML documents from either a file located from the filesystem or from a stream of characters from an in-memory location. Your typical XML parser does not really care where the actual character data comes from. If it comes from a file from the filesystem, then there is no particular required filename format just as long as the data is encoded in a text encoding that the XML parser understands. Having said that, most developers use the three letter extension 'xml' (all lowercase) to signify XML documents. One important rule to follow is that the data cannot be in binary format. If the character data comes from a stream, the only requirement is that the stream is terminated properly so that the XML parser knows to stop parsing.

Treatment of Whitespace

XML parsers treat whitespace simply as content. This is important to remember when writing raw XML in a text editor. For example, the following element

```
<paragraph> Charles River Media </paragraph>
```

actually contains one space character before the word Charles and one space character after the word Media. Any application reading in the content of this element would, therefore, have to strip the outer whitespace characters from the paragraph element's content if it did not want the whitespace as part of the text.

We've actually inserted a large amount of whitespace in our examples. The indenting we've been adding to our XML documents has simply been for aesthetic reasons only. For example, we can easily read

```
<?xml version="1.0" encoding="UTF-8"?>
<record id="r23423" created="2005/05/10" sales-rep="JLP">
  <customer id="c238423">
    <first-name>Arron</first-name>
    <last-name>Ferguson</last-name>
  </customer>
</record>
```

because we've inserted whitespace for indenting. But the same document without any whitespace at all is difficult to read

```
<?xml version="1.0" encoding="UTF-8"?><record id="r23423" created="
2005/05/10" sales-rep="JLP"><customer id="c238423"><first-name>Arro
n</first-name><last-name>Ferguson</last-name></customer></record>
```

An XML parser does not need (nor does it care) about whitespace. In fact, indenting can actually slow the XML parser down (if there's enough of it) because it has to read more characters in. It is important, however, to remember that whitespace in XML is considered significant, and even one space character is considered content.

If you have any experience with HTML you may find this treatment of whitespace to be different. HTML parsers (and Web browsers) collapse whitespace. For example, when an HTML parser encounters 23 space characters and two tab characters, it replaces all of those characters with one space character. XML parsers, on the other hand, don't collapse the extra characters and forward all whitespace characters.

Programmer's Perspective

It is important to understand that most software developers will never write an XML parser. Instead, developers will write an application and use an XML parser. Unfortunately, there is enough misinformation on the Web that suggests that it is typical practice to write an XML parser. What most of these documents refer to is the process of writing a software application that *use* the XML parser to load the XML content. The software application then processes the XML content in memory and creates data structures that can be manipulated with program code.

Namespaces

There are times when two or more XML documents may need to be combined either in memory or in a persistent state such as a file in a filesystem. Although this does not cause any parsing errors (assuming none of the rules of well-formedness are broken), it can cause semantic errors for applications that rely on particular XML elements having a particular meaning.

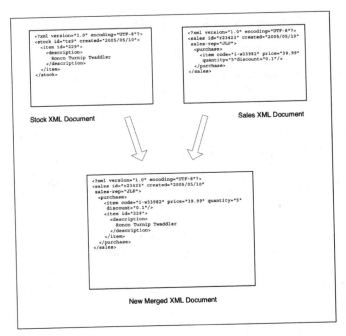

FIGURE 4.1 Example of merged XML documents causing naming collision.

Figure 4.1 gives an example of two XML documents that need to be merged. The document on the left contains stock information with an `item` element that has an `id` attribute and a child element labeled `description`. The document on the right side contains sales information with a `purchase` element, which contains an `item` child element. This child element contains `code`, `price`, `quantity`, and `discount` attributes. The document on the bottom of Figure 4.1 shows both documents merged to create a new document. This new document contains both `item` elements. Although this document is well-formed, the semantics of the document are ambiguous. Are we always to assume that the `item` element from the sales document is to be first? What if there are multiple `item` elements from the sales document? What about multiple `item` elements from both documents? Do we interleave them? This would present a problem to a company that requires processing of merged content from both documents.

The solution can easily be obtained by using namespaces in XML. Like many programming languages, XML comes with the ability to place one or more elements into a namespace. The following format applies a namespace to an element

```
<prefix:element xmlns:prefix="uri">
...
</element>
```

where

- `xmlns` is the attribute used to define a namespace and starts the namespace declaration.
- `prefix` is a label associated with the namespace (the prefix name is restricted to the same naming convention for elements and attributes).
- `uri` is any Universal Resource Identifier (URI) and is called the namespace name.
- when the namespace is in use (e.g., `prefix:element`), the element name (on the right side of the colon) is called the local part or QName (which stands for qualified name).

TIP

A URI is any resource on the Internet, which can by anything from a file, an email address, and a news message, to even a program. It is a common practice to use a specific type of URI such as a Uniform Resource Locator (URL).

Given this information, we can easily solve the problem with the solution given in Figure 4.2. Now that both documents contain namespaces, they can help to eliminate ambiguities between elements of the same name but that contain different semantic meaning. The stock document (on the left side) has the prefix `stores`, which is associated with the namespace `http://www.agf.ca/centralstores`. This namespace is mapped to the `item` element and, therefore, applies to the `item` element and all of item element's child elements. The sales document (on the right side) has the prefix `salesdept`, which is associated with the namespace `http://www.agf.ca/salesdept`. This namespace is mapped to all elements of the sales document because it starts at the top level (root element).

There are a few observations that we can make about Figure 4.2. First, the namespace in the stock document is declared at a different position than in the sales document. This was done for two reasons: (1) only the `item` element from the stock document is used in a document merge so there's no need to add the namespace to all the other elements, and (2) because the `item` element contains the namespace declaration already, there is no need to later on add it programmatically when the documents are merged (which would have been required because the namespace declaration is required in order to use a namespace).

Also, we can observe that the namespace names are unique. This is important because it ensures that elements will not have naming collisions. Another observation is that the namespace names are URLs, where each URL given contains a specific (and

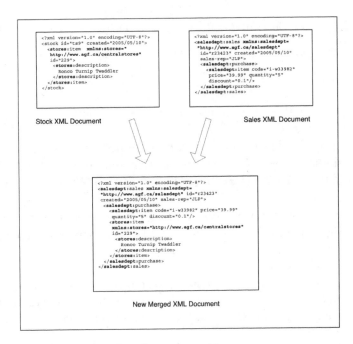

```
<?xml version="1.0" encoding="UTF-8"?>          <?xml version="1.0" encoding="UTF-8"?>
<stock id="ts9" created="2005/05/10">           <salesdept:sales xmlns:salesdept=
  <stores:item   xmlns:stores="                   "http://www.agf.ca/salesdept"
  http://www.agf.ca/centralstores"                 id="r23423" created="2005/05/10"
  id="229">                                        sales-rep="JLP">
    <stores:description>                           <salesdept:purchase>
      Ronco Turnip Twaddler                          <salesdept:item code="i-w33982"
    </stores:description>                            price="39.99" quantity="5"
  </stores:item>                                     discount="0.1"/>
</stock>                                            </salesdept:purchase>
                                                 </salesdept:sales>
```

Stock XML Document   Sales XML Document

```
<?xml version="1.0" encoding="UTF-8"?>
<salesdept:sales xmlns:salesdept=
  "http://www.agf.ca/salesdept" id="r23423"
  created="2005/05/10" sales-rep="JLP">
  <salesdept:purchase>
    <salesdept:item code="i-w33982" price="39.99"
    quantity="5" discount="0.1"/>
    <stores:item
    xmlns:stores="http://www.agf.ca/centralstores"
    id="229">
      <stores:description>
        Ronco Turnip Twaddler
      </stores:description>
    </stores:item>
  </salesdept:purchase>
</salesdept:sales>
```

New Merged XML Document

FIGURE 4.2 Merging documents with namespaces.

unique) path denoting the different departments associated with each type of document. This is standard practice.

TIP

There are a couple of common misconceptions made concerning namespace URLs, such as all namespace names must be URLs. This is not true. It is common practice, but not a requirement of any XML parser. The only requirement is that the namespace name is a URI. Another misconception is that the XML parser (or supporting application) actually looks up the URL. No network connections are made, nor are any attempts made by the XML parser to check whether there is such a Web site. The URL format is used simply because URLs are considered to be unique names (can't have two URLs of the same name).

However, some XML formats require that a specific URL be used. An application processing the XML document checks the namespace name (URI) to ensure that it is a specific value. But this requirement is outside of the scope of both the XML parser and the XML recommendation by the W3C.

It is important to note that XML parsers are only concerned that the namespace is the correct syntax. It is the applications using XML parsers that are interested in the semantic meaning of elements. In our example in Figure 4.2, we were dealing with stock items (possibly from the warehouse) and sales items from a customer purchase. The application (not the XML parser) would benefit from the namespaces because it would have the ability to differentiate between the two types of elements, which would help in further data processing.

To quickly summarize, here are some of the features of XML namespaces:

- A namespace can be assigned to any element at any level of the XML document.
- An element can contain multiple XML namespaces.
- A namespace defined at a particular element in an XML document is visible only to that element and all of its child elements (parent elements are outside of the namespace scope).
- A default namespace (with no prefix) can also be given.
- Namespace prefixes can be used within attribute values.

Default Namespace

There is the feature of being able to create what is called the *default namespace*. The default namespace is unnamed and, therefore, does not use a prefix. An example of using a default namespace is found in Listing 4.10.

LISTING 4.10   Default Namespace

```
<?xml version="1.0" encoding="UTF-8"?>
<record xmlns="http://www.agf.com" id="r23423"
 created="2005/05/10" sales-rep="JLP">
  <customer id="c238423">
    <first-name>Arron</first-name>
    <last-name>Ferguson</last-name>
  </customer>
</record>
```

Now whenever any elements are declared within this document and they do not have a prefix in front of them, they are assumed to be within the default namespace. Although this looks like a convenience, it can cause problems because only elements are considered part of the default namespace and not attributes. It is a good practice to avoid using the default namespace in your documents.

Namespaces Defined at Any Level

A namespace can be declared at any element within the XML document. As shown in Figure 4.2, both this

```
<?xml version="1.0" encoding="UTF-8"?>
<stock id="ts9" created="2005/05/10">
  <stores:item xmlns:stores="http://www.agf.ca/centralstores"
    id="229">
```

```
    <stores:description>
      Bronco Turnip Twaddler
    </stores:description>
  </stores:item>
</stock>
```

and the following are correct uses of namespaces

```
<?xml version="1.0" encoding="UTF-8"?>
<salesdept:sales xmlns:salesdept= "http://www.agf.ca/salesdept"
 id="r23423" created="2005/05/10" sales-rep="JLP">
  <salesdept:purchase>
    <salesdept:item code="i-w33982" price="39.99" quantity="5"
     discount="0.1"/>
  </salesdept:purchase>
</salesdept:sales>
```

Elements Can Contain Multiple Namespaces

An element can contain multiple namespaces as well. In Listing 4.11 the course-outline element contains two namespaces. This allows topic elements from different namespaces to be used within the same document and any application processing this document can differentiate between the two. There may be a need to process each course topic slightly differently based on different credential requirements.

LISTING 4.11 XML Element with Multiple Namespaces

```
<?xml version="1.0" encoding="UTF-8"?>
<mmsd:course-outline xmlns:mmsd="http://www.multimedia.bcit.ca/"
 xmlns:cst="http://www.computing.bcit.ca/cst">
  <mmsd:topic>Java Network Programming</mmsd:topic>
  <cst:topic>C Programming</cst:topic>
</mmsd:course-outline>
```

Namespace Scope Limitation

Whenever a namespace is defined at a particular level (element) within the XML document, all child elements can see and, therefore, use that namespace. However, parent elements do not see the namespace. So correct use of namespaces in scope would be

```
<?xml version="1.0" encoding="UTF-8"?>
<record id="r23423" created="2005/05/10" sales-rep="JLP">
  <sales:customer xmlns:sales="http://www.agf.com" id="c238423">
    <sales:first-name>Arron</sales:first-name>
    <sales:last-name>Ferguson</sales:last-name>
  </sales:customer>
</record>
```

whereas the following is incorrect because the namespace is out of scope

```
<?xml version="1.0" encoding="UTF-8"?>
<sales:record id="r23423" created="2005/05/10" sales-rep="JLP">
  <sales:customer xmlns:sales="http://www.agf.com" id="c238423">
    <sales:first-name>Arron</sales:first-name>
    <sales:last-name>Ferguson</sales:last-name>
  </sales:customer>
</sales:record>
```

The namespace is declared in the `customer` element but used in the `customer's` parent element.

Namespace Prefixes Used in Attributes

Sometimes an XML document can contain attribute values that reference elements from other XML documents or formats. It is perfectly fine to use the namespace prefix within the attribute value, as in Listing 4.12.

LISTING 4.12   Namespace Prefix in Attribute

```
<?xml version="1.0" encoding="UTF-8"?>
<xs:schema xmlns:xs='http://www.w3.org/2001/XMLSchema'>
  <xs:element name="e-mail-address">
    <xs:complexType>
      <xs:attribute name="name" type="xs:string"/>
      <xs:attribute name="address" type="xs:string"/>
    </xs:complexType>
  </xs:element>
</xs:schema>
```

It is assumed that the `string` element is part of (and found within) the namespace defined by `http://www.w3.org/2001/XMLSchema` or at least recognized by the application that uses this namespace.

VALIDATION WITH DTDS

One important need when creating a metadata format in XML is the ability to describe and force XML documents to conform to a certain order and limited choice of elements. Without this ability, we would have difficulty describing metadata because we would be at the mercy of the information and content designers who may forget the order, name, and number of elements allowed in a document. To address this need, we have DTDs. Recall from the beginning of the chapter that the acronym DTD stands for Document Type Definition.

A DTD can really be considered a schema or at least schema-like. DTDs constrain XML documents to a certain order of XML elements and attributes. Any XML document that refers to a DTD must adhere to the rules specified in the DTD. Failing to do so causes errors during the parsing process. When an XML document contains a reference to a DTD (referred to as a *document type declaration*) and that document conforms to all of the rules specified by the DTD, that XML document is said to be *valid*. A document that refers to a DTD and does not conform to the rules in that DTD is said to be *invalid*. It is important not to confuse the terms valid and well-formed, as they mean two completely different things.

XML parsers usually call upon another application or process to perform validation. This is because validation software can usually be large and complex. Therefore, separating the software into separate applications or processes can help speed up the parsing process.

Creating a DTD is about as simple as creating an XML document. The DTD is simply a text document, DTD syntax is not the same as XML, but on the positive side, the syntax is not that hard to learn.

Document Type Declarations

In order to make an XML document reference a DTD, the XML document must contain one document type declaration. The document type declaration must be after the XML declaration, but before the root element. Listing 4.13 shows an example of this.

LISTING 4.13 A Document Type Declaration

```
<?xml version="1.0" encoding="UTF-8" standalone="no"?>
<!DOCTYPE contacts SYSTEM "http://www.agf.com/dtd/contact.dtd">
<contacts>
  <contact>
    <name>
      <first-name>Arron</first-name>
      <last-name>Ferguson</last-name>
    </name>
    <mugshot>./geek-kit.jpg</mugshot>
    <e-mail>arron_ferguson@bcit.ca</e-mail>
    <e-mail>aferguson@bcit.ca</e-mail>
  </contact>
  <page-break/>
</contacts>
```

There are a few things to note about the XML document in Listing 4.13. First, the XML declaration contains a new attribute called `standalone`. The `standalone` attribute's value is set to no. This means that the XML document is using a DTD and, therefore, requires a reference to one (standalone set to yes means no DTD is associated with this document). Second, the DOCTYPE statement contains the name contacts, which is the name of the root element. If the name of the root element in the document type declaration does not match the actual root element that is used inside of the XML document, an error occurs, based on the validation process. The validating software needs to know which element is considered root so it can start validating the XML document against the rules stated inside of the DTD. It is important that this be correct. The next part of the declaration contains the keyword SYSTEM. There's actually a choice between using the SYSTEM keyword and using the PUBLIC keyword (not shown).

Using SYSTEM

The SYSTEM keyword simply means that the DTD being referred to is not publicly available and is usually located on the local filesystem (although it could be found on the Web). The important point is that the DTD is not being shared as a public document with many other users. When creating document type declarations, this is the more common way to refer the DTD. In Listing 4.13, the DTD file is found on a Web site based on the URL http://www.agf.com/dtd/contact.dtd. The URL could have also been a location on the local filesystem.

Using PUBLIC

The PUBLIC keyword states that the DTD being used is highly publicized, such as the case of a standard. For example, a typical HTML document may contain the following:

```
<!DOCTYPE HTML PUBLIC "-//W3C//DTD HTML 4.01 Transitional//EN"
    "http://www.w3.org/TR/html4/loose.dtd">
```

Right after the PUBLIC keyword is a statement in double quotes (in this case it is "-//W3C//DTD HTML 4.01 Transitional//EN"). This is considered the *public ID* and should be unique. The public ID is almost like a command because it lets an XML parser (and validation software) know which particular DTD should be used. The second part of the statement is the URI that points to the DTD to use in case the XML parser does not understand the public ID or cannot find its own copy of the DTD associated with that public ID.

When specifying a URI for a DTD, specifically a URL, there are a couple of things to watch out for. First, if a relative URL is given (e.g., "./contacts.dtd"), the XML document has to be from the same location. This applies to the situation where the DTD document is found on the local filesystem, as well as the situation where the DTD document is found on a server.

Another problem to avoid is accidentally using a filesystem-specific syntax for the URI. For example, the string C:\work\cmsdev\ch4-material\contacts.dtd is not accepted by most XML parsers and validation software and causes a validation error. This is because no protocol has been given nor is the syntax correct. The correct syntax (assuming a URL) would be file:///C:/work/cmsdev/ch4-material/contacts.dtd.

Defining Elements

Defining elements within a DTD takes the form:

```
<!ELEMENT element-name (content)>
```

Element declarations start with the less than sign followed by the exclamation point and the name ELEMENT (in all caps). The next part of the definition is the name of the element you are defining. The element name follows the rules that we discussed earlier in the chapter. The content can either be other elements, or character data and is surrounded in parentheses.

Specifying Multiplicity

Up until now, we're skirted around the issue of content. Content can be other elements, character data (called parsed character data), or a combination of both. DTD syntax allows us to specify:

- parsed character data
- exactly one
- an ordered list
- zero or more
- one or more
- zero or one
- a choice of one or the other
- nested choices
- no content at all
- a choice of any element or parsed character data (or any combination thereof)
- mixed content

Specify Parsed Character Data

One of the simplest types of content to specify is character data (referred to as parsed character data). This is done by using the key term #PCDATA in the content section:

```
<!ELEMENT first-name (#PCDATA)>
```

This would allow for the following in the XML document:

```
<first-name>Arron</first-name>
```

It would be an error to place any child elements into the `first-name` element because the element defined in the DTD only allows for parsed character data.

Specify Exactly One

To specify exactly one element requires that the element name be defined in the DTD:

```
<!ELEMENT first-name (word)>
```

where `word` is an element defined somewhere else in the DTD:

```
<!ELEMENT word (#PCDATA)>
```

The XML to conform to this would look like:

```
<first-name><word>Arron</word></first-name>
```

Based on the `first-name` element's requirement of only one child element, it would be an error to place parsed character data.

When creating DTD documents, the order in which you define your elements within the DTD is not significant. You can, for example, create an element that refers to another element that is defined later on in the document. The validation software takes care of this.

Specify an Ordered List

A more practical use of multiplicity is to create an ordered list. An ordered list requires that the child elements referenced be defined within the DTD:

```
<!ELEMENT contact (first-name, last-name, e-mail)>
<!ELEMENT first-name (#PCDATA)>
<!ELEMENT last-name (#PCDATA)>
<!ELEMENT e-mail (#PCDATA)>
```

The `contact` element requires a very specific order of the `first-name` element, followed by the `last-name` element, followed by the `e-mail` element. To place these elements in any other order in the XML document would be an error. As well, no parsed character data is allowed nor are any other elements. The XML that conforms to this looks like:

```
<contact>
  <first-name>Arron</first-name>
  <last-name>Ferguson</last-name>
  <e-mail>arron_ferguson@bcit.ca</e-mail>
</contact>
```

Specify Zero or More

Sometimes it is useful to be able to allow for no elements, one element, many elements, or any combination in between. This can be useful for an element that can contain several children but doesn't have to contain anything during certain times during the addition of content. An example of this would be:

```
<!ELEMENT contacts (contact)*>
```

The asterisk character specifies that the contacts element can contain zero or more contact elements. The contacts element becomes a placeholder for zero or more (as many as we want) contact elements. The XML looks like:

```
<contacts>
  <contact>
    <first-name>Arron</first-name>
    <last-name>Ferguson</last-name>
    <e-mail>arron_ferguson@bcit.ca</e-mail>
  </contact>
<contacts
```

Specify One or More

There may be the need to satisfy a business rule, which requires at least one child element to exist. In order to fulfill this need, we use the DTD syntax:

```
<!ELEMENT contact (first-name, last-name, (e-mail)+)>
```

The plus character is used to specify one or more. What we've done is updated our contact element to allow for multiple e-mail child elements to be specified at the end as in:

```
<contact>
  <first-name>Arron</first-name>
  <last-name>Ferguson</last-name>
  <e-mail>arron_ferguson@bcit.ca</e-mail>
  <e-mail>aferguson@bcit.ca</e-mail>
</contact>
```

Although we are allowed to place one or more (as many as we want) child elements of type e-mail, we must always have at least one e-mail child element. Without at least one, the XML document would be invalid.

Although the outer parentheses are required when defining the content for an element within a DTD, the inner sets of parentheses are optional. They are only there to make the DTD easier to read.

Specify Zero or One

Another restriction we can place on multiplicity is the ability to say that either zero or one of something is allowed. We use the question mark to place this restriction:

```
<!ELEMENT contacts (contact)*>
<!ELEMENT contact (first-name, last-name, (mugshot)?,
 (e-mail)*)>
<!ELEMENT first-name (#PCDATA)>
<!ELEMENT last-name (#PCDATA)>
<!ELEMENT mugshot (#PCDATA)>
<!ELEMENT e-mail (#PCDATA)>
```

This addition means that we can either have one `mugshot` element or none at all. Again, we've added it to the `contact` element and, therefore, the sequence given must be adhered to. The XML for this looks like:

```
<contact>
  <first-name>Arron</first-name>
  <last-name>Ferguson</last-name>
  <mugshot>./geek-kit.jpg</mugshot>
  <e-mail>arron_ferguson@bcit.ca</e-mail>
  <e-mail>aferguson@bcit.ca</e-mail>
</contact>
```

Specify a Choice of One or The Other

Providing options can also be done within the DTD syntax. An example of a choice would be:

```
<!ELEMENT contact ((first-name | nick-name), last-name,
 mugshot, (e-mail)*)>
<!ELEMENT first-name (#PCDATA)>
<!ELEMENT last-name (#PCDATA)>
<!ELEMENT mugshot (#PCDATA)>
<!ELEMENT e-mail (#PCDATA)>
<!ELEMENT nick-name (#PCDATA)>
```

The `contact` element now allows for either the `first-name` element or the `nick-name` element at the beginning. One or the other, but not both. The XML conforming to this looks like:

```
<contact>
  <first-name>Arron</first-name>
  <last-name>Ferguson</last-name>
```

```
  <mugshot>./geek-kit.jpg</mugshot>
  <e-mail>arron_ferguson@bcit.ca</e-mail>
  <e-mail>aferguson@bcit.ca</e-mail>
</contact>
```

or:

```
<contact>
  <nick-name>Ronron</nick-name>
  <last-name>Ferguson</last-name>
  <mugshot>./geek-kit.jpg</mugshot>
  <e-mail>arron_ferguson@bcit.ca</e-mail>
  <e-mail>aferguson@bcit.ca</e-mail>
</contact>
```

Both are valid choices.

Specify Nested Choices

Nesting (placing within) elements is useful when grouping is needed. Grouping certain elements is a good practice when the elements being grouped share the same characteristics or belong to the same category. Carrying on with our contact format, we can nest the first name (or nickname) along with the last name into a name element[4]:

```
<!ELEMENT contacts (contact)*>
<!ELEMENT contact (name, mugshot, (e-mail)*)>
<!ELEMENT name ((first-name | nick-name), last-name)>
<!ELEMENT first-name (#PCDATA)>
<!ELEMENT last-name (#PCDATA)>
<!ELEMENT mugshot (#PCDATA)>
<!ELEMENT e-mail (#PCDATA)>
<!ELEMENT nick-name (#PCDATA)>
```

The nesting is done using parentheses and allows us to treat a group of elements the same way we would treat one element. The XML for this looks like:

```
<contact>
  <name>
    <first-name>Arron</first-name>
    <last-name>Ferguson</last-name>
  </name>
  <mugshot>./geek-kit.jpg</mugshot>
  <e-mail>arron_ferguson@bcit.ca</e-mail>
  <e-mail>aferguson@bcit.ca</e-mail>
</contact>
```

Although it looks like we've simply added complexity to the document, if we look at this from a programming perspective, we've separated the name elements into a separate group. This can actually be beneficial, especially with large element groups, because program code can load and manipulate a smaller number of elements.

Specify No Content at All

Recall that there are times when the element name itself contains the information or message. Earlier in the chapter we saw this in XML. In order to specify this in the DTD, we use the syntax

```
<!ELEMENT page-break EMPTY>
```

The content type is empty and, therefore, no content is allowed. This means that we cannot place elements or parsed character data into the element. An element that is defined as empty in the DTD can actually be stated in XML using two forms. The first form is the empty element tag:

```
<page-break/>
```

The second form uses both the begin and end tags:

```
<page-break></page-break>
```

It is important to note that there is a big different between

```
<page-break></page-break>
```

and

```
<page-break>
</page-break>
```

Although it may appear that they are the same, they are not. Remember that XML parsers treat all whitespace as being significant. Therefore, one space character (or one new line character and four space characters, in this case) between the two tags is considered content nonetheless. If you specify that an element is empty, then you must ensure (either by typing or programmatically) that no content, not even space characters for indenting, is inserted between the begin and end tags of the empty element.

Specify Anything

Sometimes an XML format (and the accompanying application that uses it) allows for another XML format to be inserted into it. When this happens, it is convenient to specify that any element can be inserted. For example,

```
<!ELEMENT component (ANY)>
```

allows any element name to be inserted into component element. Actually, the ANY content type allows not only elements but parsed character data to be inserted, too. The catch with elements is that they must be defined within a DTD.

Multiple DTDs is covered at the end of the chapter.

NOTE

The use of the ANY type should be kept to a minimum. Specifying that any element is allowed is usually a sign that the DTD is not completed, or that the information or content designer is not fully aware of the full data set.

TIP

Specify Mixed Content

There are times when we want mixed content to be allowed into an element. When we say mixed content, we really mean that we wish to allow both parsed character data and child elements. Most of the examples that we've looked at so far haven't had much call for mixed content. They've mostly been structures such as transaction records and phone contacts. For example, if we think of a document that contains paragraphs, the paragraphs can contain regular character data, characters that are bold, italic, hyperlinks, and so on. We can specify mixed content in a DTD, but we must do it in a particular fashion:

```
<!ELEMENT paragraph(#PCDATA | bold)*>
```

The rules for specifying mixed content state:

- Parsed character data must be defined first.
- There must be a choice between parsed character data and an element using the or (|) symbol.
- There must be any combination of choices between parsed character data and child elements specified (zero or more of either parsed character data, child elements or both).

At first glance, these rules seem to be restrictive. However, once used, it's easy to see that in fact the mixed content rule is too flexible, as it does not allow for the restriction of how many elements, how many times parsed character data is allowed, or even the order of each.

The rule can actually be expanded to include multiple elements, such as

```
<!ELEMENT paragraph(#PCDATA | bold | italic | hyperlink)*>
```

which states that either parsed character data is allowed or a bold element or an italic element or a hyperlink element or any combination or order or number of any of them. We can reword the DTD definition using nesting to make the rules a little easier to read (although the meaning has not changed at all):

```
<!ELEMENT paragraph(#PCDATA | (bold | italic | hyperlink))*>
```

Mixing It Up

Up until now we've only been using the rules by themselves. DTD multiplicity can be used to define some fairly complex relationships by combining the rules we've just discussed. For example we could state:

```
<!ELEMENT purchase (account-no, date, (discount |
(account-price | bulk-discount))?)>
```

This requires a purchase element to contain an exactly one account-no element which must come first, followed by exactly one date element which must come second, followed by a choice of either a discount element or a choice of either an account-price element or a bulk-discount element either zero or once. This would be useful to model a business transaction. We could also create a format for a game to keep track of player's scores. Listing 4.14 shows the DTD and Listing 4.15 shows the XML that conforms to the DTD.

LISTING 4.14   The High Scores DTD

```
<!ELEMENT high-scores (top-ten, daily-highs)>
<!ELEMENT top-ten (entry)*>
<!ELEMENT daily-highs (entry)*>
<!ELEMENT entry (name, score, level)>
<!ELEMENT name (#PCDATA)>
<!ELEMENT score (#PCDATA)>
<!ELEMENT level (#PCDATA)>
```

LISTING 4.15   The High Scores XML Document

```
<?xml version="1.0" encoding="UTF-8"?>
<!DOCTYPE high-scores SYSTEM "Listing4-14.dtd">
<high-scores>
  <top-ten>
    <entry>
      <name>agf</name>
      <score>1234213</score>
      <level>4</level>
    </entry>
    <entry>
      <name>jlp</name>
      <score>1134213</score>
      <level>3</level>
    </entry>
```

```
    </top-ten>
    <daily-highs>
    </daily-highs>
  </high-scores>
```

Another possible scenario would be to create a DTD that describes graphical user interfaces. The format could describe the containment hierarchy of GUI components. A processing application could read in the XML document and build a GUI on the fly based on the XML document. This would be useful because it would eliminate much of the required code that a software developer would have to generate to create the GUI. In fact, anyone who understands XML and understands what the XML format is describing could create a GUI. A possible DTD found in Listing 4.16 describes the metadata rules for the XML document in Listing 4.17.

LISTING 4.16   DTD Describing a GUI

```
<!ELEMENT form (menubar?, panel*)>
<!ELEMENT menubar (menu)*>
<!ELEMENT panel (button | checkbox | radiobutton-group | list |
  combobox | text-field | text-area)*>
<!ELEMENT menu (menu-item)*>
<!ELEMENT menu-item (#PCDATA)>
<!ELEMENT button (#PCDATA)>
<!ELEMENT checkbox (#PCDATA)>
<!ELEMENT radiobutton-group (#PCDATA)>
<!ELEMENT list (#PCDATA)>
<!ELEMENT combobox (#PCDATA)>
<!ELEMENT text-field (#PCDATA)>
<!ELEMENT text-area (#PCDATA)>
```

LISTING 4.17   XML Document for GUI DTD

```
<?xml version="1.0" encoding="UTF-8"?>
<!DOCTYPE form SYSTEM "Listing4-16.dtd">
<form>
  <menubar>
    <menu>
      <menu-item>Open</menu-item><menu-item>Save</menu-item>
      <menu-item>Exit</menu-item>
    </menu>
  </menubar>
  <panel><button>Ok</button><button>Cancel</button></panel>
  <panel><text-field>insert name here</text-field> </panel>
</form>
```

Defining Attributes

Up until now, we've been completely oblivious on how to specify attributes. Being able to constrain attributes is just as important as the ability to constrain elements. For starters, there are four different attribute modifiers for specifying how and if an attribute needs to be stated. Table 4.2 lists them.

TABLE 4.2   Attribute Modifiers

Modifier	Description
#FIXED	The attribute has a fixed value (which must be provided in the DTD) and cannot be changed to a different value. Even if the attribute value is not stated in the defined element, it is still assumed to be there and to contain the fixed value that was specified in the DTD.
#IMPLIED	Implied means that the attribute is optional. It can be defined or not.
#REQUIRED	Required does just as its name implies. It requires any attribute with this modifier specified to be included every time the element is defined. Although the attribute itself is required, an empty value could be given (e.g., an empty string).
Default value	A default value given (that is a string literal) states that the attribute exists even if not stated in the defined element within the DTD. If the attribute is not explicitly given in the element in the XML document, the default value provided in the DTD is used as a default value.

In addition to the modifiers, there are ten different data types that attributes can be defined as. Table 4.3 lists them.

NOTE

Although there are ten listed data types that can be used for element attributes in the DTD, we are only going to be looking at seven of them. We downplay the ENTITY, ENTITIES (which are unparsed entities), and NOTATION types because few XML formats ever actually make use of these data types. Also, many XML developers downplay their usefulness. And lastly, it is the opinion of this author that their usefulness is limited at best.

TABLE 4.3 Attribute Data Types

Type	Description
CDATA	Character data can be any character data that conforms to the rules of legal character data for attributes as discussed earlier in this chapter.
ENTITIES	A whitespace separated list of unparsed entities.
ENTITY	An unparsed entity.
ENUMERATION	Enumeration is a list of values given separated by the vertical or symbol. Only values listed in the enumeration are valid in an XML document.
ID	A string value that can contain a string value. However, the actual value must conform to the same restrictions as XML element names (cannot start with a period or a numeric value). Additionally, any values given in the ID data type must be unique. That is, no other ID data type must have the same value within that document. The validation software will report errors if there are two ID attributes with the same value. ID values must be either `#IMPLIED` or `#REQUIRED`.
IDREF	A string value that references an ID within the same XML document. If the ID value does not exist, the validation software reports an error.
IDREFS	A whitespace-separated list of ID references. Again, the ID values must exist within the XML document or the validation software reports an error.
NMTOKEN	Name token follows almost the same rules for XML element names, however, name tokens are a little more flexible than XML element names. For example, recall that XML names may not begin with a period or a numeric character. Name tokens allow the value to start with a period or a numeric character.
NMTOKENS	Same as name token, however, instead of just one name token, the value given is a list of name tokens, each one separated by whitespace.
NOTATION	References a notation that has been defined within the DTD.

#Fixed **Attribute Modifier**

The #FIXED attribute modifier is useful if you need to specify a certain value that never changes. For example, we could specify that our GUI XML format has a version attribute that contains a specific value to signify which version of the format we are using:

```
<!ELEMENT form (menubar?, panel*)>
<!ATTLIST form version CDATA #FIXED "1.0 Version — XML GUI">
```

This value would have to be used in the XML:

```
<form version "1.0 Version — XML GUI">
...
</form>
```

If the version attribute wasn't specified, then the XML parser would assume the attribute value given in the DTD. Any other value given would cause a validation error.

#Implied **Attribute Modifier**

#Implied allows for the option of using the attribute or not. There are times when it is useful to have an optional attribute. Referring back to our GUI format, we could specify that our menu-item element contains a quick-key attribute which allows the user to make use of a keyboard command to execute the action associated with the GUI menu item:

```
<!ELEMENT menu-item (#PCDATA)>
<!ATTLIST menu-item quick-key CDATA #IMPLIED>
```

This is useful because not all menu items contain (or should contain) quick key commands.

#Required **Attribute Modifier**

There are times when it is sensible to require that a particular attribute be given. With the form root element, which represents a GUI form, we would definitely want to always know the size of the form—it should be specified:

```
<!ELEMENT form (menubar?, panel*)>
<!ATTLIST form width NMTOKEN  #REQUIRED
               height NMTOKEN #REQUIRED>
```

Multiple attributes can and should be defined together. Attributes can be defined anywhere within the DTD, although it is a good practice to list attributes right after the element. However, it is not wrong to define them, for example, at the bottom of the DTD.

Default Value Attribute Modifier

Sometimes an attribute may not be explicitly included in the XML document, but its value is just as important to include nonetheless. Beefing up our form element, we've now added a lang attribute (for the chosen language) to be used.

```
<!ATTLIST form width    NMTOKEN #REQUIRED
               height   NMTOKEN #REQUIRED
               version  CDATA   #FIXED "1.0 Version - XML GUI"
               lang     NMTOKEN "English">
```

Although most users may not wish to include this value, it is important that it exist because the application processing this document needs to know which language the GUI should be displayed in.

Putting It All Together

A revamped version of our GUI DTD now includes attributes and is found in Listing 4.18.

LISTING 4.18 GUI DTD Revised with Attributes

```
<!ELEMENT form (menubar?, panel*)>
<!ATTLIST form width   NMTOKEN #REQUIRED
               height  NMTOKEN #REQUIRED
               x       NMTOKEN #REQUIRED
               y       NMTOKEN #REQUIRED
               menubar IDREF   #IMPLIED
               visible (true | false) #REQUIRED
               title   NMTOKEN #IMPLIED
               version CDATA   #FIXED "1.0 Version - XML GUI"
               lang    NMTOKEN "English">
<!ELEMENT menubar (menu)*>
<!ATTLIST menubar id ID #REQUIRED>
<!ELEMENT panel (button | checkbox | radiobutton-group | list |
  combobox | text-field | text-area)*>
<!ELEMENT menu (menu-item)*>
<!ELEMENT menu-item EMPTY>
<!ATTLIST menu-item quick-key CDATA #IMPLIED
                    text      CDATA #REQUIRED>
<!ELEMENT button EMPTY>
<!ATTLIST button label CDATA>
<!ELEMENT checkbox EMPTY>
<!ATTLIST checkbox label   CDATA          #REQUIRED
                   checked (true | false) #REQUIRED>
<!ELEMENT radiobutton-group (radiobutton)+>
<!ELEMENT radiobutton EMPTY>
<!ATTLIST radiobutton label   CDATA          #REQUIRED
                      checked (true | false) #REQUIRED>
<!ELEMENT list (list-item)+>
```

```
<!ELEMENT list-item EMPTY>
<!ATTLIST list-item label CDATA #REQUIRED>
<!ELEMENT combobox (combobox-item)*>
<!ELEMENT combobox-item EMPTY>
<!ATTLIST combobox-item label CDATA #REQUIRED>
<!ELEMENT text-field (#PCDATA)>
<!ELEMENT text-area (#PCDATA)>
```

Creating Entities

Recall that the less than sign is not a legal character data to place inside of an element, due to the less than sign being used as part of the markup syntax. The solution was to use the predefined entity < in its place. We can also define entities of our own. First, we need to understand the different types of entities.

Internal Entities

Internal entities (also known as internal general parsed entities) are for replacing text within an XML document. There are several reasons for doing this:

- The text cannot be displayed due to the text having illegal characters in it (e.g., "<").
- The text is commonly used within the document (or documents), and it is important that the text is spelled and written correctly each time it is used (consistency).
- The text may be a symbol that is difficult to reproduce with the keyboard.
- The text is part of a different character set other than the one(s) supported by the computer and its operating system.

Internal entities are defined within a DTD and used in XML documents. For example, we could create an internal entity for the copyright symbol:

```
<!ENTITY copyright "&#169;">
```

The value given in double quotes is the Unicode value in decimal for the copyright character. Alternatively, we could also use the hexadecimal value &#xA9. The hexadecimal value uses the extra "x" to indicate that the Unicode value is being given in hexadecimal. In general the syntax for defining an internal entity is:

```
<!ENTITY entity-name "replacement text in double quotes">
```

Like elements in the DTD, the internal entity definition takes on a similar syntax. To use the entity in XML:

```
<paragraph>
All material is copyright &copyright; 2006 Charles River Media.
</paragraph>
```

This is a convenience because we do not have to use a utility to find the particular character (in this case the copyright sign) using a character utility in our operating system. This is because most keyboards do not have a key for typing the copyright sign. We could, however, take this a step further and decide that we wish to use a general entity for the entire copyright notice. This would help maintain consistency in the XML document and ensure we didn't spell the name wrong or forget the year of the copyright:

```
<!ENTITY copyright "All material is copyright &#169; 2006 Charles
    River Media.">
```

Actually, what we've just demonstrated is that internal entities can use other internal entities. Using this entity is just the same:

```
<paragraph>&copyright;</paragraph>
```

Actually, we could even include an entire legal notice in the DTD, which would help eliminate accidental changes made to the legal notice in any referring XML documents.

External Entities

The previous idea of a legal notice being included in a general entity is good but what if the notice includes XML content not just text? We can solve this problem by using an external entity (shown in bold) as found in Listing 4.19.

LISTING 4.19 XML Document with DTD and External Entity

```
<?xml version="1.0" encoding="UTF-8"?>
<!DOCTYPE document [
  <!ENTITY legal SYSTEM "./Listing4-20.xml">
  <!ELEMENT document (legal-notice, (section)*)>
  <!ELEMENT legal-notice (text)*>
  <!ELEMENT text (#PCDATA)>
  <!ELEMENT section (paragraph)*>
  <!ELEMENT paragraph (#PCDATA)>
]>
<document>
  &legal;
  <section>
    <paragraph>All material posted on this Web site is Copyright
      &#169; 2004 Arron Ferguson</paragraph>
  </section>
</document>
```

The format for external entities is slightly different than from general entities:

```
<!ENTITY entity-name SYSTEM "Listing4-20.xml">
```

PUBLIC can replace the term SYSTEM as discussed earlier. The code in Listing 4.19 shows the external entity making a reference to the XML data found in Listing 4.20.

LISTING 4.20   Referenced XML Data

```
<legal-notice>
  <text>Unless otherwise stated, all materials contained on this
  Site are copyright by the author and may not be used to endorse
  products, people or organizations without written permission by
  the author.</text>
  <text>No material may be modified or edited unless the materials
  fall under a license that states otherwise.</text>
</legal-notice>
```

The XML parser (at runtime) pieces together the full document based on the reference to the external entity. This approach is useful if the content to be generated is coming from multiple sources. An entire book could be constructed by piecing together various different XML documents as per the references in the DTD to external entities.

CAUTION

You must ensure that you do not make circular references to XML documents. This will cause a parsing error.

Parameter Entities

Parameter entities only appear in DTDs and use the format:

```
<!ENTITY % entity-name "doc.dtd">
```

You'll notice the percent sign used. This signifies that the entity is a parameter entity. Parameter entities can only be used (not just defined) within a DTD.

External Parameter Entities

Sometimes the DTD data structure becomes large (i.e., there is a large number of elements and the content model is complex). Splitting up the DTD into separate documents where each DTD document addresses a certain set of functionality can help improve readability. For example, we could split our GUI format that we specified in Listing 4.18 into three separate DTD documents: (1) the form itself, (2) the atomic components (e.g., buttons, etc.), and (3) all menu components. Splitting up the DTD content would be helpful if there were three different developers working on each different section of DTD content. Listing 4.21 shows the main DTD. This main DTD contains the form element and the parameter entities (shown in bold).

Listing 4.22 shows the atomic component elements, and finally Listing 4.23 shows the menu component elements.

LISTING 4.21 Top-Level DTD with External Parameter Entities

```
<!ELEMENT form (menubar?, panel*)>
<!ATTLIST form width    NMTOKEN #REQUIRED
              height   NMTOKEN #REQUIRED
              x        NMTOKEN #REQUIRED
              y        NMTOKEN #REQUIRED
              menubar  IDREF   #IMPLIED
              visible (true | false) #REQUIRED
              title    NMTOKEN #IMPLIED
              version  CDATA   #FIXED "1.0 Version - XML GUI"
              lang     NMTOKEN "English">
<!ENTITY % atomic SYSTEM "Listing4-22.dtd">
<!ENTITY % menu SYSTEM "Listing4-23.dtd">
%atomic;
%menu;
```

LISTING 4.22 Atomic Components DTD

```
<!ELEMENT panel (button | checkbox | radiobutton-group | list |
  combobox | text-field | text-area)*>
<!ELEMENT button EMPTY>
<!ATTLIST button label CDATA>
<!ELEMENT checkbox EMPTY>
<!ATTLIST checkbox label   CDATA            #REQUIRED
                  checked (true | false) #REQUIRED>
<!ELEMENT radiobutton-group (radiobutton)+>
<!ELEMENT radiobutton EMPTY>
<!ATTLIST radiobutton label   CDATA            #REQUIRED
                     checked (true | false) #REQUIRED>
<!ELEMENT list (list-item)+>
<!ELEMENT list-item EMPTY>
<!ATTLIST list-item label CDATA #REQUIRED>
<!ELEMENT combobox (combobox-item)*>
<!ELEMENT combobox-item EMPTY>
<!ATTLIST combobox-item label CDATA #REQUIRED>
<!ELEMENT text-field (#PCDATA)>
<!ELEMENT text-area (#PCDATA)>
```

LISTING 4.23 Menu Components DTD

```
<!ELEMENT menubar (menu)*>
<!ATTLIST menubar id ID #REQUIRED>
<!ELEMENT menu (menu-item)*>
<!ELEMENT menu-item EMPTY>
<!ATTLIST menu-item quick-key CDATA #IMPLIED
                   text      CDATA #REQUIRED>
```

Functionally these three DTDs are no different than the original DTD found in Listing 4.18. Parameter entities that refer to external DTD documents are (not surprisingly) called *external parameter entities.*

Internal Parameter Entities

Sometimes portions of the DTD are repeated continually. For example, several elements may contain the same set of attributes. It is convenient to create a parameter entity within the DTD and simply refer to it within each element definition. We gain two advantages to using the parameter entity this way. First, we save ourselves extra time typing. Second (and more important), we save ourselves from accidentally changing the common attribute(s) that the parameter entity is defining. The savings in this case is guaranteed consistency (either all consistently wrong or all consistently correct). For example, if we've decided that all of the atomic components from Listing 4.22 require an ID attribute, then we can create a parameter entity that defines the ID attribute. Listing 4.24 shows how to do this.

LISTING 4.24 DTD with Internal Parameter Entities

```
<!ENTITY % id_attr "id  ID #REQUIRED">
<!ELEMENT panel (button | checkbox | radiobutton-group | list |
  combobox | text-field | text-area)*>
<!ATTLIST panel %id_attr;>
<!ELEMENT button EMPTY>
<!ATTLIST button label CDATA #REQUIRED
                 %id_attr; >
<!ELEMENT checkbox EMPTY>
<!ATTLIST checkbox label    CDATA           #REQUIRED
                   checked (true | false) #REQUIRED
                   %id_attr; >
<!ELEMENT radiobutton-group (radiobutton)+>
<!ELEMENT radiobutton EMPTY>
<!ATTLIST radiobutton label    CDATA          #REQUIRED
                      checked (true | false) #REQUIRED
                      %id_attr; >
<!ELEMENT list (list-item)+>
<!ATTLIST list %id_attr;>
<!ELEMENT list-item EMPTY>
<!ATTLIST list-item label CDATA #REQUIRED
                    %id_attr; >
<!ELEMENT combobox (combobox-item)*>
<!ATTLIST combobox %id_attr;>
<!ELEMENT combobox-item EMPTY>
<!ATTLIST combobox-item label CDATA #REQUIRED>
<!ELEMENT text-field (#PCDATA)>
<!ATTLIST text-field %id_attr;>
<!ELEMENT text-area (#PCDATA)>
<!ATTLIST text-area %id_attr;>
```

Although Listing 4.24 only shows the parameter entity used to define a common attribute, we can use parameter entities to define any part of the document (element content, attributes, or any combination). We do, however, need to ensure that we do not introduce any circular references with our entities.

One difference between internal and external parameter entities is that internal parameter entities do not use the SYSTEM identifier.

We've completely skipped over the topic of unparsed external entities. This is because XML parsers are not obligated to do anything with unparsed external entities except to inform the application using the parser that it encountered one. Unparsed external entities most often are used for the inclusion of binary data. There are more clever ways to deal with binary data with XML documents, such as to create an element that simply uses a URI to link to the binary file or to use an encoding like Base64 or BinHex. Both of these choices are better than using unparsed external entities.

Content Models

When specifying the content within a particular XML element, we are implicitly defining a content model. The content model constrains the particular type of content that is allowed within an element.

Element Content Model

An element content model is one that only allows elements as content. We've already seen this defined, but it makes sense to apply a formal name to the practice. The following are all examples of element content models:

```
<!ELEMENT menubar (menu)*>
<!ELEMENT panel (button | checkbox | radiobutton-group | list |
  combobox | text-field | text-area)*>
<!ELEMENT list (list-item)+>
```

As shown in Chapter 5, the type of content model we create can help us determine the use of our XML format.

Mixed Content Model

As we saw, mixed content allows us to mix both parsed character data in with elements. This is useful for a format that includes character data mixed in with other elements, as was found in the word processing format in Listing 4.1:

```
<paragraph id="p23">An <i>XML tag set/specification</i> and
accompanying <i>Java API</i> that allows developers to create
GUI's by describing the interface via XML.
<link uri="http://geekkit.bcit.ca/xui" font-style="italic"
font-highlight="underlined">Purnama XUI </link> supports
dynamic binding of business logic (at runtime), multiple
namespaces, runtime validation and a rich GUI widget toolset.
Purnama XUI was originally made to address the Semantic Web's
lack of a presentation layer and was built for my B.Tech.
practicum.</paragraph>
```

The paragraph element can contain both parsed character data as well as child elements.

Internal DTDs

DTDs can also be specified within an XML document, although this practice is not entirely useful. Listing 4.25 shows the high-score DTD and XML file in one document.

LISTING 4.25 DTD and XML File as One Document

```
<?xml version="1.0" encoding="UTF-8"?>
<!DOCTYPE high-scores [
  <!ELEMENT high-scores (top-ten, daily-highs)>
  <!ELEMENT top-ten (entry)*>
  <!ELEMENT daily-highs (entry)*>
  <!ELEMENT entry (name, score, level)>
  <!ELEMENT name (#PCDATA)>
  <!ELEMENT score (#PCDATA)>
  <!ELEMENT level (#PCDATA)>
]>
<high-scores>
  <top-ten>
    <entry>
      <name>agf</name><score>1234213</score><level>4</level>
    </entry>
    <entry>
      <name>jlp</name><score>1134213</score><level>3</level>
    </entry>
  </top-ten>
  <daily-highs>
  </daily-highs>
</high-scores>
```

The whole purpose of a DTD is to standardize and constrain XML documents (emphasis on plural) to a specific pattern and rule set. If we include the DTD in an XML document, we are defeating the purpose of the standard. For example, individual XML documents may be changed and so, too, the internal DTD. If this happens, the rule set will be out of sync and several XML documents adhere to different rules. Another problem is that if the DTD represents a specification, it may not be clear where to find the official version of the DTD. If instead the DTD is on a central server (and not an internal DTD), then it is clear where to locate the official version. In the least there is an increase in bandwidth when sending XML documents because every XML document includes the DTD. If the DTD is large, this can have an adverse affect on bandwidth.

Using Multiple DTDs

Finally, we can create multiple DTD documents to describe the different aspects of an XML format. This is especially useful when the format is large and there are certain sections of it that may be useful either on their own or within other formats. As we saw previously with external parameter entities, we can cause DTDs to reference other DTDs. Our GUI format was split up into three files (Listing 4.21, Listing 4.22, Listing 4.23). Any XML documents that refer to the top-level DTD file (Listing 4.21) require no changes, even though the DTD content has been split into three files. This is definitely an advantage because it means that if we create one top-level DTD file (even if it contains next to no DTD content), any XML documents referring to it require no changes.

Limitations Of DTDs

It's easy to get starry-eyed knowing the features that we have at our fingertips when using DTDs. Unfortunately there are a few things that we cannot do with DTDs:

- Although we can state that a particular attribute is required, attributes cannot specify a minimum or maximum character length or minimum or maximum value within a range.
- Attributes cannot be forced to conform to a particular regular expression.
- Elements cannot specify a particular number of child elements (other than zero, one or many).
- Elements cannot specify *scalar data types* (such as int, float, char, byte, etc.) like the data types that are available within various programming languages.
- DTD syntax does not directly support namespaces (although a kludge to the solution is to include the prefix and colon as well as the QName for the element name).

- Mixed content, although it looks restrictive enough, does not allow further restrictions as to the order of elements and parsed character data.
- DTD constraints and multiplicity rules do not necessarily map directly to multiplicity and cardinality rules of other data model rules, such as *Data Definition Library* (*DDL*) statements for RDMSs, or to the rules that can be stated in object models such as in an *Object Oriented Programming* (*OOP*) language (e.g., Java).
- DTD syntax is different from XML syntax. Therefore, we must remember to keep the two syntaxes separate.
- Attribute ID values must start with either an alphabetic or an underscore character. For applications that require an integer value for an ID, this limitation adds complexity to any program that will eventually store the value as an integer.
- DTDs do not elegantly deal with the possibility of an XML document, including binary data. At best, all we can do is include a URI to the binary data and let the application using the XML parser deal with the binary data.
- DTDs do not inform which character encoding is to be used for the XML documents that conform to it and cannot even inform an XML parser or validation software which character encoding the DTD itself has been encoded in.

SUMMARY

In this chapter, we looked at the XML syntax, as well as how to ensure that an XML document is well-formed. We also looked at the rules of validation with DTDs, how to define elements, attributes, and some of the restriction rules of child elements and parsed character data. We also looked at internal DTDs, created and used multiple DTDs, created entities, and saw the difference between content models. As well, we looked at encoding. Looking forward, the next chapter helps us to apply what we've learned in XML to our CMS data model and explains how to perform data modeling. This is important because our CMS data model is built in the next chapter.

ENDNOTES

1. The coverage of XML in this book is meant to be thorough enough to be able to create and manipulate XML. If you are interested in a more academic perspective of XML you may wish to visit the W3C's Web site at *http://www.w3c.org/*.
2. It may appear as though we are contradicting ourselves by defining an XML element to be the smallest chunk of metadata that can be formed, when, in fact, we have element attributes. Element attributes cannot exist

on their own: they require elements. For this reason, the element is still the smallest chunk of metadata considered atomic.

3. Although we have not yet covered XML parsers, suffice it to say that an XML parser is an application that reads XML documents and sends the XML data to other applications.

4. Actually, we were already using nesting with the choice we presented between the `first-name` element and the `nick-name` element. That particular use of nesting allowed us to create a choice between two elements.

5 Data Modeling with XML

In This Chapter

- Different types of data models
- How to perform data modeling using XML
- How to create data structures using XML
- How to define data relationships using XML
- Creating a CMS data model using XML

ata modeling is an important step when developing software—even if the software application is a simple phonebook application. Even more important is choosing a data model because different data models offer different features and have different limitations. By understanding each type of data model, it becomes easier to make practical choices as to which data model suits a project's needs. Having acquainted ourselves with XML and DTDs, we can apply both to our CMS data model, which we do in this chapter. We need to create a data model so that we can consistently store our content (specifically text in our CMS). The example source code listings referenced in this chapter are located on the CD-ROM in the *Chapter 5* folder. The DTDs that are created at the end of the chapter in the section entitled *Creating the CMS Data Model* are located on the CD-ROM in the folder *CMS-project\src\CMS-dtds*.

ON THE CD

DATA MODELS IN GENERAL

When we refer to a data model, we are referring to a structure of data that has been agreed upon by data modelers, systems analysts, and software developers alike. A software application that stores 3D architectural building designs requires a much different data model than a software application that stores compressed video. Additionally, a specialized software application, such as a sound-editing program, requires a much more specific data model than, for example, an RDBMS, which allows data models to be built within a particular data model framework. Before we start to build a data model for our CMS, we should identify the different types of data models so that we understand the data models that we are using.

Relational Data Model

The relational data model is the tried, tested, and true data model that most software developers are familiar with. This is the data model that RDBMSs use for storing data. First, the RDBMS allows the *database administrator* (DBA) to set up a *tablespace* (database). The tablespace consists of tables. Tables are created to represent entities. An entity represents some sort of "thing" that needs to be modeled within the problem domain. An entity can represent a customer, a building, or a business transaction. The table consists of rows and columns. Each row, better known as a *tuple*, represents a record of information. Each column is an attribute of any given record (e.g., first name).

When we use the term problem domain, we are really just giving a formal name to the set of requirements that our project needs us to address.

Tuples within a table most likely contain one or more attributes whose value is unique. This unique value is called a *primary key* and is a way of uniquely referring to a particular record within a table. This concept is the same as a social security number, which is a way of uniquely referring to a citizen of a country because no two people contain the same social security number. Think of the ID type for attributes defined within a DTD. Tuples within a table may also contain referencing keys (*foreign keys*) whose value refers to a primary key attribute from a different tuple, which is usually found in a different table. Again, think of IDREF data types for attributes defined within a DTD. Looking back on Figure 2.14, the ERD we created for our CMS data model did not show the many-to-many relationship because it was a logical design. Figure 5.1 is a physical design showing the relationship between Page entities and Section entities using a composite table (we've removed the Content entity for simplicity).

In the PageSection table in Figure 5.1, there are two foreign keys: PageIDRef and SectionIDRef both referencing the primary key values from the Page table and the Section table respectively. It is important to note that the most powerful part of the relational model is the ability to use these foreign keys to refer to primary keys. Looking at Figure 5.1, we could use the primary keys and foreign keys to create the following *result sets* of information:

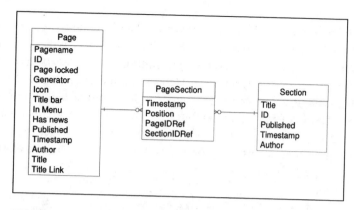

FIGURE 5.1 Physical design for `Page` and `Section` entities.

- List all pages that contain one or more sections
- List all pages where the section author and the page author are the same
- List all pages where the section has been updated (`Section Timestamp` is greater than the `Page Timestamp`)

In order to fulfill the need to query the RDBMS, a query language is needed. All RDBMSs offer some variant of SQL. Listing 5.1 shows the SQL queries for our result sets.

LISTING 5.1 SQL Queries

```
— List all pages that contain one or more sections.
SELECT Page_Name
FROM Page p, PageSection ps, Section s
WHERE p.ID = ps.PageIDRef AND s.ID = ps.SectionIDRef
ORDER BY Page_Name
SELECT Title
FROM Page p, PageSection ps, Section s
WHERE p.ID = ps.PageIDRef AND s.ID = ps.SectionIDRef
AND p.Author = s.Author
ORDER BY Page_Name
SELECT Page_Name
FROM Page p, PageSection ps, Section s
WHERE p.ID = ps.PageIDRef AND s.ID = ps.SectionIDRef
AND s.DateTimeStamp > p.DateTimeStamp
ORDER BY Page_Name
```

An RDBMS can allow for very complex relationships to be created. This ability is a powerful tool that can allow businesses to look for and find relationships found within data that may never have been obvious without being given a result set. As long as tables contain primary and foreign keys, queries can be used to refer to the tables and help users draw relationships.

Object Model

Whereas the relational model is based on tables and tuples with references to primary keys and foreign keys, the object model uses classes and objects to define how data is structured. The object model is used in Object Oriented Programming Languages (OOPLs) and describes everything in terms of classes and objects. A class is a classification of some type. A class can represent concrete real-world things such as cars, people, or fish, but can also represent more abstract things, such as transactions, application configuration information, or components of a program. Classes, both in the real world as well as in an OOPL, are simply groups of things of similar characteristics.

Objects, on the other hand, are instances of a class. In the real world, the class apple represents a grouping of like things. An instance of that class apple would be an actual apple that you have in your hand to eat. In an OOPL, the class is a chunk of program code that describes the grouping of like things. Objects of that class are called instances and remain within the program as long as it exists in memory[1]. Objects have state and behavior. This differs from entities in the relational model where the focus of entities is attributes and relationships. So objects are instances of a class. Figure 5.2 is a graphical representation of an example object model that addresses the same problem domain as the relational model that Figure 5.1 was addressing.

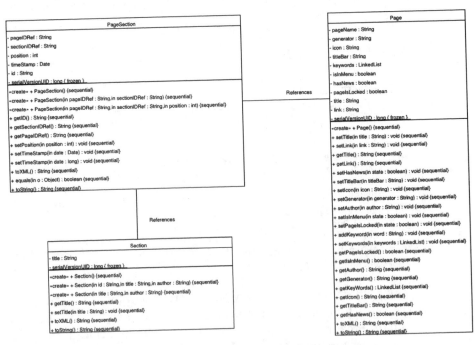

FIGURE 5.2   Example Object Model.

If you've ever taken an OOPL course, then you'll probably remember the important characteristics of the object model:

- abstraction
- encapsulation
- inheritance
- polymorphism

Abstraction in Object Oriented Programming (OOP) can take on two meanings. First, it can mean that you are using OOPL classes to represent real-world things. That is, you are creating a programmatic abstraction of the real-world things that you are modeling. More importantly, it can mean that the data types (classes) you are creating are too general to be useful or used to construct objects within a program. This is because there is not enough information given for them. In the real world, you can think of the class apple as an abstract class. Why? Because the class apple is not concrete enough for us to be able to describe what an apple is. For example, can you state what color an apple is? Or how about what an apple tastes like? Sometimes an apple is green, sometimes it is red, and sometimes it is yellow. Sometimes apples are tart, whereas other times they are sweet. We cannot answer the questions because the class that we've been given is too abstract. In OOP, an abstract class is one that cannot be used to create an object.

This is where inheritance comes into play. Inheritance is the ability to create *subclasses*. A *subclass* contains all the state and behavior of the *superclass* (the class from which the subclass is derived) plus anything else that it provides. We could create a class called apple, and then create a subclass that inherits from apple and call it Golden Delicious. The Golden Delicious subclass would be what we call a *concrete class*, which means that we can create objects from that class because there's enough information from that class to be able to do so.

Encapsulation is important in OOP programming because it allows us to hide information about a class. The implementation details of a class should not be made public to users of that class, just as you should not be expected to know how a car engine works in order for you to drive that car. If the car that you are driving has a different model, make, or uses a completely different technology for its engine, it should not change your understanding of how to use that car. This is because a standard interface has been provided (i.e., steering wheel, break pedal, acceleration pedal, etc.). The same rules apply with encapsulation in an OOPL. If the *interface* (that is the set of calls from your class) is exposed and the inner workings of a class change, any users (in this case a software developer) using this class should not have to concern themselves with the changes.

LISTING 5.2 Transaction Class Showing Encapsulation

```
public class Transaction {
    private float total;
    private int ID;
    public Transaction() {
        ID = -1;
        total = 0.0f;
    }
    public int getID() { return ID; }
    public float getTotal() { return total; }
    public void setTotal(float t) { total = t; }
}
```

For example, in Listing 5.2 a class has been made to describe a transaction. The private members total and ID are hidden (encapsulated) from users of this class—if they attempt to access the data members directly such as

```
Transaction t = new Transaction();
int x = t.total;
```

they will receive a compile time error. This is a good thing because if we change, for example, the ID type to a String but we leave the public interface (usually called the published interface) the same, the internal workings of the class have not affected the users of our class. The change is shown in Listing 5.3.

LISTING 5.3 ID Type Changed to String

```
public class Transaction2 {
    private float total;
    private String ID;
    public Transaction2() {
        ID = "";
        total = 0.0f;
    }
    public int getID() { return Integer.parseInt(ID); }
    public float getTotal() { return total; }
    public void setTotal(float t) { total = t; }
}
```

Document Object Model

The Document Object Model (DOM) is the new kid on the block. It is specific to the world of XML and is hierarchical or tree-structured.

What the DOM Is

The DOM is a data model that transforms the XML document from a tree-like data structure into program memory. Usually this is done using an OOPL where each thing in the XML document hierarchy is represented as a *node*. Depending on the DOM API you're using, a node can be anything such as an element, a processing instruction, a comment, a chunk of character data—basically anything that is found in the XML document is converted into a node. If the API is built using an OOPL, then there is usually a class called node with subclasses of type element, text, comment, etc.

The important thing to remember is that the DOM acts like a conduit that allows an XML document to be read into program memory and transformed into a tree-like data structure that can be manipulated using program code (API calls), and finally sent back out as an XML document again. The API, if it is useful, allows programmers to

- read the XML document into memory and transform it into a DOM
- add nodes
- edit nodes
- list nodes
- delete nodes
- search nodes (easily, no matter how many levels deep the document is)
- change the order of nodes
- traverse nodes (easily, no matter how many levels deep the document is)
- save the entire data model from memory to an XML document

Although this looks like a substantial wish list, these features are imperative to have because the data model is only as useful as the programming interface allows it to be. One important feature that can sometimes be overlooked is the ability to save the DOM out again as an XML document. Without this feature, changes can never be saved.

TIP

When you see the term interface describing a specification or recommendation, you should be careful not to confuse this term with GUI programming. When talking about a programming interface, we are really talking about the set of calls (i.e., function calls in a procedural programming language such as C or method calls in classes, as found in an OOPL).

One of the most commonly used DOMs for XML is the W3C's Document Object Model Recommendation, which is currently at Level 3 [Le Hégaret05]. The W3C's DOM describes both the data structure and the operations that can be performed on the data structure. They also provide an interface that implementers are required to follow in order to deliver a W3C DOM implementation in a particular programming language. The W3C DOM and API are covered in more detail in Chapter 6.

What the DOM is Not

Although the W3C provides a de facto standard DOM API and recommendation, this does not mean that the W3C's DOM is the only DOM. Anybody can create a DOM as long as they provide an interface to programmers, so that the features discussed earlier are available. The W3C's DOM is extensive—there are many different classes within the interface and the recommendation describes in detail just exactly what the data model should look like before and after being manipulated. Therefore, the W3C DOM is usually a good place to start, especially if you're new to programming with XML.

The DOM is also not a replacement for the relational data model, nor is it a replacement for the object model. It is simply another tool in the programmer's toolbox that should be used only when appropriate.

Now we can look at data modeling in XML. For the rest of this chapter, we'll take some of the modeling strategies that we have seen in both the relational data model and the object model and apply them to the DOM in XML, in addition to applying some DOM-specific strategies.

MODELING CONCEPTS

Before creating data structures in XML, there are a few concepts that need to be addressed in order to help steer our choices in the right direction.

Data-Centric

When we say that we're creating a data-centric format, we're simply saying that the data structure we're creating focuses on data. All content defined, all elements within the XML document, are simply little chunks of data. Listing 5.4 shows a data-centric document.

LISTING 5.4   Data-Centric XML Document

```
<?xml version="1.0" encoding="UTF-8"?>
<transaction>
  <customer id="c-294382">
    <name first="Arron" last="Ferguson"/>
    <phone area-code="604" prefix="432" local="8864"/>
    <shipping-address>
      <city>Burnaby</city>
      <street>3700 Willingdon Avenue</street>
```

```
      <building>SW2</building>
      <room>124</room>
      <postal-code>V5G 3H2</postal-code>
    </shipping-address>
  </customer>
  <purchase>
    <items>
      <item code="co3-4ase" brand="Bronco" product="Turnip Twaddler"
       quantity="14" discount="0.0" unit-price="$19.95"/>
    </items>
  </purchase>
</transaction>
```

There are several conclusions that we can draw and call characteristics of a data-centric document:

- We're not using mixed content (mixed content model as per the DTD format).
- Switching the order of children within any level does not change the semantic meaning of the document. For example, the `city` and `street` elements can be transposed, but the data structure still means the same thing. Additionally, we could switch `customer` and `purchase`, and again the semantic meaning has not been corrupted.
- Every innermost element contains information inside (either character data or attribute data) that can be considered meaningful. The `item` element is meaningful even if it is removed from the `items` element. The `room` element is meaningful even if it is removed from the `shipping-address` element.
- The document appears to be made of information that records either a transaction or a business process.
- Elements found within the document contain only short bursts of character data, rather than long sentences or paragraphs.
- Elements (such as the `item` element) contain more attribute data than character data.

Data-centric documents are suitable for XML formats that contain records or chunks of data that are further processed by an application. For example, transactions, messages, or data structures describing objects in an OOPL are all candidates for this type of XML document.

Document-Centric

If a data-centric format emphasizes records, a document-centric format is one where the format is structured around documents. Think of a document that is read by a word processing application. An XML format that is document-centric has several or even all of its child elements using mixed content models. Listing 5.5 shows a document-centric document.

LISTING 5.5 Document-Centric XML Document

```
<?xml version="1.0" encoding="UTF-8"?>
<document author="Arron Ferguson" created="2005/05/10"
 modified="2005/06/22" font="Times" font-size="12pt"
 left-margin="1.0inch" right-margin="1.0inch"
 top-margin="1.0inch" bottom-margin="1.0inch">
  <section id="s12" title="Purnama XUI Project">
    <paragraph id="p23">An <i>XML tagset/specification</i> and
    accompanying <i>Java API</i> that allows developers to create
    GUI's by describing the interface via XML. <link
    uri="http://geekkit.bcit.ca/xui" font-style="italic"
    font-highlight="underlined">Purnama XUI </link> supports
    dynamic binding of business logic at runtime</paragraph>
  </section>
</document>
```

Looking at the document in Listing 5.5, we can also draw conclusions about the characteristics of document-centric formats:

- Child element order is significant, and rearranging the order of child elements changes the semantic meaning of the document. For example, if we change the order of the i element with the link element, the document's semantic meaning has changed. In fact, the document's semantic meaning has been corrupted. Another example is transposing the two paragraph elements of the section element.
- Some (or sometimes many) elements contain mixed content models (as per DTD element definitions). The paragraph element contains both character data, as well as child elements (the i element and the link element).
- Many elements contain large amounts of character data with little (or sometimes no) attribute data.
- Much of the information provided in this document contains instructions on rendering for human consumption. For example, the document element's attributes for margins and fonts.
- Some of the innermost child elements lose their meaning when separated from their parent element. The i element doesn't really have any semantic meaning if it is removed from the paragraph element.

Mimicking an XML format that is document-centric in, for example, the relational model is at best difficult. This is because of the hierarchical nature of document-centric data, which doesn't fit nicely into tuples and tables. This is where the DOM excels. For a CMS, where some or much of the data found in the format is document-centric, using the DOM to manipulate data and using XML to store data offers the most elegant solution.

Elements versus Attributes

Much debate still rages on within various circles of XML experts on whether data values belong in child elements or in attributes. Some Internet support forums curtail this topic because it usually leads to unpleasant user exchanges. As you approach this question yourself you can best answer it by using the set of heuristics found in Table 5.1

TABLE 5.1   Heuristics for Using an Attribute or Element for Data

Characteristic	Element	Attribute
Data will not be exposed to the user		X
Character data is quite long in length	X	
Order is important	X	
May be more than one instance of the data	X	
Character data will be short in length		X
Data requires unique value		X
XML format is required to be compact		X
Data is part of group		X
Data contains mixed content	X	
Data contains subparts	X	
Data choice rules are complex	X	

What is important to note is that these are heuristics. Depending on your XML format, you may find that some of these apply, whereas some of them do not. Looking at some examples will help to better justify Table 5.1. If we were to create a format that represented game characters in a role playing game, we would first come up with state data for the characters as found in Table 5.2.

TABLE 5.2   State for Role Playing Game Character

State	State	State
Alive	First Name	Starting Health Value
Alias	Last Name	Max. Health Value
Age	Character type	Weapons List
Hair Color	Eye Color	Height
Weight	Race	Armor List

Based on our list of state from Table 5.2, we could create a DTD that describes this data in an XML format (see Listing 5.6).

LISTING 5.6   DTD for Role Playing Game Character

```
<!ELEMENT character (health, name, stats, weapon-list, armor-list,
                     magic-list, description)>
<!ATTLIST character id ID #REQUIRED>
<!ELEMENT health EMPTY>
<!ATTLIST health alive                 ( yes | no) #REQUIRED
                 start-health-value CDATA        #REQUIRED
                 max-health-value   CDATA        #REQUIRED>
<!ELEMENT name EMPTY>
<!ATTLIST name first CDATA #REQUIRED
               last  CDATA #REQUIRED
               alias CDATA #IMPLIED>
<!ELEMENT stats EMPTY>
<!ATTLIST stats age        CDATA #REQUIRED
                hair-color CDATA #REQUIRED
                eye-color  CDATA #REQUIRED
                height     CDATA #REQUIRED
                weight     CDATA #REQUIRED
                race
                   (human | elf | ork | dwarf | cyclops) #REQUIRED
                character-type
                   (swordsman | thief | archer | wizard) #REQUIRED
>
<!ELEMENT weapon-list (weapon)*>
<!ELEMENT weapon EMPTY>
<!ATTLIST weapon damage CDATA #REQUIRED
                 type   CDATA #REQUIRED >

<!ELEMENT armor-list (armor-item)*>
<!ELEMENT armor-item EMPTY>
<!ATTLIST armor-item protection CDATA #REQUIRED
                     type       CDATA #REQUIRED>

<!ELEMENT magic-list (magic-item)*>
<!ELEMENT magic-item EMPTY>
<!ATTLIST magic-item damage CDATA #REQUIRED
                     type   CDATA #REQUIRED>

<!ELEMENT description (#PCDATA | b | i)*>
<!ELEMENT i (#PCDATA)>
<!ELEMENT b (#PCDATA)>
```

Based on the DTD that was created in Listing 5.6, we could create an XML document, similar to Listing 5.7.

LISTING 5.7   XML Document for Role Playing Game Character

```
<?xml version="1.0" encoding="UTF-8"?>
<!DOCTYPE character SYSTEM "Listing5-6.dtd">
<character id="cw2e322">
  <health alive="yes" start-health-value="50"
    max-health-value="80"/>
  <name first="Arron" last="Ferguson" alias="geek-kit"/>
  <stats age="29" hair-color="blond" eye-color="blue"
    height="5ft.10in." weight="160lbs." race="human"
    character-type="archer"/>
  <weapon-list>
    <weapon damage="10" type="bow and arrow"/>
    <weapon damage="20" type="cross-bow"/>
  </weapon-list>
  <armor-list>
    <armor-item protection="8" type="chain-mail"/>
    <armor-item protection="6" type="steel helmet"/>
    <armor-item protection="2" type="leather boots"/>
  </armor-list>
  <magic-list></magic-list>
  <description>This character is an <b>archer</b> that has played
    all <i>three</i> of the first three levels.</description>
</character>
```

The DTD and XML document in Listing 5.6 and Listing 5.7 respectively demonstrate the use of the heuristics of Table 5.1.

- The `id` data for the `character` element is data that will most likely not be exposed to the user, therefore, we've made it as an attribute.
- The `description` data has been made as an element because the data is quite long in length (therefore, this information is better suited to an element).
- The description data contains mixed content which means that order is important.
- The `weapon` data, `armor` data, and `magic` data are all found in elements rather than attributes because there may be more than one instance of the data. If we were to use a comma-separated list within an attribute (instead of the elements that we're currently using for these pieces of data), we would have to perform further parsing, which would ultimately defeat the purpose of storing the data in XML.
- Data for first name, last name, and alias are all attributes because the values for those pieces of data are small in length (i.e., they are not sentences or paragraphs).
- The `id` data for the character is an attribute because we require a unique value. Remember, we can take advantage of the DTD validation software, which checks for uniqueness for `id` values.

- Because this format is read in by a *real-time* application, the format should not be overly verbose. We've tried to condense it where possible.

- The data types for `alive`, `start-health-value`, and `max-health-value` are all captured within the element `health`. This makes sense because they are all part of a group (health group).

- Because the `description` data contains mixed content (character data and `b` and `i` elements), it makes sense to use an element instead of attributes. This is because we cannot determine where the `b` and `i` data chunks should be placed if we were to use attributes.

- The character data itself contains several subparts of data (`description`, `health`, `name`, `stats`, `battles-fought`, `weapons-list`, `armor-list`, `magic-list`). Because of this, it would be difficult if not impossible to capture this information in an attribute.

- The choices for a particular data type are best represented using elements. For example, we have a list of weapons, a list of armor, and a list of magic. It would be difficult to represent this with attributes. Elements in this case make the most sense.

When we look at the solution found in Listing 5.6 and Listing 5.7, we need to be careful not to take the position that this is the only solution. A more appropriate position to take is that the solution that we've provided is defensible—based on our heuristics. Each time you create a data model in XML, you can apply these heuristics to better steer your design and make it defensible.

Granularity with XML

Recall that Chapter 1 talked about granularity of content. With XML, we always need to be careful to chunk data down to a level where the data is still meaningful but at the same time the data is searchable. For example, we could decide that a customer name could be stored as:

```
<name>Arron Ferguson</name>
```

However, if the software doing the searching assumed that only the last name was present and was not using regular expressions, the character data within the element would not be found. A better solution is to re-chunk the data using a finer level of granularity:

```
<name>
  <first>Arron</first>
  <last>Ferguson</last>
</name>
```

Alternatively we could provide an attribute version as well:

```
<name first="Arron" last="Ferguson"/>
```

Now any application processing this data can search and list customers based on first name, last name, or both. Another example would be XML that stores phone numbers. The following

```
<phone-number>604-434-5734</phone-number>
```

may not be considered an acceptable level of granularity—some software applications may wish to list only phone numbers within the 604 area code. In order to accomplish this, a software application would be required to parse through the phone-number element's character data and either concatenate, perform a regular expression, or both. This defeats the purpose of using XML because it's the XML parser's job to perform parsing—why should our application be required to parse through data as well? A better (more defensible) version would be:

```
<phone-number area-code="604" prefix="434" local="5734"/>
```

This way the three parts of the phone number have been broken up and stored as a group. This would make it much easier to search phone numbers based on a particular area code or local. Another situation might be using XML to store customer addresses:

```
<address value="3700 Willingdon Avenue, Burnaby, B.C., V5G 3H2"/>
```

Although this looks compact, it requires an application to parse the value attribute. This is inefficient, and it is not harnessing the power of XML. The data needs to be re-chunked down to a finer level of granularity:

```
<address number="3700" street="Willingdon Avenue" city="Burnaby"
   province="B.C." postal-code="V5G 3H2"/>
```

A final example would be how to deal with a URL:

```
<url link="http://geekkit.bcit.ca/xml.html"/>
```

For most applications, this would be appropriate. However, there may be the need to further break down the actual value for the URL if the application requires a lower level of granularity in dealing with URLs. If this were the case, we could present the solution:

```
<url protocol="http" hostname="geekkit.bcit.ca" file="xml.html"/>
```

This solution would allow an application to differentiate easily between say `http://geekkit.bcit.ca/xml.html` and `ftp://geekkit.bcit.ca/xml.html`, as it would require no extra parsing—just a check of the `protocol` attribute.

Formatting Data

One of the issues presented with XML data is how to represent data formats from various different programming languages in the XML document. Because DTDs do not let us specify scalar types (nor how to format them), nor do they allow us to create complex rule sets, we wind up having to find inventive ways for representing and formatting data. After all, elements contain either element content models or mixed content models. Only attributes allow us any degree of control, and even that control is limited.

Currency

If we were to deal with a transaction format which contains information in it such as the total cost of the purchases, we might come up with a format that looks like this:

```
<?xml version="1.0" encoding="UTF-8"?>
<transaction id="tr-234982">
  <items>
    <item code="co3-4ase" brand="Bronco" product="Turnip Twaddler"
      quantity="16" discount="0" unit-price="$19.95"/>
  </items>
  <discounts total="0"/> <tax federal="7%" provincial="0%"/>
  <total before-tax="$319.20" after-tax="$341.54"/>
</transaction>
```

Although this looks like it satisfies all of our needs, the currency values have been given dollar signs in front of them. This causes the application processing this transaction format to parse the currency values found in the `item` element's `unit-price` attribute as well as the `total` element's `after-tax` and `before-tax` attributes. Although current programming languages such as Java and C# offer many convenience methods within their vast API libraries for manipulating strings, we would still need to spend time:

- converting the string into an array of characters
- reading the first character
- determining if the first character is a dollar sign, pound sign, etc.
- performing any conversions to whichever currency format is required.

We may be lucky, however, in being able to send the value to a formatting class, which recognizes the value as currency when it comes across the dollar sign (in Java the `NumberFormat` class offers this). However, this strips away the cross-platform and cross-language independence that we inherit from using XML in the first place. A more appropriate example would be to remove the formatting altogether:

```xml
<?xml version="1.0" encoding="UTF-8"?>
<transaction id="tr-234982">
  <currency type="Canadian" conversion-currency="USD"
   rate="0.84265"/>
  <items>
    <item code="co3-4ase" brand="Bronco" product="Turnip Twaddler"
     quantity="16" discount="0" unit-price="19.95"/>
  </items>
  <discounts total="0"/><tax federal="7%" provincial="0%"/>
  <total before-tax="319.20" after-tax="341.54"/>
</transaction>
```

Although we've made the XML transaction one line longer than it was, we've gained two things. First, the `item` element's `unit-price` attribute value, and `total` element's `before-tax`, and `after-tax` attributes are now standard floating-point numbers that can be converted to whichever format as necessary. This means no more converting to character arrays or relying on language- and platform-specific formatting features.

Second, we've stated the type of currency that is being used in this transaction in the `currency` element (shown in bold). We've additionally shown the conversion currency (`conversion-currency` attribute which is using the American dollar as stated by the value USD) and the rate at which the Canadian dollar is being traded (`rate` attribute) against the American dollar. Any application using this XML format can decide when and where to place the dollar sign in the rendering of the information to the user. Not only that, but we've inadvertently added international currency conversion to our XML transaction format because the transaction has recorded the conversion rate of the Canadian dollar against the American dollar for this particular transaction. This is a useful piece of information for any business that records international transactions.

Percentages

Going back to our transaction format, we've recorded percentage values as:

```xml
<tax federal="7%" provincial="0%"/>
```

The values for both the federal sales tax as well and provincial sales tax have the percentage sign tagged on the end of the value. This, again, requires the application software to further process these values by converting the values into character strings and stripping off the percentage sign. A more appropriate solution is to represent the values as floating-point values:

```
<tax federal="0.07" provincial="0.0"/>
```

The application processing these transaction documents can later decide how to render the values.

Floating-Point Numbers

When recording floating-point numbers, the values should not contain commas for digit grouping, nor should scientific notation be used (unless the application processing these values specifically requires this). The reason is that any software processing these values have to first parse the values and then convert them back to floating-point values. Although this is not normally complicated, it can still require additional effort from application developers, which increases cost and time for software development, as well as causes extra processing.

Date

Another data type where the formatting can cause problems is date and time values. There are so many different ways to format a date (e.g., 2005-07-30) and how to represent time (e.g., 12:08:04 PM). The best solution in an XML format is to leave the formatting for the software processing the values and to use a fine level of granularity for each chunk of date and time data:

```
<date year="2006" month="3" day="22" hour="15" minute="3"
 second="14"/>
```

This may look like overkill, but it removes any programming language or platform dependencies, and it places the responsibility of parsing on the XML parser, rather than on any application software. The final solution to our transaction XML format, after fixing all formatting issues, is found in Listing 5.8.

LISTING 5.8   Transaction Format

```
<?xml version="1.0" encoding="UTF-8"?>
<transaction id="tr-234982">
  <date year="2006" month="3" day="22" hour="15" minute="3"
   second="14"/>
  <currency type="Canadian" conversion-currency="USD"
   rate="0.81265"/>
  <items>
    <item code="co3-4ase" brand="Bronco" product="Turnip Twaddler"
     quantity="16" discount="0.0" unit-price="19.95"/>
  </items>
  <discounts total="0.0"/>
  <tax federal="0.07" provincial="0.0"/>
  <total before-tax="319.20" after-tax="341.54"/>
</transaction>
```

An alternative to this solution may be to represent the date and time value as a long value (64 bit) where the increments in time are measured in milliseconds. Doing this will, however, limit the XML format's processing to languages that can easily support converting long values into date objects.

MODELING RELATIONSHIPS

The power of the relational model gives us the ability to form relationships between records within different tables, as long as we provide primary keys and foreign keys for referencing purposes. In doing so, we can form relationships between data that may reveal purchasing trends, customer preferences, stocking problems, and even detailed statistics about various demographics. It is this key feature that we wish to duplicate within our XML format, which ultimately is used within our DOM.

Primary and Foreign Keys

Although we can create primary key values in XML (using the ID type in our DTD) and foreign key values (using the IDREF type in our DTD), we are presented with a few problems in doing so:

- The ID values must start with an alphabetic character, which means that the ID type cannot be an integer type within the programming environment—it has to be represented as a string.
- The ID values have to be unique within the document—not just within a particular type of record. This is unlike the relational model, where an ID value has only to be unique within the table that the tuple exists in (not the entire tablespace).
- Because the DOM is strictly a hierarchical data model, a problem arises pertaining to where each chunk of the record should be stored (e.g., where to store the customer information and where to store the transaction information).

The first problem is easily addressed by either creating a utility class that generates random or ordered unique alphanumeric values for the primary keys, or that appends and strips away the first alphabetic character from the primary key value as the value goes into the XML document or into the programming environment, respectively.

The second problem can also be addressed by ensuring that the software application uses unique values that are unique within the entire XML document, not just unique within all customer ID values or all purchase ID values. This can be done by appending a certain alphabetic character for customers (e.g., 'c') and appending a different character for purchases (e.g., 'p'). The third problem is much more complex and should be dealt with outside of the programming language domain. It is something that we must address within our XML document format.

Record Placement

Placement of each type of record is crucial because the hierarchical nature of the DOM insinuates ownership. Listing 5.9 gives us an example of placement and containment.

LISTING 5.9 Record Containment Problem

```xml
<?xml version="1.0" encoding="UTF-8"?>
<transaction id="t234982">
  <date year="2006" month="3" day="22" hour="15" minute="3"
    second="14"/>
  <currency type="Canadian" conversion-currency="USD"
    rate="0.81265"/>
  <customer id="c294382">
    <name first="Arron" last="Ferguson"/>
    <phone area-code="604" prefix="432" local="8864"/>
    <shipping-address number="3700" street="Willingdon Avenue"
      city="Burnaby" province="B.C." postal-code="V5G 3H2"/>
  </customer>
  <purchase id="p20902">
    <items>
      <item id="i2398" brand="Bronco" product="Turnip Twaddler"
        quantity="16" item-discount="0.0" unit-price="19.95"/>
    </items>
    <discounts><discount total="0.2"/> </discounts>
    <tax federal="0.07" provincial="0.0"/>
    <total before-tax="319.20" after-tax="341.54"/>
  </purchase>
</transaction>
```

Although Listing 5.9 addresses all of the formatting issues we were previously talking about, there are a few new problems that have arisen due to the hierarchical nature of XML. The customer, the purchase, and the item within the purchase are all found within the transaction. Although this looks harmless it isn't. The relationship between customer and transaction is a one to many. We've been forced to represent it as a compositional relationship, where the customer is part of the transaction (creating a *weak entity* in relational terms). Again, the position within the hierarchy is insinuating ownership. Either this customer element is the original, in which case all other transaction elements must refer to this transaction element's customer, or this is a copy of the original customer, in which case we leave ourselves open to inconsistencies in data (due to updates and deletions). Neither of these situations is all that appealing.

Element Pools

It is true that the level within the hierarchy insinuates ownership. After all, in order to gain access to the `customer` element in Listing 5.9, we have to first access the `transaction` element. But what if this transaction is one of many transactions found within another XML document? Perhaps there are hundreds or even thousands of transactions. This would require us to perform an exhaustive search through all transaction documents or, in the least, all `transaction` elements within the same document.

Instead, what we can do is create *element pools*. Element pools are simply groupings of like data structures or records within a document or containing element. Using this approach allows us to mimic the tuples within tables found in the relational model. Listing 5.10 contains the pool of `transaction` elements, Listing 5.11 contains the pool of `customer` elements, Listing 5.12 contains the pool of `purchase` elements, and Listing 5.13 contains the pool of `item` elements. The `transaction` element in Listing 5.10 is part of a pool of transactions (although we so far have only recorded one). Instead of a `customer` element, there is now a `customer-ref` element that contains an `idref` attribute. This `idref` attribute acts as our foreign key, pointing to the primary key of the customer element found in Listing 5.11.

LISTING 5.10   Transaction Element Pool

```
<?xml version="1.0" encoding="UTF-8"?>
<transactions>
  <transaction id="t234982">
    <date year="2006" month="3" day="22" hour="15" minute="3"
     second="14"/>
    <currency type="Canadian" conversion-currency="USD"
     rate="0.81265"/>
    <customer-ref idref="c294382"/><purchase-ref idref="p20902"/>
  </transaction>
</transactions>
```

LISTING 5.11   Customer Element Pool

```
<?xml version="1.0" encoding="UTF-8"?>
<customers>
  <customer id="c294382">
    <name first="Arron" last="Ferguson"/>
    <phone area-code="604" prefix="432" local="8864"/>
    <shipping-address number="3700" street="Willingdon Avenue"
     city="Burnaby" province="B.C." postal-code="V5G 3H2"/>
  </customer>
</customers>
```

LISTING 5.12   Purchase Element Pool

```
<?xml version="1.0" encoding="UTF-8"?>
<purchases>
  <purchase id="p20902">
    <items><item-ref idref="i2398"/></items>
    <discounts><discount total="0.2"/></discounts>
    <tax federal="0.07" provincial="0.0"/>
    <total before-tax="319.20" after-tax="341.54"/>
  </purchase>
</purchases>
```

LISTING 5.13   Item Element Pool

```
<?xml version="1.0" encoding="UTF-8"?>
<items>
  <item id="i2398" brand="Bronco" product="Turnip Twaddler"
   quantity="16" item-discount="0.0" unit-price="19.95"/>
</items>
```

By separating each pool into separate files, we separate access control to each of the individual record types. An elegant software design would be to use multiple threads, each thread controlling access to each element pool (XML document). Each time a reference is made to a particular customer element, for example, the customer pool thread performs the search, freeing up the other threads to act independently (e.g., accepting requests for other searches in parallel).

If you are unfamiliar with thread programming, this topic will be covered in more detail in Chapter 7. Threads are separate lines of execution within a program and they run in parallel.

Handling Many-to-Many

If we take the business case of renting videos to consumers, we find ourselves with a many-to-many relationship between the movies and the rental of movies. This term (many-to-many) means we borrow from the relational model and RDBMS world. That is, a movie can be rented more than once (we don't just rent the movie and then throw it away after the first rental) and a rental (really a transaction) can involve the choice of one or more movies. After all, you can rent more than one movie at a time.

When DBAs and DB designers approach the task of creating the *physical model* (another relational modeling term, which means the actual data structure that is built within the DB), they create an ERD similar to the one found in Figure 5.3. As shown in Figure 5.3, the handling of the many-to-many relationship requires an extra table (the movie-rental table). In relational terms we call it an *associative entity*.

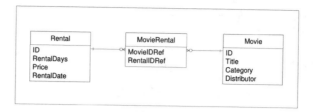

FIGURE 5.3 ERD representing movie rentals.

Seeing this, our first attempt at translating this into XML may create the format found in Listing 5.14.

LISTING 5.14 Movie Rental Transaction

```
<?xml version="1.0" encoding="UTF-8"?>
<rentals>
  <rental id="r2348232" rental-days="3" price="2.95">
    <rental-date year="2006" month="4" day="14" hour="15"
    minute="3" second="14"/>
    <movie id="m908345" title="Star Wars - Episode IV A New Hope"
     category="Science Fiction" distributor="20th Century Fox"/>
  </rental>
</rentals>
```

This first attempt, however, suffers from the same problems that we saw back in Listing 5.9. The movie element is contained and, therefore, a part of the rental. This ignores the many-to-many relationship that exists with movies and rentals, so in order to fix this, we need to mimic the table/tuple relationship and use the ERD from Figure 5.3 to create three element pools.

LISTING 5.15 Rental Element Pool

```
<?xml version="1.0" encoding="UTF-8"?>
<rentals>
  <rental id="r2348232" rental-days="3" price="2.95">
    <rental-date year="2006" month="4" day="14" hour="15"
    minute="3" second="14"/>
  </rental>
</rentals>
```

LISTING 5.16 Movie Element Pool

```
<?xml version="1.0" encoding="UTF-8"?>
<movies>
  <movie id="m908345" title="Star Wars - Episode IV A New Hope"
```

```
          category="Science Fiction" distributor="20th Century Fox"/>
        </movies>
```

LISTING 5.17   `Movie-Rentals` Element Pool

```
        <?xml version="1.0" encoding="UTF-8"?>
        <movie-rentals>
          <movie-rental movie-idref="m908345" rental-idref="r2348232"/>
        </movie-rentals>
```

Listing 5.15 gives us the `rental` element pool, Listing 5.16 gives us the `movie` element pool, and Listing 5.17 gives us the `movie-rentals` element pool. Again, by breaking these up into three separate files, we can use a software design that splits up access to these files using a multithreaded application allowing for searches and updates to be performed in parallel. On a data modeling level, each `movie-rental` element in Listing 5.17 records each movie rented within a transaction. By doing this, we model the associative entity, shown in Figure 5.3. We now have the ability to easily search and update transactions that deal with a many-to-many relationship.

Querying

One of the useful features of the relational model is the ability to easily perform queries using SQL. This is because the relational model and the world of RDBMSs are well established. XML and its data model unfortunately do not share this degree of stability and recognition. But there are a few choices that can be made in querying an XML data model.

XPath

XPath 2.0 is a command-like syntax that offers the ability to reference nodes within the data model it uses. If you've grown accustomed to using command-line navigation within your typical operating system, you'll feel comfortable with XPath. It's most common use is found in the XSLT. Using XPath has its advantages because it, too, is a W3C Recommendation and is supported by the W3C DOM. The Java SDK version 1.5 even contains API support, so that programmers can have XPath expressions evaluated so as to return a *nodeset*. However, if you're choosing to create a custom DOM, then XPath is unavailable to you unless you yourself create XPath expression evaluation capabilities into your custom DOM—not a trivial undertaking.

XQuery

XQuery is a query language currently being refined by the W3C to address the need to query XML data. At the time of this writing, it is still in draft form but should be released soon because the draft is in "last call" to comments, meaning that one more round of comments is made before it progresses to a candidate recommendation. XQuery is a accumulation of previous XML query language attempts, including one called Quilt, which was based on XPath, XML Query Language (XQL), XML Query Language (XML-QL), Structured Query Language (SQL), and Object Data Management (ODMG). Both XPath and XQuery share the same data model as defined by the W3C. Whereas XPath feels much more like a command-like syntax, XQuery feels more like an actual query language.

Custom API Calls

Although this choice offers the most flexibility, it also involves the most work. It means that you'll either be required to rely on the API provided to you (e.g., W3C DOM) or that you'll have to provide API calls yourself. In turn, these API calls are made by the application—usually under direct control from user interaction. If the application that you are creating is quite specific in its needs, then it may be appropriate to create your own API because a general-level query language or API may be overkill. We investigate custom API calls in Chapter 6.

MODELING OBJECTS

So far, most of the data modeling has been either making use of the specific abilities of the DOM or in mimicking the features found in the relational model. Another need may be to model instances of classes within the object model. Listing 5.18 displays a simple Employee class.

LISTING 5.18   Employee Class (Employee.java)

```
public class Employee {
    private String firstName;
    private String lastName;
    private static final int classID = 12342323;
    private int ID;
    public Employee() {
        firstName = "";
        lastName = "";
        ID = -1;
    }

    public Employee(String firstName, String lastName,
        int ID) {
        this.firstName = firstName;
        this.lastName = lastName;
        this.ID = ID;
    }
```

```
    public String getFirstName() { return firstName; }
    public String getLastName() { return lastName; }
    public int getID() { return ID; }


}
```

In XML we would not be so much interested in representing the OOPL class as we would be interested in representing an object of that class. This is because we want the ability to make objects persistent. Making an object persistent means to gather state information of an object during runtime and save that state to the file system for later use. This allows us to load that object at a later date, while still maintaining its state. In order to perform this, we would record certain key pieces of state. In our `Employee` class, we're interested in the `firstName`, `lastName`, and the `ID` of the employee as well as the `classID`. Listing 5.19 records this information.

LISTING 5.19 Employee XML Format

```
<?xml version="1.0" encoding="UTF-8"?>
<class name="Employee" classID="12342323">
  <fields>
    <field access="private" name="firstName" type="String"
     value="Arron"/>
    <field access="private" name="lastName" type="String"
    value="Ferguson"/>
    <field access="private" name="ID" type="int"
     value="12345678"/>
  </fields>
</class>
```

What we've recorded is the state only. No reference is made to constructors or other methods. This is intentional. Storing behavior would require us to create a programming language within our XML format, which would be an entirely different and large undertaking in itself (also another whole book). The `classID` is useful because it allows us to distinguish between different versions of the `Employee` class. This reduces errors when loading object state because we can check if we're dealing with the correct version. It may first appear that the ability to get the state information of a class would be a difficult task to accomplish. After all, how do we write functionality into our program that takes an object of a class and saves it as an XML document? We can give our `Employee` class the ability to save instances of itself easily by adding just one method:

```
public String toXML() {
    StringBuilder sb = new StringBuilder();
    sb.append("<?xml version=\"1.0\" encoding=\"UTF-8\"?>"
        + "\n");
    sb.append("<class name=\"Employee\" classID=\""
```

```
        + classID + "\">\n");
    sb.append("  <fields>\n");
    sb.append("    <field access=\"private\" "
        + "name=\"firstName\""
        + "type=\"String\" value=\"" + firstName + "\"/>"
        + "\n");
    sb.append("    <field access=\"private\" "
        + "name=\"lastName\""
        + "type=\"String\" value=\"" + lastName + "\"/>"
        + "\n");
    sb.append("    <field access=\"private\" name=\"ID\""
        + "type=\"int\" value=\"" + ID + "\"/>\n");
    sb.append("  </fields>\n");
    sb.append("</class>\n");
    return sb.toString();
}
```

We've called it the `toXML` method rather than overriding the `toString` method. This is because we want different behavior for outputting a string of each instance and outputting and XML version of each instance. Because our `toXML` method returns a string, we can easily send instances of the `Employee` class to output streams. We've even added *pretty formatting* so that when the instance is output to a string, it is properly indented and contains new line characters at the end of each element. If this type of an object were included in a larger document, we could remove the XML declaration and add to the class a variable for keeping track of which level in the XML document the object starts at, so as to correctly adjust the indenting. It's easy to get enthralled with this new ability. However, we must be careful that we make note of several limitations when using XML to make objects persistent:

■ We cannot save behavior (e.g., the statements and expressions within constructors and methods). This would cause us to develop an XML format that would contain elements that describe the various different programming language constructs. Essentially we would be creating a programming language, and we'd have to build a compiler and/or interpreter to read this language. This would not be trivial.

■ The state information we record and save cannot be based on complex timing issues. For example, it wouldn't make sense to try and record the state of a thread or to save the position of the mouse cursor on the screen. Neither would it be useful to save the state of a network socket. These state values are volatile.

■ The state information we are saving is going to be programming-language specific. We can't help this. Integer values can be signed or unsigned, characters can be 8 bit or 16 bit. The specific details of the data types depends on the programming language that we use. We would have a difficult time doing data conversions with scalar types (e.g., from C++ to Java). Additionally, complex types such as classes (a.k.a. reference types) that are found in one programming language may not be found in another programming language (e.g., `ArrayList` in Java). We could create lookup tables for both scalar types as well as complex types, but again, we're committing to language-specific formats.

CREATING THE CMS DATA MODEL

Having covered some ideas as to how to approach records and relationships between elements in XML, we can now apply these ideas to our data model that we created in Chapter 2.

Content Model DTDs

In Chapter 2, we created a series of ERDs that displayed our data model. We borrow the ER diagramming techniques from the relational world, but we can still apply them to our XML data model. We can start off by applying the look-and-feel entity that we'll call template because we'll be using XSL templates to do the transforms. Listing 5.20 shows the Templates DTD. We have created an element pool using the `Templates` element, which contains all of the `Template` elements. All `Template` attributes are required, and we've made the `id` attribute of type `ID` so that the validation software informs us if we've accidentally inserted duplicate `id` values.

LISTING 5.20 cms-templates.dtd

```
<!ELEMENT Templates (Template)*>
<!ELEMENT Template EMPTY>
<!ATTLIST Template fileName     CDATA #REQUIRED
                   id           ID    #REQUIRED
                   templateName CDATA #REQUIRED
                   copyright    CDATA #REQUIRED
                   author       CDATA #REQUIRED
                   thumbnailURL CDATA #REQUIRED>
```

TIP

DTDs help us to ensure that when we create XML documents based on the DTDs, the XML documents fully conform to the rules we've specified in the DTDs. This applies to XML documents that we create either manually or programmatically. In the case of XML documents that are created programmatically, we use the DTDs to ensure our program code is creating valid XML documents. Once we know that our program code is creating valid XML documents, we no longer have any need to validate the XML documents. This is because we know that the program code is ensuring valid XML. Another reason we don't want validation during runtime is that it costs in performance. We want the processing of XML documents to be quick. For this reason, validation should only be done during the development stage and not during regular runtime of the software.

However, once we are live and running, we don't abandon our DTDs. The DTDs show the design and better yet, offer extra documentation that others can refer to if there is a need for future development. DTDs help information designers understand the data model; so we really do want to keep the DTDs handy.

The User element pool is found in Listing 5.21. Most of the attribute types are CDATA, except for the id (which again is of type ID), and accountType and loggedOn, which are both enumerated types. This ensures that only those values are allowed to be entered in as attribute values.

LISTING 5.21   cms-users.dtd

```
<!ELEMENT Users (User)*>
<!ELEMENT User EMPTY>
<!ATTLIST User firstName    CDATA                  #REQUIRED
               lastName     CDATA                  #REQUIRED
               login        CDATA                  #REQUIRED
               password     CDATA                  #REQUIRED
               since        CDATA                  #REQUIRED
               lastEdited   CDATA                  #REQUIRED
               accountType  (admin|author|user)    #REQUIRED
               id           ID                     #REQUIRED
               loggedOn     (true|false)           #REQUIRED>
```

Next is Listing 5.22, which gives us the ForumPost element. The ForumPost element has a recursive nature in that it allows ForumPost elements to be placed inside of ForumPost elements. This makes sense when we realize that a post allows for replies, and that the replies are the same in data structure. A ForumPost always has its comment first and then all other ForumPost child elements.

LISTING 5.22   cms-forum.dtd

```
<!ELEMENT Forum (ForumPost)*>
<!ELEMENT ForumPost (Comment, (ForumPost)*)>
<!ATTLIST ForumPost    id                 ID    #REQUIRED
                       user               CDATA #REQUIRED
                       user-account-type
                          (admin|author|forum-user) #REQUIRED
                       timeStamp          CDATA #REQUIRED
                       subject            CDATA #REQUIRED>
<!ELEMENT Comment (#PCDATA)>
```

The remainder of the DTDs deals with the core CMS content. Because some of the elements use the same data structures, we're going to make use of parameter entities. In Listing 5.23, we see the Stamp element, which encapsulates a date/time stamp for all content elements that need to report a date created value and a date modified attribute.

LISTING 5.23 cms-common-core.dtd

```
<!ELEMENT Stamp EMPTY>
<!ATTLIST Stamp dateCreated  CDATA #REQUIRED
                dateModified CDATA #REQUIRED>
```

In Listing 5.24 we see the element definition for the CodeBlock element. It uses the Stamp element and, therefore, must refer to the DTD that contains the Stamp element (called cms-common-core.dtd). The Code element contains the Stamp element and then a child element called CodeContent, which contains the actual textual data. The reason for creating a CodeContent child element is due to the limitation of DTD mixed content models. Recall that we are not allowed to specify order of elements within a mixed content model with DTDs. The parameter entity is defined at the top and, therefore, we are free to use the Stamp element because it has been imported with our parameter entity.

LISTING 5.24 cms-code.dtd

```
<!ENTITY % Common-core SYSTEM "./cms-common-core.dtd">
%Common-core;
<!ELEMENT CodeBlocks (Code)>
<!ELEMENT Code (Stamp, CodeContent)>
<!ATTLIST Code id      ID      #REQUIRED
               author  CDATA   #REQUIRED>
<!ELEMENT CodeContent (#PCDATA)>
```

In addition to the date and timestamp that is common to our CMS content types, there are a few other elements that are common to other DTDs. Listing 5.25 contains the elements used for text. It contains the HyperLink element for hyperlinks within text, the Hint element that displays a description about a particular term (usually displayed in the form of a pop-up label when the mouse cursor rolls over the term within the text), the B element for bold text, the I element for italic text, and the Text element for textual data. These elements are used in the DTDs that define list, paragraph, table, and page content elements. Therefore, it makes sense to keep these elements together in one file rather than redefine them each time in each separate file.

LISTING 5.25 cms-common-text.dtd

```
<!ELEMENT HyperLink EMPTY>
<!ATTLIST HyperLink url  CDATA #REQUIRED
```

```
                         text CDATA #REQUIRED>
<!ELEMENT Hint EMPTY>
<!ATTLIST Hint term          CDATA #REQUIRED
               description   CDATA #REQUIRED>
<!ELEMENT B (#PCDATA)>
<!ELEMENT I (#PCDATA)>
<!ELEMENT Text (#PCDATA)>
```

Listing 5.26 gives us the Image element. The url attribute is for defining the path where the image is located (in the filesystem).

LISTING 5.26   cms-image.dtd

```
<!ENTITY % Common-core SYSTEM "./cms-common-core.dtd">
%Common-core;
<!ELEMENT Images (Image)*>
<!ELEMENT Image (Stamp)>
<!ATTLIST Image url       CDATA     #REQUIRED
                id        ID        #REQUIRED
                author    CDATA     #REQUIRED>
```

Listing 5.27 shows the ImageGallery element. This structure is rather complex. It requires a Stamp element (for the date/time), as well as at least one row of images (ImageRow element). Each row requires at least one thumbnail (Thumbnail element). An image gallery displays the thumbnails of the images, each having a link (link attribute) to the actual image to be viewed. By showing small thumbnails of the actual images (the actual thumbnail images are referred to by the Thumbnail's url attribute), a user can browse the image gallery without having to load all the images which could take quite awhile, depending on the bandwidth constraints as well as the number and size (in bytes) of the actual images.

LISTING 5.27   cms-image-gallery.dtd

```
<!ENTITY % Common-core SYSTEM "./cms-common-core.dtd">
%Common-core;
<!ELEMENT ImageGalleries (ImageGallery)*>
<!ELEMENT ImageGallery (Stamp, (ImageRow)+)>
<!ATTLIST ImageGallery caption   CDATA    #REQUIRED
                       id        ID       #REQUIRED
                       author    CDATA    #REQUIRED>
<!ELEMENT ImageRow (Thumbnail)+>
<!ELEMENT Thumbnail EMPTY>
<!ATTLIST Thumbnail url       CDATA  #REQUIRED
                    link      CDATA  #REQUIRED
                    caption   CDATA  #REQUIRED>
```

NOTE

At this point, we might be tempted to place some attributes in our image and image gallery DTDs that deal with whether clicking on an image causes a new Web browser window to pop up (using the target attribute for anchor tags in HTML). While this feels like a good feature to support, it is outside of the context of our data model. Our data model is describing data in a presentation-neutral manner. By referring to a target attribute, we would be binding our data model to a specific presentation format: HTML. This would be useful in HTML, but it may not be useful in another presentation format, such as a portable document format (PDF) file or a PostScript file. This issue is resolved during the presentation design phase, which we look at in Chapter 11.

Listing 5.28 displays the Table element. The Table element is similar to the ImageGallery element, except that the Table element has an extra row for the header of the table (represented by the TableHeader element). As well, each cell in the table can contain either text (Text element) or a hyperlink (the HyperLink element). This works well when a list of files is given complete with links to the actual files and descriptions of what those files are.

LISTING 5.28 cms-table.dtd

```
<!ENTITY % Common-text SYSTEM "./cms-common-text.dtd">
%Common-text;
<!ENTITY % Common-core SYSTEM "./cms-common-core.dtd">
%Common-core;
<!ELEMENT Tables (Table)*>
<!ELEMENT Table (Stamp, (TableHeader)?, (TableRow)+)>
<!ATTLIST Table id        ID       #REQUIRED
                caption   CDATA    #REQUIRED
                author    CDATA    #REQUIRED>
<!ELEMENT TableHeader (Text)*>
<!ELEMENT TableRow (Text | HyperLink)*>
```

Listing 5.29 gives us the List element. The List element has the type attribute which defines what type of list is being defined (bulleted, numbered, or a definitions list). A list consists of ListItem elements, each of which contains a Term element that is used for presenting a term, and a Text element that gives the description of the term. Again, we note that we are not interested in giving any sort of presentation formatting in this document. We are only defining the actual content, which is completely independent of all formatting and presentation metadata.

LISTING 5.29 cms-list.dtd

```
<!ENTITY % Common-text SYSTEM "./cms-common-text.dtd">
%Common-text;
```

```
<!ENTITY % Common-core SYSTEM "./cms-common-core.dtd">
%Common-core;
<!ELEMENT Lists (List)*>
<!ELEMENT List (Stamp, (ListItem)*)>
<!ATTLIST List type       (bulleted|numbered|definitions) #REQUIRED
               heading    CDATA                           #REQUIRED
               id         ID                              #REQUIRED
               author     CDATA                           #REQUIRED
>
<!ELEMENT ListItem (Term, Text)>
<!ELEMENT Term (#PCDATA)>
```

Listing 5.30 displays the `Paragraph` element. The `Paragraph` element, like the `CodeBlock` element, requires a `Stamp` element as well as textual content, making its content model mixed. Therefore, to enforce the `Stamp` element always coming first, we create a child element called `ParagraphContent`, which contains various different types of paragraph content including regular text, bold text, italic text, hyperlinks, and hints. Without the child element `ParagragphContent`, software that unmarshalls the XML document into memory would have to search for the `Stamp` element because it could be anywhere, based on our inability to specify what order the `Stamp` element is in. This would create unneeded (and unwanted) complexity in our software.

LISTING 5.30   `cms-paragraph.dtd`

```
<!ENTITY % Common-text SYSTEM "./cms-common-text.dtd">
%Common-text;
<!ENTITY % Common-core SYSTEM "./cms-common-core.dtd">
%Common-core;
<!ELEMENT Paragraphs (Paragraph)*>
<!ELEMENT Paragraph (Stamp, ParagraphContent)>
<!ATTLIST Paragraph id      ID      #REQUIRED
                    author  CDATA   #REQUIRED>
<!ELEMENT ParagraphContent
    (#PCDATA | Hint | HyperLink | B | I | Code)*>
```

The `ParagraphContent` element can contain character data, `Hint` elements, `HyperLink` elements, `B` elements (bold), `I` elements (italic), and `Code` elements inside of it. This allows the paragraph to contain rich text, which is something that is important for a CMS to support.

The complex structures have been left for last. The `Section` element does not contain any specific information in it relating to the chunks of content that can be placed within it (Listing 5.31). This is because we have a many-to-many relationship with `Section` elements and the subchunk elements (e.g., `Paragraph`).

LISTING 5.31 `cms-section.dtd`

```
<!ENTITY % Common-core SYSTEM "./cms-common-core.dtd">
%Common-core;
<!ELEMENT Sections (Section)*>
<!ELEMENT Section (Stamp)>
<!ATTLIST Section title    CDATA    #REQUIRED
                  id       ID       #REQUIRED
                  author   CDATA    #REQUIRED>
```

Listing 5.32 displays the `Page` element which does contain a number of attributes:

`author`: the author that created the page.

`generator`: the program that generated the page (in this case is the software that comes with this book: Kucing CMS).

`hasForumLogin`: a boolean value that specifies whether a page contains a form that allows the user to log into the forum portion of the CMS.

`hasNews`: a boolean value that specifies whether a page contains a link with news items.

`hasSearchLink`: a boolean value that specifies whether a page contains a link to the search page.

`icon`: a URL that references an icon. The icon is displayed in URL text field of the Web browser.

`id`: the unique identifier for each page (assigned by the CMS).

`isInMenu`: a boolean value that specifies whether or not the page is found in the menu of the CMS. This is important to differentiate because some pages (such as a copyright page) may not be included in the menu.

`link`: a link to the page itself (usually specified by a relative URL. e.g., `./index.html`)

`pageName`: the name of the page within the filesystem (e.g., `./index.html`).

`title`: the title of the page as shown in the page itself. Some layouts may require that each page have a banner at the top of which contains the name of the page.

`titleBar`: the title of the page but displayed in the title bar of a Web browser. This may or may not be the same value as what is found in the title.

A page also contains a containing element called `Keywords`, which holds `Keyword` child elements. Each `Keyword` child element lists some sort of word that can be used as a way of categorizing this page once it is displayed on the Web. We'll see how to place this information in HTML in Chapter 10.

LISTING 5.32   `cms-page.dtd`

```
<!ELEMENT Pages (Page)*>
<!ELEMENT Page (Stamp, Keywords)>
<!ATTLIST Page pageName     CDATA           #REQUIRED
               id           ID              #REQUIRED
               generator    CDATA           #REQUIRED
               icon         CDATA           #REQUIRED
               titleBar     CDATA           #REQUIRED
               isInMenu     (true|false)    #REQUIRED
               hasNews      (true|false)    #REQUIRED
               hasForumLogin (true|false)   #REQUIRED
               hasSearchLink (true|false)   #REQUIRED
               author       CDATA           #REQUIRED
               title        CDATA           #REQUIRED
               link         CDATA           #REQUIRED>

<!ELEMENT Keywords (Keyword)*>
<!ELEMENT Keyword EMPTY>
<!ATTLIST Keyword text CDATA #REQUIRED>
```

One piece we've missed is the information that goes in each page footer as well as the news section. Listing 5.33 gives us a DTD defining these elements. The CommonPageElements element for this document is really just there to satisfy the need to have a root element. It contains a Footer element and a NewsSection element. All pages for the CMS share the same footer information and the same news section. The Footer element contains four child elements: Copyright, PrivacyPolicy, Contact, and Feedback. Each of these elements provides a link to a separate page. These elements simply contain HyperLink elements that link to the actual pages.

LISTING 5.33   `cms-common-page.dtd`

```
<!ENTITY % Common-text SYSTEM "./cms-common-text.dtd">
%Common-text;
<!ELEMENT CommonPageElements (Footer, NewsSection)>
<!ELEMENT Footer ((Copyright)?, (Contact)?, (Feedback)?,
    (PrivacyPolicy)?)>
<!ELEMENT Copyright EMPTY>
<!ATTLIST Copyright url  CDATA #REQUIRED
                    text CDATA #REQUIRED>
<!ELEMENT PrivacyPolicy EMPTY>
<!ATTLIST PrivacyPolicy url  CDATA #REQUIRED
                        text CDATA #REQUIRED>
<!ELEMENT Feedback EMPTY>
<!ATTLIST Feedback url  CDATA #REQUIRED
                   text CDATA #REQUIRED>
<!ELEMENT Contact EMPTY>
<!ATTLIST Contact url  CDATA #REQUIRED
                  text CDATA #REQUIRED>
```

```
<!ELEMENT NewsSection (NewsItem)*>
<!ATTLIST NewsSection title CDATA #REQUIRED>
<!ELEMENT NewsItem (Text, (HyperLink)?)>
<!ATTLIST NewsItem date CDATA #REQUIRED>
```

Finally, we can see what our composite XML elements look like. Listing 5.34 shows the composite table between Section elements and the subchunk content elements, such as Paragraph, Image, ImageGallery, List, CodeBlock, and Table. The chunk-idref attribute references an id value from any of the subchunk elements. The section-idref attribute references the Section id. This XML document allows us to create the many-to-many relationships we need between sections and sub-chunks. We also keep a position attribute and a timestamp attribute. Although at first glance both of these attributes appear to be superfluous, they are indeed required. The position attribute is important because without it we have no way of knowing where the particular chunk should be placed when it is rendered within a section. Although within the individual data stores order is not significant, when we render pages, the order is significant. The timestamp is also important because it gives us a separate date and time, not for when the section or subchunk was created, but when the actual subchunk was assigned to the section. This extra information helps us to determine updates on sections and content.

LISTING 5.34 cms-section-chunk.dtd

```
<!ELEMENT SectionChunks (SectionChunk)*>
<!ELEMENT SectionChunk EMPTY>
<!ATTLIST SectionChunk chunk-idref    IDREF #REQUIRED
                       section-idref  IDREF #REQUIRED
                       position       CDATA #REQUIRED
                       timestamp      CDATA #REQUIRED>
```

Lastly, Listing 5.35 gives us the same sort of relationship between Page elements and Section elements.

LISTING 5.35 cms-page-section.dtd

```
<!ELEMENT PageSections (PageSection)*>
<!ELEMENT PageSection EMPTY>
<!ATTLIST PageSection pageIDRef     IDREF #REQUIRED
                      sectionIDRef  IDREF #REQUIRED
                      position      CDATA #REQUIRED
                      timestamp     CDATA #REQUIRED>
```

Dynamic Content Generation

Up until now, we've only been dealing with the data store and how content is placed into it. Obviously when the CMS displays content as a collection of Web pages, there has to be some mechanism that extracts the chunks of content and places them into one sequential document. Figure 5.4 visualizes for us the set of steps that brings us to presenting a full page of content to the viewer of the CMS.

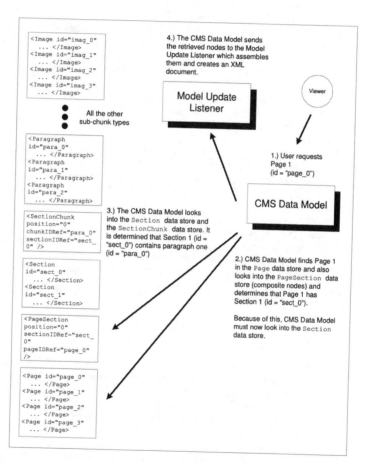

FIGURE 5.4   Dynamic content-generation process of the CMS.

The assembled XML document that the ModelUpdateListener generates (later on) is used to transform the content using an XSLT. These assembled XML documents are temporary cached documents that represent the relationships between pages, sections, and section chunks. When an administrator makes a change to any of the content chunks (via the admin applet), the ModelUpdateListener reflects these changes in the cached XML documents. An example output document might look like Listing 5.36. In the process, the ModelUpdateListener generates some new elements, namely the MenuItem elements.

LISTING 5.36 Example Dynamic Content-Generation XML Document

```xml
<?xml version="1.0" encoding="UTF-8"?>
<Page pageName="index" id="page_0"
  icon="./media/images/mr-kucing-16x16.ico"
  generator="Kucing CMS v1.0" titleBar="Kucing CMS Home"
  isInMenu="false" hasNews="true" author="Arron Ferguson" title="Home"
  link="./index.html" hasForumLogin="true" hasSearchLink="true">
  <Stamp dateCreated="1127721270890" dateModified="1127721270890"/>
  <Keywords>
    <Keyword text="Creating Content Management Systems in Java"/>
    <Keyword text="Charles River Media"/>
  </Keywords>
  <Footer>
    <Copyright url="./copyright.html" text="Copyright Notice"/>
    <Contact url="./contact.html" text="Contact"/>
    <Feedback url="./feedback.html" text="Feedback"/>
    <PrivacyPolicy url="./privacypolicy.html" text="Privacy Policy"/>
  </Footer>
  <NewsSection title="What&apos;s New!">
    <NewsItem date="2006-04-01">
      <Text>Creating Content Management Systems in Java by Arron
        Ferguson. Publisher </Text>
      <HyperLink url="http://www.charlesriver.com/Books/Features.aspx"
        text="link ..."/></NewsItem>
  </NewsSection>
  <Menu>
    <MenuItem><HyperLink url="./index.html" text="Home"/></MenuItem>
  </Menu>
  <Sections>
    <Section author="Arron Ferguson" id="sect_3" title="Welcome">
    <Stamp dateCreated="1135222438706" dateModified="1135222438706"/>
    <Paragraph author="Arron Ferguson" id="para_53" >
    <Stamp dateCreated="1135222662284" dateModified="1135819657546"/>
      <ParagraphContent>Welcome to <B>Kucing CMS 1.0</B>! Kucing
        <Hint term="CMS" description="Content Management System"/> is
        built using <HyperLink url="http://www.javasoft.com"
        text="Java"/>™ technology as well as various <Hint term="XML"
        description="Extensible Markup Language"/> technologies
        including <Hint term="XSLT" description="Extensive Stylesheet
        Language Transformation"/>.</ParagraphContent>
    </Paragraph>
    </Section>
  </Sections>
</Page>
```

For sake of completion, we've created a DTD (Listing5-37.dtd) that shows the format of the temporary cached XML documents. Listing 5.37 is located on the CD-ROM in the Chapter 5 folder. This DTD is not for runtime validation purposes, but rather a contract between the programmer and the XML data designer, so that both can agree upon the same format and XML grammar. This ensures that the outputted XML documents are consistently and correctly following the DTD rule set. The outputted XML files are used to dictate the XSL templates and how they transform, but that's not until Chapter 11.

SUMMARY

In this chapter, we looked at several different data models, including the relational model, the object model, and the document object model. We approached some modeling concepts, such as how a data-centric model differs from a document-centric model. We looked at heuristics to help us determine whether a chunk of data should be an element or an attribute, granularity within XML, formatting elements, and then we moved into modeling relationships with our XML documents using primary keys, foreign keys, and handling many-to-many relationships. We also looked at how to model objects with XML. Finally, we began creating our CMS data model by defining DTDs that our XML will conform to. Looking toward the next chapter, we sift through the different XML APIs that are available and choose one for our CMS. The right XML API allows us to create an efficient application.

ENDNOTE

1. Chapter 6 shows there are ways to make an object persistent (allow it to exist even after the program has finished running in memory).

6 Programming with XML

In This Chapter

- Three competing parser technologies: model driven parsers, event-driven parsers, and push parsers
- Comparing push versus pull parsers
- The W3C DOM Levels 1, 2, and 3
- SAX 2.0
- XPP and MXP
- Designing our own custom DOM

XML is a powerful technology, but without program code to perform some operations on it, the XML documents we so carefully designed are nothing more than text files. Additionally, choosing an appropriate API is just as important as choosing the appropriate data model. Although there are a limited number of APIs to process XML, it helps to understand the strengths and weaknesses of each in order to make an informed decision about which one to use. This assists us in our choice of which XML API to choose for our CMS data model. Without an informed choice, we may choose an XML API that does not meet our needs or possibly introduces additional constraints (such as memory constraints)—something that can hamper our development process. Careful choice of API is, therefore, important if we are to successfully manage and manipulate our data model. The example source code listings referenced in this chapter are located on the CD-ROM in the *Chapter 6* folder. The Java classes that are created at the end of the chapter in the section entitled *Coding the CMS Data Model* are located on the CD-ROM in the *CMS-project\src\org\kucingCMS\contentmodel* sub-folder.

ON THE CD

PARSER TECHNOLOGIES

While there are many different XML formats to date, there are few APIs for parsing XML. It should not be surprising because creating an API can take months, whereas creating an XML format may only take a couple of days, depending on the complexity of the format. However, the parsing APIs available do differ considerably, both in their API calls as well as how they approach the parsing process. It helps us to understand the strengths and weaknesses of each type so that we can choose the right tool for the job.

Model-Driven Parsers

One of the more complex parsers is the model-driven XML parser. This type of parser has the distinction that it reads the entire XML document into memory and creates in-memory objects within the programming language and environment that the parser is running in. This has a great advantage because the software developer simply requests objects from the parser through API calls. We call this a document object model. Figure 6.1 shows how a model-driven parser loads XML content. Each XML element is represented by an object (for example, of type `Element`). This in-memory hierarchical representation of the document is useful, but it does require a substantial API with many convenience methods in order to retrieve XML content from the objects that represent the XML.

W3C DOM API

A good example of a model-driven XML parser is the W3C DOM Recommendation. It was a great step toward formalizing a document object model.

W3C DOM Level 1

The W3C DOM was released as a W3C Recommendation on October 1, 1998, and was called Level 1. It came with both a good description as to what the DOM encompassed, how to manipulate the content inside of the DOM, and language bindings in IDL, Java, and ECMA Script.

TIP

To better understand what is being discussed with the DOM and its API, it is helpful to have the DOM API Javadocs available for viewing as we cover the W3C DOM–specific calls. If you don't have a local copy of the Javadoc documentation on your computer, you can access the DOM API docs at http://java.sun.com/j2se/ 1.4.2/docs/api/org/w3c/dom/package-summary.html.

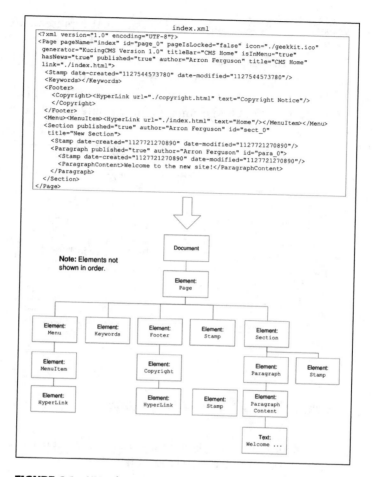

```
                              index.xml
<?xml version="1.0" encoding="UTF-8"?>
<Page pageName="index" id="page_0" pageIsLocked="false" icon="./geekkit.ico"
  generator="KucingCMS Version 1.0" titleBar="CMS Home" isInMenu="true"
  hasNews="true" published="true" author="Arron Ferguson" title="CMS Home"
  link="./index.html">
  <Stamp date-created="1127544573780" date-modified="1127544573780"/>
  <Keywords></Keywords>
  <Footer>
    <Copyright><HyperLink url="./copyright.html" text="Copyright Notice"/>
    </Copyright>
  </Footer>
  <Menu><MenuItem><HyperLink url="./index.html" text="Home"/></MenuItem></Menu>
  <Section published="true" author="Arron Ferguson" id="sect_0"
    title="New Section">
    <Stamp date-created="1127721270890" date-modified="1127721270890"/>
    <Paragraph published="true" author="Arron Ferguson" id="para_0">
      <Stamp date-created="1127721270890" date-modified="1127721270890"/>
      <ParagraphContent>Welcome to the new site!</ParagraphContent>
    </Paragraph>
  </Section>
</Page>
```

FIGURE 6.1   XML document converted into in-memory objects.

Implementers of the DOM language bindings were then free to choose the approach in which the language bindings were implemented. The inheritance hierarchy for the DOM Level 1 is shown in Figure 6.2.

There are a few interesting things to note about the inheritance hierarchy:

■ All of the classes are pure abstract classes (Java interfaces).
■ Node is the top-level interface from which all of the other interfaces derive (inherit).
■ There are interfaces for each and every type of XML element that is found when parsing an XML document: document type declaration (represented by the DocumentType interface), Entity, Element, ProcessingInstruction, Notation, EntityReference, attribute (represented by the Attr interface), and different types of text such as CharacterData, Text, Comment, and CDATASection.

- Document, which is actually the interface that represents the XML document itself being read into memory, is a sub-interface of Node. Although this looks unusual, it makes perfect sense because a node in an XML document is pretty much anything within the hierarchical structure.
- The Node interface makes use of a NodeList interface and a NamedNodeMap interface, which are for child elements and attribute lists respectively.

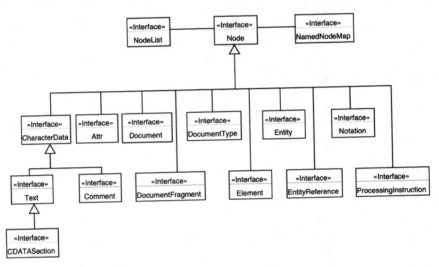

FIGURE 6.2   Class diagram of the W3C DOM.

We can look at the W3C DOM Level 1 in a different perspective: aggregation or informally known as a "has a" relationship in UML-speak. Figure 6.3 shows an aggregation diagram. The Document contains a NamedNodeMap (for attributes) and a NodeList. The NodeList has any number of child nodes, each of which can contain more nodes, which each contain NodeLists, and so forth. It helps to see these two diagrams because it can be easy to confuse the relationships, especially with the Document interface and the Node interface.

Another important issue that causes frustration with new users to the W3C DOM concerns the three method calls getNodeName, getNodeValue, and getAttributes of the interface Node. Each of these methods returns different values or objects based on the sub-interface type. Table 6.1 lists the methods along with the types and what the output values are for each. One valuable detail to remember is that getNodeName returns different string values depending on the sub-interface type. For example, for the Attr (attribute) interface, the actual attribute name is returned. For the Comment interface, the string literal #comment (not the textual content) is returned, and for the Element interface, the actual tag name is returned.

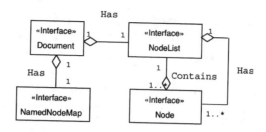

FIGURE 6.3   Aggregation diagram of the W3C DOM.

TABLE 6.1   Return Values Table

Interface	getNodeName	getNodeValue	getAttributes
Attr	attribute name	attribute value	null
CDATASection	"#cdata-section"	textual content	null
Comment	"#comment"	textual content	null
Document	"#document"	null	null
DocumentFragment	"#document-fragment"	null	null
DocumentType	name of root element	null	null
Element	tag name of element	null	NamedNodeMap
Entity	name of entity	null	null
EntityReference	name of entity referenced	null	null
Notation	notation name	null	null
Processing Instruction	PI target	PI data	null
Text	"#text"	textual content	null

An even more valuable detail to remember is what the method getNodeValue returns because it doesn't always return what you might think. Looking back at Table 6.1, it may appear odd that the Element interface would return a null value, especially if it has text. But if we look back to Figure 6.1 and see our ParagraphContent element, we notice that it contains a Text node. This is exactly how the W3C DOM works. *Everything* is a node. If we were to programmatically retrieve the textual content found in the ParagraphContent element in Figure 6.1, we would have to take the following steps (assuming we start at the top of the document):

1. Ask the Document Node for its NodeList
2. For each Node in the Document element's NodeList, ask for nodes that are of type Element and whose node name is Page
3. Ask the Page element for its NodeList
4. For each Node in the Page element's NodeList, ask for nodes that are of type Element and whose node name is Section
5. Ask the Section element for its NodeList
6. For each Node in the Section element's NodeList, ask for nodes that are of type Element and whose node name is Paragraph
7. Ask the Paragraph element for its NodeList
8. For each Node in the Paragraph element's NodeList, ask for nodes that are of type Element and whose node name is ParagraphContent
9. Ask the ParagraphContent element for its NodeList
10. For each node in the Paragraph element's NodeList, ask for nodes that are of type Text

This is an involved process, but it illustrates that everything is treated as a node. Even text. Every piece of textual data is considered a node. Even whitespace. This is the source of many misunderstandings as to the index of a node within a node list. Listing 6.1 shows a simple XML document. The question to ask is how many child nodes does the customer element have?

LISTING 6.1 Simple XML Document

```
<?xml version="1.0" encoding="UTF-8"?>
<customer id="c23423">
  <firstName>Arron</firstName>
  <lastName>Ferguson</lastName>
</customer>
```

Relying on an intuitive guess, you may speculate two. Not so! There are five nodes. Although this sounds like science fiction, five is the correct answer. Really! Figure 6.4 shows where the hidden three nodes are. Right after the customer begin tag is a new line character followed by two spaces for indenting. This is the first child node and is of type Text. This is followed by the firstName element followed by another Text node containing another new line character and two spaces—again for indenting. Now, if we were to ask how many child nodes of type Element does the customer element contain, we would be correct in our initial guess of two. Because you cannot be guaranteed how much whitespace is found between Element nodes, it is best not to assume. Therefore, whenever we are traversing the DOM, we must always be mindful of what particular sub-interface of node we are looking for and what nodes are we coming across.

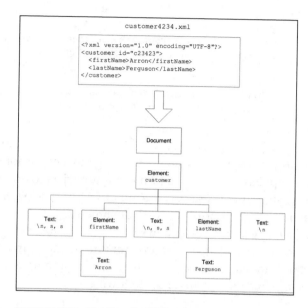

```
customer4234.xml

<?xml version="1.0" encoding="UTF-8"?>
<customer id="c23423">
  <firstName>Arron</firstName>
  <lastName>Ferguson</lastName>
</customer>
```

FIGURE 6.4   Finding the hidden text nodes.

Before going any further, it makes sense to see the context in which these calls are made. When instantiating a W3C DOM parser, a common method is to use the classes javax.xml.parsers.DocumentBuilderFactory and javax.xml.parsers.Document-Builder. These classes are from Sun's JAXP API and are commonly used; so it's fine to get accustomed to calling them. The dp1.java source code file demonstrates usage:

```
DocumentBuilderFactory dbf =
    DocumentBuilderFactory.newInstance();
dbf.setValidating(true);
dbf.setNamespaceAware(true);
dbf.setIgnoringElementContentWhitespace(true);
DocumentBuilder db = dbf.newDocumentBuilder();
db.setErrorHandler(new DOMErrorHandler());
Document doc = db.parse(file);
```

One thing to note is the setErrorHandler method call that is made. By default there is no error handler; so programmers are required to implement the ErrorHandler interface in order to access the errors that the parser may report in the case of malformed XML. A simple example would be something like:

```
class DOMErrorHandler implements ErrorHandler {
    public void error(SAXParseException spe) {
        System.out.println(spe.getMessage());
```

```
        }
        public void fatalError(SAXParseException spe) {
            System.out.println(spe.getMessage());
        }

        public void warning(SAXParseException spe)  {
            System.out.println(spe.getMessage());
        }
    };
```

All this is doing for us is simply printing the message for each error to the console. In an application, it would be more appropriate to bring up a dialog box, or if this were being run on a server, to send this error to a log file and record the date, time, user, and the name of the XML document.

So, having gotten a parser and set up an error handler, we're now ready to see how to manipulate what we just brought into memory. In order to do this, we use the methods found in the Document interface. In order to add elements and add attributes to elements, we can do the following:

```
Attr textAttr = doc.createAttribute("text");
textAttr.setValue("Click on me!");
Attr urlAttr = doc.createAttribute("url");
urlAttr.setValue("http://geekkit.bcit.ca");
hyperLink.setAttributeNode(textAttr);
hyperLink.setAttributeNode(urlAttr);
doc.getDocumentElement().appendChild(hyperLink);
```

As we read in the comments, it's important to remember to always ask the Document object for its root element by calling getDocumentElement. Otherwise, we wind up with runtime errors because you cannot append more than one node to the Document—there can only be one root element for each XML document.

One of the shortcomings of the W3C DOM Level 1 was the lack of convenient methods for retrieving nodes. For example, there was no easy way to drill down several levels within the DOM to retrieve elements, other than to write a custom method using recursion. Java programmers that first started using DOM Level 1 quickly learned how to use recursion whether they liked it or not. An example of how one might retrieve the first Element node based on a particular element name (tag name) would be:

```
public Element getElementByName(Node node, String tagName) {
    Element e = null;
    if(node.getNodeType() == Node.DOCUMENT_NODE) {
        Node rootNode = ((Document)node).getDocumentElement();
        e = getElementByName(rootNode, tagName);
    }
    if(node.getNodeType() == Node.ELEMENT_NODE) {
        e = (Element)node;
```

```
        if(e.getNodeName().equals(tagName))   return e;
        NodeList list = e.getChildNodes();
        int count = list.getLength();
        for(int i = 0; i < count; i++) {
            e = getElementByName(list.item(i), tagName);
            if(e != null)
                if(e.getTagName().equals(tagName)) return e;
        }
    }
    return e;
}
```

This works for one element, but what if one was interested in getting a list of elements? The solution would be to alter the recursive method and pass it a list that could be populated by Element nodes based on a particular tag name. An example:

```
public Element getElementsByName(Node node, String tagName,
    LinkedList<Element> elementList) {
    if(elementList == null) return null;
    Element e = null;
    if(node.getNodeType() == Node.DOCUMENT_NODE) {
        Node rootNode = ((Document)node).getDocumentElement();
        e = getElementsByName(rootNode, tagName, elementList);
    }
    if(node.getNodeType() == Node.ELEMENT_NODE) {
        e = (Element)node;
        if(e.getNodeName().equals(tagName))
            elementList.add(e);
        NodeList list = e.getChildNodes();
        int count = list.getLength();
        for(int i = 0; i < count; i++) {
            e = getElementsByName(list.item(i), tagName,
                elementList);
        }
    }
    return e;
}
```

This method returns to us a flattened list of element nodes based on the name given to the method. We could of course alter this method to search for element nodes that contain particular attributes or Element nodes that contain attributes with particular values, and so on. Any Java programmer who used the W3C DOM Level 1 would usually keep these methods in their arsenal of programming tricks and bring them up when needed.

W3C DOM Level 2

When the W3C released DOM Level 2, they addressed several of the concerns programmers had with the original DOM, one of them being the lack of traversal support in the API. To address traversal, they added the following interfaces:

DocumentTraversal: A simple interface that generates NodeIterator objects and TreeWalker objects based on parameters passed to it.

NodeFilter: An interface that defines a filter pattern to narrow searches of nodes (e.g., only element nodes where the tag name is Paragraph). There is no concrete implementation of this interface; so software developers need to define their own.

NodeIterator: An iterator which is really a flattened, ordered list of the nodes. Implementations of this interface recursively search and grab all nodes of a particular type that were listed (e.g., list only element nodes).

TreeWalker: Contains the same list of nodes searched but instead maintains the hierarchical tree structure.

These interfaces show up in the org.w3c.dom.traversal package. Let's say we want to list only element nodes from an XML document. To do this, we could write something similar to what's found in the dp2.java source code file:

```
Document doc = db.parse(file);
DocumentTraversal traversable = (DocumentTraversal)doc;
NodeIterator iterator =
    traversable.createNodeIterator(doc,
        NodeFilter.SHOW_ELEMENT, null, true);
Node node = null;
while((node = iterator.nextNode()) != null) {
    System.out.println(node.getNodeName());
}
```

Once a Document object is received from the DOM parser, the Document object is cast to a DocumentTraversal. Unfortunately, this little detail has been left to implementers to decide how to create DocumentTraversal objects. In the Xerces package from Apache, the DocumentImpl class (which implements the Document interface) also implements the DocumentTraversal interface, thus making this a legal cast. What would have been nice is if the W3C had made as part of their language bindings, a factory class that returned DocumentTraversal objects rather than leaving it to implementers to figure out how to do this. Once a programmer is in possession of a DocumentTraversal object, NodeIterator objects can be created and used. When asking a DocumentTraversal object for a NodeIterator, the following parameters must be passed to the createNodeIterator method:

node: The node from which to start the search.

whatToShow: An integer flag that states what to show (e.g., comments, elements, notations, etc.).

filter: a node filter that allows for further refinement (e.g., only elements where the tag name is Paragraph). This value can be null if no filter is required.

entityReferenceExpansion: a boolean value which states whether or not entity reference nodes are expanded.

The NodeIterator can be used in a loop to retrieve all nodes. When there are no more nodes left in the set, the nextNode method returns a null value. In order to duplicate our behavior that we so painstakingly did with recursion, we still, however, need to implement the NodeFilter interface with one of our own concrete classes. For example, we may wish to search for Element nodes of a particular tag name:

```
public class ElementNameFilter implements NodeFilter {
    private String tagName;
    public ElementNameFilter(String tagName) {
        this.tagName = tagName;
    }

    public short acceptNode(Node node) {
        if(node.getNodeType() != Node.ELEMENT_NODE)
            return FILTER_REJECT;
        else {
            Element e = (Element)node;
            if(e.getTagName().equals(tagName))  return FILTER_ACCEPT;
        }
        return FILTER_REJECT;
    }
};
```

The constructor allows us to keep an instance variable that contains the search string (i.e., tag name, in this case) we want to use. The one method that belongs to the NodeFilter interface is acceptNode, and it returns a short value, which helps the NodeIterator choose which nodes to present during iteration. The short value that is returned from this method is either NodeFilter.NODE_ACCEPT or NodeFilter.NODE_REJECT. This allows programmers to create custom determiners for choosing nodes. We would use this class by passing an instance of it to the createNodeIterator of the DocumentTraversal object:

```
DocumentTraversal traversable = (DocumentTraversal)doc;
NodeIterator iterator =
    traversable.createNodeIterator(doc,
        NodeFilter.SHOW_ELEMENT,
            new ElementNameFilter("Paragraph"), true);
```

Another example would be to create a filter that searches Element nodes that contain an attribute named id and search for a particular value within that attribute:

```
public class ElementIDAttributeFilter implements NodeFilter {
    private String idValue;
    public ElementIDAttributeFilter(String idValue) {
```

```
            this.idValue = idValue;
        }
        public short acceptNode(Node node) {
            if(node.getNodeType() != Node.ELEMENT_NODE) return FILTER_REJECT;
            else {
                Element e = (Element)node;
                NamedNodeMap attributes = e.getAttributes();
                if(attributes == null) return FILTER_REJECT;
                Attr attribute = (Attr)
                    attributes.getNamedItem("id");
                if(attribute == null) return FILTER_REJECT;
                if(attribute.getValue().equals(idValue))
                    return FILTER_ACCEPT;
            }
            return FILTER_REJECT;
        }
    };
```

This example is similar to the last one, except it drills down a little further and checks for an id attribute and compares the string literal with the value that is contained within the id attribute. In an example of using this filter, we could create an instance of this filter and pass it to the DocumentTraversal object's createNodeIterator method:

```
DocumentTraversal traversable = (DocumentTraversal)doc;
NodeIterator iterator =
    traversable.createNodeIterator(doc,
        NodeFilter.SHOW_ELEMENT,
            new ElementIDAttributeFilter("p1"), true);
```

W3C DOM Level 3

While node iterators and filters took care of traversal, there were still outstanding features that were left to programmers to figure out on their own: loading and saving XML and the ability to validate the in-memory DOM. Therefore, the W3C came up with Level 3 for the DOM which addressed both of these needs. For loading and saving, the issue was twofold. First, there had been no standardized way of instantiating a parser. Sun created JAXP for this reason. What's left of JAXP is the DocumentBuilderFactory and the DocumentBuilder classes (shown earlier). Apache's Xerces had its own set of classes for doing this. Second, there was the issue of how to save a DOM out as an XML document. Again, there was no easy way. Programmers had learned early (using Level 1) to create toXML methods in their classes and simply used that method to output the objects as XML—the returned string could simply be attached to a Writer in Java. Eventually, Sun later released some classes to address this issue. The new way of instantiating an XML parser in DOM Level 3 is shown in the dp3.java source code file:

```
System.setProperty(DOMImplementationRegistry.PROPERTY,
    "org.apache.xerces.dom.DOMXSImplementationSourceImpl");
DOMImplementationRegistry reg =
    DOMImplementationRegistry.newInstance();
DOMImplementationLS domImpl =
    (DOMImplementationLS)reg.getDOMImplementation("LS");
LSParser parser =
    domImpl.createLSParser(
        DOMImplementationLS.MODE_SYNCHRONOUS, null);
Document doc = parser.parseURI(file);
```

These calls either come from the `org.w3c.dom.bootstrap` package or the `org.w3c.dom.ls` (the "ls" in the last part of the namespace stands for load and save). Setting the system property allows the `DOMImplementationRegistry` to find the appropriate implementation class. Once a `DOMImplementationRegistry` is acquired, we call up its `getDOMImplementation` method by passing it the string literal `LS` which tells it the implementation to use (Xerces specific) which returns to us a `DOMImplementationLS`—a factory that gives us load and save objects.

The `DOMImplementationLS`'s `createLSParser` method is called by passing it two arguments. The first argument tells the factory that the `LSParser` should be synchronous. We could also choose asynchronous, meaning the call would return immediately even if the processing is not finished. This may be useful in a multithreaded situation. The second argument passed is a string and is a literal value to inform the factory that the `LSParser` uses a specific schema language during the loading of a document. If you use the string literal `http://www.w3.org/TR/REC-xml`, the DTD schema language is used. If you use the string literal `http://www.w3.org/2001/XMLSchema`, the XML schema language is used. If you pass null (like we did in our example), the `LSParser` uses whatever schema language is required. Lastly, after acquiring the `LSParser`, the `parseURI` method is called up by passing it a string value pointing to the file to open, and if all goes well, you are given a `Document` object. The next step is, of course, going back out to a file. This is accomplished by:

```
LSSerializer serializer = domImpl.createLSSerializer();
serializer.writeToURI(doc, "test.xml");
```

Going back out looks easy, however, it has the advantage that the `DOMImplementationLS` and the `DOMImplementationRegistry` have already been set up. Of course, if you cannot acquire a version of the Xerces API, then you are forced to live without support for Level 3, in which case you'll require Sun's method of outputting to file (found in the `dpsun.java` source code file):

```
FileOutputStream fos = new FileOutputStream("1-" + file);
TransformerFactory tf = TransformerFactory.newInstance();
Transformer transformer = tf.newTransformer();
transformer.setOutputProperty("media-type", "text/plain");
```

```
transformer.setOutputProperty("indent", "yes");
DOMSource source = new DOMSource(doc);
StreamResult result = new StreamResult(fos);
transformer.transform(source, result);
```

The last issue to look at is the in-memory validation. Looking at the W3C DOM Level 3 API, we're provided with several new classes. The code for doing in-memory validation is found in the dp3.java source code file:

```
SchemaFactory factory = SchemaFactory.newInstance(
    XMLConstants.W3C_XML_SCHEMA_NS_URI);
Source schemaSource = new StreamSource(
    new File("./xui.xsd"));
Schema schemaGrammar = factory.newSchema(schemaSource);
Validator validator = schemaGrammar.newValidator();
validator.validate(new DOMSource(doc));
```

The four packages we introduce in order to create this are javax.xml.transform.dom, javax.xml.transform, javax.xml.validation, and javax.xml. As usual, a factory class (in this case, it's SchemaFactory) is used to retrieve an instance of something. An object of the Schema class is retrieved. A Schema object is an abstraction for a schema grammar that is used to validate XML. Most people either use a DTD or an XML schema to validate, although there are other XML schema formats in existence. A Source object is passed to the SchemaFactory, which informs the Schema object as to which schema document to use. The implementation of Source, in this case, is a StreamSource, which is simply a stream of XML markup.

Once we've retrieved a Schema grammar, we then ask the Schema grammar to spit out a Validator object. The Validator is the object that finally performs the validation. Again, we must make use of one of the source implementations. The Validator is passed a DOMSource which, instead of a stream of XML markup, is based on a DOM Node. Because a DOMSource can be based on the Node interface, we can pass it any Node type we want including Document, Element, etc. Therefore, with this feature, we have the ability to create in-memory objects and validate them as we go, ensuring that when we output the document to a file, it is valid—something that couldn't have been done previously. However, one must ensure that there is either a DOCTYPE declaration or an XML schema namespace declared within the XML passed to the Validator, or no validation will be performed.

DOM Shortcomings

While the W3C DOM is an open standard which has grown with many API calls over the last five or more years, there are still disadvantages to using the DOM:

Whole XML document loaded into memory: Although this sounds like an advantage, it can become a big disadvantage if the XML document being loaded into memory is large (one megabyte or more). Each XML node can mean many objects are created in memory. This doesn't even begin to count all of the supporting classes that are part of the DOM either such as validation classes (for DTDs and XML schemas), namespace support, XPath, DOM Level 1, 2, and 3, and all of the other classes that are part of the bundle. In fact, in an enterprise system which loads several XML documents into memory in any given moment, the burden could easily be too much on system resources.

Still not widely accepted: The DOM Level 2 has more or less reached an acceptance level within the Java platform. However, Level 3 is still not (at the time of this writing), even though it has been out for more than a year. It is still not part of the Java SDK 1.5 and, therefore, extra libraries are required for download (e.g., Xerces from Apache). This can cause problems if there are difficulties or restrictions about additional libraries within a tier. One last note is that many of the examples showing how to do in-memory validation still show an XML document being loaded using `DocumentBuilder` rather than the new load and save classes and interfaces from Level 3.

Traversal still not effortless: Although DOM Level 2 offers classes for dealing with traversal, a programmer can still spend many hours writing functionality with `NodeFilter` implementations. While this design does promote reusability, it does suffer from a lack of convenience methods that accept tag names, attribute names, and values for searches. Typically, a lacking of convenience methods results in less acceptance of a standard even if it is an open standard.

Implementation guessing game: As we've seen, most of the actual implementation classes are hidden from us either by the use of Java interfaces or abstract classes. We really have no clue which implementation class objects we're given. Although this is a nice design pattern, it can wreak havoc in a multitiered environment where objects are sent back and forth from one tier to another. In other words, one tier may be using one implementation class, and another tier may be using another implementation class. The only way we'll find this out is at runtime, which causes much troubleshooting.

Event-Driven Parsers

Where the model-driven parser loaded everything into memory, the event-driven parsers work in an entirely different fashion. Instead of loading the entire XML document into memory and creating in-memory objects that offer a hefty API to access them, an event-driven parser simply informs the user application of events as it parses through the XML document. Some examples of possible events are:

- Start of the document
- End of the document
- Start of an element
- End of an element
- Character data from the XML element
- Start of a namespace
- End of a namespace

The user application typically has to register itself as a listener of the event-driven parser via the observer design pattern. The event-driven parser generates an event (e.g., when encountering the beginning of an element) and forwards the data of that event to the listener (user application). The user application is then responsible for doing something meaningful with the data it just received. Although this leaves the responsibility of building a DOM in the application developer's hands, it buys several advantages:

- The application developer can decide to ignore certain elements, thus saving space in memory on large documents.
- The application developer can create a much customized DOM that is specific to the problem domain. The W3C DOM may be overkill or even nonviable due to memory constraints, in the case, for example, of a cell phone where memory is limited.
- The event-driven model is typically faster because it does not load the entire XML document into memory. In fact, it only scans the XML document and informs the user application of events.

SAX API

The Simple API for XML (SAX) was released in 1998 as an alternative to the W3C DOM. David Megginson was the driving force behind this API. Currently at 2.0, SAX offers application developers the ability to register as ContentHandlers and receive events as the parser scans through the document. Figure 6.5 pictorially shows what takes place when a user application uses a SAX parser. After registering itself as a listener to parsing events, the user application calls the parse method on the SAX parser. The SAX parser then flies through the XML document calling up the appropriate methods (e.g., startDocument) in the user application. The user application is then responsible for doing something meaningful with the data it receives from the SAX parser.

In order to be a listener of SAX events, the user application must have one of its classes implement the ContentHandler interface. Figure 6.6 shows the class diagram for the ContentHandler interface. Each method in the ContentHandler is called as each event takes place. There are actually several different interfaces to implement based

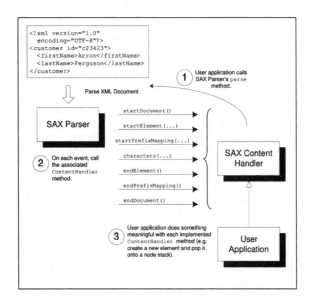

FIGURE 6.5 SAX Parser parsing an XML document.

on what types events are desired. The following interfaces should give a good feel for the listener capabilities within SAX[1]:

ContentHandler: All XML content found within the XML document (e.g., start and end of an element, start and end of the document, start and end of a namespace and character data).

ErrorHandler: All warnings, errors (both fatal and non-fatal) based on the parsing process.

DTDHandler: A bit of a misnomer, this interface provides two methods to receive notification when a notation declaration is encountered and when an unparsed entity is received.

EntityResolver: Allows the user application to handle external entities.

DeclHandler: All declarations in the DTD that are encountered. Although this reports the declarations, it is up to the user application to tokenize and interpret the DTD statements, which may not prove as useful as it could be.

Because the interfaces can contain many methods to implement, the designers of SAX have a convenience class called DefaultHandler which implements most of the listener interfaces (EntityResolver, DTDHandler, ContentHandler, and ErrorHandler). This pattern should be familiar to GUI programmers in Java who use similar classes like java.awt.event.MouseAdapter. Therefore, programmers only need to override the

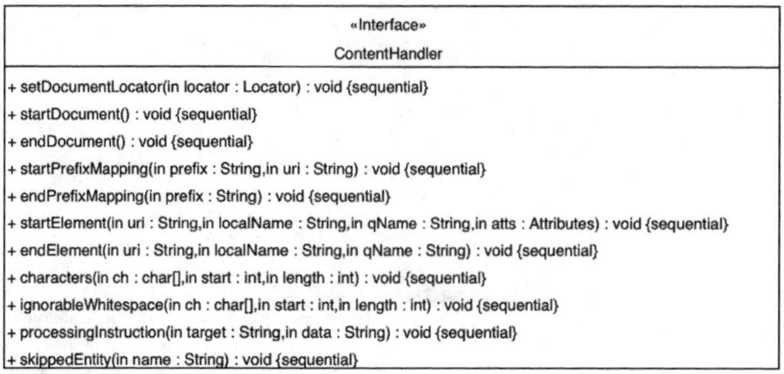

| «Interface» |
| ContentHandler |
| + setDocumentLocator(in locator : Locator) : void {sequential} |
| + startDocument() : void {sequential} |
| + endDocument() : void {sequential} |
| + startPrefixMapping(in prefix : String,in uri : String) : void {sequential} |
| + endPrefixMapping(in prefix : String) : void {sequential} |
| + startElement(in uri : String,in localName : String,in qName : String,in atts : Attributes) : void {sequential} |
| + endElement(in uri : String,in localName : String,in qName : String) : void {sequential} |
| + characters(in ch : char[],in start : int,in length : int) : void {sequential} |
| + ignorableWhitespace(in ch : char[],in start : int,in length : int) : void {sequential} |
| + processingInstruction(in target : String,in data : String) : void {sequential} |
| + skippedEntity(in name : String) : void {sequential} |

FIGURE 6.6 `ContentHandler` interface.

needed methods for their user application and, thus save wear and tear on keyboards and fingers. To listen to SAX events, a programmer can just extend the `DefaultHandler` class like the code found in the `xv.java` source code file:

```
public class xv extends DefaultHandler {
    public void characters(char[] ch, int start, int length) {
        String data = new String(ch, start, length);
        System.out.println("text: |" + data + "| length: " +
            length);
    }
}
```

The preceding code demonstrates the `characters` method. Whenever overriding (or implementing this method if you're just using the `ContentHandler` interface), it is important to remember to use the start and length parameters because they give the exact position of the character string that was retrieved by the parser. Calling up the parser is straightforward:

```
SAXParserFactory spf = SAXParserFactory.newInstance();
spf.setNamespaceAware(true);
spf.setValidating(true);
SAXParser sp = spf.newSAXParser();
sp.parse(file, this);
```

Although this simple example demonstrates how to listen to events, it does not help us understand how to build our own custom DOM from the SAX parser. Figure 6.7 offers a class diagram of a potential custom DOM user application.

The classes (that we created) in our class diagram are as follows:

CustomDOMBuilder: A class that extends the `DefaultHandler` class and overrides methods for handling of elements and character data, as well as the start and end of the document.

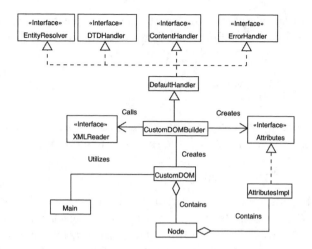

FIGURE 6.7 Custom DOM class diagram.

CustomDOM: A class that contains the root node and all its children. Although in our custom DOM implementation the CustomDOM is not a node itself, it functions much like the Document interface in the W3C DOM API, in that it represents an abstraction of the XML document and offers several overloaded marshalCustomDOM methods for saving the in-memory data model back out to an XML document to the filesystem. It also offers some convenience methods for retrieving nodes, based on a tag name or by level within the hierarchy.

Node: The abstraction for a DOM node. In our example, the Node type is a concrete class that can be used without having to deal with interfaces. It offers convenience methods for getting children (recursively), asking for an attribute value, pretty formatting (proper indenting within a tree), adding a namespace to it, and even marshalling it back out as XML via the toXML method.

Main: This class is a simple driver class that demonstrates our ability to use the custom DOM. Nothing more.

It is useful to dive into the details as to how one builds this custom DOM. In order to handle the creation of a hierarchical structure in memory, there are two classes that we can make use of in Java: HashTable and Stack. First, the HashTable class allows us to handle namespaces. The Node class must be capable of recording its own list of namespaces that are assigned to it. The CustomDOMBuilder must also have a HashTable so that it can record the namespaces and pass them to each Node as it encounters the namespace. The CustomDOMBuilder must also use the Stack class. This is important for creating the tree. For example, when the startElement method is called, any previous node that was being edited (e.g., adding character data to it), must be pushed onto the stack and a new node created, thus becoming the new currently manipulated node. Looking at excerpts from the `CustomDOMBuilder.java` source code file:

```
Node e = new Node(localName);
nodeStack.push(e);
```

The `push` method is called when we encounter a new node. Whenever the `endElement` method is called, the stack must be popped:

```
nodeStack.pop();
```

This pushing and popping of the stack happens in Last In, First Out (LIFO) order. Once the model is created, a `CustomDOM` object can be retrieved and used. The application user is then free to add nodes, query for a particular node by name, by attribute value, and marshal out the XML as a document. An example of this in action is found in the `Main.java` source code file:

```
CustomDOMBuilder builder = new CustomDOMBuilder();
builder.parse(args[0]);
CustomDOM dom = builder.getCustomDOMDocument();
Node root = dom.getRoot();
List<Node> panels = dom.getNodesByName("Panel");
int size = panels.size();
for(int i = 0; i < size; i++) {
    Node panel = panels.get(i);
    String idValue = panel.getAttributeValue("id");
    if(idValue != null) {
        Node button = new Node("Button", "xui",
            "http://xml.bcit.ca/PurnamaProject/2003/xui");
        button.addAttribute("width", "1");
        panel.addChildNode(button);
        dom.marshalCustomDOM("1-" + args[0]);
    }
}
```

Finally, creating a custom solution offers the advantage of not having to duplicate code or objects. For example, if a developer were creating a custom DOM where each XML element represented a GUI component in a UI, then the DOM would contain a lot of duplication. There would be the W3C DOM memory structures as well as the UI component hierarchy. There would also be the requirement for additional code to wire the two models together in order for the ability to keep manipulation of the hierarchies in sync. So if a component were programmatically added to the GUI containment hierarchy, an appropriate DOM element would also be added at the same position within the DOM. Figure 6.8 demonstrates this problem.

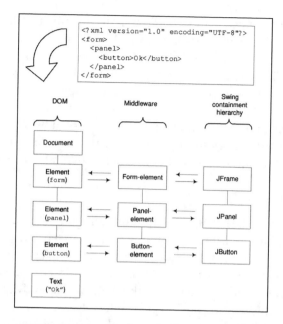

FIGURE 6.8   W3C DOM and UI containment hierarchy.

SAX Shortcomings

While SAX offers the features of being fast to load and minimal in memory, it also comes with a price: lack of convenience. Whenever using SAX, the application developer is required to come up with a custom solution in order to do something meaningful with the content parsed. This means that the following is left up to the application programmer:

- Create the entire in-memory DOM
- Provide real-time validation of the in-memory DOM
- Offer methods for accessing, deleting, inserting, and manipulating elements and element attributes
- Provide support for marshalling out the DOM to an XML document
- Provide support for namespaces

Although a simple custom solution does not require the complexity of the W3C DOM, it nonetheless requires more than a day's worth of development time. Developing a custom solution can actually take several weeks or even months, due to the specific support required and the complexity of the data model represented.

A point to make about a lacking in the SAX parser is that once the parser has been started, we cannot stop it. That is, once we call the parse method on the SAX parser, it continues all the way through the document calling up our registered content handler's methods, whether we like it or not. This could be a problem if our user application is multithreaded and time-based—for example, an application that handles socket requests from remote clients. If the SAX parser got farther ahead than what the socket connection was capable of transmitting, we would have to send a wait signal on the socket connection, rerun the SAX parser on the same document, and wait for it to cue up to the spot at which we left off. This would be very cumbersome, especially if the document was large (over a megabyte in size). The next section shows another alternative that takes care of this problem.

Push versus Pull

You may have heard of the terms push and pull in other contexts, but still within the computer industry. For example, on the Web, the approach to sending Web pages to a Web browser is considered pull. A Web browser pulls (requests) the content and the Web server does not serve content unless there is a request. The bottom line is that you have to ask for it. Alternatively, push technology is where the content is sent to you at regular intervals. A streaming media server such as an Internet radio station uses push technology. You do not have to continually request each kilobyte of digital sound, each second of play, or each song or musical piece of digital sound. Once you make that request, the content is sent to you until you make a conscious effort to request that the media server stop sending content.

The last parser we looked at was the SAX parser. It is most definitely a push parser: once you request an XML document, there is nothing stopping that SAX parser from sending the content to you short of turning off your computer. You cannot tell the SAX parser to stop. If you missed something halfway through, you'll simply have to tell the parser to parse that document over again. If the document is quite large, this costs in time. A pull parser, on the other hand, requires the user application to continue to make requests for content. Figure 6.9 shows a pictorial representation of how a pull parser operates.

A pull parser is almost identical in function as the next frame function or step function on a DVD player. By pressing the next frame button on the remote control, the user can view the next frame of video. The pull parser can step forward as well—to the next event (e.g., start element, end element, character data, etc.). In the pull parser, if the user wishes to continue stepping through events, then a program loop (e.g., while statement) must be used on the user application to keep requesting the next step through the XML document. This is analogous to one keeping the step button depressed on a DVD player's remote control, which informs the DVD player to keep stepping forward one frame at a time. Like the DVD player, once the requests stop, the pull parser stops sending content. And like the DVD player's step function, the pull parser cannot step backwards. It's a one-way-only function: forward.

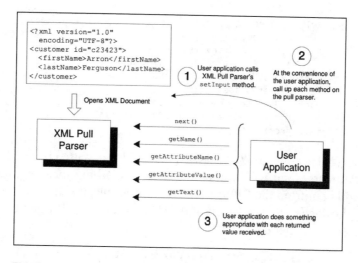

FIGURE 6.9   XML pull parser parsing an XML document.

XPP 3

In order to get a good look at an example of a pull parser, we can use XML Pull Parser (XPP) API version 3.0 by Stefan Haustein and Aleksander Slominski, which is released under an Apache style license. The XPP API is what you would call minimalist, as it only comes with four classes:

- `XmlPullParser`
- `XmlSerializer`
- `XmlPullParserFactory`
- `XmlPullParserException`

Both `XmlPullParser` and `XmlSerializer` are interfaces and, therefore, have no implementation. Because of this, there needs to be an implementation; so the author's of XPP have ensured that it comes with a reference implementation that they call the "maximum performance, minimum size pull parser" or MXP for short. Because of the simplicity of the API, it is extremely easy to pick up and start using, especially if you compare the XPP API to the SAX or the W3C DOM APIs. It is fast (visit their Web site for results) and comes with very few classes (they even have a minimal runtime version bundled in a 25 KB JAR file that contains only three classes). Like many of the examples from the previous two APIs we've looked at, gaining access to a parser looks similar in XPP because XPP uses a variation on the factory method design pattern node. The example is found in the `px.java` source code file:

```
XmlPullParser parser;
int eventType;
XmlPullParserFactory factory =
    XmlPullParserFactory.newInstance();
factory.setNamespaceAware(true);
factory.setValidating(false);
parser = factory.newPullParser();
parser.setInput(new FileReader(file));
this.processXML();
```

That last method (processXML) is something written by us (the application programmers), and which hopefully does something meaningful with the content coming in from the XPP parser. In our example, it simply prints the start and end of the document, the names of the elements, along with element attributes and element character data:

```
public void processXML() throws XmlPullParserException,
    IOException {
    eventType = parser.getEventType();
    while(eventType != parser.END_DOCUMENT) {
        if(eventType == parser.START_DOCUMENT)
            System.out.println("Document beginning ...");
        if(eventType == parser.START_TAG) {
            System.out.println("\nElement: " + parser.getName());
            int count = parser.getAttributeCount();
            if(count > 0) {
                System.out.println("  attrs:");
                for(int i = 0; i < count; i++) {
                    String value = parser.getAttributeValue(i);
                    String name = parser.getAttributeName(i);
                    System.out.println("    " + name + " = "
                        + value);
                }
            }
        }
        if(eventType == parser.TEXT) {
            String text = parser.getText();
            if(!(text.matches("\\s+"))) {
                System.out.println("CDATA: " + text);
            }
        }
        eventType = parser.next();
    }
    System.out.println("Document end.");
}
```

The loop in this method relies on a new event type condition that it receives by calling the parser's next method which breaks the loop by encountering the parser.END_DOCUMENT value. Within the loop, we can check for various conditions (start element, end element, parsed character data). Although this looks similar to the way we did in using SAX, there is a difference: it is our user application that is calling the parser explicitly by using its next method. We are in control of the parsing. The SAX parser required us to register a content handler exposing the event handling that SAX performs. The XPP parser offers us one simple method to step forward and then check values from the parser by calling accessors.

One last observation to make is that when we gather text from a text event, we should check to see whether we're simply acquiring whitespace or not. To do this we use the condition:

```
if(!(text.matches("\\s+"))) {
    System.out.println("CDATA: " + text);
}
```

This makes use of Java's string class which offers the ability to use regular expressions. The regular expression "\\s+" checks for anything that is whitespace. So if what we're receiving is not just whitespace, then we're assuming that it is meaningful character data and, therefore, we're interested in it.

XPP Shortcomings

Although the XPP parser is fast, small, and easy to learn, it isn't a W3C Recommendation, nor has it gained widespread approval within the XML community. This may not seem like much of a problem, but if the authors abandon the project, developers are faced with either having to take on the responsibility of maintaining it or accept an old version and keep using it. Another problem is that the implementation parser that comes with it (MXP) does not perform validation, does not report attribute namespaces, nor does it report document type declarations.

CODING THE CUSTOM DOM

Getting one step closer to developing a fully working CMS, it's time to think about which set of APIs is used, the features required and used by the data model, and how to marshal the content.

Rule Set Considerations

The rule set that we are talking about with our custom DOM deals with the rules from the DTDs we created in Chapter 5. Here are some of the rules that we wish our model to follow:

Object marshal capability: Each object that represents an XML node must have the ability to marshal itself out as XML.

Timestamp format: Any content node must keep a consistent format for representing date and time information.

ID uniqueness: Each node derived from the AbstractNode class must contain a unique string-based id value.

Object Marshal Capability

Although the three APIs that we looked at offer marshalling (also known as serializing), the XML content out to an XML document, we're going to go with our own custom solution. This is because we're writing very specialized nodes where each node type has specific needs (e.g., unique string id values, date time stamps, etc.). If we were to use the provided serialization features found in the APIs, we would have to intervene with the serializing process—essentially adding middleware code that would modify the XML before it was sent out to a document. Because of this, providing our own marshalling winds up being less work in the long run. Recall from Chapter 5 we presented a method in the class that had the ability to marshal out the state information from a class out as a string that could later be sent to a Writer. This is exactly what we will do for our CMS data model.

Although the AbstractNode class has to define the toXML method (from the ModelNode interface), it cannot present an implementation because it is abstract. Therefore, the toXML implementation must be found in each subclass of AbstractNode. A simple example would be the implementation code found in the Bold.java class:

```
public String toXML() {
    StringBuilder sb = new StringBuffer();
    sb.append("<B>" + EntityResolver.replaceIllegalCharacters(text)
        + "</B>");
    return sb.toString();
}
```

We're making use of the StringBuilder class, which provides efficiency when dealing with large character strings or character strings that are constantly being appended to. The StringBuilder class is a relatively new addition to the Java runtime (introduced in the Java 1.5 version) and is a faster version of the StringBuffer class, with the difference being that the StringBuilder class is not synchronized, unlike the StringBuffer class. One thing that we've added as a feature is the checking for illegal characters in our textual content within elements and attributes.

A class called EntityResolver (EntityResolver.java) offers a static method called replaceIllegalCharacters, which accepts a string and returns the same string with illegal XML characters replaced with entities (e.g., the less than symbol replaced with <):

```
public static String replaceIllegalCharacters(String str) {
    StringBuilder result = new StringBuilder();
    char[] cdata = str.toCharArray();
    int size = cdata.length;
    for(int i = 0; i < size; i++) {
        switch(cdata[i]) {
            case '<': result.append("&lt;"); break;
            case '>': result.append("&gt;"); break;
            case '\'': result.append("&apos;"); break;
            case '"': result.append("&quot;"); break;
            case '&': result.append("&amp;"); break;
            default: result.append(cdata[i]);
        }
    }
    return result.toString();
}
```

A more detailed example of a toXML method is found in the Paragraph.java class:

```
public String toXML() {
    StringBuilder sb = new StringBuilder();
    sb.append("        <Paragraph published=\"" + published + "\" "
        + "author=\""
        + EntityResolver.replaceIllegalCharacters(author) + "\" "
        + "id=\"" + id + "\" >\n");
    sb.append(dts.toXML());
    sb.append("        <ParagraphContent>");
    int size = content.size();
    for(int i = 0; i < size; i++) {
        Object o = content.get(i);
        if(o instanceof String) {
            String s = (String)o;
            sb.append(EntityResolver.replaceIllegalCharacters(s));
        } else {
            sb.append(((ModelNode)o).toXML());
        }
    }
    sb.append("</ParagraphContent>\n");
    sb.append("        </Paragraph>\n");
    return sb.toString();
}
```

Attributes where the value is a boolean or an id do not need to be checked by the EntityResolver because they have never been edited by the user, therefore, they do not contain illegal characters. Each Paragraph object can contain many different child nodes (regular, bold, italic character data, hyperlinks, and hint elements as well). These items need to be iterated through via a loop to check for illegal characters.

Timestamp Format

The `DateTimeStamp.java` class represents each timestamp saved in milliseconds which records both the date and time the node was created, as well as the data and time that the node was last edited. For this, we use the Java `long` type:

```java
public String toXML() {
    StringBuilder sb = new StringBuilder();
    sb.append("        <Stamp date-created=\"" + dateCreated.getTime()
        + "\" date-modified=\"" + dateModified.getTime() + "\"/>\n");
    return sb.toString();
}
```

This class offers two methods, one that gets the current time (used when a new `DateTimeStamp` is created in memory)

```java
public DateTimeStamp() {
    dateCreated = new Date();
    dateModified = new Date();
}
```

and one that is intended to be used when an object has to be constructed based on the XML being read in by the parser:

```java
public DateTimeStamp(long created, long edited) {
    dateCreated = new Date(created);
    dateModified = new Date(edited);
}
```

ID Uniqueness

In order to support unique `ids` for each element, we need a central distributor of `id` values so that we can maintain consistency and uniqueness among `id` values. This requirement is, however, complicated due to the fact that the client program has the ability to create new elements, such as `Page` elements, `Paragraph` elements, and so forth. That means that the client program will contain the model classes. But the model classes need to refer to the `IDFactory` in order to create `ids`. Here lies the co-nundrum. To address this problem, we have a class called `IDFactory.java`, which looks after distributing `id` values to objects. We've given it a method for adding `id` values to its private list of `ids` for when the XML parser loads all the elements and extracts each element's `id` attribute (for those that have one):

```java
public synchronized void addID(String id) {
    IDs.add(id);
}
```

There is also a method called `generateUserID` that creates an `id` value based on a given prefix:

```
public synchronized String generateUserID(String userIDPrefix) {
    int IDCounter = 0;
    String id = userIDPrefix + "_" + IDCounter;
    if(IDs.size() > 0) {
        while(IDs.contains(id)) {
            IDCounter++;
            id = userIDPrefix + "_" + IDCounter;
        }
        IDs.add(id);
        return id;
    } else {
        IDs.add(id);
        IDCounter++;
        return id;
    }
}
```

This method uses the prefix (e.g., "page_") and appends a counter number to the end of the prefix (e.g., "page_37"). The method keeps track of previously stored id numbers and starts the counter at the next available position. The problem we have with calling this in the AbstractNode class is that in order for subclasses of AbstractNode (such as Paragraph), to call this method, the IDFactory class would have to be bundled with the client application. If we do this, we take a chance of some programmer accidentally (or worse, intentionally) instantiating a remote copy of the IDFactory class and starting a new set of id values. This would wreak havoc on our system when the changes are sent back to the server because there's a good possibility that we'll have id values that are identical and not unique. To solve this problem what we've done is created a class called IDFactoryProxy which uses Java's powerful feature known as reflection. The IDFactoryProxy's method getID is what we call in the AbstractNode class and only the IDFactoryProxy.java class is bundled with the software that is sent to the client. The getID method looks like this:

```
public static String getID(String idPrefix) {
    String generatedID = "error";
    try {
        Class cls =
            Class.forName("org.kucingCMS.contentmodel.IDFactory");
        Method getInstance = cls.getMethod("getInstance",
            new Class[0]);
        Object o = getInstance.invoke(null, new Object[0]);
        Method generateUserID =
            cls.getDeclaredMethod("generateUserID", new Class[]
                { String.class } );
        generatedID =
            (String)generateUserID.invoke(o, idPrefix);
    } catch(ClassNotFoundException cnfe) {
        cnfe.printStackTrace();
    } catch(NoSuchMethodException nsme) {
```

```
        nsme.printStackTrace();
    } catch(InvocationTargetException ite) {
        ite.printStackTrace();
    } catch(IllegalAccessException iac) {
        iac.printStackTrace();
    }
    return generatedID;
}
```

By doing it this way, the client application can be bundled without the `IDFac-tory` class and when a request is made for a new subclass of the `AbstractNode` class, the client requests the object (or objects) from the server and receives a new object (or objects) from the server with appropriately sequenced `id` values. Additionally, we have encapsulated the actual `id` generation implementation and could turn around and change the `id` generation implementation without even needing to re-compile the client side because it doesn't even know about how the `IDFactory` class generates the `id` values.

Choosing the API

A useful approach to choosing the API is to plot out what we need and check it against what each parser offers. Table 6.2 checks our CMS requirements against the features offered by each parser.

TABLE 6.2   CMS Requirements to Parser API Features

Feature	CMS Req.	SAX	W3C DOM	XPP/MXP
Element namespace support	no	yes	yes	no
Attribute namespace support	no	yes	yes	no
Validation	no	yes	yes	no
Customized DOM	yes	yes	no	yes
Fast parsing	yes	yes	no	yes
License supports distribution	yes	yes	yes	yes
Small memory footprint	yes	yes	no	yes
In-memory validation	yes	N/A	yes	N/A
Convenience access methods	yes	N/A	yes	N/A

Looking at our table, the XPP/MXP solution fits like a glove, as per our CMS requirements. Going through these, we are not interested in namespace support for either elements or attributes. This is because our XML solution does not need to be merged with other XML formats. If we needed to merge our XML format with other XML formats, we would be wishing to use namespaces. Validation during runtime (as we discussed in Chapter 5) is usually not a good thing unless we are using untrusted XML. Validating during runtime causes a slowdown because the validation software must perform this task. Because we're going to perform testing of our classes against the DTDs we created in Chapter 5, we won't need runtime validation.

We are very much interested in a custom DOM. We need it based on our specialized element types and elements referencing other elements (like a database). This should rule out any APIs that already contain a prebuilt DOM because we would just be adding redundancy with a larger memory footprint. The CMS requires fast serving of content. This becomes an issue as the number of pages and the number of content chunks grows. We need speed. We need to be able to include the API with the CMS that comes on the CD-ROM for this book. The CMS should not take up gobs of memory as it runs because there could be large numbers of documents that need to be processed.

We do require in-memory validation of the DOM; but because we're writing our own custom DOM, we can control what goes into an element simply by providing the appropriate accessors and mutators for each class and offer error checking that ensures that only the appropriate types of content go into each node in memory. And because there will be so many references to elements to each of the data stores, we will need convenience methods that make it easy to drill down and recursively search for a node. Additionally, we want convenience for accessing particular attributes of nodes, too. Based on the requirements and features matrix, we can easily justify XPP/MXP for our CMS because it satisfies most of our requirements.

Don't worry if you're wondering why we haven't covered how to build a custom DOM with XPP/MXP. That is our next step because we are using it for our CMS. We are going over all of the implementation details including how to serialize objects, creating the protocol, and many other topics.

SUMMARY

We have explored three different leading technologies for XML parsers. We looked at the model-driven parser technology and viewed the W3C's DOM API covering DOM Level 1, 2, and 3. We looked at the event-driven parser technology and discussed how to create a custom DOM while using SAX. We looked at a pull parser called XPP and looked at the reference implementation known as MXP. We also started in on the code of the model and covered some of the finer points in code for the data model including marshalling the objects out to XML. Finally we looked at the features of each of the APIs and decided on XPP/MXP for our custom DOM implementation. The next chapter dives into the implementation of the CMS server side, and we'll actually set up the project build structure that is the foundation of the entire project build process.

ENDNOTE

1. These are not all of the interfaces for listening to events in SAX, but they are the core interfaces and should give a good feel for what is available in the API.

7 Server Technologies

In This Chapter

- Web server technology and what features are expected of Web server technology
- The servlet model and how multithreaded servlet containers interact with servlets
- Setting up the CMS project
- Using Ant to create a build file for our project
- Building the server classes for our CMS

W eb server technologies have evolved greatly since the early 1990s, starting off with offering a simple request-response model providing files, and advancing all the way to supporting various different runtime environments, languages, and protocols which allow for a great deal of customization. In this chapter, we'll be looking at how we can use the Java runtime environment along with Apache's Tomcat Web server in order to serve and support our CMS as a Web application. The example source code listings referenced in this chapter are located on the CD-ROM in the *CMS-project\src\org\kucingCMS\server* sub-folder.

ON THE CD

ABOUT WEB SERVER TECHNOLOGY

Web server technology has simple beginnings. The initial model was a simple consumer-producer model where the consumer requests something, and the producer either replies back with the requested thing or a message saying why the requested thing could not be returned. A Web server in its most simple form answers the request for some sort of a resource from a client application such as a Web browser. A resource could be an HTML document, a text file, a video clip, a sound clip, some sort of interactive animation file, or any type of binary file. A sharp programmer (assuming a working knowledge of the HTTP protocol) could write a basic Web server in an afternoon. Figure 7.1 shows the simplicity of the core of what a Web server offers.

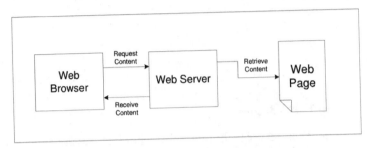

FIGURE 7.1 Simple Web server request-response model.

Features

There are, however, many other things that we come to expect a Web server to do in addition to simply sending things for which we ask. At the least, we want the Web server to give us a listing of the things it has in its possession. This is accomplished by sending a list of the resources that it contains. But again, this is pretty fundamental and doesn't offer anything new or anything that we can't find with an FTP server.

Dynamic Content Processor

What we really want to see is the ability to offer some key piece of architecture that allows us to send a request to a specialized application that can process the request from the client (consumer). For example, the Web server is perfectly capable of digging up some HTML documents and sending them to the Web browser. But what if the request from the Web browser is for information that comes from a database? We could (if we were so inclined) read all of the information from the database and meticulously type the contents into several dozen (or hundred) HTML documents. But this would be inefficient, prone to error, and when the database records changed, we'd have to go through this entire procedure all over again.

Dynamic content processing allows us to forward a request from the Web server onto a specialized application by using some sort of third-party interface. When Web server technology was created, this was kept in mind and such an interface was offered. They called it the Common Gateway Interface (CGI) and it allowed the Web server to forward requests from the Web browser over to an application that could handle the request. Figure 7.2 shows the layers of architecture. The CGI allows an interface to the Web server from custom-built applications that wish to handle requests. Recall multitiered architecture from Chapter 6 and that the CGI allows the server to communicate with an application that can accept the request, perform some processing (query a database, for example), and return a result set—usually formatted in HTML so that the Web browser can properly display the content to the user.

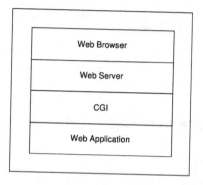

FIGURE 7.2 Web architecture with CGI.

When CGI came out (with the Web), it opened up new possibilities for delivery of content. Suddenly software developers were creating Web applications that were querying databases, filtering directory listings, creating images on-the-fly, and answering the requests of users who were logging into the Web server using Web forms. The Web server became a playground for developers, and it quickly became apparent that Web servers could do much more than was originally anticipated. All that was needed was some sort of custom application working behind the curtain to answer the requests and quietly (and hopefully quickly) respond with some sort of content. Figure 7.3 gives an updated picture for answering requests for both static content (Web documents that exist within the filesystem) and dynamic content (content that is transformed from one format into Web document form).

The Web server receives the request. If the request made by the Web browser maps to a CGI application (more on how this mapping is done), the CGI application processes and returns content to the Web server which, in turn, forwards the generated content to the Web browser. If the request is a simple request for *static content* (i.e., content that already exists), then the file is retrieved and sent to the Web browser.

Security

Providing security is imperative when limiting access to resources. Remember, based on what we just mentioned, it's not simple files such as HTML documents, but it may be user-sensitive content that comes from a database.

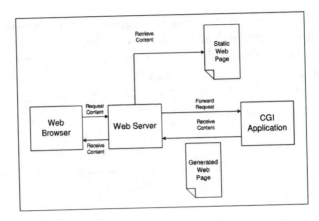

FIGURE 7.3   Requests and response and CGI.

Account-Based Control

When we mention the topic of accounts on a Web server, the first thing we most likely think of is user accounts that have access to particular resources that are managed by a specific Web application. While this is one facet of account control, this aspect is not specific to the Web server itself. What we are really talking about is accounts that administer the Web server itself—not the resources that a Web application manages. A full-featured Web server comes with the ability to manage certain aspects of the Web server itself including:

- Adding, editing, deleting various accounts
- Assigning roles to accounts (e.g., administrator, manager, etc.)
- Configuring Web application characteristics such as auto deployment, path, libraries
- Setting up data sources and access to data sources
- Logging of errors within the server itself, as well as Web applications and whether these errors are reported via email

Clearly, this goes beyond the simple request-response model, but it makes administration of the server much more efficient. This is extremely important for companies that host possibly dozens of different Web sites on one server and need to ensure that all Web applications are up, running, and not causing any errors on the Web server itself.

Resource Listings Restricted

One of the most common mistakes new Web administrators make is forgetting to restrict directory listings on the server. This may sound rather innocent, but there may be files that are meant to be restricted from the public view. For example, an instructor may set up a Web site for his students and accidentally upload an exam document. If directory listings are denied, then only those that know the exact name of the file are able to download the file. If directory listings are allowed, then simply typing '/' after the name of the directory lists all files found in that directory, allowing users to visibly see all files by name, their file extension, and size. Of course the real solution is to not upload sensitive files. A quick example of how many Web server administrators forget to turn off directory listings is made visible by going to your favorite search engine and typing in "index of cgi-bin" (include the quotes).

Secured Connections

With the ability to restrict access to both administrative functions of the Web server, as well as Web applications, comes the need to ensure secure connections. The Secure Socket Layer (SSL) is the feature required to do this. SSL is a protocol that allows content to be sent using encryption, which ensures that it is almost impossible (highly improbable) for hackers to intercept transmitted data and decipher the data because of the encryption. For sending regular content from a Web server, this is not needed. However, if a Web server is supporting Web applications that process transactions with customers where credit card numbers are sent to the server, then this is quite important for protection against fraud. In the least the Web server should support the ability to install SSL components that allow the Web server to use the protocol.

Configuration Scripts

Configuration scripts act similar to configuration files for regular desktop applications: they provide customization of the application. Looking at the Tomcat Web container/Web server, there are several different files pertaining to customization.

Because we are building our CMS as a Web application that runs with JSPs and servlets, we can choose to be specific with Tomcat. Having said that, Tomcat is a reference implementation servlet container and so any Web server that supports the both of these specifications uses the same technology, thus not requiring you to learn a whole new approach to configuring your CMS.

NOTE

Web Application Deployment Descriptor

A Web application deployment descriptor is another XML file that allows for customization on the server but is specialized for Web applications. The file is named web.xml and the whole deployment descriptor specification (including DTD) is part of the Java Servlet Specification (currently at version 2.3). When deploying your Web application (covered later in this chapter), the web.xml file is bundled with the Web app. The deployment descriptor allows us to specify things such as:

- Error pages (e.g., for 404 messages)
- Servlets that are mapped to URL patterns
- MIME type mapping
- Session timeout value
- Parameters passed to servlets
- Welcome file list (e.g., `index.html`)
- Security constraints to resources

An example of a deployment descriptor might look like:

```
<?xml version="1.0" encoding="ISO-8859-1"?>
<!DOCTYPE web-app
    PUBLIC "-//Sun Microsystems, Inc.//DTD Web Application 2.3//EN"
    "http://java.sun.com/dtd/web-app_2_3.dtd">
<web-app>
  <servlet>
    <servlet-name>ForumManager</servlet-name>
    <servlet-class>org.kucingCMS.server.ForumManager
    </servlet-class>
    <load-on-startup>1</load-on-startup>
  </servlet>
  <servlet-mapping>
    <servlet-name>ForumManager</servlet-name>
    <url-pattern>/forum.html</url-pattern>
  </servlet-mapping>
  <error-page>
    <error-code>404</error-code>
    <location>/404.html</location>
  </error-page>
  <mime-mapping>
      <extension>css</extension>
      <mime-type>text/css</mime-type>
  </mime-mapping>
</web-app>
```

This brief Web deployment descriptor maps the class `org.kucingCMS.server.ForumManager` to the alias `ForumManager`, which is mapped to the relative URL pattern `/forum.html`. Therefore, whenever a user types that resource name along with the full URL of the Web server, they (hopefully) get redirected to the `org.kucingCMS.server.ForumManager` servlet. We'll take a look at customizing our Web deployment descriptor later in this chapter.

Handling of Content Types

When we mention content type what should come to mind is the Multipurpose Internet Mail Extensions (MIME) specification. MIME was originally created for email servers and email clients so that the correct type of content could be agreed upon and recognized without error. It was, however, adopted by the Web and is used in HTTP in order for Web servers to convey to the Web browsers what type of content is being sent—same reason as email. A Web server will store metadata about content types and associated file formats. The deployment descriptor for Tomcat specifies many expected supported types, although more can be added to either the Tomcat 5.5 deployment descriptor or an individual Web application's deployment descriptor. The format for defining a MIME type is:

```
<mime-mapping>
    <extension>gif</extension>
    <mime-type>image/gif</mime-type>
</mime-mapping>
```

There may be tens if not hundreds of different MIME type mappings within a deployment descriptor. When the Web server sends a requested file, it sends along a header with the requested file, the content type, so that the Web browser knows what to do with the file. An example of what might be found within the header returned from the Web server to the Web browser:

```
File: http://www.bcit.ca/images/logo.gif
Response: HTTP/1.1 200 OK
Date: Wed, 19 Oct 2005 02:29:31 GMT
Server: Apache/1.3.27 (Unix) mod_ssl/2.8.12 OpenSSL/0.9.6b
    PHP/4.3.0
Last-Modified: Tue, 07 Dec 2004 21:21:36 GMT
ETag: "47b2e-be8-41b61ee0"
Accept-Ranges: bytes
Content-Length: 3048
Keep-Alive: timeout=15, max=100
Connection: Keep-Alive
Content-Type: image/gif
```

The content type (found in bold) lists the type, which is an image, and the image is encoded in the GIF format. It may seem like superfluous information for the server to send, but it is important because the file sent may not have an extension attached. If this were to happen, the Web browser would simply not know what to do with the file and would probably default to text. If you've ever found your Web browser displaying odd data within the content panel, then you've probably experienced a problem where either the Web server was not reporting what the mime type is, or the Web browser has been improperly configured, or both.

Logging of Requests

It is useful to see just who is visiting your site as well as what is actually being requested. At the least, it can be interesting to see just who in the world is accessing your Web site. However, logging has many more uses other than simply satisfying one's curiosity:

- Ensuring that no one is *hot linking*[1] to certain resources on your site
- Statistical reporting which can help answer questions such as which pages, resources, articles, and authors are drawing the most viewers
- Giving the ability to see suspicious access attempts (e.g., a particular restricted resource where access attempts are being repetitiously made)

At the least, it is useful to have the Web server report these accesses to resources to a file found within one of the directories for the server. Typically, the following types of information are found in a log entry:

- The IP address of the client
- The date and time of the request
- The resource requested (e.g., HTML document or GIF image)
- The protocol used (e.g., HTTP 1.1)
- The client's application and version number
- The client's operating system

Example log entries may look something like:

```
127.0.0.1 - - [18/Oct/2005:21:49:25 -0700] "GET / HTTP/1.1" 200
    8442
127.0.0.1 - - [18/Oct/2005:21:49:30 -0700] "GET /kucing/ HTTP/1.1"
    200 3375
127.0.0.1 - - [18/Oct/2005:21:49:32 -0700]
    "GET /kucing/multimedia.html HTTP/1.1" 200 6365
127.0.0.1 - - [18/Oct/2005:21:49:33 -0700]
    "GET /kucing/projects.html HTTP/1.1" 200 6184
127.0.0.1 - - [18/Oct/2005:21:49:38 -0700]
    "GET /kucing/media/images/gumbo3.jpg HTTP/1.1" 200 129143
```

A useful Web application could then read and parse these log files at regular intervals (once a day, week, or month depending on the frequency of requests) and format this information in a Web page, or convert the data into a tabular data format which could be further processed and analyzed by the Web site administrator and printed in a report.

The level of support for logging on a Web server may vary from simple log files all the way to tools that report requests as formatted documents. Tomcat 5.5 supports logging by offering a class called `org.apache.catalina.valves. AccessLogValve` which, as you might have guessed, logs requests. Because Tomcat is so highly configurable, and so well documented, all it takes to enable this service is to go into your `server.xml` file and uncomment the following:

```
<Valve className="org.apache.catalina.valves.AccessLogValve"
       directory="logs"  prefix="localhost_access_log."
       suffix=".txt" pattern="common" resolveHosts="false"/>
```

As the requests pour in, so, too, do entries in the file called `localhost_access_log.yyyy-mm-dd.txt`, where `yyyy` represents the year, `mm` represents the month, and `dd` represents the date. But this only offers us the raw data (text files). In order to do something meaningful with this data, we would either have to write our own application that parses and processes this data or use a tool that does it for us. Luckily, we have options that support both choices.

In the case of using pre-existing tools, AWStats is a standalone tool open source (GPL license) that can generate statistics from Web, as well as FTP and mail servers. It can be called using CGI or it can be called from the command line. A Java application could make use of it by calling `System.exec` within the Web application. It generates graphs, HTML, and even PDF, although it does require the Practical Extraction and Reporting Language (PERL) runtime. Another option is to use the Webalizer[2], which is another log analysis tool. The Webalizer supports and parses Apache's common log file format, as well as several variations of the combined log file format (also from Apache), which is what Tomcat 5.5 uses. Unfortunately, the Webalizer is command line and so must be run as a separate process (like AWStats).

In the case of writing it ourselves, we can either create our own solution (based on either the common log file format or the combined log file format) that reads the data in, formats it, and creates graphs and reports, or we can use a framework such as Log4j which is yet another tool from the Apache Software Foundation. Log4j is a framework complete with Javadocs which allows a developer to tie the framework into the Web application. Of course, meaningful formatting and analyzing is still required.

Logging Errors

Although this doesn't specifically deal with logging of requests, it may help to quickly discuss logging errors in this section for completeness sake because some of the requests made may be based on erroneous assumptions. In the case of our protocol, we are using object serialization to send and receive data to and from the server. There may be a case where, during object deserialization, the class of an object is not found or a class cast exception occurs. Although this type of error should not occur (assuming the administration applet is the same version as the one we compiled), we should still handle logging this type of error request because, in the least, it means that a client applet was the wrong version (worst case we have a hostile client applet). To look after the error logging we can make use of the `java.util.logging` package provided for us and use a `Logger`:

```
try {
    FileHandler handler = new FileHandler(webAppRoot + "WEB-INF"
        + File.separator + "error.log", true);
    logger = Logger.getAnonymousLogger();
    logger.addHandler(handler);
```

```
    } catch(IOException ioe) { ioe.printStackTrace(); }
Later on in our exception handling code, we can write to the logger:
    catch(ClassNotFoundException cnfe) {
        logger.log(Level.WARNING, "doAdmin: class List not found. ", cnfe);
        cnfe.printStackTrace();
    } catch(ClassCastException cce) {
        logger.log(Level.WARNING, "doAdmin: not a java.util.List. ", cce);
        cce.printStackTrace();
    }
```

This prints any errors (in this case we've simply flagged them as warnings), to a log file called `error.log`, which is placed in the Web app root directory. We'll look at where files go in a Web application later on in the chapter.

Request Forwarding

This is a useful feature because it allows either the Web server itself or another process or thread running on the Web server to forward the request to another resource (URL) found within the current Web application. In the case of doing this in Java, we use the `javax.servlet.RequestDispatcher` interface by calling it's `forward()` method:

```
if(pageNotFound) {
    RequestDispatcher disp = req.getRequestDispatcher(
        "./404.html");
    disp.forward(req, res);
}
```

The `req` variable is of type `HttpServletRequest` and is given to us in our `doGet` method from one of our servlet classes (more on servlets and the `HttpServletRequest` class later).

Forwarding vs. Redirecting

It is important not to confuse forwarding with redirecting, as they are different in functionality. A forward works within the context of the current Web application only. It does not allow sending to URLs found in other Web applications. As we saw, the forwarding capability in Java is done by using the `RequestDispatcher` class that we receive from a `HttpServletRequest`. Redirecting, however, is different in that it allows us to send the request to a different URL that is not necessarily found within the same Web application context. In Java, we can do this by calling the `javax.servlet.http.HttpServletResponse`'s `sendRedirect()` method. The other difference is that the redirect causes the Web browser to receive an empty response (the HTTP protocol contains several 300-level response codes; we'll look at the HTTP protocol in more detail in Chapter 8) which simply informs the Web browser to go somewhere else.

Session Tracking

Because HTTP doesn't record high-level states, such as usernames, passwords, and other types of data structures (including, but not limited to, shopping cart data), we need a way to trace or track user navigation and choices. Serving simple static pages doesn't require this type of functionality, but a dynamic site with many users and many different types of user and electronic transactions most definitely requires a solution. Session tracking gives us the ability to track users and electronic transactions. We can record and save information about where the user has come from, where the user is going, who the user is, and any other data that we deem suitable for recording during the visit to the server. Session tracking gives us the ability to:

- Restrict or allow access using authorization via usernames and passwords
- Track choices such as configuration information with online user accounts
- Support purchases where multiple items can be selected from many different URLs
- Allow the user to personalize the pages
- Customize content to an individual user

There are several different solutions that address session tracking—each with their own strengths and weaknesses.

Cookies

A cookie is a chunk of data that is recorded about a user's choice or selection and is stored on the user's side (Web browser). In the Java servlet API, we can access cookies by retrieving cookies from the `HttpServletRequest` objects `getCookies()` method. This returns an array of `javax.servlet.http.Cookie` objects. We can set all kinds of data into the cookie object, including its age (so that it expires after a certain time period), a comment, a value, and a version. Because the servlet API in Java offers an extremely convenient and easy set of calls, cookies can be implemented easily. However, cookies are not always the best solution for several reasons:

- Because the value is stored on the Web browser, the user may intentionally (or not) delete the cookie value. If it is expected to be there at a later date and isn't, all data will be lost and the session information needs to be resubmitted.
- There is the problem of privacy where if the Web browser is being shared by several users, cookie values could be viewed by other users. Some users may consider this a privacy issue.
- Some users turn off cookie support in their Web browsers. This causes any server-side logic to fail because it will not be able to track sessions.

Hidden Form Fields

This method of session tracking probably offers the most convenient solution because there's nothing in the Web browser that can disable hidden fields. In HTML, we can create Web forms which contain inputs. One of the input types can be hidden. This is simply a field that is placed within the form that is not displayed to the user (i.e., not rendered as part of the HTML). An example form with a hidden field may look something like this:

```
<form action="./submit.html">
  <input type="hidden" value="loginForm" id="123"/>
  <label for="loginName">Login Name:</label>
  <input type="text" name="loginName" id="loginName"/>
  <label for="password">Password:</label>
  <input type="password" name="password" id="password"/>
  <input type="submit" value="Submit"/>
</form>
```

This value can later be retrieved (just like any other input) within the servlet. While hidden form fields offer a solution that can't be turned off by the Web browser, they require further processing in order to contain information in them that is anything other than static in nature. That is, the value found in the hidden form field either has to be generated using a client-side scripting language (such as Javascript) or placed there by server code that generated the HTML in the first place. While this is not an overwhelming amount of complexity, it requires the programmers who are writing the server code that dynamically generates HTML to remember to place the appropriate values into the hidden form fields that are found within the HTML.

URL Rewriting

URL rewriting is a technique where the URL that the user originally refers to is somehow modified (by the server) to support some extra information in the URL, such as a session id value. The modified URL is then sent to the user's Web browser. We can place any type of information into the URL that we want, but the most common data placed in the URL are items such as session id values or choices within a form.

When rewriting URLs, we need to ensure that we know what each separate part of the URL means and what each separate part is called. For example, a URL such as http://www.charlesriver.com/Books/Features.aspx contains the protocol (http), the colon, and the two forward slashes, the host name (www.charlesriver.com), and the path (Books), and finally the file name (Features.aspx). We can also include a section which refers to a position within the file itself by including the id attribute

value of an HTML element prefixed with the hash symbol ('#'). We can also include an additional colon and port number right after the host name (e.g., http://www.charlesriver.com:80/). Most Web servers default to port 80; so we don't normally need to include the port number unless the Web server is running on a different port. URLs aren't just for Web servers. We can just as easily be defining an FTP server (e.g., ftp://www.bcit.ca).

Remembering that the URL format follows the format

```
protocol://hostname[:port]/path/filename#section
```

we can proceed to append to our URL further information, which must follow the format:

```
?param1=value1&param2=value2...paramN=valueN
```

So, if we wanted to append the session id value of the user to a URL, we would do it like this:

```
http://www.charlesriver.com/users?sessionid=23488&name=arron
```

We've included two pieces of information in here: the session id (with a value of 23488) and a name parameter (with a value of arron). These two pieces of information are sent from the server to the client who can then use these values to send back to the server for authentication and session tracking.

Although this technique seems simple enough, it does have its limitations. For example, for large amounts of data, URL rewriting would be impractical. Although the specification for the HTTP protocol (RFC 2616) does not specify a limit for URLs, Web browsers may have limits in what they accept as a length. For example, the Microsoft Internet Explorer has a limit of 2,083 characters. Other browsers may support more or less. If large amounts of information are being sent, another alternative should be used other than URL rewriting.

Custom Solutions And APIs

Of course we can use our own custom solutions which require us to create data structures that grab the parameters from within the server context and retrieve all parameters that were sent from the form in the client's Web browser. However, with current server technology and language support, we rarely have to use a custom solution because the commonly used programming languages and environments offer us API support.

In Java, the servlet API contains session-tracking capability. This makes our work easy because there's already a framework there to support our needs. For example, if we were handling the request from a form to allow the user to log into a forum, we may have the following HTML code:

```html
<form method="post" action="./forum.html">
  <h3>Forum Login</h3>
  Login name:<input name="name" type="text"/><br/>
  Password:<input name="password" type="password"/><br/><br/>
  <input value="Submit" type="submit"/>
  <input value="login" name="action" type="hidden"/>
</form>
```

The hidden form field contains a parameter called action with a value of login. This value allows the server to discern what request is being made. On the server side, we could handle this request using the following code:

```java
public void doPost(HttpServletRequest req, HttpServletResponse res)

        throws ServletException, IOException {
    String actionType = (String)req.getParameter("action");
    if(actionType == null) return;
    if(actionType.equals("login")) {
        String nameFromForm = (String)req.getParameter("name");
        String passwordFromForm =
            (String)req.getParameter("password");

        if(nameFromForm != null & passwordFromForm != null) {
            // create a session if none exists
            HttpSession session = req.getSession(true);
            boolean authenticated = UserManager.getInstance().
                loginUser(nameFromForm, passwordFromForm,
                session.getId());
            if(authenticated) {
                session.setAttribute("user", nameFromForm);
                session.setAttribute("password", passwordFromForm);
                session.setAttribute("accounttype",
                    UserManager.getInstance().
                    getAccountType(nameFromForm));
                doForumPage(res, nameFromForm);
            } else {
                session.invalidate();
                doForumMessagePage(res, "Login Failed.");
            }
        }
    }
}
```

In this code, we're dealing with the doPost() method of the HttpServlet class (more on this later), and we're calling the HttpServletRequest object's getParameter() method. This method returns the value of the parameter (based on the string name we pass in) or `null` if that parameter was not included in the post. This is why we check for a `null` value and return if that value is `null`. After that check, we can see if the value of the `action` parameter contains the `login` value that we are looking for. From there, we can check for the login name and password that the user supplied. Again, we check for `null` values because we want to ensure that someone was not using an altered version of our form with no username and password fields. If these values are not `null`, then we proceed to perform validation.

When we call the `getSession()` method of the `HttpServletRequest` object, we can pass in a boolean value which, if set to true, creates a new session if none was sent (from the client's Web browser). This is handy because we don't have to perform a check first to see if there is already a session created. Either way we receive a session. After we have the username, password, and a session, we can use our own classes and functionality to perform authentication. In our CMS, we've created a class called `UserManager`, which authenticates users based on accounts that have been created with the administration applet. The `UserManager` only allows the user to log in once at any given time (no multiple sessions allowed). This is why we pass the session `id` value (using the `HttpSession`'s `getId()` method)—so that we can check the current session with any session id values already recorded in the `UserManager`.

Our authenticated boolean value is true if our `UserManager` class has accepted the username and password (assuming the user is not already logged). With success, we can add whatever values to the session object that we want. In our CMS example, we're adding `user`, `password`, and `accounttype` attributes and giving them the values that the user logged in, with the exception of the `accounttype` attribute which we get from the `UserManager`. At this point, we can forward the functionality to another method and allow the user into the forum. If the authentication failed, we invalidate the session and forward the user to a different page—usually back to the login page so that the user can retry if he wants.

One really interesting aspect of session tracking in Java is the ability to listen to the binding and unbinding of session events. We may, for example, wish to be informed when a user's session has timed out. A timeout may occur if the user did not properly log out but instead simply closed the Web browser. Or if the user left the Web browser open without interacting with the browser for a specified amount of time. With a simple forum (and forum accounts), this usually isn't a problem. However, if we have resources that have been somehow locked by a user and he has failed to properly log out of the server or perhaps an error occurred, we need the ability to unlock the resources that were held by the user and his account, as well as officially logout the user's account. Otherwise all resources would stay indefinitely locked. In Java, we can implement the `HttpSessionListener` interface to handle when sessions time out:

```
public class CMSSessionListener implements HttpSessionListener {
    public void sessionCreated(HttpSessionEvent se) {
        ; // not used
    }

    public void sessionDestroyed(HttpSessionEvent se) {
        HttpSession session = se.getSession();
        String sessionID = session.getId();
        String user = (String)session.getAttribute("user");
        String password = (String)session.getAttribute("password");
        if(user != null && password != null) {
            UserManager.getInstance().logoffUser(user, password,
                sessionID);
        }
        CMSDefaultModel.getInstance().unlockContent(sessionID);
    }
}
```

The HttpSessionEvent object offers us a way of getting the session that is associated with this event by calling the getSession() method. At this point, we can retrieve the session id and any other attribute values that were placed in the session. It is important to remember that this is our last chance to grab the values of this session because it is about to expire. In our example code, we use the UserManager to log out the user. Lastly, we need to unlock any resources that may have been held by this user by calling the CMSDefaultModel's unlockContent() method, which accepts a session id value. This call may take a while to process by the server, based on how much content was locked; but the advantage is that no content remains locked indefinitely. Of course, in our Web deployment descriptor we need to tell the Web server that our Web application actually contains a class for handling such things:

```
<listener>
  <listener-class>org.kucingCMS.server.CMSSessionListener
  </listener-class>
</listener>

<session-config>
  <!— Number of minutes to time out after inactivity —>
  <session-timeout>15</session-timeout>
</session-config>
```

Virtual Hosting

Virtual hosting is the ability to treat one server as several different servers by offering more than one domain name on the same server and IP address. This allows small providers to host several different Web sites for various different companies, organizations, and individuals.

Virtual Hosting In Tomcat

Apache's Tomcat 5.5 has come a long way and now offers an elegant architecture (and solution) that makes the process of configuring easy to deal with. Figure 7.4 shows the architecture of Tomcat 5.5 and how each of the architectural components fit in and relate to one another.

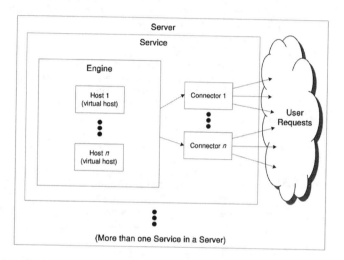

FIGURE 7.4   Tomcat 5.5 architecture.

A server, which represents the entire servlet container, can contain one or more services. A service is the grouping of one or more connector components, each of which must belong to only one engine. Connectors are what allow Web browsers and other user agents to connect to the server. The engine is considered the request processing machinery. It performs all processing for resources and can be considered the heart of the Web server. Only one engine can be found within a service. Each engine can have one or more hosts. Hosts represent virtual hosts. With Tomcat 5.5, the configuration file that contains this information (in the form of an XML file), is found in the $CATALINA_HOME/conf/server.xml file, where $CATALINA_HOME is the root directory in which you installed Tomcat 5.5. A basic install server.xml file may look something like:

```
<Server port="8005" shutdown="SHUTDOWN">
  <Listener className=
    "org.apache.catalina.mbeans.ServerLifecycleListener"/>
  <Listener className=
    "org.apache.catalina.mbeans.GlobalResourcesLifecycleListener"/>
  <Listener className=
```

```
         "org.apache.catalina.storeconfig.StoreConfigLifecycleListener"
      />
   <GlobalNamingResources>
     <Environment name="simpleValue" type="java.lang.Integer"
        value="30"/>
     <Resource name="UserDatabase" auth="Container"
        type="org.apache.catalina.UserDatabase"
        description="User database that can be updated and saved"
        factory="org.apache.catalina.users.MemoryUserDatabaseFactory"
        pathname="conf/tomcat-users.xml" />
   </GlobalNamingResources>
   <Service name="Catalina">
     <Connector port="8080" maxHttpHeaderSize="8192"
        maxThreads="150" minSpareThreads="25" maxSpareThreads="75"
        enableLookups="false" redirectPort="8443" acceptCount="100"
        connectionTimeout="20000" disableUploadTimeout="true"/>
     <Connector port="8009" enableLookups="false"
        redirectPort="8443" protocol="AJP/1.3" />
     <Engine name="Catalina" defaultHost="localhost">
       <Realm
          className="org.apache.catalina.realm.UserDatabaseRealm"
          resourceName="UserDatabase"/>

       <Host name="localhost" appBase="webapps" unpackWARs="true"
          autoDeploy="true" xmlValidation="false"
          xmlNamespaceAware="false">
       </Host>
       <Host name="www.kucingcms.org" appBase="/home/www/kucingcms"
       unpackWARs="true" autoDeploy="true" xmlValidation="false"
       xmlNamespaceAware="false" unpackWARs="true">
          <Alias>kucingcms.org</Alias>
          <Alias>www.kucing-cms.org</Alias>
          <Valve className="org.apache.catalina.valves.AccessLogValve"
             directory="logs"  prefix="kucingCMS_access_log." suffix=".txt"
             pattern="common" resolveHosts="false"/>
       </Host>
     </Engine>
   </Service>
</Server>
```

In this server.xml file ,we start off with a few Listener elements that implement the org.apache.catalina.LifecycleListener, which are for the server itself. The GlobalNamingResources element allows configuration details to be made for the Java Naming and Directory Interface (JNDI). Adhering to what Figure 7.4 showed us, we place a Service element inside of the Server element. Within the Service element, we can now start placing Connector elements, which, as mentioned before, connect the outside world with user requests. We have two Connector elements, the first one is the default, which states several different values, including the number of maximum threads that allow connection to the engine. The second Connector element contains a value of AJP for its protocol attribute. Apache JServ Protocol (AJP) is used for connecting to other Web servers and is to be used if Tomcat is only being used to serve up dynamic content, leaving the other server only to perform the task of static content.

Within the `Engine` element, we finally have our `Host` elements, one for localhost (referring to it locally) and one set up to answer Domain Name Service (DNS) directs because we've provided a network name (`www.kucingcms.org`) that can be referenced on the Web. The `Host` element with the name `www.kucingcms.org` also contains two `Alias` elements, each allowing a slightly different name to be used on the Web to refer to our server (`kucingcms.org` and `www.kucing-cms.org`). Using aliases is handy because it allows more than one name to map to the same IP address and, specifically, host. It is important to remember that although you can map more than one `Host` element inside of an `Engine` element, you must have at least one `Host` element, and one of the `Host` elements must have a value for their `name` attribute that matches the `Engine`'s attribute `defaultHost` value. In our example, it's simply using localhost. The `Valve` element allows us to perform logging (recall earlier our discussion on logging).

NOTE

The default installation of Tomcat 5.5 contains a directory meant to house Web applications. This directory is called $CATALINA_HOME/webapps. Users wanting to access Web applications from different directories have to change the Host element's `appBase` *attribute. The* `appBase` *attribute's default value is webapps. You can, for example, change this to a value of C:\files\projects\cmsdev (assuming the Microsoft XP operating system) or ./usr/webapps (assuming a Unix operating system).*

The Servlet Model

Our CMS is built on servlet technology, so it helps to understand what goes on under the hood. From a high-level perspective, Java servlets are simply Java classes that answer requests that originally came from a user agent (Web browser) and have been forwarded to the servlet by the Web container (in our case Tomcat). A Java servlet contains no main method, extends javax.servlet.http.HttpServlet, and is lightweight because it does not create processes on each request that is made on it.

From a functionality perspective, servlets can do anything that any other Java class can do, like open files, read and write data from and to a database, create images, access directories, and anything else you can think of doing in code. Servlets do require the existence of a Web container in order to run in. Unlike a regular Java class with a main method, servlets cannot be called up by the command line. Servlets require the comfort of the Web container that offers the supported framework.

Run Servlet, Run

A servlet is born into the world by being instantiated by the servlet container within the Web service. One instantiated, the servlet's `init()` method is called. This is usually one of the methods that servlet developers need to override in order to offer initialization functionality. Once a servlet is running, it handles requests that are passed to it by the Web container (Web server with servlet support). The servlet handles requests until its `destroy()` method is called, or the server simply shuts down abruptly. For the most part, it is rather odd to take down a servlet unless it is misbehaving. A simple servlet example (the token "hello world" servlet) looks like:

```java
import java.io.IOException;
import javax.servlet.http.HttpServlet;
import javax.servlet.http.HttpServletRequest;
import javax.servlet.http.HttpServletResponse;
import javax.servlet.ServletException;
import javax.servlet.ServletOutputStream;
import javax.servlet.UnavailableException;

public class MessageDisplayer extends HttpServlet {
    public void init() throws UnavailableException {
        // initialize the servlet
    }
    public void doGet(HttpServletRequest req,
        HttpServletResponse res) throws ServletException,
        IOException {
        // handle HTTP GET requests
        ServletOutputStream out = res.getOutputStream();
        out.println("<html><head></head><body><p>Hello World!"
            + "</p></body></html>");
    }
    public void doPost(HttpServletRequest req,
        HttpServletResponse res) throws ServletException,
        IOException {
        // handle HTTP POST requests
    }
}
```

The `doGet()` method accepts two objects: a `HttpServletRequest` object and a `HttpServletResponse` object. The `HttpServletRequest` object represents an abstraction of the user agent request and contains functionality for querying the request via method calls. As we saw earlier when dealing with session tracking, an `HttpServletRequest` object can be queried for parameters that come from the form sent by the Web browser. Some (but not all) of the other types of information we can retrieve are:

- cookies (using the `getCookies()` method)
- the HTTP method that was used to make the request (using the `getMethod()` method). This helps us to determine what request was made by the Web browser (e.g., GET, POST)

- attribute names which are the names of the attributes available to the request (using the `getAttributeNames()` method)
- the MIME type (using the `getContentType()` method)
- the user's IP address (using the `getRemoteAddr()` method)

If the `HttpServletRequest` was the abstraction for the data coming into our little servlet world, then the `HttpServletResponse` represents the abstraction for the data that we are sending back to the user. With this class we can do things like:

- add a cookie (using the `addCookie()` method)
- add a date header (using the `addDateHeader()` method)
- send an error response (using the `sendError()` method)
- set the content length (using the `setContentLength()` method)

Threading And Servlets

Because servlets live within a server that is constantly handling requests from multiple clients, we have to manage code and realize that the code exists in a more complex environment than a simple standalone application. Our servlet has to handle the situation of a multithreaded environment where multiple threads are accessing the servlet itself.

Although we are only creating one servlet instance ourselves, that one instance is being accessed by multiple threads that exist on the servlet container. Figure 7.5 shows the relationship between threads and the servlet. Within the servlet container there exist (or can exist) many different threads—each thread representing requests from users.

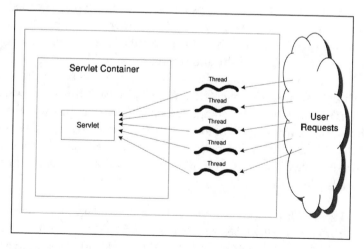

FIGURE 7.5   Threads and their relationship to a servlet.

While this has no direct impact on what we do with our servlet class on its own, it does have an immense impact on any resources our servlet may access. Resources can be in the form of other objects, or they can be files that are accessed directly by the servlet. Let us explore a simple example. Listing 7.1 gives us a simple servlet that displays a count variable within the HTML page.

LISTING 7.1   Simple Count Servlet (`CountDisplayer.java`)

```java
import java.io.IOException;
import javax.servlet.http.HttpServlet;
import javax.servlet.http.HttpServletRequest;
import javax.servlet.http.HttpServletResponse;
import javax.servlet.ServletException;
import javax.servlet.ServletOutputStream;
import javax.servlet.UnavailableException;

public class CountDisplayer extends HttpServlet {
    private int count;
    public void init() throws UnavailableException {
        count = 0;
    }
    public void doGet(HttpServletRequest req,
        HttpServletResponse res)
        throws ServletException, IOException {
        // handle HTTP GET requests
        ServletOutputStream out = res.getOutputStream();
        out.println("<html><head></head><body><p>Accessed:"
            + count++ + " times.</p></body></html>");

    }
}
```

We've created a private instance variable of type int called count. To understand what happens next, we need to understand a bit about the Java Virtual Machine (JVM) and how it handles threads. Java threads are (like threads in other environments) lightweight and, therefore, only require a program counter (PC) and a stack, which is not unlike a conventional stack in a programming language such as C. As threads are created in the JVM, each thread is awarded its own stack that is private to that thread and, therefore, no other thread has access to it. Within this stack are things such as local variables, partial results, and return values of any methods that the thread has previously invoked. The heap, on the other hand, stores all class instances as well as arrays. Unlike stacks, the heap is visible to all threads within the JVM.

NOTE   *Java has two basic types: primitives and references types. Primitive types are, for example, int, float, boolean, double, long, char, byte. Primitive types are passed by value and so are not actually found in the heap. Reference types are found in the heap. There are three different sub-types for reference: class, array, and interface.*

Where things can go awry is when non-local variables (class and instance) are being accessed by multiple threads. Looking back at Listing 7.1, if we were to envision two threads accessing the servlet at roughly the same time, we may get into trouble. The problem is shown in Figure 7.6. Thread one increments the count variable. Just after thread one increments the count variable, thread two comes along and does the same thing. The problem is that thread one is going to read (and display) a value that has been incremented twice. This may not cause too much strife with our access counting servlet, but if this value were the number of available seats on an airplane that have been sold, we may undersell the number of seats available. Other scenarios could have dire consequences based on our lack of concurrency control.

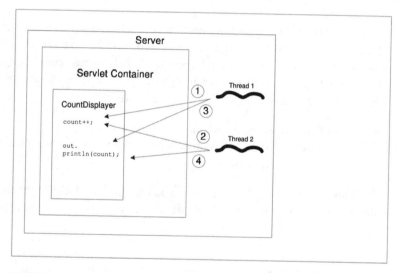

FIGURE 7.6 Threads and race condition.

The solution is to serialize access to the count variable. We do this using Java's monitor support. Listing 7.2 shows the servlet solution for fixing this problem.

LISTING 7.2 Simple Count Servlet With Synchronization (CountDisplayerSynchronized.java)

```
import javax.servlet.http.HttpServletResponse;
import javax.servlet.ServletException;
import javax.servlet.ServletOutputStream;
import javax.servlet.UnavailableException;
```

```
public class CountDisplayerSynchronized extends HttpServlet {
    private int count;
    public void init() throws UnavailableException {
        count = 0;
    }
    public void doGet(HttpServletRequest req,
        HttpServletResponse res)
        throws ServletException, IOException {
        // handle HTTP GET requests
        ServletOutputStream out = res.getOutputStream();
        synchronized(this) {
            out.println("<html><head></head><body><p>Accessed:"
                + count++ + " times.</p></body></html>");
        }
    }
}
```

We've used the keyword `synchronized`, which serializes access to whatever code block we wrap it around using an object monitor. This ensures that if there are two (or more) threads attempting to access this synchronized code, that only one thread has access to this critical section at a time. What we should now be aware of is that any resources that our servlets access must either:

■ be local variables found within methods or;
■ have some sort of serialized access control wrapped around the resource (using the synchronized keyword in Java).

This is important to remember when we look at the data model access that we allow not just one servlet to have access to, but several different threads to have access to.

SETTING UP THE CMS PROJECT

For our CMS project, we'll need to make sure we have all of the necessary files and place them in proper directories as well as making a build file. We don't want to have to compile all of these files by hand and have to perform all of the procedures manually. In this part of the chapter, we'll walk through setting up the project so that it can be rebuilt quickly, easily, and consistently.

Directory Structures

A typical build for a software system contains several different directories each containing a different group of files or a different part of the software build. At this point, it helps to identify the files that we'll need:

- Source code that we're writing for our CMS. We'll need three parts to this (admin tool, data model, and the server-side logic).
- Although not mandatory for running the software, it will be useful to include the DTDs in the build or at least in the build directories.
- Other source code that we'll be bundling up with ours. In our case, we'll be compiling and bundling the JGoodies Forms and JGoodies Looks libraries.
- CSS files for the look-and-feel templates we'll be using.
- Deployment descriptor that describes the Web app.
- Any JSP files.
- The licenses for our software and the other libraries we've included.
- Any supporting media such as images and icons.
- XSLT style sheets that we'll use for the look-and-feel.
- Any third-party libraries that our Web app will require in order to run.

Figure 7.7 shows the directory structure of our CMS Web application. There are two main directories under the CMS-Project directory: src and thirdparty which contain the source of our project and the third-party libraries that our Web application use, respectively. Looking from top to bottom, the client directory is actually empty but is used when we start the build process.

FIGURE 7.7   Build directory structure for the CMS Application.

The admin applet will temporarily be placed in there right before we generate our Java Archive (JAR) file, and then place the JAR file into a Web Archive (WAR) file. We've included the DTD files, although they won't be bundled in the WAR file at the end. It's important to group all project files together so that we have a quick and easy way of referencing all files.

It is important to note that the directory structure found in Listing 7.7 is only considered our build directory structure and not the Web app directory structure that will be created once our CMS has been deployed.

The com directory contains all source code files from the JGoodies Forms and the JGoodies Looks libraries. These source code files are already found on the CD-ROM under the *CMS-project\src\com* directory. However, the actual bundles from where these source code files have come from are also found on the CD-ROM under the *software* directory on the CD-ROM (`forms-1_0_6.zip` and `looks-2_0_1.zip` files). Additionally, you can download the newest versions by going to the JGoodies Web site and visiting their download page at: *http://www.jgoodies.com/downloads/libraries.html.* Figure 7.8 shows the directory structure of the JGoodies Forms and JGoodies Looks packages. You do not need to do anything to these files other than leave them in the directory, which allows them to be added to the project when it is built.

FIGURE 7.8 JGoodies source code subdirectories.

The deployment descriptor (`web.xml`) is placed in the `deploydesc` directory. At this point, we can name it anything we want, although we should continue with it being a file with the extension `xml`. The downloads directory can be for any files that you wish your Web app to offer users for downloading. The `jsp` directory stores Java Server Pages (JSPs). We do not write these ourselves because our CMS will auto-generate them for us. Our only JSP file will be the one for the admin page, which we'll look at later in Chapter 10. JSPs are compiled into servlets by the Web container (Tomcat in our case). The licenses directory should contain all licenses, including all libraries that we'll be using, and even our own license.

The media directory contains all media needed to support displaying Web pages. This includes (but is not limited to) images of various sorts, icons, sound, thumbnail images, sound, and video. In our CMS, the `thumbs` directory contains thumbnail images that are auto-generated by the CMS itself. Therefore, this directory should not be used to store anything else. The `org/kucingCMS` directory contains all of our files from our project. Within the `org` directory, we have three subdirectories: `admin`, `contentmodel`, and `server`. They each contain the files for the admin applet, the data model for our CMS, and the server code, respectively.

The templates directory contains the XSLT style sheets that we'll create for the CMS. XSLT style sheets are covered in Chapter 11. The `xml` directory houses all of the data store files that the server needs in order to write all content to. The `xml` directory also contains a `cache` subdirectory. This directory is used by the CMS, so it shouldn't be used, nor should files found in that directory be edited manually.

The About the CD-ROM section covers how to edit and change the build project so as to use different data for the CMS.

NOTE

Required Libraries

The `thirdparty` directory contains a subdirectory called `libs` which has all of the libraries that the server needs in order to run. This directory contains the following libraries:

ON THE CD

- Apache's Xalan library which offers the Java support for XSLT style sheet transforms (the `serializer.jar` file and the `xalan.jar` file, which both come from the compressed archive `xalan-j_2_7_0-bin.zip` found in the `software` directory on the CD-ROM)
- Apache's Xerces library which offers XML parsing (the `xercesImpl.jar` file and the `xml-apis.jar` file that are also found in the compressed archive `xalan-j_2_7_0-bin.zip` found in the `software` directory on the CD-ROM)
- XPP/MXP library which offers the fast XML parser used by our CMS data model (the `xpp3_min-1.1.3.4.0.jar` file which comes from the compressed archive `xpp3-1.1.3.4.C_all.zip` found in the `software` directory on the CD-ROM)
- JSP™ Standard Tag Library (JSTL) package which offers functionality in JSPs, such as calling XML parsers and XSLT transformers—specifically Xalan (the `jstl.jar` file, and the `standard.jar` file are also found in the compressed archive `jakarta-taglibs-standard-1.1.2.zip` which is found in the `software` directory on the CD-ROM)

NOTE

ON THE CD

All of the libraries (JAR files) have already been placed in the thirdparty/lib direc-tory within the build directory on the CD-ROM. The compressed (ZIP) archives are also found on the CD-ROM in the software directory, for sake of completion. You can always visit the Web sites of each of the software providers to ensure that you have the newest version of their libraries. About the CD-ROM lists the sites (URLs provided) and the software archives that you can download.

Configuring the Deployment Descriptor

Our deployment descriptor (a.k.a. our `web.xml` file) requires the following types of information to be placed in it:

- Registering servlets within our Web app so that they are seen within the servlet container
- Mapping servlets to certain URLs
- Choosing a default URL for certain error pages (e.g., 404 messages for page not found)
- Blocking access to certain directories
- Setting up a listener to session events (i.e., session timeouts)

All examples for our deployment descriptor are taken from the Kucing CMS 1.0 deployment descriptor, found on the CD-ROM in the *CMS-project\src\deploy-desc* subdirectory. We need to register the following servlets:

`MessageDisplayer:` This servlet handles all HTTP 404 messages and displays a message to the user informing him that there is no resource by the name typed by the user.

`ConnectionManager:` The servlet that handled all calls from the admin applet.

`JSPtoHTMLServlet:` The servlet that simply offers aliases to the JSP files that our CMS generates. Kucing CMS 1.0 generates JSP files which contain references to the cached XML files that contain the page content and the XSLT style sheets that transform the XML to XHTML. Rather than forcing the user to remember to type ".jsp" at the end of each document name, we're hiding the fact that the files are of type JSP and simply offering ".html" extensions as aliases.

`SearchEngine:` The search engine servlet that handles all search requests by the user.

`ForumManager:` The servlet that manages the forum. It deals with logging in, posts, replies, and listing of posts within the forum.

In order to register a servlet with our Web application, we need to add the following XML elements:

```
<servlet>
  <servlet-name>MessageDisplayer</servlet-name>
  <servlet-class>org.kucingCMS.server.MessageDisplayer
  </servlet-class>
  <load-on-startup>1</load-on-startup>
</servlet>
```

We're registering our `MessageDisplayer` servlet and specifying that it will be loaded on startup. If we wish to map that servlet to a particular URL, then we are required to offer the following:

```
<servlet-mapping>
  <servlet-name>MessageDisplayer</servlet-name>
  <url-pattern>/404.html</url-pattern>
</servlet-mapping>
```

This maps the servlet (based on the name we gave it) to the URL pattern `/404.html`. Whenever a user agent attempts to access the resource within our Web application (e.g., `http://geekit.bcit.ca/kucingCMS/404.html`), the Web container redirects the request to our `MessageDisplayer` servlet. As a last measure, what we can do is ensure that whenever a 404 error is encountered within the context of our Web app, we can inform the server that we wish for it to access a particular URL pattern. In this case we can say:

```
<error-page>
  <error-code>404</error-code><location>/404.html</location>
</error-page>
```

These three steps have just ensured that whenever users choose a URL that is not found within our Web app, the server redirects it to our `MessageDisplayer` servlet. The same works for other servlets that will handle specific URLs. For example, our `SearchEngine` should always be mapped to the relative URL `./search.html`. To do this, we create the following XML structure in our deployment descriptor:

```
<servlet>
  <servlet-name>SearchEngine</servlet-name>
  <servlet-class>org.kucingCMS.server.SearchEngine</servlet-class>
  <load-on-startup>1</load-on-startup>
</servlet>
<servlet-mapping>
  <servlet-name>SearchEngine</servlet-name>
  <url-pattern>/search.html</url-pattern>
</servlet-mapping>
```

Another clever step we can take is for the disabling of listing and accessing files within certain directories. We know that users will want access to our `download` directory, our `media` directory (and its subdirectories), our `client` directory (where the admin applet will be found), and the `css` directory (where the CSS files will be found). However, we want to deny access to the `xml` directory because it contains some sensitive information in it, such as the passwords for logging into our CMS admin tool. In order to do this, we need to tell the Web server that a certain URL pattern is sent to a specific servlet. In this case, our `MessageDisplayer` servlet:

```
<servlet-mapping>
  <servlet-name>MessageDisplayer</servlet-name>
  <url-pattern>/xml/*</url-pattern>
</servlet-mapping>
```

By specifying `/xml/*`, we are redirecting all requests for listings or access to individual files within that directory. All requests are sent to the `MessageDisplayer` servlet, which results in an error message being sent to the user. As already mentioned, our CMS generates JSP files. These JSP files are placed in the root of our Web app CMS; so whenever the user wants to access a page, he must type the name of the resource with the ".jsp" extension at the end (e.g., `http://geekkit.bcit.ca/kucingCMS/index.jsp`). Although this is not a horrible inconvenience, it is still an inconvenience. Most users are more comfortable with the ".html" extension. If we could ensure that users only have to type in the ".html" extension, we would be offering an extra level of convenience, not to mention that we'd be hiding the fact that we're even using JSP technology (not that JSPs are a bad thing!). In order to do this, we would set up the following XML structure in our deployment descriptor:

```
<servlet>
  <servlet-name>JSPtoHTMLServlet</servlet-name>
  <servlet-class>org.kucingCMS.server.JSPtoHTMLServlet
  </servlet-class>
  <load-on-startup>1</load-on-startup>
</servlet>
<servlet-mapping>
  <servlet-name>JSPtoHTMLServlet</servlet-name>
  <url-pattern>*.html</url-pattern>
</servlet-mapping>
```

This registers our `JSPtoHTMLServlet` servlet and maps all requests asking for resources which end in ".html" to the our `JSPtoHTMLServlet` servlet. Lastly, we want to register our session listener to a particular class that we create:

```
<listener>
  <listener-class>org.kucingCMS.server.CMSSessionListener
  </listener-class>
</listener>
```

```
<session-config>
  <session-timeout>15</session-timeout>
</session-config>
```

This maps the `CMSSessionListener` class to the listener for session events (i.e., timeouts) and sets the session timeout quantum to 15 minutes. We'll see later on in the chapter what these servlets do and how they do it.

Creating the CMS Build File

Chapter 2 introduced us to the installation procedure of setting up Ant. Ant is yet another offering from the Apache Software Foundation. It is a build tool that allows us to manage large Java projects, although it can also be used to manage projects written in other programming languages such as C# and even C and C++. If you're familiar to make (the build tool used in the C and C++ world), Ant may seem a little foreign to you, although in the end it offers the same output: a built software project. The syntax that Ant uses is, of course, based on XML; so if you've been enjoying the XML technology that we've been using so far in this book to create our CMS, creating build files should not cause any anxiety—at least from a syntax point of view. We'll use Ant and create a build file for our CMS project so that it compiles our code and builds an entire Web Archive (WAR) file for deployment of our CMS.

The Build Process

The build process is based on what are called *tasks*. Each task represents a certain action to perform (e.g., compile, generate documentation, build a JAR file, etc.). Before each task is executed, it is checked to see if it has dependencies on other tasks. It appears to have a waterfall effect, as Figure 7.9 shows.

In Figure 7.9, all of our CMS build tasks are shown. When Ant starts executing the build file, it looks at the first task (which is the default task to start). In Figure 7.9, the Deploy CMS task is shown on top as the first task to execute. However, Deploy CMS has a dependency: Clean. Therefore, Ant attempts to execute the Clean task. But Clean also has a dependency (Create Distribution) and so once again Ant looks at the next dependency. This iterative process takes place until Ant cannot find anymore tasks with dependencies at which point it executes the first task not containing any dependencies.

This process has a recursive bubbling up behavior, and if you can feel comfortable with that, then building projects in Ant (no matter how large they are), should not seem intimidating. With the flow of tasks covered, its now a good time to look at the actual XML script that defines these tasks. The Ant build file (called `build.xml`) is found on the CD-ROM in the *CMS-project folder*. All sample code in this section references this file.

ON THE CD

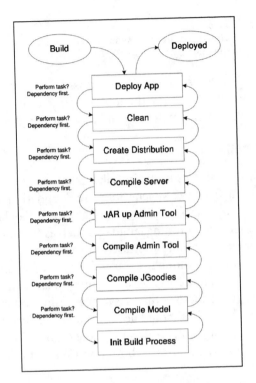

FIGURE 7.9 The Ant build process.

Declaring Properties

Ant allows us to define properties which can be referenced throughout the build script. This comes in handy when we're referring to files or directories more than once. That way, if the directory changes, then we'll only have to make one change and it will be at the top of the file where we've declared all of our properties. The Kucing CMS build file has the following properties:

```
<property name="deploy-dir"
   location="C:\work\apache-tomcat-5.5.16\webapps"/>
<property name="servlet-api"
   location="C:\work\apache-tomcat-5.5.16\common\lib\
   servlet-api.jar"/>
<property name="build-dir" location="./build"/>
<property name="dist-dir" location="./"/>
<property name="licenses-dir" location="./src/licenses"/>
<property name="src-code-dir" location="./src/org/kucingCMS/"/>
<property name="src-dir" location="./src"/>
<property name="jgoodies-src-dir" location="./src/com/jgoodies"/>
<property name="application" location="kucingCMS-1.0.war"/>
```

All of these properties refer to directories (relative) found in our base build directory (e.g., where to find the licenses or source code). There are two properties here that we're especially interested in because they are properties that we'll need to change the values of in order to get our CMS to build on computers with different configurations and paths. The first property is the `deploy-dir` property. This property we are using to specify the deployment directory, which is where Ant places the built WAR file. A default installation of Tomcat has the `webapps` directory as a subdirectory of the Tomcat directory. For your project to build correctly on your computer, you need to change this value to point to where you've installed Tomcat. In the example file, the value has been set to `c:\work\apache-tomcat-5.5.16\webapps`.

The second property that we are interested in is the `servlet-api` property. This property specifies where to find the servlet API that is used for all servlets (`servlet-api.jar`). We need to reference this library because many of our server-side classes reference classes from this library. We're referencing the `servlet-api.jar` file found at `C:\work\apache-tomcat-5.5.16\common\lib\servlet-api.jar`. Tomcat has this file, so we don't need to download it.

Init Build Process Task

At the bottom of Figure 7.9 we see the Init Build Process task. This task starts the ball rolling. The XML that performs this task is:

```
<target name="init-build" description="Create directories">
  <mkdir dir="${build-dir}"/>
</target>
```

We've given the task a name (`init-build`) and a description, which is useful for applications that may wish to display this process to a GUI or if we simply wish to see the descriptions at the command line. The element `mkdir` allows us to create a directory. The directory created is a temporary directory used to place compiled files into before they are bundled up and placed in a JAR or WAR file.

Compile Model Task

Compiling the model uses the `javac` element in Ant:

```
<target name="compile-model" depends="init-build"
description="Compile the model code">
  <javac srcdir="${src-code-dir}/contentmodel"
    destdir="${build-dir}"/>
</target>
```

We offer it the source directory from where to find the source code for the model. We've referenced a property by using the property name and prepending the dollar sign to the beginning of it (`${src-code-dir}`). This tells Ant that we're referencing a property. We can use a mixture of property values and string literals, which is what we've done in the `srcdir` attribute. We've done this so that we can reuse the same base source code directory property for all three packages for our CMS project (model, server, and admin applet).

Compile JGoodies Task

The JGoodies source code has been extracted and placed in the `com` subdirectory of the `src` directory. We're compiling this code instead of simply including the JAR file with the compiled classes because a JAR file cannot contain references to classes inside of an inner JAR file. For this reason, we're compiling these classes, and we're going to place them in the same JAR file (the admin jar file) along with the admin tool and CMS model classes. Temporarily (and like the model code for our CMS) the class files are placed within the `build` directory that the Init Build Process task created at the start of our build process.

```
<target name="compile-jgoodies" depends="compile-model"
  description="Compile the server code">
  <javac srcdir="${jgoodies-src-dir}" destdir="${build-dir}"/>
</target>
```

Compile Admin Tool Task

Now that we have the CMS model code compiled and the JGoodies source code compiled, we can compile our admin tool because it references both of the previous groupings of packages:

```
<target name="compile-admin" depends="compile-jgoodies"
  description="Compile the JGoodies libraries">
  <javac srcdir="${src-code-dir}/admin" destdir="${build-dir}" />
</target>
```

JAR Up Admin Tool Task

Another element we can use is the `jar` element in Ant. It allows us to specify that the task will be building a JAR file for us. Within the jar element, we can specify `fileset` elements, which list files that we wish to be included in the JAR. The XML for doing this looks like:

```
<target name="jar-admin" depends="compile-admin"
  description="Put the admin tool in a JAR file">
  <jar destfile="${src-dir}/client/kucingCMS-admin.jar"
    basedir="${build-dir}" excludes="org/kucingCMS/server/*.class">
    <fileset dir="${src-dir}">
      <include name="org/kucingCMS/admin/*.png"/>
      <include name="org/kucingCMS/admin/*.gif"/>
```

```
      </fileset>
      <fileset dir="${src-dir}">
        <include name="com/jgoodies/looks/common/*.png"/>
        <include name="com/jgoodies/looks/plastic/icons/*.png"/>
        <include name="com/jgoodies/looks/plastic/icons/*.gif"/>
        <include name="com/jgoodies/looks/windows/icons/*.gif"/>
        <include name="com/jgoodies/looks/windows/icons/xp/*.png"/>
      </fileset>
    </jar>
  </target>
```

Here we are including all images of type PNG and GIF found in either our admin subdirectory based on what we created for our applet, as well as any images of the same type that are part of the JGoodies build process. The jar element contains the destfile attribute, which is both the directory that the JAR file should be placed in (the client subdirectory of our project) and the name of the JAR file itself. The basedir attribute allows us to tell Ant where the files we're placing in our JAR file go and an excludes attribute which allows us to tell Ant to exclude certain files. Here we're excluding the server files from being included in the JAR file because they're not part of the admin tool runtime (which will be loaded on within the Web browser).

Compile Server Task

Next, we compile the server with the following XML:

```
<target name="compile-server" depends="jar-admin"
  description="Compile the server code">
  <javac srcdir="${src-code-dir}/server" destdir="${build-dir}">
    <classpath>
      <pathelement
        path="./thirdparty/libs/xpp3_min-1.1.3.4.0.jar"/>
      <pathelement path="${servlet-api}"/>
    </classpath>
  </javac>
</target>
```

This, again, places a bunch of files (directories, subdirectories, and class files) into the build directory. We reference the MXP/XPP parser library because this is the parser that we're using in our code. We also need to link to the servlet API (using the servlet API property).

Create Distribution Task

This is one of the last tasks and is also the biggest. This is where we create the WAR file. The WAR file contains all files, directories, and even the client admin applet, which has already been JARred up. This task creates our WAR and places it in the directory of our choosing. If we place it in a directory that is visible to our Web container (Tomcat 5.5) and the Web container is set to auto deploy, then command run within a batch or script file could cascade the entire build process, including placing our WAR file in the proper Web application directory causing the application to be automatically run as soon as it has been compiled. The XML for this gives us:

```
<target name="create-distro" depends="compile-server"
  description="Generate the distribution">
  <war destfile="${application}"
    webxml="./src/deploydesc/kucingCMS.xml">
    <classes dir="${build-dir}">
      <exclude name="com/**"/>
      <exclude name="${src-code-dir}/admin/**"/>
    </classes>
    <lib dir="thirdparty/libs"/>
    <zipfileset dir="${src-dir}/licenses" prefix="downloads"/>
    <!- More zip file sets here ... see CD-ROM ->
    <zipfileset dir="${src-dir}/client" prefix="client"/>
  </war>
</target>
```

Like the jar element, the war element contains a destfile attribute that contains both the directory and the name of the archive to make (in this case a WAR not JAR). The webxml attribute tells Ant where to find the deployment descriptor; in our case, we've called it kucingCMS.xml. The classes element contains a list of files to exclude. We're excluding everything in the com directory and subdirectories (these are the JGoodies classes which we've already placed in the JAR file, and there's no reference to these look-and-feel or forms classes in the server code), and all files in the admin directory of our project because these have already been JARred up in the admin applet.

We also included the lib element, which tells Ant to include libraries (i.e., JAR files) in the WAR—we include the third-party libraries (e.g., Xalan, Xerces, and XPP/MXP). The remaining elements are the zipfileset elements, which help us to include entire directories into the WAR. We specify the directory to grab (using the dir element), and we specify the actual placement of that directory in our WAR file (using the prefix element).

Clean Task

Lastly, we perform clean up, which involves the deletion of created directories:

```
<target name="clean" depends="create-distro"
  description="Remove build directory">
  <delete dir="${build-dir}"/>
  <delete file="${src-dir}/client/kucingCMS-admin.jar"/>
</target>
```

We need to be careful not to delete our project files because this operation is not reversible.

Deploy App Task

Finally, we deploy, which is the step taken to move the WAR file that we created to the destination directory, which could be a live Web application directory where the WAR is auto deployed:

```
<target name="deploy-CMS" depends="clean" description="Deploy the WAR">
  <move todir="${deploy-dir}" file="${application}"/>
</target>
```

Building an Ant build file does take some time, but for large projects it can literally save a developer many hours of time having to recompile, open directories, navigate to the correct directory at the command line, and move files around. Ant's way of representing tasks is logical and maps nicely to each step of the development way when creating software.

CREATING THE SERVER-SIDE LOGIC

Recalling our design from Chapter 2, our server-side logic consists of several servlets and a few supporting classes that are called upon by the servlets. In this section, we'll be looking at how these servlets can successfully call up other classes within a multiuser environment using Java's monitor capability to ensure serialized access to resources.

The Connection Manager

The connection manager is the servlet that handles all requests from the admin tool. The development of the admin applet is covered in detail in Chapter 9. One of the first things that we must do in our connection manager servlet is initialize all classes that are to be used. This takes place inside of the init method of our servlet. Recall that this is one of the methods that we really should override from the HttpServlet class. Inside of the init method we retrieve a ServletContext object, which we use to get the actual path of where our Web application is situated:

```
ServletContext ctx = getServletContext();
String webAppRoot = ctx.getRealPath("/");
```

This is important for when we write to files (relative paths). Next, we set ourselves up a logger which will log all unusual issues, such as class cast exceptions or improper use of our application protocol. At the least, this is useful to us in the debugging process as well as when we are running and we wish to check if we've had some unusual access attempts:

```
try {
    FileHandler handler = new FileHandler(webAppRoot + "WEB-INF"
        + File.separator + "error.log", true);
    logger = Logger.getAnonymousLogger();
    logger.addHandler(handler);
} catch(IOException ioe) { ioe.printStackTrace(); }
```

The next few lines of code call up the data model, which is really a bootstrapping process:

```
userManager = UserManager.getInstance();
userManager.loadUsers(webAppRoot);
model = CMSDefaultModel.getInstance();
model.loadStores(webAppRoot);
PageCacheGenerator generator = new PageCacheGenerator(webAppRoot);
generator.constructPages();
XMLPageCacheGeneratorThread generatorThread =
    new XMLPageCacheGeneratorThread(generator);
model.addModelListener(generatorThread);
templateManager = TemplateManager.getInstance();
templateManager.loadTemplates(webAppRoot);
```

Most of the classes that we're referencing are being referenced using a class method called getInstance(). This method returns one and only one instance of the class. Recall that we are dealing with a servlet that is called up by many different threads. This is one step we need to take in order to ensure data integrity and concurrency. We instantiate the user manager and tell it to load the users (passing it the real path of the Web app so it can find the XML file). We also instantiate the data model (CMSDefaultModel) itself, the page cache generator (PageCacheGenerator) which upon startup generates temporary XML files representing the actual Web pages, the page cache generator thread (XMLPageCacheGeneratorThread) which creates the JSP files that refer to the XML cached files, and finally the template manager (TemplateManager) which provides the logic for generating the JSP files (which is called upon by the XMLPageCacheGeneratorThread class).

The doPost() method actually redirects to the doAdmin() method which retrieves the serialized object stream with the following:

```
ObjectInputStream ois =
    new ObjectInputStream(req.getInputStream());
List message = (List)ois.readObject();
ois.close();
String messageType = (String)message.get(0);
```

The message type is then checked using an `if-else` conditional section:

```
if(messageType.equals(ProtocolConstants.LOGIN)) {
    doLogin(req, res, message);
} else if(messageType.equals(ProtocolConstants.LOGOUT)) {
}
```

Each situation must be handled separately, such as logging in, logging out, creating, adding/deleting users, listing templates, applying templates, or any of the commands that are part of the content management admin applet requests.

The details of this protocol are covered in Chapter 8.

Looking at the section where logging in takes place, we have:

```
protected void doLogin(HttpServletRequest req, HttpServletResponse res,
    List message) throws IOException, ClassNotFoundException {
    String user = (String)message.get(1);
    String password = (String)message.get(2);
    HttpSession session = req.getSession(true);
    session.setAttribute("user", user);
    session.setAttribute("password", password);
    List responseMsg = new LinkedList();
    if(UserManager.getInstance().loginNonForumUser(user, password,
        session.getId())) {
        responseMsg.add(ProtocolConstants.LOGIN_ACK);
        responseMsg.add(session.getId());
        responseMsg.add(UserManager.getInstance().getUser(user,
            password));
    } else {
        responseMsg.add(ProtocolConstants.LOGIN_NACK);
        session.invalidate();
    }
    sendMessage(res, responseMsg);
}
```

The variable labeled message (which is of type `java.util.List`) is passed in from the `doAdmin()` method from earlier. It contains the list of objects that make up the protocol. Because the first position in the list is always the protocol request, the next two protocol values are the username and password. It should be safe to cast these to strings, but if this doesn't work, there is exception-handling in place that will trigger a new log entry. The server then refuses to respond to the requesting client, which will abort the transaction. This is fine because if any client tool is not using the established sequence of data structures in the protocol, we can assume that the requests are being made by a hostile source.

An `HttpSession` object is created, which is assigned to current session, or unless the logging in action fails, in which case it will be invalidated. The user manager is called up and the username, password, and session id value are passed in. We're passing in the session id value because we wish to check whether this user is already logged in. The user manager returns false if the session id does not match with the current session id (assuming there is one). If this fails, the request is denied, and the user is sent a response (ProtocolConstants.LOGIN_NACK).

NOTE

ON THE CD

For a more detailed look at what the source code does, use a source code editor (such as JEdit) to open and view the files found on the CD-ROM in the CMS-project\src\org\kucingCMS\server subfolder.

Data Stores

Based on our design from Chapter 2, we decided that there was based functionality amongst all data stores and, therefore, we saw the need to use inheritance in order to reuse code.

The DataStore Base Class

The data store classes all derive from the base class DataStore, which contains a list of ModelUpdateListener objects (for listening to updates within each data store). There is also a list (java.util.List) of ModelNodes, which are the direct child nodes of the root. One common method that all data store objects share is the loadStore() method, which loads all XML from file:

```
public void loadStore(String path, String file) {
    try {
        String webAppPath = path;
        this.storeFile = webAppPath + "xml" + File.separator
            + file;
        parser = new MXParser();
        parser.setFeature(XmlPullParser.FEATURE_PROCESS_NAMESPACES,
            false);
        parser.setInput(new FileReader(storeFile));
        parseDocument();
    } catch(XmlPullParserException xppe) { xppe.printStackTrace();
    } catch(FileNotFoundException fnfe) { fnfe.printStackTrace();
    } catch(IOException ioe) { ioe.printStackTrace();
    }
}
```

This starts the parsing up by calling up the MXP parser from the XPP/MXP library that we downloaded. The method parseDocument() steps through the document:

```
protected void parseDocument()
    throws XmlPullParserException, IOException {
    int eventType = parser.getEventType();
    while(eventType != parser.END_DOCUMENT) {
```

```
            if(eventType == parser.START_TAG) {
                parseStartElement();
            } else if(eventType == parser.END_TAG) {
                parseEndElement();
            } else if(eventType == parser.TEXT) {
                parseText();
            }
            eventType = parser.next();
        }
    }
```

The `parseStartElement()`, `parseEndElement()` and `parseText()`, are all abstract in the `DataStore` class and are declared as such. This is because at this level we have no idea as to the specific parsing behavior that is required for each of the data store types. Although this commits the code to the XML data format we've created (not allowing the code to be useful with other XML formats), it does offer us efficiency and the ability to ignore particular events that we know we'll never be interested in. For this reason, there are several other methods found in the `DataStore` class which include `updateStore()`, `getNodes()`, `deleteNode()`, and several others that are specific to the XML data structure being encapsulated.

The `DefaultDataStore` Class

One of the subclasses of the `DataStore` class is the `DefaultDataStore` class, which represents all stores whose type is an `AbstractNode` such as `Page`, `Section`, `Paragraph`, and so on. We can't use the `DefaultDataStore` class for types such as `Footer` or `NewsSection` because they do not contain the same types of information in them or are not considered to be certain types (e.g., `Searchable`, `Lockable`, to name a few).

As far as loading goes, because we've ensured that all XML types in our data model have the ability to marshal themselves out as XML, our `updateStore()` method is easy to implement:

```
public void updateStore() {
    try {
        FileWriter writer = new FileWriter(storeFile);
        StringBuffer sb = new StringBuffer();
        sb.append("<?xml version=\"1.0\" encoding=\"UTF-8\"?>\n");
        sb.append("<" + rootElementName + ">\n");
        int size = nodes.size();
        for(int i = 0; i < size; i++) {
            ModelNode node = (ModelNode)nodes.get(i);
            sb.append(node.toXML());
        }
        sb.append("</" + rootElementName + ">\n");
        writer.write(sb.toString());
        writer.flush();
        writer.close();
    } catch(IOException ioe) { ioe.printStackTrace(); }
}
```

At this point, there should be warning bells going off suggesting that we're forgetting about our servlet and how multiple threads may be accessing our data store. However, what we've done is place the serialized control one level above the data stores: at the CMS data model level. All requests to change, list, delete, and add nodes of any sort trickle down from the ConnectionManager, to the CMSDefaultModel, which synchronizes all calls. Doing it at a higher level simplifies the logic within the data stores themselves, and also allows the data model to be in control of concurrency because it does manage all data stores.

Adding a node is simple as well. When a node (of type AbstractNode) is passed in to be added to the appropriate data store, the java.util.List is updated, the XML file that offers the persistence for this store is updated, and any listeners to model events are informed of the change:

```java
public boolean addNode(ModelNode node) {
    String nodeID = ((AbstractNode)node).getID();
    nodes.add(node);
    this.updateStore();
    this.updateListeners(ModelUpdateListener.NODE_ADDITION);
    return true;
}
```

Retrieving nodes in the form of a list generates a new list. We need this because retrieving nodes is based upon the search criteria of a session id value. The list, therefore, can only contain those nodes that have a match on the session id value:

```java
public List getNodes(String sessionID) {
    List list = new LinkedList();
    int size = nodes.size();
    for(int i = 0; i < size; i++) {
        AbstractNode node = (AbstractNode)nodes.get(i);
        if(node.getSessionID() == null
            || node.getSessionID().equals(sessionID))
            list.add(node);
    }
    return list;
}
```

We only return nodes whose session id value is null (meaning not locked by a session), or the session id value is the same as the one being passed in (which means it's the same session, and, therefore, the same user). Returning nodes that match and that are not locked means that users will not be able to see nodes (content) that are locked by other users. Deleting is similar, but we have to check both the session id as well as the id value of the node itself:

```java
public boolean deleteNode(ModelNode n) {
    if(n == null) return false;
    String sessionID = ((AbstractNode)n).getSessionID();
```

```
String nodeID = ((AbstractNode)n).getID();
int size = nodes.size();
for(int i = 0; i < size; i++) {
    AbstractNode node = (AbstractNode)nodes.get(i);
    if(node.getID().equals(nodeID)
        && node.getSessionID().equals(sessionID))
    {
        nodes.remove(i);
        this.updateStore();
        this.updateListeners(
            ModelUpdateListener.NODE_DELETION);
        return true;
    }
}
return false;
}
```

We cast the `ModelNode` to an `AbstractNode` so that we can retrieve the values for its session id and its node id. Both of these values are used as we cycle through the current data stores list of nodes to see if both the node id and the session id match. If so, we can proceed to delete a node, update the underlying XML document, and update all interested listeners of the event.

The `PageDataStore` Class

Looking at one of the implementing classes of the `DefaultDataStore` class, `PageDataStore`, we're offered a glimpse into how it handles parsing:

```
protected void parseStartElement() {
    currentElementName = parser.getName();
    if(currentElementName.equals("Page")) {
        currentElement = new Page(
            parser.getAttributeValue(null, "id"),
            parser.getAttributeValue(null, "author"),
            parser.getAttributeValue(null, "icon"),
            parser.getAttributeValue(null, "titleBar"),
            parser.getAttributeValue(null, "pageName"),
            Boolean.parseBoolean(parser.getAttributeValue(null,
                "isInMenu")),
            Boolean.parseBoolean(parser.getAttributeValue(null,
                "hasNews")),
            parser.getAttributeValue(null, "title"),
            parser.getAttributeValue(null, "link"),
            Boolean.parseBoolean(parser.getAttributeValue(null,
                "hasForumLogin")),
            Boolean.parseBoolean(parser.getAttributeValue(null,
                "hasSearchLink"))
        );
    } else if(currentElementName.equals("Stamp")) {
        DateTimeStamp stamp = new DateTimeStamp(
            parser.getAttributeValue(null, "dateCreated"),
```

```
        parser.getAttributeValue(null, "dateModified")
    );
    currentElement.setDateTimeStamp(stamp);

    } else if(currentElementName.equals("Keyword")) {
    currentElement.addKeyword(parser.getAttributeValue(null,
        "text"));
    }
}
```

For each XML element read in, a check is made to see if it is a Page element. We need to perform this check because Page elements contain child elements (Stamp, Keywords, or Keyword). If the element is a Page element then we extract the attribute values and place them in a new Page object. If the current element read in is a Stamp (timestamp), then we instantiate a new Stamp object. At all times for this data store, the current element can remain of type Page because we dig no deeper with other elements other than to add them to the Page object itself in memory. The endElement() method requires us to watch and see if the end element is a Page element, and if so, this is our cue that we can now add this element to the list of nodes this data store contains because we've come to the end of any more data that it may contain.

```
protected void parseEndElement() {
    currentElementName = parser.getName();
    if(currentElementName.equals("Page"))
        nodes.add(currentElement);

    currentElementName = "";
}
```

Because all other elements that are encountered within the Page element are empty elements, we do not need to handle any text events.

SUMMARY

ON THE CD

At this point, it is left up to the reader to explore the CD-ROM, specifically the *CMS-project\src\org\kucingCMS\server* subfolder, where many different server-side classes exist. Of particular interest may be the search engine (SearchEngine.java), the forum manager (ForumManager.java), and the page cache generator (PageCache-Generator.java). The code for these classes is complete and can be viewed for a better understanding as to how the server managed the content.

In this chapter, we've looked at how Web servers handle requests for various types of resources, and we've explored the interaction between a Web server and supporting technologies, such as Java servlets. We also looked at some of the features that are expected to exist for generating dynamic content generation, such as the ability to provide session tracking, forwarding, and configuring files. We explored the servlet model and how a multithreaded Web server interacts with our servlets and how we have to provide serialized access to our resources in order to provide concurrency with our resources and data. We also looked at setting up deployment descriptors and creating Ant build files, and we created both for our CMS project. Finally, we looked at some of the classes that are part of the CMS server-side logic. The next chapter helps make clear some of the communications between the server and the admin applet, as it explores the application protocol used to connect the two.

ENDNOTES

1. Hot linking falls under the category of stealing one's bandwidth. Creating a hot link is the procedure of linking to resources that are not actually on your site (usually images) but making it look like they are by simply referencing the resource directly in your HTML document. Typically the worst offenders are users of blogs where bandwidth and storage space are limited.
2. The Webalizer is open source software under the GPL and is found at: *http://www.mrunix.net/webalizer/.*

8 Protocol Topics for CMS Development

In This Chapter

- The HTTP protocol status codes
- The HTTP request and response headers
- Programmatically generating HTTP requests and responses using Java
- HTTP tunneling using a custom application protocol for our CMS

Creating programs that communicate with each other requires the use of some sort of protocol. A protocol is simply an agreed upon set of rules for sending data between two or more computers. In this chapter (and within the context of our CMS), we'll be investigating how to create a protocol. As mentioned in Chapter 2, we'll be using HTTP as the application-level protocol and building our custom CMS protocol on top of HTTP < , which allows our CMS to handle requests using conventional Web browser technology. The example source code listings referenced in this chapter are located in the *Chapter 8* folder on the CD-ROM and in the *CMS-project\src\org\kucingCMS\admin* and *CMS-project\src\ org\kucingCMS\server* subfolders on the CD-ROM.

ON THE CD

UNDERSTANDING HTTP

HTTP is the application protocol used on the Web to transport all content. It is a stateless protocol, meaning that there is no direct method of being able to store persistent data although other means can provide this functionality. At its core, HTTP is a simple request/response protocol that allows a Web server to answer requests with responses which contain the resource sought or a message stating why the resource was unavailable (via a number of message codes). HTTP can keep connections opened (via `Connection: keep-alive` in the protocol), but only if HTTP 1.1 is used instead of the older 1.0 version. Most of the interactions within the HTTP protocol are considered to be *idempotent*, which simply means that if a particular action occurs more than once, the same outcome should be expected. The following types of request methods are available in HTTP:

GET: A request method to retrieve whatever resource that is requested in the URL given.

HEAD: Similar to the GET request method; however; it only asks for the head of the HTTP protocol rather than the actual content that would normally come with it (as would in the case of the GET request method). This is a useful method for debugging or development where only the head value of the protocol itself is required.

POST: A request method to post some data to the server. The request method is applied to a particular resource based on the URL given by the client making the request. This request method simply logically adds a resource to the URL—not necessarily asking questions about whether it will replace whatever is currently there. A POST request method is useful when the resource(s) being sent is appending to existing resource(s).

PUT: PUT is similar to POST, although PUT is considered idempotent, whereas POST is not. With PUT, if the resource already exists, then PUTting again simply replaces the existing resource with what you are currently PUTting. With a POST, the request could be appending or replacing, it is not necessarily guaranteed.

DELETE: The DELETE request method is supposed to delete any resource that may exist on the server. This request method is rarely implemented (most likely due to the fact that a DELETE request is only a suggestion—the request may be overridden).

TRACE: This request method is a loop-back method and is only useful for performing diagnostics as to who is involved in the chain as far as requests. For example, if there any intermediate servers such as proxy servers intervening between the originator of the request and the server that accepts the request.

CONNECT: Used for connecting to a proxy that can dynamically switch to being a tunnel (i.e., SSL tunneling).

Status Codes

Along with the request methods, there are different types of status codes that are used within the protocol. It is important to know what these different status codes are, or at least what the most common status codes are, so that when your developing your own Web applications you can understand what the status is of any particular request.

Informational Status Codes (1xxx)

The 100-level codes convey information and do not contain anything else (sometimes not even the header). These status codes are not commonly encountered, but it is good to know what they mean because you may need to use them if your application-specific protocol you are building requires their functionality.

100 Continue: This is an interim response which simply tells the client to either send the rest of the request, or if the client has already done so, to sit tight and wait for the server to respond back

101 Switching Protocols: A request (from the client) to switch protocols. Usually used when a client is requesting to switch from HTTP 1.0 to HTTP 1.1.

Successful Status Codes (2xxx)

This class of requests is for being able to inform the client that the server has received the request and that the request was successfully received, understood, and accepted.

200 OK: Request succeeded. If a GET request method was made, then the information was sent to the client from the server. If a POST request method was made, then the information sent to the server from the client was accepted.

201 Created: A new resource was created on the server side. The server has sent a new URL for that particular resource that was created on the server side.

202 Accepted: The request has been accepted by the server. This request method is dubious because it may or may not be completed due to being denied by user intervention or another process intervening.

203 Non-Authoritative Information: Suggests that the resource requested is being gathered up (by the server) from third-party providers.

204 No Content: The request has been made (and is successful) but there is no content to provide to the client.

205 Reset Content: This is mostly used for when the client sends (either via PUT or POST) data to the server. This is a way for the server to tell the client to refresh its view (e.g., clear all input fields).

206 Partial Content: Only part of the content was sent to the client from the server from a GET request method.

Redirection Status Codes (3xxx)

This class of status codes requires the client (user agent) to take more action. Note that this doesn't necessarily suggest that the user personally has to instigate this—as long as the user agent automatically performs this task on the user's behalf.

300 Multiple Choices: This status code informs the user agent that there are a set of choices for the resource and that a choice needs to be made.

301 Moved Permanently: The resource being requested has been moved and one of the URLs provided in the response back offers the new location of the resource. The user should make note of this because this resource redirection may not be available in the future.

302 Found: The requested resource has been given a different temporary URL. The user should take action to go to that temporary URL.

303 See Other: Another URL contains the same resource and that other URL should be used instead. If a GET request was made, it is fine for the user agent to automatically redirect.

304 Note Modified: The client has made a GET request and the resource has not been modified (the client may have expected it to be via a POST).

305 Use Proxy: The requested resource must be accessed via a proxy (location provided).

306 (Unused): This status code was used in an older version of HTTP but is no longer being used (deprecated).

307 Temporary Redirect: The resource requested has temporarily been given a different URL. Added in HTTP 1.1 as a replacement for 302.

Error Status Codes (4xxx)

This class of status codes represents errors that have taken place. These codes can be applied to any request.

400 Bad Request: This type of error message is given when a malformed URL is given.

401 Unauthorized: This request requires user authentication and none was given.

402 Payment Required: Not used. For future use.

403 Forbidden: The request was refused but the server is not wishing to elaborate as to why the request was refused.

404 Not Found: The requested resource was simply not found at this point in time. Could be available later. Most common type of error message to the point where Web servers usually build a particular template page for 404 messages.

405 Method Not Allowed: The method request was not allowed (e.g., PUT).

406 Not Acceptable: This is usually due to the user agent requesting a resource that is not compatible with the types the user agent suggested it was capable of accepting from the beginning of the request.

407 Proxy Authentication Required: This status code is similar to 401 but is specific to authentication with a proxy server.

408 Request Timeout: The client did not make a request within the quantum that the server was expecting the request to be made in.

409 Conflict: This type of request is usually used with PUT method requests where an incorrect or unacceptable version of the resource was PUT on the server.

410 Gone: The resource is no longer available on the server and there is no forwarding address. More permanent than a 404 which indicates that the resource may be up later.

411 Length Required: The server requires that the request contain the Content-Length field, which states the actual length of the resource being sent.

412 Precondition Failed: A precondition given in one or more of the request header fields evaluated to false on the server.

413 Request Entity Too Large: What is being sent (i.e., the resource) is too large for the server to accept or process or both. This could be useful for the POST or PUT method requests when the user is attempting to send (for example) an image file that is quite large (e.g., 10 MB or more).

414 Request-URI Too Long: Although rare, this could happen with a POST being converted to a GET with URL rewriting being used.

415 Unsupported Media Type: The format of the resource is not supported by the request method being used.

416 Requested Range Not Satisfiable: The client included an unsatisfiable Range field value in the request header.

417 Expectation Failed: The value in the Expect header field could not be met.

Server Error Status Codes (5xxx)

This class of status codes provides error codes specific for servers to return if they are incapable of processing a particular request. With dynamic content generation, these types of status codes arise from some sort of programming error from the Web application.

500 Internal Server Error: Some sort of unexpected condition arose from the request. With Java servlets, it usually means that something inside of the Java servlet code failed to handle the request (application programming error).

501 Not Implemented: The functionality required to fulfill the request is not there (e.g., no implementation for the PUT or POST requests).

502 Bad Gateway: The server which was contacted is a proxy server and received an invalid response further down the stream from another server.

503 Service Unavailable: The server cannot perform the processing for the request due to maintenance or overloading of the server itself.

504 Gateway Timeout: A server, which is acting as a proxy, did not receive a response further upstream from the server whose resource is being requested.

505 HTTP Version Not Supported: The type of request made (along with the combination of header fields) was not supported by the currently supported version of HTTP.

Example Interactions

Seeing some of the interactions between the server and the client can help demystify what is being done, even though in Java we have many classes available to us in order to abstract some of the details (at least with the syntax) of HTTP.

The GET Request Method

When a user types in a URL inside of the Web browser, clicks a hyperlink based in a previously loaded Web page or selects a bookmark link from the menu, a request is made for content using the GET request method. A typical GET request from the Web browser looks something like:

```
GET / HTTP/1.1
Host: www.bcit.ca
Connection: keep-alive
Accept-Encoding: gzip
Accept: text/xml,application/xml,application/xhtml+xml,text/html;
   q=0.9,text/plain;q=0.8,image/png,*/*;q=0.5
Accept-Language: en-us,en;q=0.5
Accept-Charset: ISO-8859-1,utf-8;q=0.7,*;q=0.7
User-Agent: Mozilla/5.0 (Windows; U; Windows NT 5.1; en-US;
   rv:1.8.0.1) Gecko/20060111 Firefox/1.5.0.1
```

The top of the header consists of the type of request being made, along with the URL to the resource (in this case the '/' is given, which states we want the root of the resource) with the version of HTTP being used. The next few fields offer us some insight into what the Web browser is expecting. For example, the host (server) that should be found is www.bcit.ca, which is where to grab the root resource. The Connection field accepts the value close or the value keep-alive. The value keep-alive is the default for HTTP 1.1 and is useful because it keeps the connection opened between the client (Web browser) and the server so that if there are multiple requests being made, they are all made within the same socket connection. This is more efficient than creating new socket connections for each request, which costs in time. Rarely is only one request made because Web pages contain images, mul-

timedia content, and other types of files linked inside of them that should be downloaded and viewed by the Web browser.

*It is important to understand that when a Web browser makes a request for a Web
page, it is actually making several requests. If the Web page requested contains
many different resources such as images, interactive animation files, references to
Cascading Style Sheets (CSSs), or Javascript files, the Web browser has to make a
request for each file. However, when the user chooses a Web page to view, the user
sees this all happen as one complete atomic operation. This is an illusion but a convenient one because it would be painstakingly monotonous for users to have to
make requests for each resource found or associated with a page.*

The OK Response Method

The server, of course, must respond. If the resource is found, then the server usually responds with a status code of 200 in the header and then proceeds with the
actual content. A requested page response may look something like:

```
HTTP/1.1 200 OK{CRLF}
Date: Wed, 15 Mar 2006 01:54:45 GMT{CRLF}
Server: Apache/1.3.27 (Unix) mod_ssl/2.8.12 OpenSSL/0.9.6b
  PHP/4.3.0{CRLF}
Connection: close{CRLF}
Transfer-Encoding: chunked{CRLF}
Content-Type: text/html{CRLF}
{CRLF}
<!doctype html public "-//W3C//DTD HTML 4.01 Transitional//EN">
{CRLF}
{CRLF}
<!- Page Updated by Marqui on 3/9/2006 10:53:08 AM p58s100 0 ->
{CRLF}
<html>{CRLF}
<head>{CRLF}
</head>{CRLF}
  ...
<html>{CRLF}
```

We've included {CRLF} to represent carriage return and line feed couples, which
are found at the end of each line because these characters are non-printable. In the
case when the server is sending data back to the client, there needs to be a percep-
tible boundary between the HTTP header and the content that flows after the
header. For example, we need a clear distinction between the header itself (and its
fields) and the actual data that makes up the content sent (e.g., a JPEG image). The
protocol (as per the HTTP specification from the W3C) requires that a blank line
with only the pair carriage return/line feed (CRLF) be found with nothing preced-

ing the two, which is then followed by the actual content data [Fielding99]. Another example, this time with an image, would look like:

```
HTTP/1.1 200 OK{CRLF}
Date: Tue, 14 Mar 2006 22:43:05 GMT{CRLF}
Server: Apache/1.3.27 (Unix) mod_ssl/2.8.12
  OpenSSL/0.9.6b PHP/4.3.0{CRLF}
Last-Modified: Tue, 07 Dec 2004 21:21:36 GMT{CRLF}
ETag: "47b2e-be8-41b61ee0"{CRLF}
Accept-Ranges: bytes{CRLF}
Content-Length: 3048{CRLF}
Connection: close{CRLF}
Content-Type: image/gif{CRLF}
{CRLF}
4749463839616801 3000F7A200C1C1C1
4444449F9F9F7171 71E3E3E3D7D7D7AA
AAAA5B5B5B888888 4F4F4FB5B5B5CCCC
...
4FFBDADF2420003B
```

The image request offers us a status code of 200, which tells us the server successfully returned the resource. The date is given, the server type, and a few other pieces of information including the content type, which is of type image/gif which is the MIME type. Although we didn't specify this type as being acceptable it is assumed because GIF is one of the earlier formats to gain Web acceptance. Right after the content type is given, we have a blank line with only a carriage return and line feed. This signals that the header is completed, and that what remains is the actual content. We're showing the actual image data as a series of Unicode values (in hexadecimal) in eight byte groupings (16 bytes on a row), and we remind ourselves that the first sequence of values found in a GIF image file is the version of GIF used. This case we have GIF89a (Unicode value 47 for 'G', Unicode value 49 for 'I', Unicode value 46 for 'F', and so on).

HTTP in Java

Now that we've seen the low-level details, we can appreciate the API calls that we can use so that we don't have to write this data out manually. On the client side, we could put together the following code snippet to send a GET request and retrieve the header as well as the content as found in Listing 8.1.

LISTING 8.1   ClientRequestTest.java

```
import java.net.*;
import java.io.*;
```

```java
public class ClientRequestTest {
    public static void main(String[] args) {
        try {
            URL url = new URL(args[0]);
            HttpURLConnection urlConnect = (HttpURLConnection)url.
                openConnection();
            urlConnect.setRequestMethod("GET");
            String headerName = "";
            String headerValue = "";
            int index = 0;
            while(true) {
                headerName = urlConnect.getHeaderFieldKey(index);
                headerValue = urlConnect.getHeaderField(index);
                index++;
                if(headerName == null && headerValue == null)
                    break;
                else if(headerName == null)
                    System.out.println(headerValue);
                else
                    System.out.println(headerName + ": "
                        + headerValue);
            }
            InputStream is = urlConnect.getInputStream();
            StringBuilder sb = new StringBuilder();
            int ch;
            while((ch = is.read()) != -1) {
                sb.append((char)ch);
            }
            System.out.println(sb.toString());

        } catch (Exception e) { e.printStackTrace(); }
    }
}
```

The code in Listing 8.1 gives us the basis for a Web browser, although we'd have to add a significant amount of code to process the content. The receiving end, of course, requires that requests for content are handled. The starting point for code that we'd want to create for a Web server would need to handle the requests for content. Listing 8.2 offers us that.

LISTING 8.2 ServerResponseTest.java

```java
import java.net.*;
import java.io.*;

public class ServerResponseTest {
    public static void main(String[] args) {
        try {
            ServerSocket server = new ServerSocket(80);
            while(true) {
```

```
                    ResponseThread rt =
                        new ResponseThread(server.accept());
                }
            } catch (Exception e) { e.printStackTrace(); }
        }
    }

    class ResponseThread implements Runnable {
        private Thread thread;
        private Socket socket;
        public ResponseThread(Socket socket) {
            this.socket = socket;
            thread = new Thread(this);
            thread.start();
        }
        public void run() {
            String CRLF = "\r\n";
            try {
                StringBuilder sb = new StringBuilder();
                String text = "";
                BufferedReader br = new BufferedReader(
                    new InputStreamReader(socket.getInputStream()));
                while(!(text = br.readLine()).equals(""))
                    sb.append(text + "\n");
                PrintWriter pw =
                    new PrintWriter(socket.getOutputStream(), true);
                pw.println("HTTP/1.0 200 OK\r\n");
                pw.println("<html>\n  <head></head>\n  <body>\n");
                pw.println("    <h2>Client Request:</h2>\n");
                pw.println("    <pre>" + sb.toString() + "</pre>");
                pw.println("  </body>\n</html>");
                pw.flush();
                pw.close();
                br.close();

            } catch(Exception e) { e.printStackTrace(); }
        }
    };
```

Listing 8.2 shows a class that performs nothing more than using a ServerSocket (which is listening on port 80) to receive requests from client connections. The ResponseThread class implements the Runnable interface and contains its own thread for running as a separate line of execution. This way, each request is handled by a separate thread (how most Web servers operate). The run method of each ResponseThread object reads the input coming in from the Socket (using the Socket's input stream), and sends out a response. In this case, all that is being returned is the information that was found in the request header, although a real Web server would be retrieving resources such as Web pages, images, and other requested types of files and resources.

Protocol Tunneling

With the Internet being such a common part of home computing, network and computer security is paramount. Because of this, most computers are behind firewalls. A *firewall* can be either a hardware device or a software application that really acts as the gatekeeper to connectivity by either allowing or denying data to or from a computer or group of computers. From an application programming perspective, the sending and receiving happens via a *socket* connection, which is really just a software abstraction representing an open communication connection with another computer. Establishing the connection to another computer requires the socket to choose a *port*. A port is another software abstraction (because each port does not actually map one-to-one to a hardware port) which acts much like a channel or frequency to which both the end points (computers) can use to send data to each other. Firewalls can restrict data from being sent to or being sent from particular ports for security reasons, as well as restrict certain types of data from being sent or received based on the protocols being used.

Typical firewall configurations (specifically home office networks) allows for certain ports and certain types of data to be sent and received. One of the common types of data in particular is Web content via the HTTP protocol—which we've been looking at in this chapter. Web traffic is considered to be safer than unknown content and streams and port 80 is known as the default port in which Web servers offer their service on. Based on this knowledge, we can, therefore, ensure that our application is accessible behind firewalls by using what is called *protocol tunneling,* or in the case of a Web application, *HTTP tunneling.* HTTP tunneling is the technique of slipping data into a stream of what appears to be typical Web data. Recall that we've so far seen the data that comes in from requests and responses, and we've even created a couple of simple applications (a client and a server) which can connect to each other (or other programs) using HTTP as the application-level protocol.

With Java servlets, we can gain access to the input and output streams and fire off data that may not normally be considered normal Web content. Recall from Chapter 7 that we were able to write to a servlet's output stream using the following code:

```
public void doGet(HttpServletRequest req,
    HttpServletResponse res)
    throws ServletException, IOException {
    ServletOutputStream out = res.getOutputStream();
    out.println("<html><head></head><body><p>Hi!"
        + "</p></body></html>");
}
```

This gave us the ability to write back to the requestor (the Web browser) Web data. Additionally, we can also accept data from a servlet using the servlet's input stream:

```
public void doGet(HttpServletRequest req,
    HttpServletResponse res)
    throws ServletException, IOException {
    BufferedInputStream bis =
        new BufferedInputStream(req.getInputStream());
    // do something with the data
}
```

The `HttpServletRequest` class offers us an intput stream of type `ServletInputStream`, which allows us to receive the data coming in from the client. The `HttpServletResponse` class offers us an output stream of type `ServletOutputStream`, which allows us to send to the client. With these classes in hand, we can turn toward creating a very specialized stream of data: serialization of objects.

Using object serialization is a handy feature because it requires little work on our part. Serializing objects in Java allows us to save the state of an object from the JVM to a more persistent state such as a file that is saved to the filesystem. By doing this, we can later on deserialize the object and continue to use it. Using object serialization within an application protocol allows us to quickly and easily save objects (such as our data model) and forward those objects to another application. In the case of our CMS, we can pass the custom built object model that represents XML nodes from the server to the client. The only stipulation we are presented with is that the client must have the same classes that the server's objects were generated from. However, not only must the classes exist on the client, but they must also be the same versions of the classes that were generated during a compile time build.

Tunneling with the Client

From the client side, we can bundle up a request as a `java.util.List`, which contains a collection of objects and sends it using an `HttpURLConnection` object:

```
public void sendMessage(List message) throws
    MalformedURLException, ClassNotFoundException, IOException {
    URL url = null;
    url = new URL("http://localhost:8080/admin.connection");
    HttpURLConnection con =
        (HttpURLConnection)url.openConnection();
    con.setRequestProperty("Content-Type",
        "application/x-java-serialized-object");
    con.setRequestMethod("POST");
    con.setDoOutput(true);
    con.setDoInput(true);
    con.setUseCaches(false);
    con.setDefaultUseCaches(false);
```

```
    ObjectOutputStream oos =
        new ObjectOutputStream(con.getOutputStream());

    oos.writeObject(message);
    oos.flush();
    oos.close();
    ObjectInputStream ois = new
ObjectInputStream(con.getInputStream());
        List response = (List)ois.readObject();
    }
```

We must ensure that we set the MIME type, in our case application/x-java-serialized-object. We also must ensure that we're setting the request method to POST because that's what our application is doing. We create an object output stream, pass it the HttpURLConnection object's output stream, and then tell the object output stream to write the objects.

Tunneling with the Server

On the server side, we're operating within the context of a servlet. The servlet offers us the input and output streams that are necessary to communicate with the client. The servlet interface offers us a tidy abstraction which shields us from the details of the HTTP protocol. The servlet's response to the client looks something like:

```
public void doPost(HttpServletRequest req, HttpServletResponse res)
        throws ServletException, ClassNotFoundException,
        ClassCastException, IOException {
    ObjectInputStream ois =
        new ObjectInputStream(req.getInputStream());
    List message = (List)ois.readObject();
    ois.close();
    ObjectOutputStream oos =
        new ObjectOutputStream(res.getOutputStream());
    List messageResponse = new LinkedList();
    oos.writeObject(messageResponse);
    oos.flush();
    oos.close();
}
```

We must always remember to return something back because that is part of the requirement of the HTTP protocol. All of the details of HTTP headers have been hidden from us, other than setting a few things on the client side such as POST and the MIME type. However, all of the other details such as length, appropriate numbers of carriage return and line feed characters, and which particular header fields we place in the stream are completely hidden from us. Best of all, our protocol tunnels through HTTP and so it should work without any problems even if the CMS server is operating behind a firewall.

CREATING THE CMS PROTOCOL

Using HTTP tunneling with object serialization as the data stream for our CMS communication protocol, we must now define the particulars of how the client and server interact.

Protocol Design

As mentioned earlier, the communications between the client and the server must always be confined within the limits of the HTTP protocol, which is a stateless protocol. Additionally when a client makes a request, the server must respond in the least with an error code. Working in that context, we can define a set of requests and responses that offer the functionality we are interested in providing. For the remainder of this chapter, all examples are from either the *CMS-project\src\org\kucingCMS\admin* or the *CMS-project\src\org\kucingCMS\server* subfolders on the

ON THE CD

CD-ROM.

Because we are sending and receiving objects, we need to define an organized grouping of objects for both requests and for responses. Figure 8.1 shows the request groupings with objects in our serialized protocol. When we create a `java.util.List`, the contents follow one of those formats.

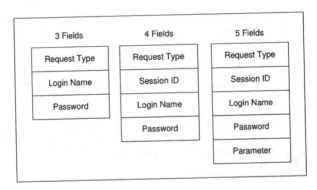

FIGURE 8.1 Request format for the CMS protocol.

Additionally, we need to specify a format for responding to the requests. This ensures that clients are able to decipher the data sent back. Figure 8.2 offers the response types. With these groupings, we can start applying them to each specific request/response scenario.

For consistency and a mind for a reduction in time spent debugging, we define a class called `ProtocolConstants`, which contains a bunch of string constant values that represent each type of request and response message that can be made. This

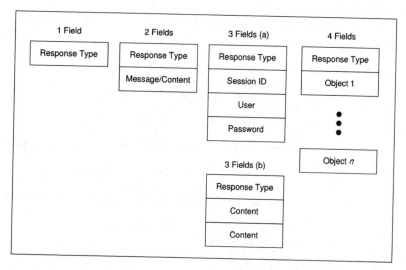

FIGURE 8.2   Response format for the CMS protocol.

way, both the client and the server can consistently communicate using the exact same values.

Login-Logout Requests

Because we're using HTTP and our own custom protocol (i.e., object serialization), we do need to manage our own session id values somewhat. As well, every request made after login must require that the user attempting to log in provides a valid session id. If the session id is not valid, then entry into the CMS is denied and a message back is given. We'll first look at how to log in a client.

Client Login Request

The very first thing any user needs to do in order to perform any actions is to log in. A login consists of sending the login request, the login name, and the password. A login request on the client side (within the AdminTool class) looks like:

```
List request = new LinkedList();
request.add(ProtocolConstants.LOGIN);
request.add(userName);
request.add(password);
ObjectInputStream ois = this.sendMessage(request);
```

The sendMessage() method accepts a java.util.List and fires it off to the server via HTTP tunneling. This follows the three field format for requests from Figure 8.1. The userName and the password variables retrieve the actual values that the user typed into the text fields. Meanwhile, on the server side, the request is received by the ConnectionManager class:

```java
String user = (String)message.get(1);
String password = (String)message.get(2);
HttpSession session = req.getSession(true);
session.setAttribute("user", user);
session.setAttribute("password", password);
List responseMsg = new LinkedList();
if(UserManager.getInstance().loginNonForumUser(user, password,
    session.getId())) {
    responseMsg.add(ProtocolConstants.LOGIN_ACK);
    responseMsg.add(session.getId());
    responseMsg.add(UserManager.getInstance().getUser(user, password));
} else {
    responseMsg.add(ProtocolConstants.LOGIN_NACK);
    session.invalidate();
}
sendMessage(res, responseMsg);
```

And the server either sends back a value of LOGIN_ACK, a session id, and a copy of the user object that exists on the server. This copy is a useful data structure for the client so that the individual values (login name, first name, last name, password, etc.) do not have to be managed separately.

Client Logout Request

When a client requests to logout (handled by the AdminTool class), the client sends a request in the form of:

```java
List request = new LinkedList();
request.add(ProtocolConstants.LOGOUT);
request.add(sessionID);
request.add(user.getLogin());
request.add(user.getPassword());
// Now get the response back:
ObjectInputStream ois = this.sendMessage(request);
```

The server (ConnectionManager) receives the request as:

```java
String sessionID = (String)message.get(1);
String user = (String)message.get(2);
String password = (String)message.get(3);
List responseMsg = new LinkedList();
HttpSession session = req.getSession(false);
if(UserManager.getInstance().logoffUser(user, password, sessionID))
{
    session.invalidate();
    CMSDefaultModel.getInstance().unlockContent(sessionID);
    responseMsg.add(ProtocolConstants.LOGOUT_ACK);
```

```
    } else {
        responseMsg.add(ProtocolConstants.LOGOUT_NACK);
    }
    sendMessage(res, responseMsg);
```

This allows the server to log out the user, assuming that the login name, password, and session id are all correct. When the server returns with a response, the message is either in the form of an acknowledgement (agreement and, therefore, the request was successful) or a non-acknowledgement, which means that that the request was denied.

User Account Requests

Managing user accounts requires adding users, editing the current account, and deleting user accounts. Each request is different and, therefore, needs to be handled separately. We'll just look at the process of adding a user and leave it to the reader to explore the other requests by looking at the source code provided on the CD-ROM.

Add User Request

Adding a user actually requires a two-step process that the end user never actually sees. Recall that Chapter 5 discussed that all objects must be created on the server side. This is to ensure that id values are not duplicated. Because of this, when we add user accounts, we're actually performing two requests at once: create a user, add the user to the data store. The first step (creating a user) is requested first on the client side via the AddUserPanel class:

```
User user = caller.getUser();
List request = new LinkedList();
request.add(ProtocolConstants.CREATE_USERS);
request.add(caller.getSessionID());
request.add(user.getLogin());
request.add(user.getPassword());
request.add(1);
ObjectInputStream ois = caller.sendMessage(request);
List response = (List)ois.readObject();
String msg = (String)response.get(0);
List userList = (List)response.get(1);
ois.close();
if(msg.equals(ProtocolConstants.CREATE_USERS_ACK)) {
    User newUser = (User)userList.get(0);
    List addUserRequest = new LinkedList();
    addUserRequest.add(ProtocolConstants.ADD_USERS);
    addUserRequest.add(caller.getSessionID());
    addUserRequest.add(user.getLogin());
    addUserRequest.add(user.getPassword());
    List newUsersList = new LinkedList();
    newUsersList.add(newUser);
```

```
addUserRequest.add(newUsersList);
ObjectInputStream ois2 =
    caller.sendMessage(addUserRequest);
List response2 = (List)ois2.readObject();
String msg2 = (String)response2.get(0);
String details = (String)response2.get(1);
if(msg2.equals(ProtocolConstants.ADD_USERS_ACK)) {
    this.resetFields();
} else if(msg2.equals(ProtocolConstants.ADD_USERS_NACK)) {
    JOptionPane.showMessageDialog(this, "Failed.",
        "Failed to add user.", JOptionPane.ERROR_MESSAGE);
}
ois2.close();
} else {
    caller.setBackToLoginForm();
    JOptionPane.showMessageDialog(this, "Request failed.",
        "Error", JOptionPane.ERROR_MESSAGE);
}
```

We first tell the server that we're interesting in creating a user (CREATE_USERS). We pass our session id, login name, and password, as well as the number of user objects we want to create (one in this case). We send our message and await a response. If the server told us that it was successful (CREATE_USERS_ACK), then we attempt to extract the newly created user object and populate its members by grabbing the form field values (not shown). We tell the server that we want to add a user to the system (ADD_USERS) and send it off with again our session id, username, and password, and we bundle the user object in list. Although our client applet only creates one user at a time, the protocol with the server supports multiple user additions based on the fact that it accepts a list of users to add instead of just one user. This is handy if we later on decide that we wish to add that functionality within the admin applet. This all gets bundled and sent off again to the server via our sendMessage() method. If the server responds with an acknowledgement (ADD_USERS_ACK), we clear the fields and allow the user to do it again if he desires. If the server responded with a no acknowledgement (ADD_USERS_NACK), then we retrieve the error message and display it to the user.

The server handles these requests separately. First, the create request is handled by the ConnectionManager class:

```
String sessionID = (String)message.get(1);
String user = (String)message.get(2);
String password = (String)message.get(3);
List responseMsg = new LinkedList();
if(UserManager.getInstance().authenticateUser(user, password,
    sessionID)) {
    responseMsg.add(ProtocolConstants.CREATE_USERS_ACK);
    Integer numberOfUsers = (Integer)message.get(4);
    List users = new LinkedList();
```

```
    for(int i = 0; i < numberOfUsers.intValue(); i++) {
        User u = new User("", "", "", "", User.FORUM_USER);
        users.add(u);
    }
    responseMsg.add(users);
} else {
    responseMsg.add(ProtocolConstants.CREATE_USERS_NACK);
}
sendMessage(res, responseMsg);
```

What's important to note on the create request is that none of these objects are actually added to any data store. It would be an error to add them at this point because the complete transaction may fail, in which case we would have to roll back the request; this could cause problems if other clients are updating as well because the data store could get tied up for some time. The add request is then performed by the ConnectionManager class:

```
String sessionID = (String)message.get(1);
String user = (String)message.get(2);
String password = (String)message.get(3);
List responseMsg = new LinkedList();
if(UserManager.getInstance().authenticateUser(user, password,
    sessionID)) {
    responseMsg.add(ProtocolConstants.ADD_USERS_ACK);
    List usersToAdd = (List)message.get(4);
    int size = usersToAdd.size();
    StringBuilder sb = new StringBuilder();
    for(int i = 0; i < size; i++) {
        User u = (User)usersToAdd.get(i);
        if(UserManager.getInstance().addUser(u))
            sb.append("User: " + u.getLogin() + " added.");
        else
            sb.append("User: " + u.getLogin() + " add failed.");
    }
    responseMsg.add(sb.toString());
} else {
    responseMsg.add(ProtocolConstants.ADD_USERS_NACK);
}
sendMessage(res, responseMsg);
```

Content Management Requests

For a detailed example of adding a content chunk, we'll look at the image gallery content chunk type because it requires some extra abilities.

Listing Images On Server Request

The ImageGalleryPanel class needs to first display to the user the list of files that are found within the server's set of folders. The client first makes a request for the file list with the following code:

```
listRequest.add(ProtocolConstants.IMAGE_FILE_LISTING);
listRequest.add(caller.getAdminTool().getSessionID());
listRequest.add(user.getLogin());
listRequest.add(user.getPassword());
ObjectInputStream ois =
    caller.getAdminTool().sendMessage(listRequest);
List listResponse = (List)ois.readObject();
String msg = (String)listResponse.get(0);
ois.close();
if(msg.equals(ProtocolConstants.IMAGE_FILE_LISTING_ACK)) {
    List imageList = (List)listResponse.get(1);
    int size = imageList.size();
    for(int j = 0; j < size; j++) {
        imageFilesListModel.addElement(imageList.get(j));
    }
    caller.getAdminTool().showContentForm();
} else {
    caller.getAdminTool().setBackToLoginForm();
    JOptionPane.showMessageDialog(this,
        "File listing denied",
        "List Request Denied.",
        JOptionPane.ERROR_MESSAGE);
}
```

The client, through the `ImageGalleryPanel` class, requests a file list (`IMAGE_FILE_LISTING`) and packages up the session id, login, and password (as per our design from earlier). In the case where the request succeeded, a list is extracted from the second position in the list that was sent as a response. The list simply contains file names. These file names can be displayed to the user so that he can choose these file names for the image gallery. On the server side, this is handled by the `CMSDefaultModel` class:

```
response.add(ProtocolConstants.IMAGE_FILE_LISTING_ACK);
java.util.List fileList = new LinkedList();
String imageDirectory = webAppPath + File.separator + "media"
    + File.separator + "images";
File dir = new File(imageDirectory);
String[] imageFiles = dir.list();
int size = imageFiles.length;
for(int k = 0; k < size; k++) {
    String name = imageFiles[k];
    String lower = name.toLowerCase();
    if(lower.endsWith(".bmp") || lower.endsWith(".gif") ||
        lower.endsWith(".jpg") || lower.endsWith(".jpeg") ||
        lower.endsWith(".png") || lower.endsWith(".tif") ||
        lower.endsWith(".tiff"))
    fileList.add(name);
}
response.add(fileList);
```

The server checks the images directory and filters all file names by only choosing files that end with `bmp`, `gif`, `jpg`, `jpeg`, `png`, `tiff`, or `tif` (and any case combinations of these names). We send them back as a response. Although we don't see any validation taking place here, the `CMSDefaultModel` class only sees any requests that have been authenticated by the `ConnectionManager` class earlier.

Adding Image Gallery Content Chunks Request

The `ImageGalleryPanel` class offers the functionality of adding new image galleries although some of its functionality is found in its superclass `ContentChunkPanel`. Within the `ImageGalleryPanel` class, the action event-handling method simply contains two calls to the superclass `ContentChunkPanel`:

```
super.createContent(ModelNode.IMAGE_GALLERY);
packageImageGallery();
super.addContent();
resetFields();
```

Like creating user objects on the server, we must first perform a create request and then add them. The code in the `ContentChunkPanel` class offers us the following code for creating a new content chunk:

```
List createRequest = new LinkedList();
createRequest.add(ProtocolConstants.CREATE_CONTENT);
createRequest.add(caller.getSessionID());
createRequest.add(user.getLogin());
createRequest.add(user.getPassword());
List nodesToCreate = new LinkedList();
nodesToCreate.add(nodeType);
nodesToCreate.add(new Integer(1));
nodesToCreate.add(ModelNode.SECTION_CHUNK);
nodesToCreate.add(new Integer(1));
createRequest.add(nodesToCreate);
ObjectInputStream ois =
    caller.sendMessage(createRequest);
List createResponse = (List)ois.readObject();
String msg = (String)createResponse.get(0);
ois.close();
if(msg.equals(ProtocolConstants.CREATE_CONTENT_ACK)) {
    chunk = (AbstractNode)createResponse.get(1);
    sc = (SectionChunk)createResponse.get(2);
} else {
    caller.setBackToLoginForm();
    JOptionPane.showMessageDialog(this,
        "Create Content Chunk Failed!",
        "Create Content Chunk Request Denied.",
        JOptionPane.ERROR_MESSAGE);
}
```

As usual, we send user information. We create another list, which contains an integer number stating the number of content chunks to create. We're passing a variable called nodeType, which was passed in by the subclass ImageGalleryPanel as ModelNode.IMAGE_GALLERY. This helps the superclass method become generic enough that we can use it with all subchunk content types. The next step is to request another type of object (ModelNode.SECTION_CHUNK). We need this because our data model contains many-to-many relationships. The client has to display to the user the appropriate relationship between the content chunk and the section it belongs to. We then package this all up (the nodesToCreate list is placed inside of the createRequest list) and send it to the server. If the response is an acknowledgement, then we can retrieve the content chunk (chunk variable) and the section chunk (sc variable) which is processed by the admin applet and displayed in the UI. The server side handles the request with:

```
response.add(ProtocolConstants.CREATE_CONTENT_ACK);
java.util.List nodeListingsRequests =
    (java.util.List)request.get(4);
int size = nodeListingsRequests.size();
for(int i = 0; i < size; i++) {
    String nodeType = (String)nodeListingsRequests.get(i);
    i++; // increment
    Integer integer = (Integer)nodeListingsRequests.get(i);
    int numberOfNodes = integer.intValue();
    for(int j = 0; j < numberOfNodes; j++) {
        ModelNode node = this.createNode(nodeType);
        if(node != null) response.add(node);
    }
}
```

Each type and number of that type is extracted and the server attempts to fulfill the request. The server contains the call

```
ModelNode node = this.createNode(nodeType);
```

which returns an object of the appropriate requested type. Again, note that, at this point, we are not adding content to the server, we're merely creating them and passing them over to the client (admin applet). In the event that the user disconnects, these content chunks will be lost, although this won't cause any problem on the server other than a break in the contiguous numbering id values of certain nodes. Adding content is similar to the previous example where we added user objects to the server. To see the protocol in more detail, the CD-ROM contains all of the source code from the CMS project.

ON THE CD

SUMMARY

In this chapter, we've looked at the HTTP protocol by studying the status codes it uses and what they mean. We've also looked at what HTTP request headers look like and what HTTP response headers look like, as well as how to programmatically request and respond to HTTP protocol events. We discussed how HTTP tunneling can be used to send application-specific data within HTTP, which helps eliminate the problems of firewalls. Finally, we looked at some of the finer points within our CMS protocol for the admin applet and the CMS server to communicate with one another. In the next chapter, we'll be looking at how to build the admin applet for our CMS so that we can manage the content, manage users, and also change the look and feel of the entire CMS with the single click of a button.

9

Implementing the Admin Applet

In This Chapter

- Performing client-side validation, such as bounds checking
- Building the CMS administration applet
- Creating layouts with Abeille Forms Designer
- Sending and receiving model data
- Creating the login form, the managing content form, and the administration applet itself

U ser interface design is an entire field of study on its own, so we will only be looking briefly at this area as it applies to our administration applet that allows users to manage the content in our CMS. The example source code listings referenced in this chapter are located on the CD-ROM in the *Chapter 9* folder. The Java classes created at the end of the chapter, in the section *Creating The Admin Tool* are located on the CD-ROM in the *CMS-project\src\org\kucingCMS\ admin* and *CMS-project\src\org\kucingCMS\contentmodel* subfolders.

ON THE CD

CLIENT-SIDE VALIDATION

Performing validation in forms is the process of ensuring that what the user enters as data is within the bounds or range of acceptable values. As mentioned earlier, we can prevent incorrect values to be entered by restricting how the user enters data. For example, instead of entering a date value in by hand, the user can choose the date by using combo boxes, or even better would be a calendar component that allows the user to choose a date from an interactive calendar. However, some data needs to be entered in by the user. We also have situations where a particular sequence of data choices has to be made. For example, a user may have to choose between a credit card payment and money order. If the user chooses credit card payment, then he has to fill out the fields for the credit card form. Otherwise, these fields can be left blank.

All of these checks made should happen on the client-side for several reasons. First, the server shouldn't be required to know the details of particular client-side functionality. This would cause an extra level of complexity if there were more than one type of client-side application. The server would have to know the difference between various different client-side applications. Second, if the server handles many different clients per minute or worse, per second, the burden placed on the server to handle validation may affect server response times.

Another reason is that the server software grows in size because it has to handle the validation rules increasing the size in memory of the server application. From a design perspective, including validation on the server is not an elegant solution because it requires the server to know about particular UI components—the server has to know which field was left blank, for example.

While the validation should be left to the client-side, this does not mean that the server performs no error checking. If the server does no checking, we risk the possibility of inconsistent data in the least. Worse case, we may have opened up a potential security hole in our software allowing hostile client applications to exploit the security hole. The important difference is that error checking focuses on the data and the data structures that house the data, whereas validation focuses on the UI components that support the entry of data. The server-side software can still refuse to accept data that is either corrupt or incomplete even though the user interface has validated the data (or not).

Bounds Checking

When we perform bounds checking, we're not necessarily checking for errors (although errors can be part of it). We're restricting the bounds or range of acceptable values that the user is allowed to type in.

Number Bounds

Checking number values is one of the easier bounds checking operations to perform because the use of an equality operator will suffice—especially if the number values are integer numbers instead of real (floating point) numbers. If we were allowing a user to type in the number of orders of a particular product like in Figure 9.1 that he wanted to purchase, there may exist a business rule that restricts that user from ordering more than 10 items.

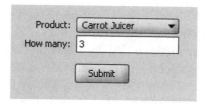

FIGURE 9.1   Number bounds check in order form.

Our code (in Java) should handle a negative number, zero, a positive number over 10, or a floating point number (you can't order 2.5 items) and any non-integer numbers:

```java
String value = howMany.getText();
int intValue = 0;
boolean valid = false;
try {
    intValue = Integer.parseInt(value);
    if(intValue < 0)
        JOptionPane.showMessageDialog(null,
        "Numbers cannot be negative.", "Item Number Error",
        JOptionPane.ERROR_MESSAGE);
    else if(intValue == 0)
        JOptionPane.showMessageDialog(null,
        "Can't select zero items.", "Item Number Error",
        JOptionPane.ERROR_MESSAGE);
    else if(intValue > 10)
        JOptionPane.showMessageDialog(null,
        "Max item count is 10.", "Item Number Error",
        JOptionPane.ERROR_MESSAGE);
    else
        valid = true;
} catch(NumberFormatException nfe) {
    JOptionPane.showMessageDialog(null,
        "Please enter a whole number.", "Item Number Error",
        JOptionPane.ERROR_MESSAGE);
}
if(valid) submitRequest(); // submits request
```

We can make use of the exception handling capability as well as the parsing ability of the Integer class in Java. We should offer descriptive feedback (remember one of our heuristics); so it makes sense to split up the cases of greater than 10, less than zero, and zero so that we can offer up separate messages.

String Bounds

In Java, checking bounds with string values is easy because the `string` class offers many convenience methods that eliminate the mechanics of writing string manipulation methods ourselves. With string values, we are usually attempting to ensure the size of a string. A common check is to ensure that a username and password are both a certain number of characters long. This is something that the client-side can easily do, so it would be a waste of bandwidth and processing to force the server-side to process this. We can easily perform this check by writing the following:

```
String value = loginTextField.getText();
if(value.length() < 8)
    JOptionPane.showMessageDialog(null,
        "Login name must be 8 characters or more.",
        "String Error", JOptionPane.ERROR_MESSAGE);
else submit();
```

Date Bounds

Date values can be correct in format, but a business rule may require a form of validation. In Figure 1.24 (Chapter 1), we saw a form that allowed the user to enter in their birth date for validation. This may be required for an online submission form for purchasing a product, such as a movie or a computer game with an 'R' rating (restricted), or using a credit card which requires an adult over the age of 18. We can validate by retrieving the values from the combo boxes (assuming we placed `Integer` objects in them in the first place):

```
Integer day = (Integer)dayComboBox.getSelectedItem();
Integer month = (Integer)monthComboBox.getSelectedItem();
Integer year = (Integer)yearComboBox.getSelectedItem();
Calendar DOBCalendar = new GregorianCalendar(year.intValue(),
    month.intValue(), day.intValue());
Calendar currentCalendar = Calendar.getInstance();
int yearDiff = currentCalendar.get(Calendar.YEAR)
    - DOBCalendar.get(Calendar.YEAR);
int monthDiff = currentCalendar.get(Calendar.MONTH)
    - DOBCalendar.get(Calendar.MONTH);
int dayDiff = currentCalendar.get(Calendar.DATE)
    - DOBCalendar.get(Calendar.DATE);
if(yearDiff >= 18 && monthDiff >=0 && dayDiff >= 0) submit();
else
    JOptionPane.showMessageDialog(null,
        "Sorry, you are not old enough to purchase this product.",
        "Age Validation Error", JOptionPane.ERROR_MESSAGE);
```

This code uses two `Calendar` objects (concrete class is `GregorianCalendar` because `Calendar` is an abstract class). The first calendar places the date of birth value in by extracting the combo box values for year, month, and date. Another calendar object is created, which has the current date. We compare the two by checking the difference between the integer values for year, month, and date. If they are all either zero or non-negative numbers, the user has entered in a date of birth value that is at least 18 years of age.

CREATING THE ADMIN TOOL

Based on our requirements from Chapter 2, our CMS administration tool is a Java applet. It's safe now to cover the frontend because we've already chosen a parser API, built the model code, built the server-side logic, and implemented a protocol. We also looked at Abeille Forms Designer which allows us to build UIs using drag-and-drop (DnD) features instead of having to write all of the code for the UI by hand. Recall that Abeille Forms Designer uses a grid where components are placed within the grid and can span multiple rows and multiple columns. Additionally, rows and columns can be of a fixed size or can be set to fill a particular area. With this in mind, it helps to first visualize what the UI should look like.

Based on what we've mentioned about converting functional requirements to UI features, we can come up with the following list of forms needed:

- Login form
- Menu form
- Look-and-feel form
- Users add, edit, and delete forms
- Edit content form for paragraphs, tables, images, image galleries, list, and code chunks

Overall Layout

In order to make sure that the layout fits as well as provide ease of use, it helps to create a rough design that shows where in the applet each of the forms are positioned. The login form is straightforward because it does not share screen real estate with other forms. The menu form is also independent of other forms, and so is the look-and-feel form. However, the user account form consists of adding user accounts, changing attributes of the existing account, and deleting other user accounts. The interaction with each of these user account features does not require dependence on other forms. For example, if we add a user, we can do so without needing to display to the user the edit current user account or deleting user accounts. Although these three forms are considered part of the same area of functionality, they can exist in separate panels. Therefore, each is placed into a tabbed pane where the user can select each tab to perform the required operation (refer back to Figure 1.19 to see the user account tabs).

When we get to the area of managing the actual content for the CMS, however, we find ourselves at a place where we need to think the functionality and interactivity out carefully before proceeding.

Menu

We know that the user needs to see several key pieces of information:

Menu: A menu for carrying out actions, such as list all content from the server.

Create a page: Create a page on the server and update client view.

Delete a page: Delete a page on the server and update client view.

Create a section: Create a section (once a page is selected) on the server and update the client view.

Delete a section: Delete a section (once a page is selected) on the server and update the client view.

Create a content chunk: Create any of the following types of content chunks: paragraph, image, image gallery, table, list, or code chunk (once a section is selected), and update client view.

Delete a content chunk: Delete a content chunk of the following types of content chunks: paragraph, image, image gallery, table, list, or code chunk (once a section is selected), and update client view.

The menu should be visible at all times. Because of this. we need to set aside screen real estate for the menu. When the user chooses to create any type of content, an appropriate editor window should be made visible within the form.

Common Tasks

The site has common content, such as the footer and the news section. We say these are common because all pages will have the footer information in them and all pages can have the news section. There isn't a news section for each page (based on our requirements). There needs to be two links that bring up editors for editing both the footer as well as the news section. Because we'll be editing either one or the other, they can both share the same area of space.

Content Navigation

The content itself can have or has a hierarchical nature. Recall in Chapter 2 that we stated our data model supported many-to-many relationships between pages and sections and sections and content chunks. However, for the purpose of our implementation, we will only be offering the client a limited view, which is a one-to-one relationship for pages and sections and a one-to-one relationship for sections and content chunks, although our data store on the server supports much more (this is only a limitation of the client administration tool).

To support a hierarchical navigation, we should really consider using a JTree in Swing because it offers expansion of visible nodes and allows the user to select pages, sections, and content chunks. This component should be visible at all times so that the user can select any content type at any level. Again, screen real estate needs to be set aside to support this.

Content Editors

We know we'll need content editors for each of the following types:

- Page
- Section
- Footer
- News section
- Paragraph
- Image
- Image gallery
- Table
- Code chunk
- List

Each editor requires a submit button that allows the user to submit either the changes (if a currently existing content chunk was selected and placed in the editor) or submit a new chunk of content. We need to remember to place a button and wrap functionality around it for each of the content editors.

We can also divide the remaining screen real estate up into functional areas in a logical fashion, so that the user isn't looking all over the screen to see where a particular editor is. For example, editing the footer and the news section can happen in one place (switching between the two). The page and section content chunk types can be edited in the same area as well because they are considered high-level content chunks (because they are containers of other content chunks). The sub-chunk types that are placed into sections (paragraph, image, image gallery, table, list, or code chunk) can also share the same area because the user can only edit one of them at a time.

Finalized Layout

Having gone over the layout needs of each area of functionality for editing content, we can come up with a layout. Figure 9.2 displays the content editor components in four quadrants. The top left consists of menu choices that can be clicked for performing operations. It is important to keep track of what has been selected so that only certain types of menu items are available (grayed out menu items mean that a particular operation is disabled). This is because many of these operations are context sensitive. For example, if no page is selected in the tree view, then there should be no ability to create sections or content chunks because you need to place the section or content chunk into its container. Additionally, if no section is selected, then there should be no ability to delete a section.

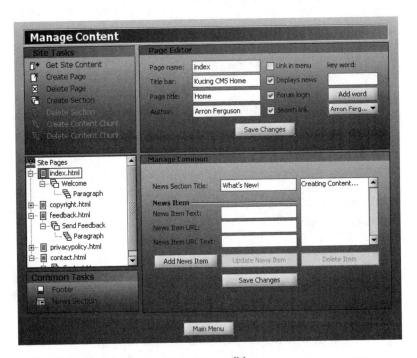

FIGURE 9.2 Layout design for content editing.

The tree view is found directly below the menu. Nothing should be visible in this tree view until the user clicks the Get Site Content menu item (top left) because this content can only be found on the server. Any content shown from previous login sessions would possibly be showing inconsistent content. Below the tree view are the two menu items for the footer and the news section. By clicking on either of these menu items, the user is presented with editors for each (but not at the same time) in the bottom right quadrant. The footer and news section editors share the same bottom right quadrant with the paragraph editor, image editor, image gallery editor, table editor, list editor, and code chunk editor. This helps us conserve screen real estate, which is at a premium, and it also helps us adhere to our heuristics of design, mentioned earlier.

The page editor and section editor share the top right quadrant. From a logical perspective, it makes sense that these two share the same space because they both are high-level containing content chunks. As well, the user is only able to (or interested in) editing one at a time; so this makes design sense.

Base Panel Class

Many of the classes that we'll be using contain similar or the same behaviors. For example, we want to use the same colors for title bars and labels; if we're offering a color background (which we are), we'll want all components to implement the same behavior for drawing the color background. Therefore, we should reuse code by taking advantage of inheritance.

Refactoring Forms Designer Code

GUI development tools historically have a habit of generating code that is neither pretty nor efficient. Abeille Forms Designer, on the other hand, actually generates code that is quite tidy and modular. Every class that Abeille Forms Designer generates for us contains some common code that is used with most components used in our GUI. For this reason, we should create a superclass that can be derived from. However, before we can do this, we need to extract the common code that the Abeille Forms Designer generates.

Generating Code in Abeille Forms Designer

Like many development tools, Abeille Forms Designer requires a project to be created. To do so, select the File menu and choose the New Project menu item to display a dialog that allows you to name a project and place it into an appropriate folder. Figure 9.3 shows the dialog box for setting up a project. With this project file now opened, we can now start designing forms. We can select the File menu and choose the New Form menu item which creates a new form. At this point, we can generate the code from this blank form.

In the Tools menu, the Code Generation menu item offers us the ability to export the design as Java source code. Figure 9.4 displays the Code Generation dialog. We need to choose the Options menu, which requires us to give the class a name and a package. Once we type a name into the Code Generation Options subdialog (any name for this class will do because we're just stripping out common code from it), we can go back to the Code Generation dialog and select Save to open a file dialog that allows us to save the source code file.

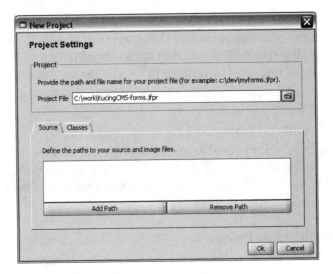

FIGURE 9.3 Project settings dialog.

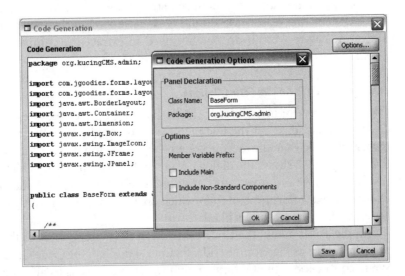

FIGURE 9.4 Abeille Forms Designer Code Generation dialog.

At this point you can open up the class that you generated. There are really only two things we want from this class, the import statements

```
import com.jgoodies.forms.layout.CellConstraints;
import com.jgoodies.forms.layout.FormLayout;
import java.awt.Container;
```

```
import java.awt.Dimension;
import javax.swing.Box;
```

and the `addFillComponents()` method

```
protected void addFillComponents( Container panel, int[] cols,
    int[] rows ) {
    Dimension filler = new Dimension(10,10);
    boolean filled_cell_11 = false;
    CellConstraints cc = new CellConstraints();
    if ( cols.length > 0 && rows.length > 0 ) {
        if ( cols[0] == 1 && rows[0] == 1 ) {
            panel.add( Box.createRigidArea( filler ), cc.xy(1,1) );
            filled_cell_11 = true;
        }
    }
    for( int index = 0; index < cols.length; index++ ) {
        if(cols[index] == 1 && filled_cell_11) { continue; }
        panel.add( Box.createRigidArea( filler ), cc.xy(cols[index]
            ,1) );
    }
    for( int index = 0; index < rows.length; index++ ) {
        if ( rows[index] == 1 && filled_cell_11 ) { continue; }
        panel.add( Box.createRigidArea( filler ), cc.xy(1,
            rows[index]) );
    }
}
```

The generated class usually contains a method called `createPanel()`, which adds all components to a container via the custom layout manager provided by the JGoodies library. An example of an empty form (i.e., no components added to the container) generated by Abeille Forms Designer might look like:

```
public JPanel createPanel() {
    JPanel jpanel1 = new JPanel();
    FormLayout formlayout1 = new FormLayout("FILL:DEFAULT:NONE,"
    + "FILL:DEFAULT:NONE,FILL:DEFAULT:NONE","CENTER:DEFAULT:NONE,"
    + "CENTER:DEFAULT:NONE,CENTER:DEFAULT:NONE");
    CellConstraints cc = new CellConstraints();
    jpanel1.setLayout(formlayout1);
    addFillComponents(jpanel1,new int[]{ 1,2,3 },new int[]{ 1,2,3 });
    return jpanel1;
}
```

The method usually creates a new local variable of type `Jpanel`, unless we explicitly rename it, in which case Abeille Forms Designer creates it as an instance variable. In either case, we're more interested in removing this and referring to the current class using the `this` keyword. Besides, we choose to do this because our form classes are all subclassing `JPanel`, so it makes little sense to have a panel inside of a panel. This means that any reference to the panel (in this case called jpanel1) has to be replaced with the this keyword. Later in our code, we will change the name of the createPanel() method to createLayout().

The CMSPanel Class

Because we're running inside of an applet, all of our forms are some sort of container. Our new class should, therefore, be a subclass of JPanel. This is fine because all we want is a container. In addition to the import statements and the addFillComponents() method that we previously copied from the generated code, we're going to place a gradient fill in the background of this superclass with a couple of colors. Our CMSPanel class is found in Listing 9.1.

LISTING 9.1 CMSPanel.java **Class**

```java
package org.kucingCMS.admin;
import com.jgoodies.forms.layout.CellConstraints;
import com.jgoodies.forms.layout.FormLayout;
import java.awt.Color;
import java.awt.Container;
import java.awt.Dimension;
import java.awt.GradientPaint;
import java.awt.Graphics;
import java.awt.Graphics2D;
import javax.swing.Box;
import javax.swing.JPanel;
public class CMSPanel extends JPanel {
    protected Color lightBlue = new Color(216, 224, 226);

    protected Color darkBlue = new Color(22, 62, 114);
    protected AdminTool caller;
    protected CMSPanel() { setOpaque(true); }
    public CMSPanel(AdminTool caller) {
        this();
        this.caller = caller;
    }
    public void paintComponent(Graphics g) {
        Graphics2D g2 = (Graphics2D)g;
        int w = getWidth();
        int h = getHeight();
        GradientPaint gradient = new GradientPaint(w/2, 0,
            lightBlue, w/2, (int)(h * 1.4), darkBlue, false);
        g2.setPaint(gradient);
        g2.fillRect(0, 0, w, h);
    }
    protected void addFillComponents( Container panel, int[] cols,
        int[] rows ) {
        Dimension filler = new Dimension(10,10);
        boolean filled_cell_11 = false;
```

```
CellConstraints cc = new CellConstraints();
if ( cols.length > 0 && rows.length > 0 ) {
    if ( cols[0] == 1 && rows[0] == 1 ) {
        panel.add( Box.createRigidArea( filler ),
            cc.xy(1,1) );
        filled_cell_11 = true;
    }
}
for( int index = 0; index < cols.length; index++ ) {
    if(cols[index] == 1 && filled_cell_11) { continue; }
    panel.add( Box.createRigidArea( filler ), cc.xy(
        cols[index],1) );
}

for( int index = 0; index < rows.length; index++ ) {
    if(rows[index] == 1 && filled_cell_11) { continue; }
    panel.add( Box.createRigidArea( filler ), cc.xy(1,
        rows[index]) );
}
}
}
```

We're overriding the `paintComponent` method so that we can add access to the `Graphics2D` context and use a `GradientPaint` to make the background fill a gradient from one color to another:

```
GradientPaint gradient = new GradientPaint(w/2, 0, lightBlue,
    w/2, (int)(h * 1.4), darkBlue, false);
```

This creates a gradient object with the starting point for the gradient being in the middle of the width and at the top of the component. Rather than use the height to end as the end of the gradient fill, we choose a value that is 1.4 times as tall as the height. This value (1.4) makes the gradient fill extend past the bottom, which has the effect of making the bottom of the screen not so dark—or at least not as dark as our end color for the gradient.

Sending and Receiving Model Data

With the base panel created we can now turn our attention to another panel that contains common behavior: the content chunk panel. The content chunk types (i.e., paragraph, image, image gallery, table, list, and code chunk) all adhere to the same set of steps for processing user requests for content creation and updates, which are:

1. Perform editing
2. Send new or edited content to server

The editing operations are specific to the type of content being edited, but we're more interested in sending either edited or new content to the server. In the case of edited material, we're simply sending objects that already exist and have been sent to us by the server. These objects (our custom DOM) have their data changed and sent back for placement into the data stores on the server. The protocol for doing so is simply for the client to bundle the content up, send to the server, wait for an acknowledgement, and then update the UI. In the case of new content however, the process is a little more involved.

Recall from Chapter 8 that the process of creating content starts on the server side. Because of this, creating content actually requires two steps:

1. Request new content chunks
2. Edit and send back the content chunks

We need to perform this because without it we would have problems with the server getting content chunks with multiple id values—something that would corrupt the data in the data stores when more than one author made changes to the content. We can create a class called `ContentChunkPanel.java` which extends the `CMSPanel` class. The `ContentChunkPanel.java` class requires the following instance variables:

```
protected AbstractNode chunk;
protected SectionChunk sc;
```

Edit Content

Performing editing requires some validation (which is implemented by each content chunk subclass), and then a call to the `ContentChunkPanel`'s `editContent()` method:

```
protected void editContent() {
    try {
        User user = caller.getUser();
        List addRequest = new LinkedList();
        addRequest.add(ProtocolConstants.EDIT_CONTENT); // (0)
        addRequest.add(caller.getSessionID());
        addRequest.add(user.getLogin());               // (2)
        addRequest.add(user.getPassword());            // (3)
        ContainerCollection collection =
            new ContainerCollection();
        List nodes = new LinkedList();
        chunk.touchModifiedDate();
        nodes.add(chunk);
        ContentContainer container =
            new ContentContainer(nodes);
```

```
            collection.addContainer(container);
            addRequest.add(collection);                    // (4)
            ObjectInputStream ois2 = caller.sendMessage(addRequest);
            List addResponse = (List)ois2.readObject();
            String msg2 = (String)addResponse.get(0);
            String details = (String)addResponse.get(1);
            if(msg2.equals(ProtocolConstants.EDIT_CONTENT_ACK)) {
                caller.showContentForm();
                JOptionPane.showMessageDialog(this,
                    details, chunk + " Edit Response",
                    JOptionPane.ERROR_MESSAGE);
            } else {
                caller.setBackToLoginForm();
                JOptionPane.showMessageDialog(this,
                    "Edit Content Chunk Failed!",
                    "Edit Content Chunk Request Denied.",
                    JOptionPane.ERROR_MESSAGE);
            }
            ois2.close();

        } catch(MalformedURLException mue) {
            caller.setBackToLoginForm();
            mue.printStackTrace();
            JOptionPane.showMessageDialog(this, mue.getMessage(),
                "URL is malformed!", JOptionPane.ERROR_MESSAGE);
        } catch(ClassNotFoundException cnfe) {
            caller.setBackToLoginForm();
            cnfe.printStackTrace();
            JOptionPane.showMessageDialog(this, cnfe.getMessage(),
                "Class not found!", JOptionPane.ERROR_MESSAGE);
        } catch(IOException ioe) {
            caller.setBackToLoginForm();
            ioe.printStackTrace();
            JOptionPane.showMessageDialog(this, ioe.getMessage(),
                "Could not connect!", JOptionPane.ERROR_MESSAGE);
        }
    }
```

The first thing we do at the top of this method is to request from the admin applet (`AdminTool` class which is covered later in this chapter) the user whose currently logged in. We need the user's login name, password, and the session ID value that was given by the server. A `java.util.LinkedList` collection is created, which is used to send the edit content request. A `ContainerCollection` is instantiated, which holds the nodes that are to be edited (recall this packaging from Chapter 8). Note that we are only placing one node (content chunk) into this collection. The client administration applet currently only supports sending one content chunk for editing, but the server's protocol has been built to support multiple nodes which we can later grow into with our administration applet, if we wish. Once packaged, we call

```
ObjectInputStream ois2 = caller.sendMessage(addRequest);
```

which sends the list to the `AdminTool` via its `sendMessage()` method. The next three lines

```
List addResponse = (List)ois2.readObject();
String msg2 = (String)addResponse.get(0);
String details = (String)addResponse.get(1);
```

unpack the response, which (based on our protocol) give us a status message and some details. A call is made to the `AdminTool`'s `showContentForm()` method which updates the tree view and editors based on the changes that were made. We wrap exception handling around this code to ensure that we catch malformed URLs (i.e., the URL does not exist on the server), class not found (i.e., the client applet does not contain the appropriate class files), a class cast exception (i.e., server and client have different compiled versions of the class files), and a general IO exception (i.e., no Internet connection found). In any case, the user is taken back to the login form, a stack trace is printed to the applet console, and a dialog is presented to the user explaining the mishap.

Creating Content

Creating content requires submitting a request to the server for some new content chunk nodes, updating them, and then sending them back to the server for updates into the data stores. The first method, `createContent()`, wraps the following code with exception handling (as was the case with editing content):

```
User user = caller.getUser();
List createRequest = new LinkedList();
createRequest.add(ProtocolConstants.CREATE_CONTENT); // (0)
createRequest.add(caller.getSessionID());            // (1)
createRequest.add(user.getLogin());                  // (2)
createRequest.add(user.getPassword());               // (3)
List nodesToCreate = new LinkedList();
nodesToCreate.add(nodeType);
nodesToCreate.add(new Integer(1));
nodesToCreate.add(ModelNode.SECTION_CHUNK);
nodesToCreate.add(new Integer(1));
createRequest.add(nodesToCreate);                     // (4)
ObjectInputStream ois =
    caller.sendMessage(createRequest);
List createResponse = (List)ois.readObject();
String msg = (String)createResponse.get(0);
ois.close();
if(msg.equals(ProtocolConstants.CREATE_CONTENT_ACK)) {
    chunk = (AbstractNode)createResponse.get(1);
    sc = (SectionChunk)createResponse.get(2);
} else {
```

```
caller.setBackToLoginForm();
JOptionPane.showMessageDialog(this,
    "Create Content Chunk Failed!",
    "Create Content Chunk Request Denied.",
    JOptionPane.ERROR_MESSAGE);
}
```

Like the `editContent()` method, we must first retrieve from the admin applet the user object so that we can gain the login name, password, and session ID values. We create a `java.util.LinkedList`, which houses the type of request being made (using `ProtocolConstants.CREATE_CONTENT`), session ID, login, and password. Next, we create another list that contains the node type we are attempting to create:

```
nodesToCreate.add(nodeType);
```

The `nodetype` variable is passed in from the subclass content type, which comes from the `ModelNode` class in the `org.kucingCMS.contentmodel` package. This allows us to use constants to specify what type we are wishing to create. We then state the number (in this case one node) and also request a section chunk type as well (using the constant `ModelNode.SECTION_CHUNK`). Remember, our data stores deal with many-to-many relationships between content chunks and sections and many-to-many relationships between sections and pages. So every time we create one of these types, we need to request an associative node to link the two together. The `sendMessage()` method is called and an `ObjectInputStream` is (hopefully) returned. A list gives us a message in the form of a string. At this point, we need to check what value the string has. If it is `ProtocolConstants.CREATE_CONTENT_ACK`, then we can attempt to extract the two objects

```
chunk = (AbstractNode)createResponse.get(1);
sc = (SectionChunk)createResponse.get(2);
```

which are the content chunk and the section chunk (associative node), respectively. Recall that these are our two instance variables of this class, and they are used by each content chunk editor for referencing the content that is to be edited and displayed.

The Login Form

We can start off by drawing a picture using graph paper if it helps us to understand better the grid concept and how to lay things out in the grid. Later when we have confidence with the tool, we can simply build the interface directly into the design view. Figure 9.5 displays the rough drawing of the login form (complete with sketched mascot).

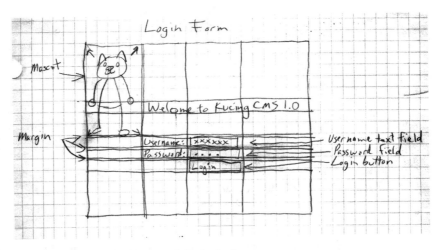

FIGURE 9.5 Rough drawing of the login form.

We have sketched in 10 rows and five columns. Three of the rows we've specified are going to be very thin, but they are there to separate each row of labels and text fields from each other because it looks too cramped if components are touching each other. A rendering of this in Abeille Forms Designer (in design mode) is found in Figure 9.6.

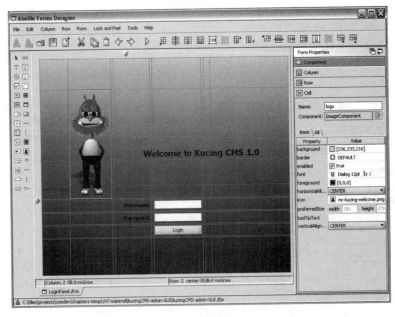

FIGURE 9.6 Login form in design view using Abeille Forms Designer.

At this point, we can generate the code from Abeille Forms Designer. The method that we are interested in from the generated code is the `createLayout()` method, which contains the following code (based on the design in Figure 9.6):

```
private void createLayout() {
    this.setName("this");
    FormLayout formLayout = new FormLayout("FILL:20DLU:GROW(1.0),"
    + "FILL:DEFAULT:NONE,FILL:4DLU:NONE,FILL:88PX:NONE,FILL:4DLU:"
    + "NONE,FILL:120PX:NONE,FILL:4DLU:NONE,FILL:DEFAULT:NONE,FILL:"
    + "100DLU:GROW(1.0)","CENTER:DEFAULT:GROW(1.0),CENTER:92DLU:"
    + "NONE,CENTER:19DLU:NONE,CENTER:40DLU:NONE,CENTER:20DLU:NONE,"
    + "CENTER:2DLU:NONE,CENTER:18DLU:NONE,CENTER:2DLU:NONE,CENTER:"
    + "18DLU:NONE,CENTER:2DLU:NONE,CENTER:18DLU:NONE,CENTER:2DLU:"
    + "NONE,CENTER:20DLU:GROW(1.0)");
    CellConstraints cc = new CellConstraints();
    this.setLayout(formLayout);
    title.setFont(new Font("Tahoma",Font.BOLD,20));
    title.setForeground(darkBlue);
    title.setName("title");
    title.setText("Welcome to Kucing CMS 1.0");
    title.setHorizontalAlignment(JLabel.LEFT);
    this.add(title,new CellConstraints(4,3,6,1,
        CellConstraints.CENTER,CellConstraints.DEFAULT));
    logo.setIcon(new ImageIcon(AdminTool.class.
        getResource("mr-kucing-welcome.png")));
    logo.setName("logo");
    logo.setHorizontalAlignment(SwingConstants.CENTER);
    logo.setVerticalAlignment(SwingConstants.CENTER);
    this.add(logo,cc.xywh(2,2,1,4));
    userNameLabel.setFont(new Font("Tahoma",Font.BOLD,12));
    userNameLabel.setName("userNameLabel");
    userNameLabel.setForeground(darkBlue);
    userNameLabel.setText("Username:");
    userNameLabel.setHorizontalAlignment(JLabel.RIGHT);
    this.add(userNameLabel,cc.xy(4,7));
    passwordLabel.setFont(new Font("Tahoma",Font.BOLD,12));
    passwordLabel.setName("passwordLabel");
    passwordLabel.setText("Password:");
    passwordLabel.setForeground(darkBlue);
    passwordLabel.setHorizontalAlignment(JLabel.RIGHT);
    this.add(passwordLabel,cc.xy(4,9));
    userNameField.setName("userNameField");
    userNameField.setSelectionColor(new Color(230,105,0));
    userNameField.setHorizontalAlignment(JTextField.LEFT);
    this.add(userNameField,cc.xy(6,7));

    passwordField.setName("passwordField");
    passwordField.setSelectionColor(new Color(230,105,0));
    passwordField.setHorizontalAlignment(JPasswordField.LEFT);
    this.add(passwordField,cc.xy(6,9));
    submitButton.setActionCommand("Login");
```

```
submitButton.setText("Login");
submitButton.setForeground(darkBlue);
submitButton.setToolTipText("Log into the CMS.");
this.add(submitButton,cc.xy(6,11));
addFillComponents(this,new int[]{ 1,2,3,4,5,6,7,8,9 },
    new int[]{ 1,2,3,4,5,6,7,8,9,10,11,12,13 });
}
```

In the `LoginForm`'s `createLayout()` method, we've added each of the components (e.g., `JLabels`, a `JTextField`, `JPasswordField`, and `JButton`) to the form. This is done by instantiating the object, setting colors and font, any alignment values, and then adding the component to the layout. The `add()` method of our panel is passed two objects:

1. The GUI component that is to be added to the layout
2. A `CellConstraints` object, which is returned by a call to one of the coordinate placement static methods of the `CellConstraints` class

The `CellConstraints` class is provided in the JGoodies library and helps the JGoodies specific layout manager (called `FormLayout`), perform placement routines to the components to ensure that they are positioned as we had them in our design view.

Login Form Event Handling

Because the login form is fairly simple (as compared to some of the content chunk editors), we only require event handling for focus and action events. We're going to implement the `FocusListener` interface so that we can provide the following:

```
public void focusGained(FocusEvent fe) {
    if(fe.getSource() instanceof JTextComponent) {
        JTextComponent t = (JTextComponent)fe.getSource();
        t.selectAll();
    }
}
```

All this does is ensure that if the user clicks one of the text component subclasses (in this case both the `JTextField` and the `JPasswordField`), that any text already found in the text component are automatically selected, so that whatever the user types replaces the existing text. It's not extremely important, but is something that users come to expect from forms. We also want to handle action events via the `ActionListener` interface:

```
public void actionPerformed(ActionEvent ae) {
    if(ae.getSource() == passwordField ||
        ae.getSource() == submitButton ||
        ae.getSource() == userNameField) {
```

```
        caller.doLogin(userNameField.getText(),
            new String(passwordField.getPassword())));
    }
}
```

All we're doing here is passing the values from the fields (login name and password to the admin tool), which we will hand over to the admin tool for further processing (covered later in this chapter).

Managing Content

Referring back to Figure 9.2, there are two components on the left side that help to manage both the content as well as manage the forms that appear within our content editing containing form. All of these panels that represent forms are aggregated in the `ManageContentPanel.java` class. However, each area of functionality is separated in order to make the code more modular.

Site Tasks Panel

As we saw earlier, our hyperlink labels are functioning as menu items and offer the ability to add and delete pages, sections, and section chunks. This class (called `SiteTasksPanel.java`) extends the `CMSPanel.java` class that we created earlier so as to take advantage of common functionality. We require two instance variables within the `SiteTasksPanel` class:

```
private ModelNode nodeToDelete;
private ManageContentPanel caller;
```

The `nodeToDelete` variable is the node that is deleted (which could be any of the CMS content chunks). In the case that the user has not selected a node to delete, this variable will be null; so we need to ensure that we check for a null value before proceeding:

```
if(nodeToDelete == null) return;
```

Deleting a node requires going through the same protocol steps that we have demonstrated earlier with edits and adding content chunks (the `ContentChunkPanel.java` class); however, we can show it here for the sake of being consistent:

```
List request = new LinkedList();
request.add(ProtocolConstants.DELETE_CONTENT);
request.add(caller.getAdminTool().getSessionID());
request.add(user.getLogin());
request.add(user.getPassword());
List nodes = new LinkedList();
nodes.add(nodeToDelete);
```

```
ContentContainer container = new ContentContainer(nodes);
ContainerCollection collection = new ContainerCollection();
collection.addContainer(container);
request.add(collection);
ObjectInputStream ois = caller.getAdminTool().sendMessage(request);
List response = (List)ois.readObject();
String msg = (String)response.get(0);
```

We're specifying that we're deleting content with `ProtocolConstants.DELETE_CONTENT`. However, once this operation finishes, and assuming the server returns a value of `ProtocolConstants.DELETE_CONTENT_ACK`, we still need to perform some updates locally because the local copy still contains the old version of the content. Deleting the content within this admin applet requires checking what type our `nodeToDelete` is. We're taking advantage of the `ContentContainer.java` class as well as the `ContainerCollection.java`, which make it easier to access collections of nodes of different types:

```
if(nodeToDelete instanceof Page)
    caller.getContainerCollection().getPagesContainer().
        deleteNode(nodeToDelete);
else if(nodeToDelete instanceof Section)
    caller.getContainerCollection().getContainer(
    ModelNode.SECTION).deleteNode(nodeToDelete);
// ...
else if(nodeToDelete instanceof Code)
    caller.getContainerCollection().getContainer(
    ModelNode.CODE).deleteNode(nodeToDelete);
caller.reloadCachedContent();
caller.getAdminTool().showContentForm();
```

Once this call is made, we need to ensure the admin applet reloads the content so that the user sees the updates.

Content Tree Panel

The tree that displays pages, sections, and content chunks is represented by a `JPanel` that contains a `JscrollPane`, which contains the `JTree`. We'll call this class the `JScroll-Tree.java`. The tree uses a `DefaultTreeModel` object which is instantiated when the scroll tree class is instantiated. One of the common methods found in the form classes that we've created is the `resetFields()` method, which initializes fields and component values. For example, text fields are cleared, combo boxes are set to the default index or cleared of model data, lists are cleared, and in the case of the `JTree`, we set its model to a string literal which simply suggests to the user to click the Get Site Content menu item:

```
public static final String LOAD_MESSAGE =
    "<Click 'Get Site Content'>";
// ...
protected void resetFields() {
    model.setRoot(new DefaultMutableTreeNode(LOAD_MESSAGE));
}
```

The process of loading content into the tree is quite involved and requires using the ContentContainer and ContainerCollection classes. The process goes like this:

1. Reset the tree's model to a string.
2. Retrieve a list of Pages, a list of Sections, a list of PageSections, and a list of SectionChunks from the container collection.
3. Cycle through an outer loop of pages from the page list.
4. For each Page object, create a new DefaultMutableTreeNode, add the Page object to the DefaultMutableTreeNode, and add the DefaultMutableTreeNode to the tree's root node.
5. Create a new PageSection list which contains only PageSections that are referenced by the current Page in the loop (call it currentPageSectionsOnly).
6. Go through the PageSection list that contains all PageSections and see if the current page (outer loop) id is found in any of the PageSections. If so, add that PageSection to currentPageSectionsOnly.
7. Sort the PageSections, which sorts based on their position values. Position is important because without it the sections that belong to a page would be placed out of order from what the user had placed them in. Although it may look like we may have duplicates, the position is always unique. This is because we're only dealing with one page with all of its sections. If we were dealing with more than one page, then we could possibly have duplicate position values.
8. Using the (sorted) currentPageSectionsOnly list, create a new inner loop and go through the Section list, using the id reference in each PageSection to reference Sections. For each Section, create a DefaultMutableTreeNode and add the Section whose id value is referenced.
9. This new inner loop now references each Section. Now match Sections in the SectionChunk list. Add SectionChunks to a new currentSectionChunksOnly list which only contains SectionChunks that have been matched to the current Section.
10. Sort the currentSectionChunksOnly list and use this list to match content chunks in the content chunk list (via the id reference).
11. For each of the matched content chunks, create a new DefaultMutableTreeNode, and add the current content chunk to the DefaultMutableTreeNode. Add this content chunk DefaultMutableTreeNode to the section DefaultMutableTreeNode.

Looking at this procedure carefully, it becomes clear that we're using Java code to perform the action of two joins in SQL. The code for performing this task is:

```java
protected void loadContent(ContainerCollection collection) {
    model = null;
    model = new DefaultTreeModel(new DefaultMutableTreeNode(
        LOAD_MESSAGE));
    tree.setModel(model);
    List pageList = collection.getPagesContainer().getContent();
    List sectionList = collection.getContainer(
        ModelNode.SECTION).getContent();
    List pageSectionList = collection.getContainer(
        ModelNode.PAGE_SECTION).getContent();
    List sectionChunksList = collection.getContainer(
        ModelNode.SECTION_CHUNK).getContent();
    List chunksList = collection.getAllContentChunks();
    ((DefaultMutableTreeNode)(model.getRoot())).
        setUserObject("Site Pages");
    int size = pageList.size();
    for(int i = 0; i < size; i++) {
        Page page = (Page)pageList.get(i);
        DefaultMutableTreeNode pageNode =
            new DefaultMutableTreeNode(page);
        ((DefaultMutableTreeNode)(model.getRoot())).add(pageNode);
        String pageID = page.getID();
        int pageSectionSize = pageSectionList.size();
        List<PageSection> currentPageSectionsOnly =
            new LinkedList<PageSection>();
        for(int j = 0; j < pageSectionSize; j++) {
            PageSection ps = (PageSection)pageSectionList.get(j);
            if(ps.getPageIDRef().equals(pageID)) {
                currentPageSectionsOnly.add(ps);
            }
        }
        Collections.sort(currentPageSectionsOnly,
            new AssociativeComparator());
        int currentPSSize = currentPageSectionsOnly.size();
        for(int k = 0; k < currentPSSize; k++) {
            PageSection ps = (PageSection)currentPageSectionsOnly.
                get(k);
            int sectionListSize = sectionList.size();
            for(int m = 0; m < sectionListSize; m++) {
                Section section = (Section)sectionList.get(m);
                String sectionID = section.getID();
                if(sectionID.equals(ps.getSectionIDRef())) {
                    DefaultMutableTreeNode sectionNode =
                        new DefaultMutableTreeNode(section);
                    pageNode.add(sectionNode);
                    List currentSectionChunksOnly =
                        new LinkedList();
                    int sectionChunksSize =
                        sectionChunksList.size();
```

```
for(int n = 0; n < sectionChunksSize; n++) {
    SectionChunk sc = (SectionChunk)
        sectionChunksList.get(n);
    if(sc.getSectionIDRef().equals(sectionID))
        currentSectionChunksOnly.add(sc);
}
Collections.sort(currentSectionChunksOnly,
    new AssociativeComparator());
int currentSCSize = currentSectionChunksOnly.
    size();
for(int p = 0; p < currentSCSize; p++) {
    SectionChunk sc2 =
        (SectionChunk)currentSectionChunksOnly.
        get(p);
    String chunkIDRef = sc2.getChunkIDRef();
    int chunkListSize = chunksList.size();
    for(int r = 0; r < chunkListSize; r++)
    {
        AbstractNode chunk =
            (AbstractNode)chunksList.get(r);
        if(chunk.getID().equals(chunkIDRef))
            sectionNode.add(
                new DefaultMutableTreeNode(
                    chunk));
    }
}
} //end if
} // end for loop for section list
}// end current PageSection list
}
}
```

The Admin Applet

As mentioned earlier, the encompassing class is an applet (JApplet to be precise), and the name of our subclass is AdminTool.java. Although all applets (JApplets too) are Panels, our subclass will not really offer any visual presentation of its own other than to simply house other components such as our forms. There are a couple of class variables of interest for the our applet:

```
private static final String adminServlet = "admin.connection";
private static final String lnf =
    "com.jgoodies.looks.plastic.PlasticXPLookAndFeel";
```

The first class variable (adminServlet) is part of a URL that points us back to the server. It's the location of the server applet that handles all applet requests. This should be a constant value, although in a future version we could contain this in a text file so that future versions of our applet read the value from a text file. This would give us the ability to change the URL to connect to without having to re-compile our source code. The second class variable offers the qualified name of the look-and-feel class that is part of the JGoodies Looks library. Later in our applet's init() method, we can set the look-and-feel—one of the more dazzling features of Java's Swing:

```
public void init() {
    try {
        UIManager.setLookAndFeel(lnf);
    } catch (Exception e) { ; }
    // create/layout all of the screens
    this.instantiateCommonComponents();
    this.setContentPane(loginPanel);
    loginPanel.invalidate();
    this.validate();
}
```

We're using the UIManager class, which (surprisingly) is the UIlook-and-feel manager. We pass it the name of the look-and-feel that we wish to set to. Although this call must be wrapped in some exception handling, we're really not too inter-ested in handling this because a failure to set the look-and-feel to something dif-ferent than the default won't be the end of the world. Actually there are four exceptions to catch: ClassNotFoundException, InstantiationException, IllegalAcces-sException, and UnsupportedLookAndFeelException.

Sending to the Server

All of the communications from forms found in the administration applet have been making use of the sendMessage() method. As mentioned in Chapter 8, the server and the client applet communicate using object serialization. The sendMessage() method in the applet looks like:

```
public ObjectInputStream sendMessage(List message) throws
    MalformedURLException, IOException {
    URL url = null;
    url = new URL(getCodeBase() + adminServlet);
    HttpURLConnection con =
        (HttpURLConnection)url.openConnection();

    con.setRequestProperty("Content-Type",
        "application/x-java-serialized-object");
    con.setRequestMethod("POST");
    con.setDoOutput(true);
    con.setDoInput(true);
    con.setUseCaches(false);
    con.setDefaultUseCaches(false);
    ObjectOutputStream oos =
        new ObjectOutputStream(con.getOutputStream());
```

```
        oos.writeObject(message);
        oos.flush();
        oos.close();
        ObjectInputStream in =
            new ObjectInputStream(con.getInputStream());
        return in;
    }
```

We start off by using a URL object, which allows us to use the code base (where the applet came from) which assists in the formation of a HttpURLConnection object. Using the URL connection (whose application protocol is HTTP) we set the MIME type to application/x-java-serialized-object. We call the setDoOutput() method and pass true (we're sending), we call the setDoInput() method and pass true (we're receiving too), and we turn off caches because we want to ensure that all data is sent and received, regardless if it looks as though it is the same content previously. Finally, we get an ObjectOutputStream, write the content to it, flush and close the stream and return an ObjectInputStream, which contains the response from the server.

SUMMARY

ON THE CD

Although we've covered some of the functionality that is found within the CMS found in this book, it is left to the reader to explore the CD-ROM, specifically the *CMS-project\src\org\kucingCMS\admin* subfolder where many different admin supporting classes exist. There are detailed examples as to how to send content from the admin applet by looking at classes such as the table panel (TablePanel.java), the image gallery panel (ImageGalleryPanel.java), and the common tasks panel (CommonTasksPanel.java).

In this chapter, we looked at validation, such as bounds checking, and we moved into the details of building the CMS administration applet. We familiarized ourselves with Abeille Forms Designer, and we saw the code it generated and figured out what particular methods were pertinent to our custom administration classes. We also studied how the administration applet sends and receives model data to and from the server. Finally, we looked at some of the actual classes that are part of the applet including the login form, managing content form, and the administration applet. We now look forward to the next chapter where we investigate HTML and CSS, which will allow us to present our content to the user in a consistent manner while also having an eye for design and look-and-feel.

10 XHTML and CSS

ON THE CD

In order to incorporate the ability of outputting Web documents from our CMS, we need to master the task of creating Web documents. This chapter focuses on the mechanics of HTML and style sheets so that we can apply the mechanics to Web page creation in the next chapter. Our CMS, after all, is a Web application, and we need the ability to generate Web pages from our CMS. The source code listings referenced in this chapter are located on the CD-ROM in the *Chapter 10* folder.

Knowing how to present our Web content not only involves knowing how to chunk, organize, and group our content, but also how to present it. In this chapter, we look at how to make our Web content (hopefully) pleasing to the eye by using current Web technology. Although our process involves a couple more steps than what would normally be required for delivering static content (i.e., content that is already formatted and ready as HTML documents), the added benefit of being able to change our content on-the-fly far outweighs the extra work we put into this process.

INTRODUCTION TO HTML TECHNOLOGIES

There are several different versions of HTML, and so before we delve into the specifics of DHTML, a talk about HTML is in order.

HTML Origins

HTML was originally started (Tim Berners-Lee) and defined loosely on the rules of SGML. We say loosely because many of the strict markup rules were easily broken, and these broken (or non-valid) HTML documents were still accepted and parsed (and rendered) by Web browsers. Recall from Chapter 4 that XML requires all open tags to have close tags as well for each element (unless we're dealing with an empty tag). Web browsers, however, allowed for such things as:

```
<html>
  <head> </head>
  <body>
    <p>Welcome to <b>Kucing CMS 1.0.</p>
  </body>
</html>
```

The previous markup contains a paragraph (the p element) with bold text (the b element), where the bold element does not have an end tag (i.e., missing </b>). For an XML parser, this would result in an error, and the parser would refuse to parse the rest of the document. However, Web browsers (still) allow for this type of sloppiness in HTML.

HTML 4.0

HTML 4.0 (most recent version is 4.01) is a W3C Recommendation that added the following features to previous versions (e.g., 1.0, 2.0, 3.0, 3.2) of HTML:

Internationalization: Allowing multiple character sets to be used. Recall Chapter 4 discussed Unicode.

Accessibility: The removal of presentation markup and document structure markup (e.g., font size vs. placement of paragraphs), Image elements support text attribute, title, and lang attributes on all elements, abbr and acronym elements, more descriptive elements, and attributes in tables.

One of the most important differences with HTML 4.0 and previous versions was the separation of presentation markup from the structure of the document. That is, all formatting such as font family, color, alignment, text size, and other presentation data is to be removed from the HTML document and placed inside of style sheets. Only the HTML structure remains intact within the document (i.e., paragraphs, tables, images, etc.). This new design offers the following advantages:

Consistency: Since presentation data is separated (usually in a separate document) from the content structure, all HTML documents can refer to the same style sheet, thus reducing the chance of inconsistent formatting. For example, if a certain font is used (e.g., Helvetica) in a style sheet, then all HTML documents that use that style sheet will have the same font.

Reduced Bandwidth: Because multiple HTML documents refer to only one style sheet, the amount of downloads is reduced—download only one style sheet instead of one style sheet for each HTML document.

Separation of Job Function: Graphic and layout designers can focus on how the document looks, whereas Web developers can focus on what information to put into the structure of the HTML document. Because these two tasks are separate, designers won't have to worry about developers making changes to the layout, and developers won't have to worry about designers changing the structure of the HTML.

LISTING 10.1   HTML and Style Together

```
<html>
  <head><title>Welcome - Kucing CMS 1.0 </title></head>
  <body bgcolor="#BDDBFB" style="font-family: arial,
    'lucida console', sans-serif">
  <h2 align="center">Welcome</h2>
  <p align="justify">Welcome to Kucing CMS 1.0. Kucing CMS 1.0 is
  a <b>Content Management System</b> written in Java(tm) and runs
  within a servlet container such as the
  <a href="http://tomcat.apache.org/" style="text-decoration:
  none; border-bottom-style: dashed; border-bottom-width: thin;">
  Apache Software Foundation's Tomcat Web server</a>.
  </p>
  </body>
</html>
```

Listing 10.1 shows presentation data and content structure together. Because they are in one document, it is more difficult to extract the actual content. Also, if there are multiple HTML documents that use the same style (e.g., same font), then care must be taken to ensure that all HTML documents use the same style.

LISTING 10.2 HTML Only

```
<!DOCTYPE HTML PUBLIC "-//W3C//DTD HTML 4.0 Transitional//EN">
<html>
  <head>
    <title>Welcome - Kucing CMS 1.0 </title>
    <link type="text/css" rel="stylesheet"
      href="Listing-10-2.css">
  </head>
  <body>
    <h2>Welcome</h2>
    <p>Welcome to Kucing CMS 1.0. Kucing CMS 1.0 is a <b>Content
    Management System</b> written in Java(tm) and runs within a
    servlet container such as the
    <a href="http://tomcat.apache.org/">Apache Software
    Foundation's Tomcat Web server</a>.
    </p>
  </body>
</html>
```

In Listing 10.2, we've removed all style data and placed it inside of a separate style sheet document (Listing 10.3). Now any other documents that require the same style can simply reference the style document found in Listing 10.3. This approach is cleaner in that the HTML is easy to read (compared to Listing 10.1) and the style data can be shared by multiple HTML documents. As well, if we wish to parse through the HTML with an XML parser, the parser won't take as long to perform the parsing because a parser won't have to process unnecessary data.

LISTING 10.3 Style Sheet Only

```
/* A simple style sheet example */
body {
  background-color: #BDDBFB;
  font-family: arial, 'lucida console', sans-serif;
}

h2 { text-align: center; }
p { text-align: justify; }
a {
  text-decoration: none; border-bottom-style: dashed;
  border-bottom-width: thin;
}
```

XHTML 1.0

XHTML was an attempt to force Web developers to adhere to the rules of XML, thus making it easier for XML-based applications to parse HTML. The W3C offers what they call three different "flavors" of XHTML:

XHTML 1.0—Strict: This version of XHTML forces all presentation data into separate style sheets as well as strict adherence to XML rules for well-formed markup.

XHTML 1.0—Transitional: Some of the rules about separating presentation from content structure can be broken (e.g., allow the center element). This flavor is a good choice if there is some need to support older Web browsers that may not be aware of style sheets.

XHTML 1.0—Frameset: Supporting the use of frames (a generally discouraged practice).

XML is a descendant of SGML (really a subset of SGML) as is HTML. However, XML is strict like SGML, whereas HTML has historically been quite lax with markup rule adherence although this is changing with the W3C's creation of XHTML.

Frames are generally discouraged because a frameset cannot be bookmarked— only one HTML document. Other problems are: previous page and next page confusion (i.e., which frame is being changed); there is a security risk if a frame is downloaded by the client's Web browser but not displayed (it could be executing some malicious script without any visual feedback); printing is difficult because only one frame at time can be printed; and search engines may index and reference pages that don't contain navigation, thereby sending the user to a page without any menu options (referred to as a black hole).

XHTML is really simply HTML 4.01 with the strictness of following the rules of well-formedness. Conforming to the XML rules means that applications that wish to parse through (and possibly store and integrate) data coming from an XHTML document may do so without having to battle parsing errors that would normally be associated with HTML documents. A quick summary of the differences between XHTML and HTML 4.0:

Documents must be well-formed: as mentioned in Chapter 4, well-formedness requires that begin and end tags are properly nested.

Lowercase: All element names and attributes must be lowercase (recognizing XML's case sensitivity rule).

Attribute values double-quoted: All attribute values must be in double quotes.

Attribute name and value given: If an attribute is placed inside of an element, it must have the equals value and a begin and end double quote.

Whitespace in attributes: when defining multiple tokens within an attribute value, all trailing and leading whitespace will be stripped.

Script and style elements: Both script and style elements may contain illegal characters (e.g., < or &). To avoid parsing errors use either marked sections or entity references (e.g., `<![CDATA[ if(x < y) ]]>` or `&amp;`).

Using `id` and `name` attributes: HTML 4.0 introduced the `id` and `name` attributes that can be placed in many different elements within HTML content. In XHTML, the data type for these is considered `ID` (DTD type) and, therefore, the values for these attributes must be unique within the XHTML document.

Entity References in Hexadecimal: All entities that reference characters using hexadecimal must be in lowercase (e.g., `&#xA9;` for the copyright symbol and not `&#XA9;`).

DHTML

DHTML is an unofficial flavor of HTML because it is not a specification, nor a W3C Recommendation. DHTML is simply a packaging of four technologies:

- HTML 4.0
- Cascading Style Sheets (CSS)
- The W3C DOM
- JavaScript

A more strict (or current) packaging of DHTML can have XHTML in place of HTML 4.0.

These four technologies really represent two pairs of tightly coupled technologies that work together. First we have HTML 4.0 and CSS. Because of the use of HTML 4.0, it is a requirement to have CSS because HTML 4.0 removes all style information from the HTML document and places it inside of the CSS technology. The second pair is the W3C DOM and JavaScript. Recall from Chapter 6 that we looked at the W3C's DOM. Although we did not explicitly look at DOM Level 2, one of the parts of the recommendation for DOM Level 2 is the support for HTML 4.0 or XHTML documents. In order words, the ability to access all nodes within an HTML document. By coupling HTML and JavaScript together, we have a dataset along with a scripting language that allows us to access and manipulate the nodes in the dataset. A simple example of DHTML in practice is found in Listing 10.4.

LISTING 10.4   DHTML with JavaScript and HTML 4.0

```
<!DOCTYPE HTML PUBLIC "-//W3C//DTD HTML 4.0 Transitional//EN">
<html>
  <head>
    <title>Welcome - Kucing CMS 1.0 </title>
```

```
  <link type="text/css" rel="stylesheet"
    href="./Listing-10-3.css">
</head>
<body>
  <h2>Welcome</h2>
  <p id="content">Welcome to Kucing CMS 1.0. Kucing CMS 1.0 is a
  <b>Content Management System</b> written in Java(tm) and runs
  within a servlet container such as the
  <a href="http://tomcat.apache.org/">Apache Software
  Foundation's Tomcat Web server</a>.
  </p>
  <script type="text/javascript">
    document.getElementById('content').style.color="#ff0000";
  </script>
</body>
</html>
```

Listing 10.4 has added a tiny script (JavaScript) that accesses the (HTML) document and sets the color of an element by referencing its `id` attribute. DHTML can be quite a powerful tool to the Web developer because it allows for the creation, manipulation, and deletion of nodes within an HTML document. Some of the uses can be:

- Create menus
- Dynamically arrange layouts
- Hide and display certain items based on context-sensitive user-driven events
- Perform client-side validation

Creating XHTML

In Chapter 4, we covered how to create XML documents and what constitutes a well-formed XML document. As we've just learned, the W3C has redirected HTML back to its roots of following well-formedness rules by creating XHTML 1.0. As we cover the HTML tagset, we can keep this in mind and ensure our HTML is well-formed.

LISTING 10.5   Simple XHTML Document

```
<?xml version="1.0" encoding="UTF-8"?>
<!DOCTYPE html PUBLIC "-//W3C//DTD XHTML 1.0 Strict//EN"
  "http://www.w3.org/TR/xhtml1/DTD/xhtml1-strict.dtd">
<html xmlns="http://www.w3.org/1999/xhtml">
  <head><title>Hello XHMTL World!</title></head>
  <body>
  </body>
</html>
```

XHTML differs slightly in what it expects. Listing 10.5 shows a simple XHTML document. The first line in Listing 10.5 shows the XML declaration (remember, this is not considered a processing instruction although it looks suspiciously like one) which, although not mandatory, it is strongly encouraged by the W3C to be included. The next line of code is the document type declaration (represented as DOCTYPE). Recall from Chapter 4 where we covered validation of XML. This declaration allows Web browsers to handle the validation based on the particular DTD rule set that is given. In XHTML, this document type declaration is mandatory—failure to provide a document type declaration results in the Web browser not treating your HTML document as XHTML. As mentioned earlier, XHTML 1.0 offers three different versions: strict, transitional, and frameset; so there are three different document type declarations that can be made:

```
<!DOCTYPE html PUBLIC "-//W3C//DTD XHTML 1.0 Strict//EN"
"http://www.w3.org/TR/xhtml1/DTD/xhtml1-strict.dtd">

<!DOCTYPE html PUBLIC "-//W3C//DTD XHTML 1.0 Transitional//EN"
"http://www.w3.org/TR/xhtml1/DTD/xhtml1-transitional.dtd">

<!DOCTYPE html PUBLIC "-//W3C//DTD XHTML 1.0 Frameset//EN"
"http://www.w3.org/TR/xhtml1/DTD/xhtml1-frameset.dtd">
```

Using the strict version of XHTML requires some changes if you've been using regular HTML for a while. The W3C has been nudging Web developers in this direction with the merging of HTML 4.0 with XHTML 1.0. It is beneficial to Web developers to move in this direction because it makes it easier to programmatically parse, read, and manipulate XHTML. In fact, the W3C Recommendation for XHTML 1.0 is called XHTML™ 1.0 The Extensible HyperText Markup Language (Second Edition), A Reformulation of HTML 4 in XML 1.0. Over time, Web developers can expect this move to strict XHTML.

If you are creating Web pages that are viewed using older Web browsers (e.g., Internet Explorer 5 or less), then your likely choice is the transitional DTD. This way you inform the Web browser that the HTML document does not necessarily conform to XHTML and may not even conform to HTML 4.0. This may be because you are allowing some of the presentation information to exist within the HTML document instead of within the CSS.

Remembering all of the new rules of XHTML can be daunting—especially if you've learned many of the bad habits that older versions of HTML allowed Web developers to get away with. The W3C offers an online validator, which reports any errors in your XHTML code. The URL is: http://validator.w3.org/.

If you are confident that your user base is using the most recent versions of Web browsers, then you may wish to go with the strict DTD. Doing so requires you to keep all presentation information in your CSS and requires your XHTML document to conform to the rules of XML. XHTML documents always contain one root element: html. This element is required and without it the Web browser does not render your document as an XHTML document. The html element contains two direct child elements: head and body.

The head Element

The head element contains information in it that is not rendered directly to the user but is considered important metadata information for describing the document. The next section looks at the elements that are allowed to be placed within the head element.

The base Element

The base element refers to a base URL in which all URLs defined within the same page can be based on. So, for example. if we have the following base element inside of the head element

```
<base href="http://www.charlesriver.com/books/"/>
```

any other elements that contain relative URLs would use the base URL that was supplied in the base element. So if the following two anchor elements are supplied

```
<body>
  <a href="./products.html">link 1</a>
  <a href="http://www.bcit.ca">link 2</a>
</body>
```

the first link (link 1) would resolve to http://www.charlesriver.com/books/ products.html, whereas the second link would simply be http://www.bcit.ca because it is supplied as an absolute link not a relative link.

The link Element

The link element offers a way to link other documents to the current XHTML document. The link element can be placed in the head element any number of times. The most common use for this element is to link CSS files that are to be used by the current XHTML document:

```
<link rel="stylesheet" type="text/css" href="geekkit-basic.css"/>
```

This statement tells the Web browser to use a CSS file called `geekkit-basic.css`. Other uses are for telling search engines where to find alternative versions of the same document

```
<link media="print" type="application/postscript" rel="alternate"
  href="http://geekkit.bcit.ca/examples.ps"/>
```

or where to find the first page of a multi-page document collection

```
<link media="print" type="text/html" rel="Start"
  href="http://geekkit.bcit.ca/titlepage.html"/>
```

The `script` Element

The `script` element allows for scripts (such as JavaScript) to be placed within a Web page. This can be useful for dynamic processing of data from a server, to handle validation of forms, or for event handling of complex UI components that are built using JavaScript and XHTML. An example of displaying the time within a Web page using JavaScript is found in Listing 10.6.

LISTING 10.6 HTML Document Using the `script` Element

```
<?xml version="1.0" encoding="UTF-8"?>
<!DOCTYPE html PUBLIC "-//W3C//DTD XHTML 1.0 Strict//EN"
  "http://www.w3.org/TR/xhtml1/DTD/xhtml1-strict.dtd">
<html xmlns="http://www.w3.org/1999/xhtml">
  <head><title>Hello XHMTL World!</title>
    <script type="text/javascript">
      function getTime() {
        var para = document.getElementById("para_0");
        para.childNodes.item(0).nodeValue = new Date();
        setTimeout("getTime()", 1000);
      }
    </script>
  </head>
  <body onload="getTime()"><p id="para_0"> </p></body>
</html>
```

 The script element is not just confined to the head element. It can also be placed in the body element. There can also be any number of script elements in either the head or the body

The `style` Element

The `style` element allows for the embedding of style information within the XHTML document itself. Although this is supported, it should be avoided because style sheets should be separate documents so that multiple XHTML documents can reference the same style sheet, thus reducing bandwidth and reducing inconsistencies in style. However, it may be acceptable if the style information is at a minimum and won't be reused by other XHTML documents:

```
<style type="text/css">
  p { text-align: justify; }
</style>
```

The `title` Element

The `title` element is used to display a title on the Web browser's title bar:

```
<title>Kucing CMS 1.0 Admin Tools</title>
```

It is usually a good idea to place some information in the title bar so that users are informed about which Web page they have visited—especially if they have multiple Web browser windows opened.

The `body` Element

The body element contains all content that is presented to the user (or at least that can be presented to the user). There are many different child elements that can be placed within the body element. We'll look at the most commonly used elements.

The `heading 1 ... 6` Elements

There are six different levels of headings that can be used within an XHTML document, each one offering a different size of text. This offers flexibility in creating sections within sections within sections of content. Listing 10.7 shows four levels deep of headings (i.e., sections within sections):

LISTING 10.7 XHTML with Headings

```
<?xml version="1.0" encoding="UTF-8"?>
<!DOCTYPE html PUBLIC "-//W3C//DTD XHTML 1.0 Strict//EN"
  "http://www.w3.org/TR/xhtml1/DTD/xhtml1-strict.dtd">
<html xmlns="http://www.w3.org/1999/xhtml">
  <head><title> new document </title></head>
  <body>
    <h1>Section 4.0 - Introduction to XML</h1>
    <p>Software development has been ...</p>
    <h2>Section 4.1 - Understanding XML</h2>
    <p>If you are quite familiar with XML  ...</p>
    <h3>Section 4.1.1 - What XML Is</h3>
    <p>Because there is much hype surrounding  ...</p>
    <h4>Section 4.1.1.1 - A Description of Metadata Structures</h4>
    <p>As we mentioned previously, XML is  ...</p>
  </body>
</html>
```

Figure 10.1 shows the display within a Web browser of the rendered XHTML content (from Listing 10.7). Although it may appear that we are applying presentation-specific formatting to our XHTML document, the heading levels are logical levels of content structure rather than specific formatting details. We can qualify this statement by realizing that at no point have we stated a font, a font size, or any other formatting rules to the heading. The Web browser has simply chosen to render the headings using its own default presentation choices. As we'll see later in this chapter, we can add our own specific presentation formatting using CSS.

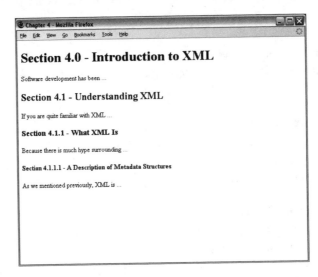

FIGURE 10.1 Web page with different levels of headings.

Paragraph Type Elements

There are several different elements that allow for the creation of paragraphs and structure within paragraphs. Listing 10.8 gives us a Web page that displays many of the paragraph type elements that are available. The paragraph element (`<p></p>`) can house straight text as well as several different types of elements including bold (`<b></b>`) and italic (`<i></i>`), which bold text and italicize text respectively. The big (`<big></big>`) and small (`<small></small>`) elements make the text slightly bigger and slightly smaller within the paragraph respectively. The `acronym` element allows Web browsers to provide a pop-up definition for the acronym provided. In Listing 10.8, when the user places the mouse cursor over the word XUI, a pop-up rectangle appears with the title `XML (based) User Interface`. This element can be useful if many different acronyms are used within a Web page document because too many definitions may make the document hard to read.

LISTING 10.8   XHTML Paragraphs and Paragraph Content

```
<?xml version="1.0" encoding="UTF-8"?>
<!DOCTYPE html PUBLIC "-//W3C//DTD XHTML 1.0 Strict//EN"
  "http://www.w3.org/TR/xhtml1/DTD/xhtml1-strict.dtd">
<html xmlns="http://www.w3.org/1999/xhtml">
  <head><title> Paragraphs And Paragraph Content </title></head>
  <body>
    <p><b>Purnama Project</b> <acronym title="XML (based) User
    Interface">XUI</acronym> is a Java <i>reference
    implementation</i> of a <big>X</big>ML <big>U</big>ser
    <big>I</big>nterface (XUI) that allows GUIs (Graphical User
    Interfaces) to be described using XML and thus platform and
    language independent. It is both an XML format (which conforms
    to <code>XML Schema</code>), and a Java <small>API</small>. As
    the author of Purnama XUI has stated:</p>
    <blockquote><p>My intention with XUI (pronounced "zooey") is to
    give developers the ability to create interactive resources
    that are independent of platform and programming languages —
    interactive resources which can easily be accessed online.</p>
    </blockquote>
    <p>In XUI the XML is unmarshalled and then turned into a GUI:
    </p>
    <pre>  // get a builder.
XUIBuilder builder =
XUIBuilderFactory.getInstance().getXUIBuilder();</pre>
  </body>
</html>
```

If a block quote of text is required within a document then the `blockquote` element can be used. Web browsers usually indent the block quote text, although the default indent value is specific to the Web browser. If there is a need for monospaced characters, the `code` element can be used. Usually the `code` element is used to embed the names of method calls or classes of a particular programming language. If, however, you need to show a block of code, then you will require the `pre` element. The `pre` element is useful because it is the only element that requests that the Web browser not collapse whitespace. Unlike regular XML parsers, XHTML parsers, and specifically Web browsers, collapse whitespace. Collapsing whitespace is not desired when displaying program code within an XHTML document. Listing 10.8 shows the `pre` element used with an indent of two spaces. Figure 10.2 shows the presented Web page from Listing 10.8.

There are still several other types of elements that can be placed within the paragraph element within HTML. However, many of the elements that provide formatting within a paragraph can easily be obtained by simply using style sheets.

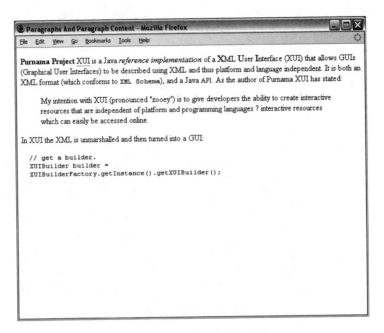

FIGURE 10.2 Paragraph text rendered in Web browser.

List Elements

XHTML offers three different types of lists. The first is an unordered list. Unordered lists are defined using the `ul` element which contains list item elements (`<li></li>`). Listing 10.9 displays the unordered list (first list). Unordered lists are not numbered and are usually represented as bulleted lists, although style sheet information can change this. The next type of list is the ordered list which numbers list items and is represented by the `ol` element. Listing 10.9 offers us an ordered list (second list). Fortunately, we are not responsible for numbering the list items ourselves—the Web browser does this for us. The last type of list is a definition list which is represented by the `dl` element. Definition lists are slightly different from unordered and ordered lists in that definition lists offer both a definition term (represented by the `dt` element) and a definition description (represented by the `dd` element) for each item. Again, looking back to Listing 10.9, the third list given shows the same three items as a definition list.

LISTING 10.9 XHTML Lists

```
<?xml version="1.0" encoding="UTF-8"?>
<!DOCTYPE html PUBLIC "-//W3C//DTD XHTML 1.0 Strict//EN"
  "http://www.w3.org/TR/xhtml1/DTD/xhtml1-strict.dtd">
```

```
<html xmlns="http://www.w3.org/1999/xhtml">
  <head><title> Lists </title></head>
  <body>
    <ul>
      <li>Content Management</li>
      <li>Introduction to Content Management Systems</li>
      <li>Licensing Issues</li>
    </ul>
    <ol>
      <li>Content Management</li>
      <li>Introduction to Content Management Systems</li>
      <li>Licensing Issues</li>
    </ol>
    <dl>
      <dt>Chapter 1</dt>
      <dd>Content Management</dd>
      <dt>Chapter 2</dt>
      <dd>Introduction to Content Management Systems</dd>
      <dt>Chapter 3</dt>
      <dd>Licensing Issues</dd>
    </dl>
  </body>
</html>
```

Figure 10.3 shows the rendered list in HTML (from Listing 10.9). The level of indenting is chosen by the Web browser at this point because we have not been adding any style information yet.

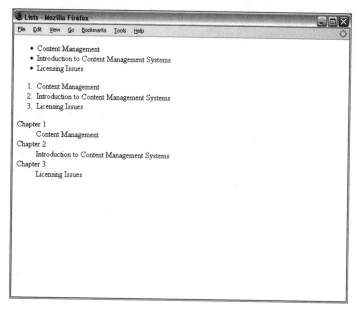

FIGURE 10.3   XHTML lists example.

The Break Element

The break element allows us to place a line break within text. This is useful if we wish to separate a list of items or create some whitespace on a page. The break element is an empty element and, therefore, has no end tag:

```
<br/>
```

The Anchor Element

One of the most important elements in XHTML is of course the hyperlink element. This element allows us to create the hyperlinks within our XHTML documents. The anchor element is represented by the a element. Anchor elements can be placed just about anywhere and house absolute URLs such as http://www.charlesriver.com or relative URLs, such as ./index.html. One important rule we must remember is that XHTML strict requires us to embed anchor elements within paragraph elements—we cannot simply place an anchor element directly into the body element of our XHTML document. Listing 10.10 displays an XHTML document which contains anchor elements (hyperlinks).

LISTING 10.10   XHTML Hyperlink Elements

```
<?xml version="1.0" encoding="UTF-8"?>
<!DOCTYPE html PUBLIC "-//W3C//DTD XHTML 1.0 Strict//EN"
  "http://www.w3.org/TR/xhtml1/DTD/xhtml1-strict.dtd">
<html xmlns="http://www.w3.org/1999/xhtml">
  <head>
    <title> Anchor Elements </title>
  </head>
  <body>
    <p>
      <a id="top" title="Go to bottom of page" href="#bottom">
        Go To Bottom Of Page</a>
      <br/><br/><br/><br/><br/><br/><br/><br/><br/><br/>
      <a title="Charles River Media"
        href="http://www.charlesriver.com/Books/Features.aspx">
          Charles River Media</a>
      <br/><br/><br/><br/><br/><br/><br/><br/><br/><br/>
      <a title="An image" href=""></a>
      <br/><br/><br/><br/><br/><br/><br/><br/><br/><br/>
      <a id="bottom" title="Go to top of page" href="#top">
        Go To Top Of Page</a>
    </p>
  </body>
</html>
```

The middle anchor takes the user to the Charles River Media Web site. This is the typical example of using a hyperlink: to take the user to another Web page. The href attribute is used to direct the Web browser to the correct URL.

```
<a title="Charles River Media"
   href="http://www.charlesriver.com/Books/Features.aspx">
   Charles River Media</a>
```

The text between the begin and end tags for the anchor element house the text that is displayed as a hyperlink. Anchor elements can also be used to direct the user to another place within the same Web page. In order to do this, another anchor element must be referenced. This is accomplished by using a relative URL to simply reference an id value of another anchor element. In Listing 10.10, the anchor labeled Go To Bottom Of Page takes the user to the bottom of the page. This is because the href attribute value of this anchor references the id attribute value of the other anchor—in this case the referenced id attribute value has a value of bottom. This value matches the id attribute value of the bottom anchor element. Note that we can also use the name attribute, as well as the id attribute to reference the anchor element from other anchor elements.

Table Elements

The use of tables within any HTML has earned a negative connotation. This is unfortunate because for several years tables in HTML were misused. With earlier versions of HTML there were no complex ways to lay out content. Web developers, therefore, turned to the table element and used the table to perform layouts within the page. This was very much a misuse of the table element. The table element is, after all, not a layout mechanism, it is for displaying tabular data. Tabular data can take many forms including statistical results from surveys, listings of personal contacts, course material, just to name a few. Listing 10.11 offers an example of a table in XHTML.

LISTING 10.11   XHTML Table

```
<?xml version="1.0" encoding="UTF-8"?>
<!DOCTYPE html PUBLIC "-//W3C//DTD XHTML 1.0 Strict//EN"
   "http://www.w3.org/TR/xhtml1/DTD/xhtml1-strict.dtd">
<html xmlns="http://www.w3.org/1999/xhtml">
  <head><title> Tables </title></head>
  <body>
    <table>
      <caption>File Listing</caption>
      <thead>
        <tr>
```

```
          <td></td>
          <td>File</td>
          <td>Topic</td>
          <td>Format</td>
        </tr>
      </thead>
      <tfoot>
        <tr>
          <td></td>
          <td>File</td>
          <td>Topic</td>
          <td>Format</td>
        </tr>
        <tr>
          <td colspan="4">File Listing</td>
        </tr>
      </tfoot>
      <tbody>
        <tr>
          <td rowspan="4">File<br/>Listing</td>
          <td><a href="./downloads/1.zip">Java-intro-to-2D.zip</a>
          </td>
          <td>2D Raster API</td>
          <td>Zipped Lecture Slides</td>
        </tr>
        <tr>
          <td><a href="./downloads/2.zip">DOMDemo.zip</a></td>
          <td>DOM Demo App</td>
          <td>Zipped Java Source</td>
        </tr>
        <tr>
          <td><a href="./downloads/3.jar">jcalendar.jar</a></td>
          <td>Java Calendar App</td>
          <td>Self-executing JAR</td>
        </tr>
      </tbody>
    </table>
  </body>
</html>
```

Tables are allowed (but not required to) contain a caption—although a caption is useful—especially if there are several different tables that represent data sets. If you're used to older versions of HTML, then this table looks slightly different. XHTML strict requires tables to be divided into three main sections within a table: header, footer, and body. Each of these three child elements represents header rows, footer rows, and the main body of rows, respectively. Although we declare the order to be header, footer, and body, the Web browser renders the header at the top of the table, the footer at the bottom of the table, and of course the body is between the two. Although this adds extra data to our document, it gives us flexibility in how we later format the different parts of a table, as well as allows us to place multiple rows within both the header as well as the footer.

Within each of these three main areas, we are allowed to add rows using the `tr` element. Table rows then contain table data for each column represented. We use the `td` cell to represent cells. We can place straight text, anchor elements, paragraphs, headings, lists, and even other tables within the table data element, although we shouldn't be placing tables within tables to perform layouts. Lastly, Figure 10.4 gives us the rendered view from the Web browser of our table (Listing 10.11). Again, the rendering attributes are the default attributes chosen by the Web browser because we have not yet applied any specific rendering attributes ourselves using style sheets.

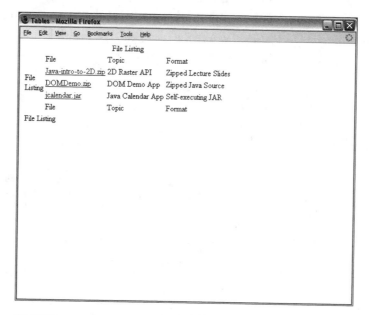

FIGURE 10.4   XHTML table example.

The *image* Element

The image element in XHTML allows for the insertion of an image within the Web content. We can, for example, place an image into the document with:

```
<img src="./portrait.jpg" alt="Self Portrait"/>
```

The `src` attribute accepts the URL that references the image, and the `alt` attribute displays an alternative message if image rendering has been disabled or if the image is not available.

Form Elements

Creating forms is one of the oldest and yet one of the most powerful features of HTML. It allows us to build an interactive Web page where users can enter data and submit that data to a server. Although the set of GUI components is rather small (compared to Java's Swing), we do have enough that we can send simple information sets, or if need be, we can create more complex layouts and forms using combinations of the existing components. XHTML forms offer us the following types of components:

input: An input can be a button, a checkbox, file, hidden, image, password, radio, reset, submit, and text

select: A selection component that presents a list of components

textarea: A text area where the user can type multiple lines of text

label: A label used to label the other types of components

Looking at Listing 10.12, we see a form that contains most of the different types of form components available.

LISTING 10.12   XHTML Form

```
<?xml version="1.0" encoding="UTF-8"?>
<!DOCTYPE html PUBLIC "-//W3C//DTD XHTML 1.0 Strict//EN"
  "http://www.w3.org/TR/xhtml1/DTD/xhtml1-strict.dtd">
<html xmlns="http://www.w3.org/1999/xhtml">
  <head><title>Form Example</title></head>
  <body>
    <form action="./submit.html">
      <p><label for="firstName">First Name:</label>
        <input type="text" name="firstName" id="firstName"/>
        <label for="lastName">Last Name:</label>
        <input type="text" name="lastName" id="lastName"/>
        <label for="password">Password:</label>
        <input type="password" name="password" id="password"/>
        <label for="address">Address:</label>
        <textarea rows="2" cols="20" id="address"></textarea>
        <label>Sex:</label>
        <input type="radio" name="sex" id="male"/>
        <label for="male">Male</label>
        <input type="radio" name="sex" id="female"/>
        <label for="female">Female</label>
        <input type="checkbox" name="like" id="likeXHTML"/>
        <label for="likeXHTML">I like XHTML</label>
        <label for="experience">Experience</label>
        <select size="1" name="experience" id="experience">
          <option value="newcomer" selected="selected">
            Newcomer</option>
          <option value="semi-experienced">
```

```
      Semi-experienced</option>
    <option value="advanced">Advanced</option>
  </select>
  <label for="chaptersList">Chapters Read</label>
  <select size="6" multiple="multiple" name="chaptersRead"
    id="chaptersList">
    <option value="ch1" selected="selected">
      Chapter 1 - Content Management</option>
    <option value="ch2" selected="selected">
      Chapter 2 - Introduction to Content Management Systems
    </option>
    <option value="ch3" selected="selected">
      Chapter 3 - Licensing Issues</option>
    <option value="ch4" selected="selected">
      Chapter 4 - Introduction to XML</option>
    <option value="ch5" selected="selected">
      Chapter 5 - Data Modeling With XML</option>
    <option value="ch6" selected="selected">
      Chapter 6 - Programming with XML</option>
    <option value="ch7" selected="selected">
      Chapter 7 - Server Technologies</option>
    <option value="ch8" selected="selected">
      Chapter 8 - Protocol Topics for CMS Development
    </option>
    <option value="ch9" selected="selected">
      Chapter 9 - User Interface Design</option>
    <option value="ch10">Chapter 10 - Web Design</option>
  </select>
  <label for="uploadComment">Upload Comment File:</label>
  <input type="file" name="uploadComment"
    id="uploadComment"/>
  <input type="submit" value="Submit"/>
  <input type="reset" value="Reset"/>
  <input type="hidden" value="basicForm" id="basicForm"/>
  <input type="image" src="./manage-content-64x64.png"
    id="manageContent"/>
 </p>
 </form>
 </body>
</html>
```

The input element can be changed to create different components. We do this by assigning different values to the input element's type attribute. For example, we can assign it a value of text which turns the input element into a text field, as seen in Listing 10.12, for the input element whose id attribute value is firstName. A rendering of the form is shown in Figure 10.5 (from Listing 10.12). We can also turn the input into a password field, which is like a text field, but each character is shown as an asterisk to mask the actual characters typed into that field. Listing 10.12 shows a password input (the input whose id attribute value is password).

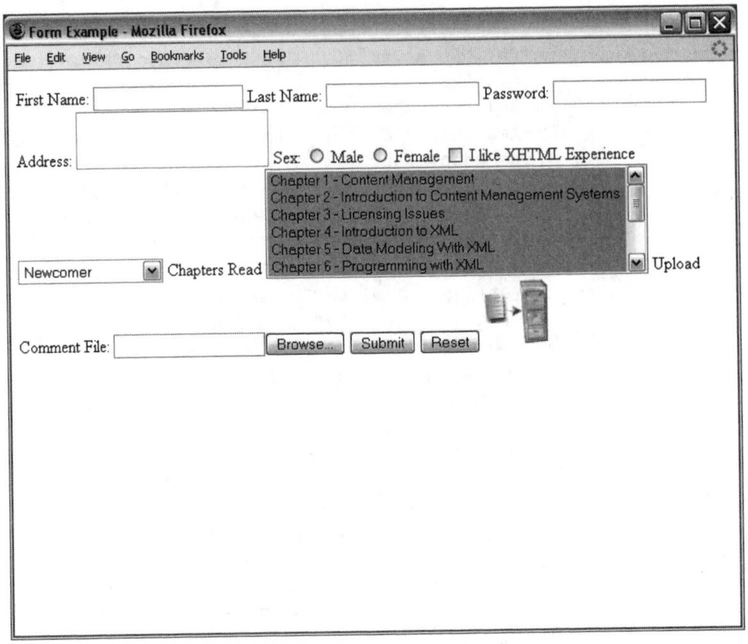

FIGURE 10.5 XHTML form.

Inputs can be grouped together as radio buttons by changing their `type` attribute value to `radio` and ensuring that all radio buttons that are to be part of a group all use the same value for their `name` attribute value. In Listing 10.12 the input elements whose `id` attribute values are `male` and `female` are part of the `sex` input element group. This means that only one of the radio buttons can be selected at a time.

Inputs can also be created as checkboxes. Checkboxes allow the user to either select the checkbox or not. Checkboxes should function independently unlike radio buttons. To make an input into a checkbox, set its `type` attribute value to `checkbox`. Listing 10.12 has a checkbox (`id` attribute value is `likeXHTML`). In order to allow users to upload files an input can be turned into a file upload input. This input has both a text field as well as a button (usually labeled `Browse`). When the button is selected a file dialog box opens and allows the user to select the name of a file. This filename (including its full path within the filesystem) is displayed in the text field. In Listing 10.12, the input whose `id` attribute value is `uploadComment` has been created as a file type input. In order to allow a form to submit the information to the server, an input that has been created as type submit is needed (`type` attribute value `submit`). In order for this to work, however, the action attribute of the form element itself must contain a URL (be it relative or absolute) of the server resource that processes the submitted request. Recall Chapter 8, where we processed requests from the client on the server.

Another useful input type is the reset type. Setting an input's `type` attribute value to `reset` turns the input into a button that allows the user to clear all fields within the form simply by selecting the reset input. Sometimes there is a need to have a hidden field (i.e., one that is not visible to the user). This may be important if we need to help the server distinguish between different forms that are attempting to send information. Listing 10.12 shows a hidden input (`id` attribute value `basicForm`). Changing the input's `type` attribute to `hidden` hides the input from being rendered in the Web page. The last type of input is the image type. This input uses an image in place of a button for rendering to the user. The drawback is that you must supply an image by linking to it using the `src` attribute of the `input` element. In Listing 10.12 (at the bottom), there is an input (`id` attribute value `manageContent`) which uses an image listed as `manage-content-64x64.png`. When the form information is sent to the server, the coordinates of where the user clicked within the image is sent as well. This can be useful if a large image is used where different regions of the image map to different resources on the server.

The Image Element

XHTML allows us to place images into the page and even specify the size we wish the image to be displayed at. Listing 10.13 shows an XHTML document with three different image elements, each element referencing the same image but changing the size presented within the document.

LISTING 10.13   Image Element Example

```
<?xml version="1.0" encoding="UTF-8"?>
<!DOCTYPE html PUBLIC "-//W3C//DTD XHTML 1.0 Strict//EN"
  "http://www.w3.org/TR/xhtml1/DTD/xhtml1-strict.dtd">
<html xmlns="http://www.w3.org/1999/xhtml">
  <head><title>Image Example</title></head>
  <body>
    <p>
      <img alt="./river.png" src="./river.png"/>
      <img alt="./river.png" src="./river.png" width="70"
        height="52"/>
      <img alt="./river.png" src="./river.png" width="35"
        height="27"/>
    </p>
  </body>
</html>
```

In order for the image element to be valid to the strict XHTML DTD, all `img` elements must contain an `alt` attribute. The `alt` attribute offers an alternative text description for any Web browsers that cannot or have been configured to not display images. Figure 10.6 shows the displayed Web page (from Listing 10.13).

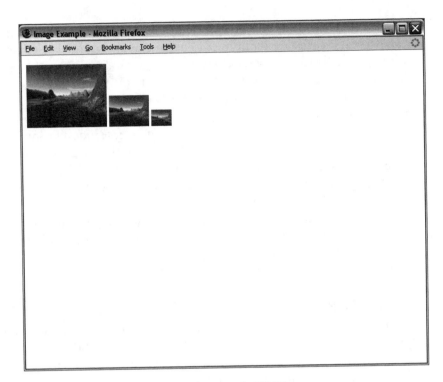

FIGURE 10.6 Rendered image elements in XHTML.

Common XHTML Attributes

XHTML inherits functionality of HTML 4.0—specifically the ability to place a few particular attributes within almost any element.

The id Attribute

The id attribute can be applied to most XHTML elements including anchor, paragraph, table, and heading elements, to name a few. The id attribute offers the ability to uniquely identify a particular XHTML element within the document. The id attribute is defined as ID within the DTD that defines the XHTML rule set; so no two id attribute values can be the same within an XHTML document. Reasons for using the id attribute on an XHTML element are:

- A style sheet selector (covered later in this chapter)
- A target anchor used with hyperlinks
- A way for a script to refer to a particular element (e.g., using JavaScript)
- External Web applications to be able to identify particular elements within an XHTML document for specialized processing needs

In the case of an `id` being used with a style sheet, we could use the `id` value to identify text that should be formatted differently. Listing 10.14 shows an anchor element (hyperlink) that uses an `id` attribute to indicate special formatting (in this case changing the color of the hyperlink text).

LISTING 10.14   The `id` Attribute Used as a Style Sheet Selector

```
<?xml version="1.0" encoding="UTF-8"?>
<!DOCTYPE html PUBLIC "-//W3C//DTD XHTML 1.0 Strict//EN"
  "http://www.w3.org/TR/xhtml1/DTD/xhtml1-strict.dtd">
<html xmlns="http://www.w3.org/1999/xhtml">
  <head><title> Home Page </title>
    <style type="text/css">
      #homeLink { color: rgb(40, 61, 123); }
    </style>
  </head>
  <body>
    <p>Visit the site at: <a id="homeLink"
      href="http://www.charlesriver.com">CRM</a></p>
  </body>
</html>
```

Specifying Text Direction

The `dir` attribute and the `bdo` element can be rather confusing as to how they work. The purpose of both of them is to correctly render Unicode text using the correct direction. For example, any characters that are rendered using English language characters should be rendered from left-to-right. In contrast, Hebrew characters should be rendered from right-to-left. By default, the Unicode specification assigns directionality to characters by using an algorithm, which determines which direction the text should take. If the Web browser (i.e., user agent) encounters right-to-left characters, then it applies what is known as a *bidirectional algorithm*. If, however, it encounters left-to-right characters, then the bidirectional algorithm is not used. The problem comes into play when characters are encountered that are both left-to-right as well as right-to-left. This type of sequence of characters is said to be *directionally neutral* and, therefore, ambiguous to the user agent. This problem is what the `dir` attribute and the `bdo` element address.

The `dir` attribute can be applied to most elements (e.g., paragraph elements, table elements, the body element), but its behavior is dependent on the character set and the element that it is placed within. For example, if the paragraph element has the `dir` attribute with a value of `rtl` (right-to-left), then the paragraph is set to align right (aligned to the right of the display pane). If a table has the `dir` attribute with a value of `rtl`, then the cells are displayed within the table in right-to-left order. Listing 10.15 offers several examples of the `dir` attribute within paragraphs and one in a table.

LISTING 10.15   The bdo Element and dir Attribute

```
<?xml version="1.0" encoding="UTF-8"?>
<!DOCTYPE html PUBLIC "-//W3C//DTD XHTML 1.0 Strict//EN"
  "http://www.w3.org/TR/xhtml1/DTD/xhtml1-strict.dtd">
<html xmlns="http://www.w3.org/1999/xhtml">
  <head><title>The dir Attribute</title></head>
  <body lang="en">
    <p>This sentence renders <b>and</b> displays characters from
      left to right. <bdo dir="rtl">This sentence renders
      characters from left to right.</bdo>
    </p>
    <p dir="rtl">This sentence displays characters from right to
      left. <bdo dir="rtl">This sentence renders <b>and</b>
      displays from right to left.</bdo></p>
    <table dir="rtl">
      <tbody>
        <tr><td>1</td><td>2</td><td>3</td></tr>
      </tbody>
    </table>
  </body>
</html>
```

The bdo element can be placed within paragraphs, headings, the div element, the pre element, and a few other less commonly used elements. Of course, in order for either to work correctly the Web browser that is rendering the text must support the dir attribute and the bdo element. The bdo element is used within conjunction with the dir attribute and forces the direction of the rendered text.

All Web browsers that support HTML 4.0 and above have the ability to correctly render text with the dir attribute and the bdo element.

Listing 10.15 shows use of the bdo element. As shown earlier, Figure 10.6 displayed the actual rendering of the XHTML document. Most times there is little need to use this feature. However, if a document contains, for example, both English and Hebrew characters, then using both the bdo element and the dir attribute help alleviate text-rendering problems.

The lang Attribute

The lang attribute can be used to specify which language is being used within a document. The body element in Listing 10.15 contains the lang attribute with a value of en for English. While not mandatory, the lang attribute can help assist search engines in determining which language a page is presented in, help user agents (Web browsers) choose the correct quotation marks, hyphens, spacing, and assist grammar checkers make more accurate suggestions.

Accessibility Attributes

Two attributes that assist in accessibility are the accesskey attribute and the tabindex attribute. First, the accesskey attribute allows for quick key access to particular elements. The accesskey can work with the anchor element (a), area, button, input, label, legend, and textarea elements. The accesskey attribute accepts a value which is the name of the particular key with which to associate. If the user presses that key on the keyboard, then the cursor jumps to that particular element within the XHTML document. Listing 10.16 contains a form that makes use of the accesskey attribute in several different elements.

NOTE

Access keys usually require another key to be pressed as well. In Microsoft Windows, the Alt key must be pressed in tandem with the access key. In the Macintosh OS, the Cmd key must be pressed.

The tabindex attribute assigns a tab index value to the particular element that the attribute is found in. The tabindex attribute can be applied to the anchor element, area, button, input, object, select, and textarea elements. The tab index allows users to press the tab button on the keyboard to cycle through and select particular elements within the XHTML document. This is useful if the user does not have a mouse or cannot use the mouse. Web browsers already allow the ability to tab through elements within a page, but the tabindex element allows the designer to change the order of the tabbing. Listing 10.16 shows a form where the tab order has been reversed.

LISTING 10.16   Accessibility Attributes in a Form

```
<?xml version="1.0" encoding="UTF-8"?>
<!DOCTYPE html PUBLIC "-//W3C//DTD XHTML 1.0
  Strict//EN" "http://www.w3.org/TR/xhtml1/DTD/xhtml1-strict.dtd">
<html xmlns="http://www.w3.org/1999/xhtml">
  <head><title>Form Example</title></head>
  <body>
    <form action="./submit.html">
      <p>
        <label accesskey="f" for="firstName">First Name:</label>
        <input tabindex="4" type="text" name="firstName"
          id="firstName"/>
        <label accesskey="l" for="lastName">Last Name:</label>
        <input tabindex="3" type="text" name="lastName"
          id="lastName"/>
        <input tabindex="2" accesskey="s" type="submit"
          value="Submit"/>
        <input tabindex="1" type="reset" value="Reset"/>
```

```
      </p>
    </form>
  </body>
</html>
```

Replacing the `applet` Element

The `applet` element is used to reference a Java applet within a Web page. This element has been deprecated, which means it is no longer to be used in XHTML strict. The replacement element is the `object` element. So, for example, if you were accessing a Java applet within a Java Archive (JAR) file within a Web page, you would have used the `applet` tag as follows:

```
<!DOCTYPE HTML PUBLIC "-//W3C//DTD HTML 4.0 Transitional//EN">
<html>
  <head>
    <title>Kucing CMS 1.0 Admin Tools</title>
    <link type="image/x-icon"
      href="./media/images/mr-kucing-16x16.ico"
      rel="shortcut icon">
  </head>
  <body>
    <p align="center">
      <applet code="org.kucingCMS.admin.AdminTool.class"
        archive="./client/kucingCMS-admin.jar" width="640"
height="520">
      </applet>
    </p>
  </body>
</html>
```

To create the same functionality, we now use the `object` element. The `object` element accepts several attributes as well as child elements. One attribute in particular is the `classid` attribute. Because of lack of a specific definition from W3C, the `classid` attribute has been interpreted differently within the Web community. For example, to follow proper XHTML form using the `object` element with the Mozilla Web browser and Mozilla FireFox Web browser, we specify the `classid` value as in Listing 10.17.

LISTING 10.17 Mozilla and FireFox Web browser Use of `Object` Element

```
<?xml version="1.0" encoding="UTF-8"?>
<!DOCTYPE html PUBLIC "-//W3C//DTD XHTML 1.0 Strict//EN"
  "http://www.w3.org/TR/xhtml1/DTD/xhtml1-strict.dtd">
<html xmlns="http://www.w3.org/1999/xhtml">
  <head>
    <title>Kucing CMS 1.0 Admin Tools</title>
    <link type="image/x-icon"
```

```
                    href="./media/images/mr-kucing-16x16.ico"
                    rel="shortcut icon"/>
          </head>
          <body>
            <p>
              <object classid="java:org.kucingCMS.admin.AdminTool.class"
                width="640" height="520">
                <param name="code"
                  value="org.kucingCMS.admin.AdminTool.class"/>
                <param name="archive"
                  value="./client/kucingCMS-admin.jar"/>
                <param name="type"
                  value="application/x-java-applet;version=1.5.0"/>
              </object>
            </p>
          </body>
        </html>
```

The value given for the `classid` (shown in bold) for Mozilla browsers uses the `java` keyword, followed by a colon, and then by the full name of the class that is to be loaded as an applet (including the package). However, Microsoft Internet Explorer uses a slightly different approach, which is shown in Listing 10.18.

LISTING 10.18   Microsoft Internet Explorer Web Browser Use of `Object` Element

```
<?xml version="1.0" encoding="UTF-8"?>
<!DOCTYPE html PUBLIC "-//W3C//DTD XHTML 1.0 Strict//EN"
  "http://www.w3.org/TR/xhtml1/DTD/xhtml1-strict.dtd">
<html xmlns="http://www.w3.org/1999/xhtml">
  <head>
    <title>Kucing CMS 1.0 Admin Tools</title>
    <link type="image/x-icon"
      href="./media/images/mr-kucing-16x16.ico" rel="shortcut icon"/>
  </head>
  <body>
    <p>
      <object classid="clsid:8AD9C840-044E-11D1-B3E9-00805F499D93"
        width="640" height="520">
        <param name="code"
          value="org.kucingCMS.admin.AdminTool.class"/>
        <param name="archive"
          value="./client/kucingCMS-admin.jar"/>
        <param name="type"
          value="application/x-java-applet;version=1.5.0"/>
      </object>
    </p>
  </body>
</html>
```

The `classid` attribute in Listing 10.18 has a completely different meaning and is not the name of the class to run. Its value is instead a unique identifier for declaring use of the Java runtime. This, of course, causes a problem because we now need to create two different solutions in order to support Microsoft's Internet Explorer and Mozilla Web browsers. Instead, we can take advantage of a little trick that allows us to slip in a conditional check within XML comments. Listing 10.19 gives us both solutions in one page. Microsoft has created a method of placing a conditional check within an XML comment. Listing 10.19 shows the condition which starts with `[if !IE]` and ends with `<![endif]`. If this page is opened with Internet Explorer, this check is performed and the first `object` element will be ignored by Internet Explorer. Internet Explorer only attempts to use the second `object` element because it is outside of the conditional check within the comment. If this page is opened with Mozilla FireFox, it does not recognize the conditional within the comment and proceeds to open the first `object` element because the first `object` element's `classid` value contains a reference to a Java class. FireFox ignores the second object element because from its perspective, it does not contain a valid Java class name.

LISTING 10.19 Multiple Values for the `classid` Attribute

```
<?xml version="1.0" encoding="UTF-8"?>
<!DOCTYPE html PUBLIC "-//W3C//DTD XHTML 1.0 Strict//EN"
  "http://www.w3.org/TR/xhtml1/DTD/xhtml1-strict.dtd">
<html xmlns="http://www.w3.org/1999/xhtml">
  <head>
    <title>Kucing CMS 1.0 Admin Tools</title>
    <link type="image/x-icon"
      href="./media/images/mr-kucing-16x16.ico"
      rel="shortcut icon"/>
  </head>
  <body>
    <p>
    <!-[if !IE]> If it's not Internet Explorer, do this: ->
    <object classid="java:org.kucingCMS.admin.AdminTool.class"
      width="640" height="520">
      <param name="code"
        value="org.kucingCMS.admin.AdminTool.class"/>
      <param name="archive"
        value="./client/kucingCMS-admin.jar"/>
      <param name="type"
        value="application/x-java-applet;version=1.5.0"/>
    </object>
    <!-<![endif]->

    <!- Microsoft Internet Explorer ->
    <object classid="clsid:8AD9C840-044E-11D1-B3E9-00805F499D93"
      width="640" height="520">
```

```
    <param name="code"
      value="org.kucingCMS.admin.AdminTool.class"/>
    <param name="archive"
      value="./client/kucingCMS-admin.jar"/>
    <param name="type"
      value="application/x-java-applet;version=1.5.0"/>
  </object>
 </p>
 </body>
</html>
```

The `div` and `span` Elements

We've saved `span` element and the `div` element until last for a good reason. These two elements offer *inline* and *block-level* structure. When we say inline, we are referring to textual content that is found within a line of text. The `span` element can be pretty much placed anywhere within any element that houses content such as paragraphs, headings, and table data. The `span` element is used with styles where there is a need to place a special style for a certain string of characters or words. An example may be a search engine that is highlighting certain words or phrases in a search result. We might find the span element in some XHTML like this:

```
<p>After a document is loaded into the DOM, <span
  class="hiliteText">XUI</span> then turns that document into a
  graphical user interface. </p>
```

Block level, on the other hand, is referring to a section of several different types of element and content structure which is being treated as one large composite. The `div` (short for division) element allows us to group several different structures together for the purpose of treating them as a composite content structure. This might be useful for a group of elements that represents something such as a menu system:

```
<div class="menuBox">
  <ul class="menu">
    <li><a href="#" class="menuItem">Home</a></li>
    <li><a href="#" class="menuItem">Projects</a></li>
    <li><a href="#" class="menuItem">XML</a></li>
  </ul>
</div>
```

Neither the `span` nor the `div` element offers any default presentation formatting. In fact, without a CSS to assign styles to these element types, a Web document looks no different with these elements inserted into the document than if they had never been there. This brings us to the need to create style using Cascading Style Sheets.

INTRODUCTION TO CASCADING STYLE SHEETS

Up until now, we've only been creating the content structure within the XHTML documents. At the beginning of the chapter, we alluded to all presentation information such as formatting details like font size, style, background colors, and such being removed from XHMLT (although this migration started with HTML 4.0). It is now time to investigate the abilities of CSS. Although CSS offers the ability to separate our presentation data from the content structure, it does force us to learn a new syntax as well as a few new concepts. Currently the standard is CSS Level 2, which was released on May 12, 1998, as a recommendation. CSS Level 2.1 is (at the time of this writing) a "last call" working draft, which simply means that most requests for feedback from the community as well as W3C members have come in; so it can be expected that CSS Level 2.1 should be released soon.

Having mentioned about working drafts, CSS Level 2.1 has seen wide adoption, even in working draft form. Most of the features laid out in CSS level 2.1 are available in the more widely used Web browsers, including Microsoft Internet Explorer 6.0, Firefox 1.0, Firefox 1.5, and Opera 8, with only a few features missing such as printing, counter selections, and some whitespace options.

For a thorough listing of features supported within the various Web browsers, visit: http://www.webdevout.net/browser_support_css.php#css2standards.

The Box Model

The W3C defines the *box model* for CSS, which is really just a way of visualizing the different parts of the XHTML document as a series of rectangular containers within other rectangular containers. This metaphor works well with our XHTML document tree because nodes within the tree contain other nodes. For example, a span element would have a box that could be placed within a paragraph which also has a box. The paragraph could then be placed within a division element which too contains a box. Each of these content elements makes up the document as a whole.

With each element's box, there are several different characteristics that we can format. Figure 10.7 shows the box model for element boxes. From the outside to the inside, we have first the margin. The margin surrounds the entire content box, ensuring that if there are several different content boxes near each other that they won't actually touch. It's like an invisible force field that surrounds the content box. It won't show any color but allows any content elements that are underneath it (e.g., parent boxes) to show through. The next level in is the border. The border can have its thickness changed, and there are actually several different styles of border including solid, dashed, and dotted. On the inside of the border is the padding. The

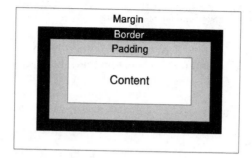

FIGURE 10.7   Box model elements.

padding ensures that there is space between the actual content, whether it be an image or text, and the border. Otherwise, the content (e.g., text) would actually touch the border, which may make it difficult to visualize the content. Later when we look at properties, we'll see how we can change the dimensions, style, and color of boxes, using the span element and the div element.

Selectors

To start, we need to consider the concept of selectors. Selectors are simply elements that are allowed to be assigned a style. There are three different types of selectors: element, class, and id. The general syntax for using selectors is:

```
selector { property: value; }
```

We must remember to place the property name and the value within braces. Whitespace is allowed; so the following is considered equivalent:

```
selector
{
  property: value;
}
```

Element Selectors

An element selector is simply one of the elements that we have available to use for rendering within XHTML. For example, we can use the paragraph element (p) as a selector:

```
p { font-size: 12pt; }
```

In this simple example, we've specified any paragraph element to have a font size of 12 points. We could also specify that all tables have a background color of blue:

```
table { background-color: blue; }
```

If we decide to have a common style applied to several different elements, we can simply group element selectors together. If, for example, we wanted all heading elements to have the color black:

```
h1, h2, h3, h4, h5, h6 { background-color: black; }
```

Class Selectors

Although element selectors are useful as a shotgun approach, they can cause problems if we don't want all instances of a particular element to receive the same style. We may decide that certain tables are to display a background color of yellow, where other tables are to display a background color of red. In order to do this, we use class selectors. Element selectors simply named the element that was to be used as a selector. Class selectors take a different approach. Instead, we create our own name of a selector and refer to it in the XHTML using the class attribute. So the CSS could name two different background colors for tables

```
table.yellow_table { background-color: yellow; }
table.red_table { background-color: red; }
```

and refer to these classes in our XHTML:

```
<table class="yellow_table">
  <tbody><tr><td rowspan="4">File Listing</td></tr></tbody>
</table>
<table class="red_table">
  <tbody><tr><td rowspan="4">File Listing</td></tr></tbody>
</table>
```

The class selectors that we created referred to the table elements (e.g., `table.red_table`). This means that the table element in XHTML has a `red_table` class and a `yellow_table` class. This is useful for the table elements. But what if we wish to extend this functionality to other elements? This is actually easy. All we need to do is remove the element name from the selector and replace it with an asterisk (or just the dot and the name of the class for those who don't wish to type the asterisk):

```
*.yellow_table { background-color: yellow; }
```

This allows any element to make use of the `yellow_table` class. So we come to an important point about naming classes. We should always be choosing names that reflect the functionality that we are trying to present—not the element names or presentation style. As an example, if all yellow tables were to represent tabular data and all red tables were to represent image gallery thumbnails, then we would be better suited to calling these classes `tabular_data` and `image_gallery` respectively.

ID Selectors

ID selectors take the opposite approach compared to element selectors. They are specific to only one selector based on the element id attribute's value. Recall that XHTML requires id attributes to be of type ID from the DTD specification that requires id values to be unique within an XHTML document. This can be useful for a style that is to be applied only once. Defining an id selector is similar to a class in that we can come up with our own name for the selector. However, with an id selector, we have to use the hash symbol at the beginning of the selector declaration:

```
#copyright { color: red; font-size: 10pt; }
```

Later on when we use the selector, we must add the id attribute to the XHTML element that is applying that style:

```
<p id="copyright">Copyright (c) 2006 Charles River Media.</p>
```

So only one element within the XHTML document can have this id value and, therefore, this style.

Contextual Selectors

Contextual selectors give us another way to be specific in how we apply style by creating certain combinations of rules. For example, we may wish to only apply a style to anchor elements within paragraph elements. The syntax for doing this would look like:

```
p a { font-size: 14pt; }
```

This style only applies to anchor elements within paragraphs and not within any other element (e.g., td, i, b). Contextual selection can be applied to class and id selectors as well. Going further with this, we could insist that only italic elements whose parent element is from the hilite class are chosen for a style (in this case, change the background color to yellow):

```
*.hilite I { background-color: yellow; }
```

Any parent element that sets its class attribute value to hilite will receive the style:

```
<p class="hilite">
  <i>Welcome to ...</i>
</p><p>
  <i>More about ...</i>
</p>
```

The first paragraph would receive the style, but the second paragraph would not. Contextual selection with the id selector works in a similar fashion:

```
#no_1 a { font-size: 10pt; }
```

In this case, we are stating that any anchor elements found within the element with an id attribute value of no_1 should have its font size changed to 10 points. The XHTML that would use this would look like:

```
<p id="no_1"> <a name="bottom" href="#top">Top</a> </p>
```

We can also group contextual selectors together:

```
h1 a, h2 a { background-color: purple; }
```

This has the effect of setting the background color of any anchor elements found within heading one or heading two parent elements to purple. This offers consistency with headings one and two in terms of background color and eliminates the need to re-declare the style for each heading we wish to affect.

Pseudo Elements and Pseudo Classes

As we're seeing so far, CSS allows us to use selectors to access elements within the XHTML document tree. We can refer to the element by name, by class, or by the unique id value. In order for us to refer to these elements, they need to exist within the XHTML document tree. In XHTML, however, there are several elements and classes that do not exist. This is where pseudo elements and pseudo class become useful. A pseudo class is a class that doesn't actually exist within the XHTML document tree. Two examples of pseudo elements are the :first-letter and the :first-line elements, which refer to the first letter in a paragraph and the first line in a paragraph, respectively. These are actually elements that can have style applied to them and yet there are no elements within the XHTML document to describe them. We could, for example, set the style for these elements by declaring:

```
p:first-line { font-weight: bold; }
p:first-letter { font-size: 200%; font-weight: bold; }
```

This would ensure that the first line (not sentence) of the paragraph was presented as bold, and that the first letter of the paragraph started with a letter that was twice as large as the currently selected font size. Another (tricky) couple of pseudo elements are the before and after pseudo elements. Current Web browser support for these elements is sketchy at best with only Opera 8.5 supporting them completely, Firefox versions 1.0 and 1.5 browsers support these elements in some scenarios and Microsoft Internet Explorer 6.0 offers no support of these two pseudo elements. For example, in order to always place the string literal e-mail in front of elements whose class selector is email, we would create the following selector:

```
*.email:before { content: "E-mail: " }
```

The content property refers to generated content of the element. We could turn around and reference this class in any element because we've used the asterisk and the dot operator in front of the class name email

```
<td><p class="email">arron_ferguson@bcit.ca</p></td>
```

which would print

```
E-mail: arron_ferguson@bcit.ca
```

Pseudo classes are like pseudo elements in that they may not exist within the XHTML document tree but do represent characteristics of a particular element. Some pseudo classes are mutually exclusive as is the case of the link and visited classes. The :link pseudo class represents anchor links that have not yet been :visited, whereas the visited pseudo class represents an anchor link that has already been visited. There is also the :hover pseudo class which represents the user using the mouse to *rollover* the component. This is useful for pointing out to the user that a particular element within the document is interactive, which is the case with a hyperlink (i.e., the anchor element). The :active pseudo element represents an element being activated by the user and the :focus pseudo element represents an element that is capable of accepting keyboard events (i.e., element has focus). We could use all of these pseudo elements together in order to create a more animated interactive experience by applying these pseudo elements to all of our anchor elements:

```
a:link { color: rgb(161, 67, 175); }
a:visited { color: rgb(101, 40, 135); }
a:hover { text-decoration: none; }
a:active { color: rgb(252, 192, 87); }
```

The previous code would allow the Web browser to change the color of the anchor's link once it has been visited, change the color of the anchor's link when the user is selecting the anchor's link, and when the mouse hovers (rolls over) the anchor's link, it removes the text decoration (usually represented by an underline). By taking advantage of these pseudo elements, we are offering our XHTML documents a little more interactivity and animation.

Properties

So far we have been focusing on the selectors but not the properties that the selectors have been using. We've seen a few properties by example, but it helps us to understand what properties we can use so that our style changes can be more effective. There are six categories of properties available:

Font Properties: Change the font style, font family, weighting, and size.

Color Properties: Assigning the color of elements (including background color).

Text Properties: Adjusting text alignment, indenting, and controlling whitespace.

Classification Properties: Used to classify styles of elements, such as what type of list is being used or how a particular class is displayed (or not).

Box Properties: Specifying the amount of padding between certain elements' bounding boxes.

Positioning: The placement of elements and details such as overflow.

Font Properties

Font properties allow us to change font characteristics of textual data. As an example, we can create a style that is to be used for standard body text:

```
*.bodyStyle {
  font-family: gill, helvetica, sans-serif; font-size: 12pt;
  font-style: normal; font-variant: normal; font-weight: lighter;
}
```

The `font-family` property allows us to choose a font family. The comma-separated list for this property allows us to offer up a list of choices that we are hoping for, starting with our first choice, and so on. The first two choices (`gill` and `helvetica`) are *family names*—specific fonts. It is suggested by the W3C that we always offer a last alternative which is a *generic family* name. The value `sans-serif` is a generic choice (recall Chapter 1, where we talked about font types). The `font-size` property has been chosen as 12 points, although we can choose any size we wish. Keep in mind that most viewers prefer a reading font to be between 10 and 14 points for reading. The `font-style` property can be set to `normal` (default setting), `italic`, and `oblique`. Oblique actually looks like the italic font because it is slanted, although oblique is simply a mathematical skew of the font, whereas italic is a separate font.

The `font-variant` property allows either the value `normal` (default) or `small-caps`, which may be useful for legal text. We can also set the `font-weight` property, which allows the font weight to be set. Weight really means the thickness of the font or boldness of the font. We can choose the following constant literal values: `normal`, bold, `bolder`, `lighter`, or we can chose numbered values such as 100, 200, 300, 400, 500, 600, 700, 800, and 900. Of course, on small point sizes little change can be seen. Lastly, we can use the font property, which is an all-in-one statement that allows us to state all of the previous properties into one statement:

```
*.bodyStyle { font: normal normal lighter 12pt helvetica; }
```

The previous example used the point unit of measure, which is a unit of measure given by the print industry to describe the size of the font. Your typical newspaper is either 10 or 11 point. Web documents are usually best read at 12 point. We can specify the following units of measure to specify font size:

Point: There are 72 points per inch. This unit of measure is from the printing industry, although it is applicable within the Web as well. The point unit of measure is an absolute unit of measure meaning that it can be guaranteed to be the same size in all environments. This unit of measure is usually considered an acceptable method of defining the size of a font (e.g., `font-size: 12pt`).

Pixel: Refers to the pixel size on the screen. Although pixels are absolute as an atomic unit, they are not considered a reasonable unit of measure for fonts because the number of pixels on a screen may vary with the resolution of the desktop environment (e.g., `font-size: 20px`).

Pica: A pica is 1/6 of an inch and the pica unit of measure is another inheritance from the printing industry. Picas are not so common for describing the size of a font, although some desktop publishers may use them. Picas are also absolute units of measure (e.g., `font-size: 2pc`).

Em space: Em space is a relative unit, and it refers to the width of the capital "M" in whatever font is currently being used (e.g., `font-size: 1.5em` which is 150 percent the normal size).

Centimeter: Sets the size of the font in centimeters (e.g., `font-size: 2cm`).

Inch: Sets the size of the font in inches (e.g., `font-size: 2in`).

Millimeter: Sets the size of the font in millimeters. Usually not very common (e.g., `font-size: 80mm`).

Percentage: A less common and relative unit of measure is to specify the size using a percentage. The percentage is a percentage of the size of the current font being used (e.g., `font-size: 50%` which sets the font to half its current size).

Relative Literals: There are two relative literals: `larger` and `smaller`, which sets the font slightly larger or slightly smaller respectively. These types should be avoided because the control of size may change from font to font.

Absolute Literals: These are literals which are roughly equivalent to the heading sizes for the heading elements: `xx-small`, `x-small`, `small`, `medium`, `large`, `x-large`, and `xx-large`. Again, these literal values should be avoided because there size is not a particular unit that can be controlled.

Color Properties

We can use style to control color. First off, we can set the color of the text such as:

```
p { color: blue; }
```

We can also change the background color using the `background-color` property:

```
p { background-color: green; }
```

Up until now, we've simply been using string literals to set the color of the background. However, we can specify color using two other units of measure: hexa-decimal values and comma-separated decimal triples. Before looking at these, it helps to understand what the values represent.

What Is Color

Color, simply put, is the perceptual effect that a certain portion of light wavelengths have on our eyes. Each wavelength is perceived as a different color. Note that the human eye can detect wavelengths within the ranges 400 nm to 700 nm). Color within the wavelength spectrum goes from violet, indigo, blue, green, yellow, orange, and finally red. On the low end of the color spectrum, we have infrared. Infrared is the light wavelength used in most remote-control devices. It is invisible to the human eye, and, therefore, we cannot see it. On the high end of the color spectrum is ultraviolet. Ultraviolet, also known as UV, is the color of violet that gives us sunburn.

Within the human retina, there are three types of color photo receptors: one type for red, one type for green, and one type for blue. There is a fourth type of photo receptor, but it is not used in determining color, but instead for night vision where there are very low levels of light. The fact that our eyes are especially sensitive to red, green, and blue has helped base the theory of three primary colors being: red, green, and blue. Incidentally, combinations of mixing the three primaries are not capable of displaying all colors available under the color spectrum. They are, however, capable of displaying many of them.

Color Models

Scientists have developed a technique for plotting various colors that are visible to the human eye. This technique uses a 3D coordinate system called *color space*. When the colors are plotted (in color space), there are different methods for arranging the many colors that we can see. These different methods for arranging the colors are referred to as *color models*. Color models allow us to categorize color in ways that best suit the way we are trying to use color.

The RGB Color Model

The RGB color model has been one of the most common standards because of the explosion of the computer industry. This is because many devices within the computer industry (with the exception of printing devices) rely on the RGB color model. It is the color model most people are familiar with.

The RGB color model uses the three primary colors red, green, and blue. The RGB color model was used to develop the Cathode Ray Tube (CRT) and other color raster graphics devices. The colors in the RGB color model are considered additive colors making the RGB color model an *additive color model*. An additive color model means that a resulting mix of color is formed by a sum of any combination of the three primaries. As an example, if you wished to create purple, you would add red and blue together to form purple. They are summed or added together. An additive color model defines pure black as being the absence of any color and pure white as being all color together.

True Color

As you know, each image is made up of pixels, which are little squares displayed on the monitor; each pixel has a color value describing its color appearance on the screen. We need a data structure that allows us to store each of the three primaries (red, green, blue). For each primary color we will assign one byte: there are 8 bits per byte. We now have one byte for red, one byte for green, and one byte for blue. Each primary color on its own is capable of being set to 256 different values. These values allow us to describe 256 individual colors. Zero represents black, and 255 represents a maximally saturated primary.

When all three colors are summed together, we are able to produce a combination of over 16 million colors. Why? If you add the three bytes together you wind up with 24 bits (3 bytes * 8 bits per byte). Because we are dealing in a binary number system, we know that all values possible are powers of two. So for 24 bits we use:

$$2^{24} = 16,777,216$$

This is why we can display over 16 million colors. It's the ability to create any color between 1 and 16,777,216. This method of describing color is referred to as

24-bit color or true color. True color means that there is a higher amount of different wavelengths than the human eye is capable of discerning from. Having an understanding of the three primary colors, we can now fully understand the units of measure.

Hexadecimal Color Values

Hexadecimal color values are written by providing the hex values of each of the red, green, and blue values making up the true color, and which are preceded by the hash symbol. For example, to specify the color red using the hexadecimal value, we would use:

```
#FF0000
```

The `ff` value is 255 in hexadecimal. The second two zeros represent green (which are turned off), and the last two zeros represent blue (which too are turned off). But not all people feel comfortable using hexadecimal values.

Comma-Separated Triples

Decimal values are much easier to use because most people are comfortable counting in tens. The syntax is slightly different than the hex value, but it boils down to the same RGB triple. To specify red in the comma separated decimal triple, we would use:

```
rgb(255, 0, 0)
```

To specify pure white, we would use:

```
rgb(255, 255, 255)
```

Using Image within a Style

So far we've only been looking at color. We can also specify that a style is to use an image. If we wish to use a background image for our Web page, we use the background-image property:

```
body { background-image: url('./background.jpg'); }
```

Note that we must provide a valid URL in order to use the image. If the image is not big enough to fill the entire background, then we can use the background-repeat property:

```
body {
  background-image: url('./background.jpg');
  background-repeat: repeat;
}
```

We can specify that the image repeats both in the x direction as well as the y direction using the `repeat` value. If we only wish for the image to repeat in the x direction (rows), then we use the value `repeat-x`. If we want the image to only repeat in the y direction (columns), we use the value `repeat-y`. We can also use the value `no-repeat`, although this is just the same as if we didn't use the `background-repeat` property at all. A rather interesting effect is to add a background image that stays stationary where the text and rest of content scroll. To do this, we use the `background-attachment` property and assign it a value of `fixed`:

```
body {
  background-image: url('./background.jpg');
  background-attachment: fixed;
}
```

Lastly, we can set the position of an image by using the `background-position` property. We can use this to specify an offset of the image within the box it is sitting in. For example, to place a background image in the exact center of the box that it is placed in, we would use the following:

```
body {
  background-image: url('./background.jpg');
  background-attachment: fixed;
  background-position: center center;
}
```

We have to remember to use the `background-position` property with the `background-attachment` property for correct results. Other values are left, bottom, right, and top.

Text Properties

While the level of control that is available on the Web comes nowhere near the level of control in printed media, CSS 2.1 does offer us some fairly detailed control over text. We can, for example, set the following:

Letter Spacing: Explicit control of the spacing between individual letters. We could create classes that control individual character strings that could possibly mimic kerning, which in desktop publishing terms is the space between certain combinations of characters (e.g., less space between the letter 't' and 'h'). Any value given is space that is in addition to the default amount of space between letters.

Line Height: The height of a line of text. We could, for example, place more space between lines within a legal document, or place less space between lines for news articles or text that contains a large font.

Text Decoration: Decorating the text with an underline, overline, line-through, and blinking.

Text Transform: capitalize (which capitalizes the first letter of each word—useful for title text), uppercase (useful for legal statements or documents), and lowercase.

Text Align: Aligns text to left, right, center, or justify (newspaper style).

Text Indent: Allows the first line of text to be indented.

Vertical Align: Changes the alignment of text within a line. Vertical alignment options are specified relative to the baseline of the box that the text is situated in. Valid values are: baseline (along the baseline of the box), middle (midpoint of the box), sub (lower than the baseline, subscript), super (raised baseline, superscript), text-top (aligned to the top of the parent's content area), text-bottom (aligned to the bottom of the parent's content area), or a percentage, or lastly a length value.

Word Spacing: Explicit control over the amount of extra space between words. This may be useful in situations where greater control over titles is needed. Any value given is space that is in addition to the default amount of space between words.

Listing 10.20 shows a CSS declaring values for these properties, Listing 10.21 shows the XHTML page utilizing the styles, and Figure 10.8 shows the rendered document.

LISTING 10.20   Using Text Properties in CSS

```
body {
  font-family: gill, helvetica, sans-serif; font-size: 12pt;
  text-indent: 1em; line-height: 1.75em;
}
body b { word-spacing: -0.1em; }
body acronym { letter-spacing: 0.1em; }
body a { text-decoration: overline; }
*.above { vertical-align: super; }
*.legal {
  text-transform: uppercase; text-align: center;
}
```

LISTING 10.21   Text Properties in XHTML

```
<?xml version="1.0" encoding="UTF-8"?>
<!DOCTYPE html PUBLIC "-//W3C//DTD XHTML 1.0 Strict//EN"
  "http://www.w3.org/TR/xhtml1/DTD/xhtml1-strict.dtd">
<html xmlns="http://www.w3.org/1999/xhtml" lang="en-CA"
  xml:lang="en">
```

```
<head>
  <title>Home</title>
  <link rel="stylesheet" href="Listing-10-20.css" type="text/css"
    media="screen"/>
</head>
<body>
  <p>Welcome to <b>Kucing CMS 1.0</b>! Kucing <acronym
  title="Content Management System">CMS</acronym> is built using
  <a href="http://www.javasoft.com">Java</a>™ technology as well
  as various <acronym title="Extensible Markup Language">XML
  </acronym> technologies including <acronym title="Extensive
  Stylesheet Language Transformation">XSLT</acronym>. Kucing CMS
  1.0 uses XML as its <i>sole</i> datastore technology. Kucing
  CMS attempts to be a <span class="above">head above</span> the
  crowd.</p>
  <p class="legal">All information in this document has been
  checked for accuracy.</p>
</body>
</html>
```

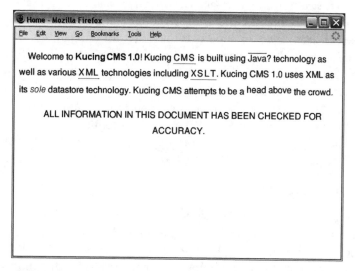

FIGURE 10.8   Text properties used within a Web page.

Classification Properties

Classification properties are available to change how whitespace is treated within XHTML. Recall that XHTML by default collapses whitespace. This may interfere with formatting within a Web page when indenting is important, as in the case when showing program code. In CSS, we can use the whitespace property, which accepts the values `normal`, `pre`, and `nowrap`, for CSS 1, and `pre-wrap` and `pre-line` in CSS 2.1 (for which at the time of this writing there is no browser support for). The pre value creates the style like the pre element, where whitespace is preserved; the nowrap value does not allow text to be wrapped (i.e., no carriage return unless a br element is placed to break the content to a new line). In order to use the pre value in the white-space property, we would declare it in our CSS:

```
*.keepAllWhiteSpace { white-space: pre; }
```

And then use it within, for example, a paragraph element:

```
<p class="keepAllWhiteSpace">The rain      in Spain
falls mainly on the
plain.</p>
```

This would actually keep all whitespace (every whitespace character, every carriage return, every line feed, and every tab character). Under classification, we can also change some of the attributes of lists. For example, we can use the list-style-type property, which accepts several different attributes for the bullet values: disc, circle, square, decimal, lower-roman, upper-roman, lower-alpha, upper-alpha, or none. The roman values are useful for legal documents, whereas for general lists we can use the disc, circle, or square. If these are not enough, the list-style-image can be used to provide an image that acts as the symbol representing the list item. The value must be supplied as a URL (e.g., list-style-image: url('bullet.gif')). Another value that allows us control over lists is the list-style-position property, which accepts the value inside or outside depending on where you want the list item symbol to be placed in. When we refer to inside or outside, we are referring to the actual list item block. It does not imply that the list item symbol (e.g., bullet) will be placed to the right of the text.

Box Properties

Recall earlier when we mentioned the box model and how we were allowed to create margins, borders, and padding around content. First, we can change the size of the margin using any of the unit types we discussed earlier. We can specify margin sizes by doing it in one statement to change all sides (top, bottom, left, and right):

```
span { margin: 1.0em; }
```

Or we may decide that we wish for the different sides of our margin to be of different sizes:

```
span {
  margin-top: 1.0em; margin-bottom: 0.5em;
  margin-left: 0.75em; margin-right: 1.2em;
}
```

For our borders, we can set the style as being dashed, dotted, double, groove, inset, outset, ridge, solid, or none. None is the default, so you'll have to set the border-style property to something other than none if you wish for the border to show up. Additionally, we can specify a thickness for our border by setting all sides as being equal:

```
span { border-style: solid; border-width: 1pt; }
```

Or, if we decide that the border sides each need different sizes, we can do the size individually as in:

```
span {
  border-style: solid; border-top-width: 1pt;
  border-bottom-width: 2pt; border-left-width: 3pt;
  border-right-width: 4pt;
}
```

The padding is also another area in which we can change the size. We may wish to create text areas that are acting as menu items and want the border to be enough space away from the actual anchor element's text:

```
span { padding: 1.0em; }
```

Again, we can assign individual values for each of the sides:

```
span {
  padding-top: 1.0em; padding-bottom: 2.0em;
  padding-left: 3.0em; padding-right: 0.0em;
}
```

The content dimensions can be changed as well. We do this with the width and height properties:

```
div {
  background-color: rgb(181, 181, 181);
  height: 200px; width: 200px;
}
```

There are two last properties that are of use: float and clear. The float property is useful with images that are embedded within text or text that is being used as menus. The item floated becomes a block-level rather than inline and is either placed to the left or right. To disable this behavior, set the float property to none. The clear property is used to state which side (or sides) do not allow for other floating elements to be placed on. It's kind of like a detracting field, which pushes away other elements from coming near the element with the clear property set. The values for clear are: left, right, none, or both.

It helps to see these values used in practice. For example, if we wish to create a Web page that contains images on the right side of a content area (possibly adverts) with all text on the left side, we may come up with a style sheet that looks like Listing 10.22.

LISTING 10.22 CSS With `Clear` and `Float`

```
body {
  font-family: gill, helvetica, sans-serif;
  font-size: 12pt; text-align: justify;
}

*.advert {
  float: right; clear: right; border-style: solid;
  border-width: 1px; margin-left: 5px; margin-right: 1px;
  margin-top: 2px; margin-bottom: 2px;
}
```

The XHTML using this CSS is found in Listing 10.23 (paragraph text-shortened in listing).

LISTING 10.23 XHTML Using `Float` and `Clear`

```
<?xml version="1.0" encoding="UTF-8"?>
<!DOCTYPE html PUBLIC "-//W3C//DTD XHTML 1.0 Strict//EN"
  "http://www.w3.org/TR/xhtml1/DTD/xhtml1-strict.dtd">
<html xmlns="http://www.w3.org/1999/xhtml" lang="en-CA" xml:lang="en">
  <head>
    <title>Home</title>
    <link rel="stylesheet" href="Listing-10-22.css" type="text/css"
      media="screen"/>
  </head>
  <body>
    <div class="contentPane">
      <img class="advert" alt="CMS Books" src="CMS-books.jpg"/>
      <img class="advert" alt="Kucing Dental Floss"
        src="kucing-dental-floss.jpg"/>
      <img class="advert" alt="Lava Storm Game"
        src="lava-storm-game.jpg"/>
      <img class="advert" alt="Need A Holiday?"
        src="need-holiday.jpg"/>
      <p>Before looking at the XUI, a quick introduction ...</p>
      <p>While at present, the Web is capable of presenting ...</p>
      <p>HTML does not support metadata other than a few  ...</p>
      <p>The Semantic Web addresses these issues by ...</p>
      <p> Based on the W3C recommendation, RDF is to use ...</p>
    </div>
  </body>
</html>
```

Figure 10.9 shows the rendered page. The adverts are all lined up on the right side of the page. This is because we've specified that the class `advert` `floats` right, and we've given the `clear` property a value of `right`, which pushes away any other elements from the right side of the adverts. This forces the next advert to jump down below the current advert.

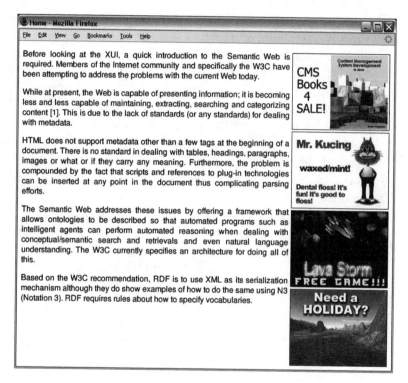

FIGURE 10.9   Rendered page using Float and Clear.

Positioning Properties

The last group of properties is for positioning elements within a Web page. We have several options, including absolute positioning. The following lists properties that are available:

left: How far a box is moved away from the left side of the parent container. Can be a unit of measure, percentage, or left as auto, which leaves it to the Web browser to figure out.

top: How far a box is moved away from the top part of the parent container. Can be a unit of measure, percentage, or left as `auto`, which leaves it to the Web browser to figure out.

overflow: Specifies how content is to be handled when the content is larger than the box that the content sits in. Choices are `visible` (which means the content is not clipped and renders outside of the box), `hidden` (content is clipped and not visible), `scroll` (content using a scroll pane that allows the user to scroll through the content), or `auto` (which is browser-dependent but should allow for scrolling).

position: Specifies whether a box can be positioned. Values are `static` (box is normal and follows normal flow—`left` and `top` are not used), `relative` (specify how much this box moves in relation to its normal position), `absolute` (the box is taken out of normal flow and positioned exactly where the left and top values specify it to be), `fixed` (does not move even if content is scrolled. Useful for those wishing to create menus that are always found in the same place but do not wish to deal with the horrors of frames).

visibility: Controls whether a box is visible or not. Values are `visible` and `hidden`. Although it may seem strange to hide content, it is useful when a scripting language is being used to switch between certain boxes (e.g., interactive menus).

z-index: Allows boxes to be rearranged in terms of their z-order or depth. This simply means the layer that the box sits on. A useful way to approach this concept is to pretend that each box is drawn on a sheet of clear plastic and placed over the top of previous sheets of clear plastic. Boxes with higher `z-index` values are considered to be on top of boxes with lower `z-index` values. Values are specified as integers. By default each box is given a successive `z-index` value.

clip: Applies to elements that are using the `overflow` property (with values other than `visible`). Values can either be `auto` (same size and location as the element's box) and a shape. Currently in CSS 2.1, the only valid shape is a rectangle (e.g., `clip: rect(5px, 5px, 5px, 5px)`).

The Cascading in CSS

One of the features of CSS is the cascading effect of style rules (also known as inheritance). If you recall, XML documents contain many inner levels of nodes including child nodes, comments, attributes, etc. It helps to remember this rule because in XHTML when a style is applied to, for example, a paragraph, then all textual data within the paragraph as well as other child elements (e.g., bold, italic) will inherit the style of the parent paragraph element. As in programming language, there is an order of operations, so there is also an order of inheritance precedence in CSS, and it assigns priority from the most specific to the most general.

Style Attribute Priority

The highest priority is given to the `style` attribute that has been placed within an element:

```
<p style="color: red">Copyright &#169; 2006 Charles River Media.</p>
```

Style Element Priority

The next highest priority is given to the `style` element itself found within the `head` element:

```
<style>
  body { color: red; color: yellow; }
</style>
```

Link Element Priority

Using the `link` element within the `head` element to link to an external style sheet takes the next level of priority:

```
<link title="Basic" media="screen" href="./Listing-10-20.css"
  type="text/css" rel="stylesheet"/>
```

Browser Defaults Priority

The last level of priority is the Web browser's default settings. These are only used if they are not overridden by any of the other priority levels of style

Exceptions to the Rule

Although the inheritance works most of the time, there are a few exceptions where a style is not inherited. The W3C suggests that these exceptions are intuitive, although unless you know about them, it may cause some confusion as to why a particular style does not work. A couple of examples are: background properties and margin-top.

Creating a Web Page Template

Having gone over some heuristics that help guide our design process, we can now work toward a template. As mentioned in Chapter 2, we are using XSLT to transform our XML to XHTML. In order to do this, we first need to create a static XHTML document to serve as a template. It's easier to focus on the details of the XHTML and CSS first and then incorporate the design into our XSLT later. Creating a layout starts with a drawing of the general layout. Figure 10.10 displays an idea for a layout. It appears with a banner across the top of the page with a menu right below it. To the bottom and right of the banner are news items, forms for login, and a link to a search page. The rest of the page contains the content. Although this is a standard layout, we can still spruce it up by choosing appropriate colors and creating a smart looking banner for it. A standard layout is also intuitive for a larger audience because it is familiar to most users.

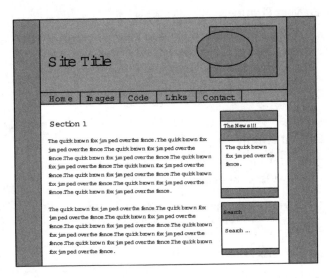

FIGURE 10.10   Layout design drawing.

Once we have an idea we need to visualize how the XHTML structures this for us, we can make use of CSS to help place certain structures in our layout. Again, we can draw out the logical structure of the XHTML element tree. Figure 10.11 displays a hierarchical content structure. Each rectangle represents a logical content structure. These aren't the names of elements found within XHTML. However, we can use CSS to assign classes to the div element, which essentially represent the structure that is shown in Figure 10.11. From this point, we can simply refer to these rectangles as classes if we think in CSS terms. The document is at the top level and contains two main classes: content and footer. While the footer only contains the information found in the footer (e.g., links to contact information, feedback page, etc.), the content class contains the rest. Within the content class are the menu, title bar, and content pane. The menu contains menu items (i.e., links to other pages within our CMS), the title bar contains any images and a title of the page, and the content pane class contains the remaining content: forms (e.g., search form, login form), the news section, and all other content.

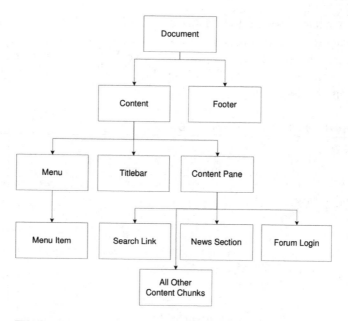

FIGURE 10.11   XHTML content class hierarchy.

The first step to realizing this design in code is start off with a valid XHTML document such as:

```
<?xml version="1.0" encoding="UTF-8"?>
<!DOCTYPE html PUBLIC "-//W3C//DTD XHTML 1.0 Strict//EN"
  "http://www.w3.org/TR/xhtml1/DTD/xhtml1-strict.dtd">
<html xmlns="http://www.w3.org/1999/xhtml">
  <head><title>Title</title></head>
  <body></body>
</html>
```

You can always check your XHTML document by going to the W3C's online XHTML validation service found at: http://validator.w3.org/check.

With a template in place, we can start placing div elements into our XHTML document that represent each type of class that we find in our diagram. If you recall from the previous chapter, we can create CSS classes that can apply style to various elements within our document. Listing 10.24 shows the base document without most of the sample content. The indenting and commenting are obviously not necessary, however, they make reading the document much easier if we are writing these types of documents by hand. Listing 10.24 demonstrates the use of div elements to represent the classes found in Figure 10.11. We've also added an additional div element (with a class attribute value of sidebar) that wraps around all of the div elements that contain forms. We've done this so that we can treat all of these div elements as a group. This is useful if we decide to change their relative position within the document.

LISTING 10.24 XHTML Template Base

```
<?xml version="1.0" encoding="UTF-8"?>
<!DOCTYPE html PUBLIC "-//W3C//DTD XHTML 1.0 Strict//EN"
  "http://www.w3.org/TR/xhtml1/DTD/xhtml1-strict.dtd">
<html>
  <head>
    <title>Kucing CMS - Template</title>
    <link rel="stylesheet" type="text/css"
      href="./css/kucingCMS.css" media="screen"
      title="Kucing CMS - Template"/>
  </head>
  <body>
    <!- Content ->
    <div class="content">
      <!- Titlebar ->
      <div class="titlebar">
        <h1>Geek-kit - Basic</h1>
      </div>
      <!- Menu ->
      <div> </div>
      <!- Content Pane  ->
      <div class="contentPane">
        <!- Sidebar - container for forms on right ->
        <div class="sidebar">
          <!- Search Box  ->
          <div class="floatBox">
            <p>A news item here.</p>
          </div>
          <!- News Section  ->
          <div class="floatBox">
            <h3>News</h3>
            <!- News Item ->
            <div><p>A news item here.</p></div>
            <!- Another News Item  ->
            <div><p>A news item here.</p></div>
          </div>
          <!- Forum Login ->
          <div class="floatBox">
            <p>Login here</p>
          </div>
        </div>
        <!- End of sidebar->
        <!- ALL OTHER CONTENT HERE ->
      </div>
```

```
      <!- End of Content Pane ->
    </div>
    <!- End of Content  ->
    <!- Start of Footer ->
    <div class="footer">
      <p><a href="#" title="Copyright page">Copyright &#169;
        2006 Charles River Media</a></p>
      <p><a href="#" title="Policies page">Policies</a></p>
      <p><a href="#" title="Feedback page">Feedback</a></p>
      <p><a href="#" title="Contact page">Contact</a></p>
    </div>
    <!- End of Footer ->
  </body>
</html>
```

Many What You See Is What You Get (WYSIWYG) HTML editors and design tools do not recognize or support XHTML strict, although this is bound to change with time. This can cause problems if you decide to create a Web page template that you wish to be XHTML strict. Even if you decide that you are more interested in designing templates using WYSIWYG tools, you still may wish to understand the syntax of XHTML and CSS because you can always correct inconsistencies with tools that may not correctly generate XHTML documents.

Styling the Document

Starting from the top level, there are a few base styles that we can apply that will trickle down to all of the other subelements, unless we decide to override them. We can apply an element selector to the body element of our document first:

```
body {
  background-color: rgb(255, 255, 255); color: rgb(22, 62, 114);
  font-family: gill, helvetica, sans-serif; font-size: 12pt;
  margin: 4px; text-align: justify;
}
```

We've set the background color to white and a text color that is prominently blue (last color value is higher than the first two). We've selected the font known as Gill, but if it's not available, we want Helvetica, and as a last resort if neither of these exist, we can use any sans serif font chosen by the Web browser. The selected font size is 12 points, which is a reasonably sized font for reading material on the Web with a four pixel margin around the content blocks; and finally, we've set the `text-align` property to `justify`, which means that it appears like newspaper articles where the words on a line are spaced out so as to fill up the entire line. We can continue adding default styles to elements that we'll use regularly, such as the `pre` element:

```
pre {
  white-space: pre-line;        /* For CSS 2.1 */
  white-space: -moz-pre-wrap;   /* Mozilla, because 1999 */
  white-space: -o-pre-wrap;     /* Opera 7 */
  white-space: -pre-wrap;       /* Opera 4 - 6 */
  word-wrap: break-word;        /* IE 5.5+ */
  padding-top: 5px;
}
```

These properties to pre are an unfortunate kludge that is required for dealing with the pre style which does not wrap text to the next line. Only the property value pre-line is actually part of the W3C Recommendation for CSS 2.1, and at the time of this writing, it is not supported by most of the Web browsers. The others are company solutions that have existed to address the problem of not being able to create a style that wraps the pre style and must be included for each Web browser.

This may beg the question why use the pre element in the first place. But the reason why we need the pre element is so that we can display text that has preserved whitespace. Remember, XHTML does collapses whitespace. If we are attempting to display some sort of program source code, we usually want to preserve whitepsace. While using pre lets us preserve whitespace, it does so purely—including not wrapping new line characters. So if a content author provides text that does not contain new line characters, the text does not wrap to the next line and, therefore, the Web browser will have a Web page that is too wide for the window, thus requiring the scroll bars. This looks messy and usually destroys the layout. This can be fixed by programmers where the server software can dictate the column at which text wraps at (by forcing a new line). However, this can still cause problems because it assumes a layout width constant—something we cannot do with a CMS that can change its look-and-feel on the fly. This is why the pre-line value for the white-space property is so welcomed.

Looking at a different need for content, we can take advantage of our knowledge of pseudo classes and offer different colors for hyperlinks (the anchor element):

```
a { color: rgb(230, 105, 0); text-decoration: underline; }

a:link, a:visited { color: rgb(230, 105, 0); }
a:hover { text-decoration: none; }
a:active { color: rgb(183, 217, 251); }
```

For the purpose of keeping our color theme simple, both the link and visited pseudo classes are using the same color, although this doesn't have to be the case. Another element to be styled consistently throughout our template is the acronym element. The CSS code for this is:

```
acronym {
  background-color: rgb(242, 148, 35);
  cursor: help; text-decoration: none;
}
```

For this inline element, we're changing the background to a deep orange. A property we didn't look at previously is the cursor property. It allows us to set the type of cursor that is being used. In this case what we're saying is that whenever the mouse cursor rolls over the acronym, the help cursor is displayed. We're also removing any text decoration that may normally appear with an acronym; so because the background color of this inline element has been changed, we don't necessarily need any other text decoration.

The Content Class Selector

Found as the first of two classes within the body of our document, the content class offers several other styles that cascade down to other child elements. The CSS code that adds style to this class is:

```
*.content {
  background-color: rgb(242, 148, 35);
  border-color: rgb(230, 105, 0);
  border-style: solid; border-width: 2pt;
  margin-bottom: 0pt; margin-left: auto;
  margin-right: auto; margin-top: 5pt;
  min-height: 550px; padding: 0px; width: 85%;
}
```

There are a few things we can discern about the content class selector:

- We've chosen a background color that is a dark orange (the first two channels have higher values, although if they had both been equal, we would have made yellow instead of orange, but a higher red value turns the yellow to orange).
- The foreground color is a lighter orange color.
- The border style is solid and has a point size of 2 points. We've chosen to apply this border style to all four sides.
- The left and right margin values are set to auto relying on the Web browser to decide the default margin value (usually between 5 and 8 pixels). The bottom margin value is zero, which offers no space and the top is set to a literal value of 5 pixels.
- The content box's minimum height is 550 pixels. This is set to ensure that right side floating boxes will appear to be placed within the containers.
- We've added a 0 pixel padding value and the width of the content box is 85 percent of the Web browser's rendering pane so that our content will appear to be a vertical ribbon.

The Titlebar Class Selector

For the `titlebar` class selector, we need to set up style information that controls the banner and the text that is found in it. The following CSS code gives us just that:

```
*.titlebar {
    background-image: url('./images/KucingCMS-banner.jpg');
    background-repeat:repeat; border-color: rgb(230, 105, 0);
    border-style: solid; border-bottom-width: 2pt;
    border-top-width: 0pt; border-left-width: 0pt;
    border-right-width: 0pt; font-weight: bold;
    height: 140px; padding-bottom: 40px; padding-left: 25px;
    padding-right: 20px; padding-top: 15px;
}
```

The background has been given an image via a URL. When creating CSS files, it is often useful to hide any media that is used in part of the style sheet. We've done this by placing the image into a subdirectory of the CSS files directory. The background-repeat property is used so that if the Web browser resizes the window larger than what the image is, the image will repeat. Because of this, it is important to ensure that any images used within this block are *tileable*. Creating a tileable image means that if the image is repeated in either the horizontal direction or the vertical direction and that the user is not able to see where the end of one image meets the beginning of another.

The border color has been set, although the border is only used on the bottom of this box. This is because the top, left and right sides already contain borders from the containing `content` class. We do not want double thick borders on the top, left, and right sides. The font weight is set to bold because all text placed within the title bar will be considered title text. The height of the title bar is set to 140 pixels to ensure enough of the background image is shown, and finally we add padding so that any text placed within this box is not flush with the edges.

The Menu Class Selector

For our menu, we'll be using menu items. Although we could simply just make a series of anchor elements, we can use one of the list types available in XHTML. Because order is not significant, we can use an unordered list to contain the menu items. This structural containment is useful because it is easy to spot menu items and also allows us to differentiate between menu items and other element types if our menu box contains other information in it. The XHTML code for our menus may look something like:

```
<div>
  <ul class="menu">
    <li><a href="#" class="menuItem">Home</a></li>
    <li><a href="#" class="menuItem">Projects</a></li>
    <li><a href="#" class="menuItem">XML</a></li>
  </ul>
</div>
```

To create style for these menu items, a possible style choice would be:

```
*.menu {
  background-color: rgb(230, 105, 0); color: rgb(255, 255, 255);
  float: left; font-size: 10pt; list-style-type: none;
  margin: 0pt; padding: 0pt; width: 100%;
}
```

First, we are using an orange background color, with a white foreground color for the text. The font size is 10 points (slightly smaller than the content text), and we're floating the content left, meaning that the content will be block versus inline content. The value left states that the element is floated to the left within the containing box. We've also set the list-style-type property to a value of none—we're turning off any list rendering-specific options. Otherwise, the list items would render bullets, numbers, or whatever type was chosen. The margin and padding have been set to zero, and the width is set to 100 percent. By setting the unordered list's width to 100 percent, we're forcing it to expand its width to the containing div element. But we're also creating a chain reaction that forces the unordered list's containing div element to expand, as well to its containing element (another div element).

Next, we need to add some style for the anchor elements as well. We do so with the following:

```
*.menu a {
  border-color: rgb(242, 148, 35); border-style: solid;
  border-width: 1pt; font-weight: bold;
  line-height:2em; text-align: center; text-decoration: none;
  width: 16%;
}
*.menu a:link, .menu a:visited {
  color: rgb(255, 255 ,255); float: left; line-height: 2em;
}
*.menu a:hover {
  background-color: rgb(242, 148, 35); color: rgb(40, 61, 123);
  float: left; line-height: 2em;
}
*.menu a:active {
  color: rgb(183, 217, 251); float: left; line-height: 2em; }
*.menu li { display: inline; }
```

These selectors are allowing us to make use of pseudo classes (once again) so that when the user mouses over (i.e., rolls over) each menu item or clicks on each of the menu items, there is some sort of change in color. This animated touch is visual feedback to the user that what they are clicking is in fact a link. We've changed the line height so that there is plenty of space (in this case orange space because the background color is orange). We're also asking that each of these elements are given 16 percent of the width of the container that they are sitting in. The last selector is to ensure that each list item has its `display` property set to `inline`. This value (`inline`) ensures that each list item has its own inline box. Without this new inline box, the 16 percent is not applied to these list items because they do not have their own inline boxes.

The Content Pane Class Selector

The content pane contains much of the bulk of the content presented to the user. The CSS code for this is:

```
*.contentPane {
  background-color: rgb(255, 255, 255); margin: 22px;
  min-height: 500px; padding: 8px;
}
```

Although some of this seems superfluous, we do need to change the background color back to white because the content class set it to an orange color. Recall that style cascades down and, therefore, our content pane (which is contained within the content box) inherits the orange color. We also need to set the minimum size of the content pane to the same minimum height that the content box was set to.

The Sidebar Class Selector

Recall that we said we were creating a containing block that holds all form blocks and the search block as well. Although we could have simply placed these block types directly into the `contentPane` class itself, we've placed them in an intermediate container called the `sidebar` class. Although this may look like nothing more than an extra level of unnecessary complexity, it does offer us ease of use—especially if we later decide that we wish to move the entire set of boxes to the left side. The CSS code for the class selector called sidebar is:

```
*.sidebar { float: right; width: 180px; }
```

We've stated that we're going to `float` the entire contents to the `right` (conforming to Figure 10.10) and that the width is 180 pixels.

The Float Box Class Selector

Within the sidebar class selector, we can now place floating boxes. That's just what our float box class selector does for us. It is used for the little boxes that sit on the right side of our content pane and display a link to the search page, the news section (with news items), and a forum login form. The CSS code for the floating box itself is:

```
*.floatBox {
    background-color: rgb(255, 255, 255);
    border-color: rgb(230, 105, 0); border-style: solid;
    border-width: 1px; float: right; font-size: 10pt;
    margin: 3px; padding-left: 4px; padding-right: 4px;
    text-align: left; width: 150px;
}
```

This draws a white box with an orange border around it with a little bit of padding and a width of 150 pixels, some padding, and a slightly smaller font size (10-points). We may wish, however, for a little banner placed at the top within the box, as well as smaller banners for sections within the box (e.g., news items). For this, we can set the style for two heading elements:

```
*.floatBox h3 {
    background-color: rgb(230, 105, 0); color: rgb(255, 255, 255);
    font-size: 1.2em; text-align: center;
}
*.floatBox h5 {
    background-color: rgb(242, 148, 35); color: rgb(255, 255, 255);
    font-size: 1.0em; margin: 0px; padding: 3px;
}
```

The larger of the two (heading 3) uses a dark orange background color with white text on it. This allows us to place a title for the box (e.g., "Forum Login" or "News Section"). Its alignment value is center. The style for heading 5 is similar but uses a lighter orange color, sets the font to a slightly larger size, and aligns left. Lastly, for the floating box we can set the margins:

```
*.floatBox p {
    margin-bottom: 16px; margin-left: 0px; margin-right: 0px;
    margin-top: 0px; padding: 0px;
}
```

The margin values are set to zero pixels for all but the top. This ensures that the news section does not take up a lot of vertical space. The only place where we want some whitespace from the margin is on the top of each paragraph because it shouldn't be too close to the orange banner above it.

The Footer Class Selector

At the bottom of the page we have our footer. For this we create a `footer` class selector. It contains links to pages that will display information such as contact information, feedback page, privacy policy information, and copyright notices. We use two selectors: a class selector and a contextual selector:

```
*.footer { font-size: 8pt; text-align: center; }
*.footer p {
    display:inline; padding-left: 10pt; padding-right: 10pt; }
```

The content in the footer is displayed outside of the main box (`content` class selector), and each inline element is centered at an 8-point font. The contextual selector (applied to the elements within `footer` class selector) add padding to the left and right sides (10-point), and the display type is `inline`, which means that the content should flow as text rather than stacked like vertical boxes on top of each other.

Both the completed XHTML documents (`Listing-10-24.html` and `kucingCMS.html` which is the finished template) and the CSS (`kucingCMS.css`) files are both located on the CD-ROM in the *Chapter 10* folder.

ON THE CD

SUMMARY

ON THE CD

For further exercise, the reader is encouraged to look on the CD-ROM in the *Chapter 10* folder and look at Listing 10.24, as well as the supporting CSS file (`kucingCMS.css`) and the example template (`kucingCMS.html`). These files offer explanation into design choices and how layouts can be performed using CSS and XHTML.

In this chapter we looked at XHTML and its roots coming from the SGML world and the different types of elements. We explored the strictness of XHTML by applying the rules of XML to it. We read about how the presentation material was removed from XHTML to form a much more comprehensive style presentation language known as CSS. We saw how CSS contains different types of selectors, and we looked at properties for various different aspects of presentation formatting, including the box model that allows designers to create layouts without having to resort to tables as layout constructs. We also looked at the cascading details which act as style inheritance within the XHTML document tree. We finally built a Web page template that was used within the CMS for presenting content. We built this template using XHTML and CSS, which allowed us to create a fairly sophisticated layout which supported our content. In the next chapter, we refactor this template and place it into an XSLT, which allows us to programmatically select content from the XML data model and output it all out as XHTML.

11

Creating Web Pages With XSLT

In This Chapter

- The transforming process found using XSLT
- Common XSLT elements that allow us to apply templates, loop within node lists, create conditional expressions, and choose attributes within an XML document
- Creating queries using XPath
- Common XPath functions for operations such as counting and checking for a position within a node set
- Refactoring a Web page into an XSLT style sheet

In the last chapter we looked at the mechanics of XHTML and CSS, which allowed us to separate document structure from the presentation data (i.e., the style). We followed the rules of strict XHTML and looked at many different XHTML elements and CSS properties. In this chapter, we apply these fundamentals to an XHTML document that we can later turn into an XSLT template. The source code listings referenced in this chapter are located on the CD-ROM in the *Chapter 11* folder.

ON THE CD

USING XSLT

One of the most powerful features of XML is the ability to integrate XML formats with other XML formats. We can mix XML elements from multiple tagsets so long as the XML formats that we are using conform to the strict rules of XML. Chapter 4 mentioned some of the areas in which we can use XML. One of those areas was the ability to perform transforms. XSLT is a W3C Recommendation currently sitting at version 1.0. XSLT is in itself XML and is used to transform other forms of XML. The result of the transform can be another XML format, but it doesn't have to be XML at all. Like other XML formats, XSLT is only useful if there is an application or an API that can read in the XSLT document and perform the transform.

For the remainder of this chapter, we will be looking at the most commonly used elements and attributes found in XSLT—not necessarily all of them. For further reading of all elements and attributes, visit the W3C Web site for XSLT at: http://www.w3.org/TR/xslt.

XSLT Concepts

One of the first things to realize is that XSLT is simply another XML format. That said, XSLT is considered a *functional programming language*[1] and is one of the three parts of the XSL Family. The other two are the XML Path Language (XPath) and the Extensible Stylesheet Language Formatting Objects (XSL-FO). We will look at XPath later on in this chapter.

XSLT Process

XSLT is based on the concept of reading a source tree, using some pattern matching mechanism to select nodes from the source tree, and copy those selected nodes (based on the pattern matching) into the result tree. When we talk about trees, you can think back to the DOM tree of nodes that we were programmatically manipulating back in Chapter 6. Pattern-matching is simply the process of selecting which nodes from the source tree will end up in the result tree. Pattern-matching is done using XPath. The process for transforming is represented within the DFD in Figure 11.1. The XML Parser retrieves the XML document and (hopefully) parses the XML, which it then sends as a source tree to the XSLT transformer, which then retrieves the style sheet. The XSLT transformer then builds a result tree, which it can pass over to a user agent (e.g., Web browser), or simply saves the data to a file.

Listing 11.1 gives us a simple XML file, which is transformed into XHTML using the XSLT style sheet found in Listing 11.2. The transformation that we create in XSLT is considered to be a style sheet. We can call it this because the XSLT function calls we make are applying styles by using formatting.

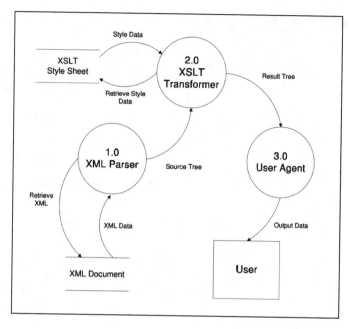

FIGURE 11.1   The XSLT process of transforming.

LISTING 11.1   Simple XML File

```
<?xml version="1.0" encoding="UTF-8"?>
<?xml-stylesheet type="text/xsl" href="./Listing-11-3.xslt"?>
<users>
  <user firstName="Arron" lastName="Ferguson" id="232"/>
  <user firstName="John" lastName="Smith" id="234"/>
  <user firstName="Dave" lastName="McDermit" id="231"/>
</users>
```

The second line within Listing 11.1 should be the only new piece of data that we have not yet seen. It is the `xml-stylesheet` processing instruction, and it is a reference within the XML to a style sheet. We're required to specify a style sheet for an XML file if we want to transform the XML. The two attributes we've used within this processing instruction are both required (based on the DTD rules). The `type` attribute allows us to specify the type of style sheet (XSLT, although it's simply given as a value of `xsl`), and the `href` attribute which should look familiar from the XHTML world (recall anchor tags) which allows us to specify a URL of where to find that particular resource.

LISTING 11.2 Simple XSLT Style Sheet

```xml
<?xml version="1.0" encoding="UTF-8"?>
<xsl:stylesheet version="1.0"
  xmlns:xsl="http://www.w3.org/1999/XSL/Transform">
  <xsl:output method="xml" indent="yes" encoding="UTF-8"/>
  <xsl:output method="xml"
    doctype-public="-//W3C//DTD XHTML 1.0 Strict//EN"
    doctype-system=
      "http://www.w3.org/TR/xhtml1/DTD/xhtml1-strict.dtd"/>
  <xsl:template match="/">
    <html>
      <head><title> Simple XSLT Transform </title></head>
      <body>
        <p>
          <xsl:for-each select="users/user">
            <xsl:sort select="./@id"/>
            <b>User:</b>
            <xsl:value-of select="./@id"/> 
            <xsl:value-of select="./@firstName"/> 
            <xsl:value-of select="./@lastName"/> <br/>
          </xsl:for-each>
        </p>
      </body>
    </html>
  </xsl:template>
</xsl:stylesheet>
```

The XSLT style sheet itself should look familiar. It, too, is XML. As mentioned in earlier chapters, it is not required but is good practice to include the XML declaration at the beginning of the document. The root element of all XSLT style sheets is the `stylesheet` element. The namespace prefix that is assigned to the XSLT tagset is usually `xsl`, although it is not wrong to use `xslt` as well. Recall that Chapter 4 mentioned that namespaces have a name (the URI), and in most `tagsets`, a namespace name can be anything that is a URI. However, the XSLT recommendation is firm with its required value of `http://www.w3.org/1999/XSL/Transform` for the name value.

The rest of the content found within the style sheet is a mixture of elements from the XSLT namespace and XHTML. Because we're using a defined namespace for XSLT, any transformer that reads this style sheet is able to sort through the XSLT elements and the non-XSLT elements (in this case XHTML). The next two are examples of using the `output` element. The first of the two tells the XSLT transformer that the output is XML, allows indenting to be inserted into the document, and is encoded using `UTF-8`. The second output element allows us to specify that we'll be inserting a document type declaration that will be based on the XHTML strict format. Both of these output elements allow an elegant way of inserting the values into the source tree without actually typing them into the document. This is important because both are required to be at the top of the document and placing the actual statements within our style sheet would cause parsing errors.

The next element in is the `template` element, which allows us to select a node within the source tree using the `match` attribute, which at this time uses the '/' that represents the top of the document (i.e., like the '/' in Unix which also represents the root level within the filesystem tree). Inside of this template, we've inserted XHTML elements. When the transformer reads through this document, it simply copies the non-XSLT tagsets and data from the source tree, and places it all to the result tree. Inside of the paragraph element, we've placed a `for-each` element which is similar to a for loop in Java. The loop selects each `user` element in the XML document and performs the statements inside of the loop. The `sort` element is a request to sort the output (in this case based on each user element's `id` attribute). Lastly, within the loop, we're selecting the `id`, `firstName`, and `lastName` attribute values from each `user` element. If we were to write a loop in Java that was considered roughly equivalent, it would look something like this:

```
int size = users.size();
Collections.sort(users);
for(int i = 0; i < size; i++) {
    User user = (User)users.get(i);
    System.out.println("User:");
    System.out.println(user.getID());
    System.out.println(user.getFirstName());
    System.out.println(user.getLastName());
}
```

This would of course assume that the `users` Java counterpart was a `java.util.List`, the `User` class implemented `Comparable`, and that printing to the output stream was considered equivalent to outputting to the result tree in XSLT. The output of the transform (using Listing 11.1 for our XML and Listing 11.2 for our style sheet) would look like this:

```
<?xml version="1.0" encoding="UTF-8"?>
<!DOCTYPE html PUBLIC "-//W3C//DTD XHTML 1.0 Strict//EN"
  "http://www.w3.org/TR/xhtml1/DTD/xhtml1-strict.dtd">
<html>
  <head><title> Simple XSLT Transform </title></head>
  <body>
    <p><b>User:</b>231 Dave McDermit<br/>
      <b>User:</b>232 Arron Ferguson<br/>
      <b>User:</b>234 John Smith <br/>
    </p>
  </body>
</html>
```

The transforming we've accomplished can actually be completed either on the client side or on the server side. Client-side transforming is generally considered a bad idea because it exposes the XML to the client and the user. This can sometimes lead to inconsistent transforms between Web browsers or no transforming at all if the Web browser does not support it. The result is raw XML, which is hard to read. Server-side transforming is considered more appropriate because it does not expose the user or the client-side software to the XML formats. All the user sees is XHTML. The disadvantage of server-side transforms is the burden placed on the server, which can be great if the server experiences high request frequencies.

About the only difference that may need to be changed within the XSLT style sheet itself is a change in the output element's method attribute. In our example we've stated that we're sending XML. This is because our XHTML is in fact XML. A Web browser, however, treats XML content differently than XHTML; so if we were insisting on doing client-side transforming, we would want to change the value of the output element's method attribute to read HTML instead of XML.

Referring To Nodes

Because we are familiar with nodes in XML, it makes it easier to understand the process that XSLT transformers go through to generate the result tree. As mentioned, the result tree is created by going through a source tree and copying nodes from it (and possibly rearranging the copied nodes). Whenever a template inside of our style sheet refers to a different node within the tree, we are changing our level and position within the node set. This is not unlike moving through directory structures within a filesystem (e.g., using the cd command to change directory). Because of this, the *current node* and the *current node set* are constantly changing. Referring back to Listing 11.2, the forward slash ('/') referred to the top level, which is the document itself. The for-each element in XSLT referred to users/user. If we were in a filesystem, this would have been equivalent to the command cd users/user. It is important to understand this concept of current node and node list because it allows us to create XSLT transforms that work properly.

Unlike operating system command-line programs that offer feedback to the user about whether a file or directory exists, XSLT transformers do not offer feedback about whether a certain node or node set was encountered. For example, if you are searching a filesystem for any files with a txt extension, the command-line console program usually provides feedback stating that no file was found of that type (extension). However, when performing transforms, if the transformer does not find any nodes of a particular name (due to being at the wrong level of the DOM tree, for example), the result tree simply is rendered as empty. This is why it is important to understand at what exact level of the tree you are in.

Creating Transforms

At the heart of all transforming operations are the two XSLT elements: `template` and `apply-templates`. We saw in Listing 11.2 the *template* element in use:

```
<xsl:template match="/">
   . . .
</xsl:template>
```

The `template` element is almost like a function call, in that it is a direct command to the transformer to perform some set of actions (which ultimately results in a transform). By using the `match` attribute of the `template` element, we are asking for a pattern match from the source tree (i.e., XML document). As mentioned, the '/' is to start at the root of the document, but we could just as easily choose a deeper element (such as users from Listing 11.1). The `match` attribute allows us to use XPath statements to perform matching within the source tree. We will look at XPath more in depth later on in this chapter. Within the `template` element, we are allowed to place other XSLT elements such as the `for-each` element for looping. The results from other inner XSLT elements produce result fragments that are placed in the result tree. However, as we've seen, we can also use other elements from other XML tagsets, if we so choose. In Listing 11.2, we included XHTML. In fact, we can place any textual content into the body of the template element. For example, if we decided to use XSLT to generate a Java class source code file based on the XML file from Listing 11.1, we could create a style sheet like Listing 11.3.

LISTING 11.3   XSLT Generating Java Source Code

```
<?xml version="1.0" encoding="UTF-8"?>
<xsl:stylesheet version="1.0"
  xmlns:xsl="http://www.w3.org/1999/XSL/Transform">
  <xsl:output method="text" indent="yes" encoding="UTF-8"/>
  <xsl:template match="/">
import java.util.*;
public class Users {
    private java.util.List list;
    public Users() {
        list = new java.util.LinkedList();
        User user = null;
        <xsl:for-each select="users/user">
        user = new User(<xsl:value-of select="./@id"/>,
          <xsl:value-of select="./@firstName"/>,
          <xsl:value-of select="./@lastName"/>);
        list.add(user);
        </xsl:for-each>
    }
}
  </xsl:template>
</xsl:stylesheet>
```

The output from this transform would look like:

```java
import java.util.*;
public class Users {
    private java.util.List list;
    public Users() {
        list = new java.util.LinkedList();
        User user = null;
        user = new User(232, Arron, Ferguson);
        list.add(user);
        user = new User(234, John, Smith);
        list.add(user);
        user = new User(231, Dave, McDermit);
        list.add(user);
    }
}
```

We could use XSLT in ways that may not even have been anticipated. We could articulate an XML format that specifies (in a language-independent way) instructions, data structures, and classes and then create a style sheet that outputs the appropriate programming language-specific source code. In fact, we could have an attribute in each XML file that specifies which programming language that the style sheet should transform to. Of course, the style sheet would need to handle all language-specific instructions in the templates. Doing so would, however, give us the power of being able to specify a program that is language independent and then have source code generated for us. Taking this idea to the outer limits, we could write a program (or a series of programs) to be responsible for invoking compilers for each source code file. We would be able to bridge cross-platform and cross-language independence.

If the `template` element was roughly equivalent to a function call, then the `apply-templates` element is a request to process all child nodes within the current selected node. The `apply-templates` element is usually used with its `select` attribute where the value of the `select` attribute is the child node (or child nodes) to select. Listing 11.4 shows the use of the `apply-templates` element.

LISTING 11.4 Using the `apply-templates` Element

```xml
<?xml version="1.0" encoding="UTF-8"?>
<xsl:stylesheet version="1.0"
  xmlns:xsl="http://www.w3.org/1999/XSL/Transform">
  <xsl:output method="xml" indent="yes" encoding="UTF-8"/>
  <xsl:output method="xml"
    doctype-public="-//W3C//DTD XHTML 1.0 Strict//EN"
      doctype-system=
```

```
              "http://www.w3.org/TR/xhtml1/DTD/xhtml1-strict.dtd"/>
          <xsl:template match="/">
            <html>
              <head><title> Simple XSLT Transform </title></head>
              <body><xsl:apply-templates select="users"/></body>
            </html>
          </xsl:template>

          <xsl:template match="users">
            <p>
              <xsl:for-each select="user">
                <xsl:sort select="./@id"/>
                <b>User:</b>
                <xsl:value-of select="./@id"/> 
                <xsl:value-of select="./@firstName"/> 
                <xsl:value-of select="./@lastName"/> <br/>
              </xsl:for-each>
            </p>
          </xsl:template>
        </xsl:stylesheet>
```

In Listing 11.4, we've matched the document with the slash, and then we've used the `apply-templates` element along with the `select` attribute to select the `users` element within the XML (assuming we're still referencing Listing 11.10. Once the `users` element is selected, the transformer then calls the template whose `match` attribute value is `users`. Using the `select` attribute of the `apply-templates` element, we're given a behavior that almost acts like a function call. If we were to use the `apply-templates` element without the `select` attribute, all applied processing would be given to the child nodes of the current selected node. This function call-like ability allows us to make our style sheets highly modular, which is covered later in the chapter.

The `value-of` element allows us to create a text node that is placed in the result tree. We do this by using the `select` attribute that defines a pattern to match. In Listing 11.4 we used the `value-of` element to select the attributes of each `user` element from Listing 11.1 (`id` attribute, `firstName` attribute, and `lastName` attribute). The result is that the attribute values are placed in the result tree, as we saw when we output the XHTML. The `value-of` element can be used to output attribute values and elements.

Looping and Conditional Elements

As shown in Listing 11.2, we have the ability to loop through a list of child nodes. Looping with the `for-each` element is somewhat equivalent to a Java for loop, with the exception that the XSLT `for-each` cannot specify the number of times that it loops through—it loops through the entire number of nodes. Using a for loop is useful because we can treat a node list as a whole so as to perform further processing. Listing 11.5 offers us a simple XML document that contains a section element with several different child elements: `paragraph`, `code`, and `italic` as well as straight text.

LISTING 11.5 Section XML Document

```
<?xml version="1.0" encoding="UTF-8"?>
<?xml-stylesheet type="text/xsl" href="./Listing-11-7.xslt"?>
<section>
  <paragraph>A paragraph element.</paragraph>
  <code>A code element.</code>
  <code>Another code element.</code>
  <italic>Here's some italic</italic>
  <paragraph>Another paragraph element.</paragraph>
  Some text at the very end.
</section>
```

Listing 11.6 shows a style sheet that contains the `for-each` element. In this example, the loop contains cases dealing with different types of elements (we'll look at the conditional element next). The `for-each` element is using the XPath function `node()`, which allows us to be general in what we select. We could have used the name of an element, but this would not help us with this example because we are dealing with a mixed content model. Recall that a mixed content model is a content model that contains both elements and text. In Listing 11.5, there are five child elements of the `section` element, and at the very end there is some text. Hence, this is a mixed content model. We need to generalize here so that we can ensure that we can grab the `value-of` text nodes in our source tree as well.

LISTING 11.6 XSLT Style Sheet with `for-each` and `if` Elements

```
<?xml version="1.0" encoding="UTF-8"?>
<xsl:stylesheet version="1.0"
  xmlns:xsl="http://www.w3.org/1999/XSL/Transform">
  <xsl:output method="xml" indent="yes" encoding="UTF-8"/>
  <xsl:output method="xml"
    doctype-public="-//W3C//DTD XHTML 1.0 Strict//EN"
      doctype-system=
        "http://www.w3.org/TR/xhtml1/DTD/xhtml1-strict.dtd"/>
<xsl:strip-space elements="section"/>
  <xsl:template match="/">
    <html>
      <head><title> XSLT - For Each &amp; If Elements </title>
      </head>
      <body>
        <xsl:apply-templates select="section"/>
      </body>
```

```
    </html>
  </xsl:template>

  <xsl:template match="section">
    <div>
      <xsl:for-each select="node()">
        <xsl:if test="self::paragraph">
          <p><xsl:value-of select="."/></p>
        </xsl:if>
        <xsl:if test="self::code">
          <pre><xsl:value-of select="."/></pre>
        </xsl:if>
        <xsl:if test="self::italic">
          <i><xsl:value-of select="."/></i>
        </xsl:if>
        <xsl:if test="self::text()">
          < <xsl:if test="string-length(self::text()) != 0">
            <p><xsl:value-of select="."/></p>
          </xsl:if>
        </xsl:if>
      </xsl:for-each>
    </div>
  </xsl:template>
</xsl:stylesheet>
```

We also have at our disposal the if element, which is almost identical to an if statement in Java, with the exception of not having an else block at the end to handle the situation of the if element's state being false. In Listing 11.6, we've included some if statements to check for the different types of child elements within the section parent element. For example, we're handling paragraph elements, code elements, italic elements, and straight text. The condition is using the *self axis*. An axis is simply the selected nodes chosen by the current context node. This takes the form:

```
axis name :: node test [predicate]
```

Where the axis name is one of 13 named axes that can be chosen, followed by the node test and an optional predicate. In Listing 11.6, we've used the self axis. The self axis is similar to the this keyword in Java where it describes the current context (class in Java, node in XML). There are five node tests in Listing 11.6. The first three node tests are based on element names: paragraph, code, and italic. The fourth and fifth tests offer a little more depth to what is possible using XSLT and XPath:

```
<xsl:if test="self::text()">
  <xsl:if test="string-length(self::text()) != 0">
    <p><xsl:value-of select="."/></p>
  </xsl:if>
</xsl:if>
```

The outer `if` element is testing whether a text node was selected within the current context (in this case the section element). If this is true (not an element, in our example), then an inner condition is checked which is to see if the string length of the current text node is not equal to zero (in other words, not an empty string). We are able to do this because at the beginning of our style sheet we've included the `strip-space` element. The `strip-space` element allows us to specify elements in the source stream whose whitespace should be collapsed.

In our case, we've included the `section` element as an attribute value (the `elements` attribute) of the `strip-space` element. Recall from Chapter 4, that a mixed content model contains text nodes, even if the text nodes are the whitespace characters we added for intending. Without this extra check, we will receive a number of empty paragraphs due to empty strings for the text nodes. However, this only works because of the use of the `strip-space` element that we've defined near the top of our style sheet. We're using the `string-length()` function of XPath to check the length of a string.

The `choose` element offers another conditional solution. The `choose` element requires one or more `when` child elements and can have an optional `otherwise` element at the end. It is most like a switch statement in Java, with the exception that only the `when` element's statements are processed unlike a Java switch statement which requires a `break` statement to stop executing instructions. Listing 11.7 contains a simple XML document of tabular data (just rows for simplicity).

LISTING 11.7 XML Tabular Data

```
<?xml version="1.0" encoding="UTF-8"?>
<?xml-stylesheet type="text/xsl" href="./Listing-11-9.xslt"?>
<table>
  <tableRow>Content Management</tableRow>
  <tableRow>Introduction to Content Management Systems</tableRow>
  <tableRow>Licensing Issues</tableRow>
  <tableRow>Introduction to XML</tableRow>
</table>
```

An XSLT style sheet that transforms this XML document to XHTML is found in Listing 11.8. We're using the `choose` element as well as the `position()` XPath function to determine the child node's position within the child node list. We're also using the `mod()` function to determine the difference between every third row and all other rows (remainder is zero on every third iteration). We're using this calculation to color each third row different for visual clarity. Although we're only using one `when` element, we could actually be using as many as we need. Again, the `choose` element is very similar to the `switch` statement in Java.

LISTING 11.8   XSLT With choose Element

```
<?xml version="1.0" encoding="UTF-8"?>
<xsl:stylesheet version="1.0"
  xmlns:xsl="http://www.w3.org/1999/XSL/Transform">
  <xsl:output method="xml" indent="yes" encoding="UTF-8"/>
  <xsl:output method="xml"
    doctype-public="-//W3C//DTD XHTML 1.0 Strict//EN"
    doctype-system=
    "http://www.w3.org/TR/xhtml1/DTD/xhtml1-strict.dtd"/>
  <xsl:template match="/">
    <html>
      <head>
        <title> XSLT - Choose Element </title>
        <style type="text/css">
          *.lightOrangeColor
            { background-color: rgb(242, 148, 35);}
          *.lightBlueColor
            { background-color: rgb(183, 217, 251);}
        </style>
      </head>
      <body>
        <xsl:apply-templates select="table"/>
      </body>
    </html>
  </xsl:template>

  <xsl:template match="table">
    <div>
      <table>
        <xsl:for-each select="./tableRow">
            <xsl:choose>
              <xsl:when test="(position() mod 3) = 0">
                <tr class="lightOrangeColor">
                  <td><xsl:value-of select="."/></td>
                </tr>
              </xsl:when>
              <xsl:otherwise>
                <tr class="lightBlueColor">
                  <td><xsl:value-of select="."/></td>
                </tr>
              </xsl:otherwise>
            </xsl:choose>
        </xsl:for-each>
      </table>
    </div>
  </xsl:template>
</xsl:stylesheet>
```

Attribute Value Templates

There are times when you need to pull out some data from your source tree and place it inside of an attribute of an element that is found in your style sheet. The first thing that should come to mind at this point is that you will use the `value-of` element. But this does not work (even if you convert the less than and greater than symbols to entities). The solution is to use attribute value templates. Attribute value templates are just that: attribute values that are serving as template processing. For example, in our style sheet, we wish to place values into our anchor element:

```
<a href=" "><xsl:value-of select="./@text"/></a>
```

The anchor element's `href` attribute cannot contain an element (or an element's attribute)—even if it is an XSLT element. Instead, we use an attribute value template:

```
<a href="{HyperLink/@url}"><xsl:value-of select="./@text"/></a>
```

Attribute value templates must be surrounded by braces. Another example may be filling the meta elements in our XHTML document with attribute values from our page element:

```
<meta http-equiv="content-type" content="application/xhtml+xml;
  charset=UTF-8" />
<meta name="author" content="{@author}" />
<meta name="generator" content="{@generator}" />
```

Introduction to XPath

Up until now we've been focusing on XSLT elements and how to perform transforms using common elements. We actually have been using XPath for many of the pattern matchings. Although XPath is not XML, it is similar to us because is looks vaguely similar to URLs. XPath looks similar to URLs for three reasons. First, the syntax looks similar (e.g., using the forward slash both as a path separator and as a way of referencing the root itself). Second, the tree-like referencing is also similar. Third, we also have the notion of absolute paths and relative paths. In XPath we can refer to the top of the document using:

```
<xsl:template match="/"> . . . </xsl:template>
```

Or we can use a relative path such as:

```
<xsl:value-of select="./Bold"/>
```

which attempts to select the current context's `Bold` element.

Using Axes

As mentioned earlier, there are 13 axes. They each give us the ability to navigate in a different direction. The thirteen axes are:

ancestor: Refers to any direct or indirect ancestor. This is useful for when you may wish to treat an element differently when it is inside of a different parent. For example, you may have a `link` element that can be placed inside of a `paragraph` element as well as a table `cell`. Different attributes are displayed in the paragraph than in the table cell. The ancestor axis contains the root node unless the current context node is the root node itself.

ancestor-or-self: Same as ancestor, but also includes the current context node.

attribute: Contains the attributes of the current context node unless the current context node is not an element, in which case this axis is empty. A shorthand representation of this axis is the '@' symbol.

child: Contains all of the children of the current context node. The child axis is considered the default axis. So, for example, in Listing 11.8 we did a pattern match (`./tableRow`) which used the implied child axis because we mentioned no axis. Additionally could have also said `tableRow`. The longhand way of writing this would have been `child::tableRow`. All three of these are equal.

descendant: Recursively contains all children nodes. However, the descendant axis does not contain attribute nodes or namespace nodes.

descendant-or-self: Same as the descendant axis, but also includes the current context node. The shorthand representation of this axis is '//'.

following: Contains all nodes that are found after (trail after) the current context node excluding descendant nodes, attribute nodes, and namespace nodes. This sounds confusing as it simply sounds as if it's only the following siblings, but it is more than that. This axis includes other nodes that are not necessarily coming from the same parent as the current context node so long as they follow the current context node.

following-sibling: This axis only includes all nodes that are found after (trail after) the current context node. If the current context node is an attribute node or a namespace node, this axis will be empty.

namespace: Contains all namespace nodes unless this axis is not an element, in which case it will be empty.

parent: Contains the parent node unless the current context node is the root, in which case the axis will be empty. The shorthand representation of this axis is two dots ('..').

preceding: Contains all nodes that are before the current context node. This excludes ancestor nodes, attribute nodes, and namespace nodes but includes nodes that may not necessarily have the same parent as this current context node has.

preceding-sibling: Contains all nodes that are siblings (i.e., same parent as the current context node) and that are found before this current context node. If the current context node is an attribute node or a namespace node, then this axis is empty.

self: the current context node. The shorthand representation of this axis is a single dot ('.').

Using XPath Functions

There are many functions that we can use with XPath and we apply to the axes when we're pattern matching in our XSLT style sheets. These functions can be grouped into the following categories:

Node Set Functions: Functions that deal with nodes.

String Functions: Functions that allow for the manipulation and inspection of strings.

Boolean Functions: Functions that deal with boolean values (includes the ability to turn a result into a boolean value).

Number Functions: Contains some standard math functions, such as floor and ceiling, as well as the ability to convert strings into numbers (assuming the string value is a number).

Date Functions: Date and time functions.

There are many other functions and we won't be covering all functions—just commonly used functions and functions that apply to our CMS style sheets. For more information on these functions see: http://www.w3.org/TR/xpath.

Many of these functions may seem familiar because they capture some of the core needs programmers have when dealing with text and numbers or in the case of the XML DOM, nodes. For example, if we wish to copy Keyword elements from the current context to the result tree, we could say something like:

```
<xsl:if test="count(child::*) > 0">
  <xsl:element name="meta">
    <xsl:attribute name="name">keywords</xsl:attribute>
    <xsl:attribute name="content">
      <xsl:for-each select="./Keyword">
        <xsl:value-of select="./@text"/>
```

```
        <xsl:if test="position() != last()">, </xsl:if>
      </xsl:for-each>
    </xsl:attribute>
  </xsl:element>
</xsl:if>
```

The first line uses the count function to count how many child nodes are found. If the number given back is greater than zero, then our processing continues. Once inside, we use a for-each element that copies the contents of each Keyword element. One last check is made and that is a check to see if the node going through the for loop is the last node (using the last() function and comparing its value to the position function which returns the current index in the loop) in the list, then we do not print the comma. This ensures that all Keyword element values printed are followed by a comma, unless of course we're encountering the last Keyword element in the node list. Back in Listing 11.8, we used the position function to give us the index of the current context node:

```
<xsl:when test="(position() mod 3) = 0">
  <tr class="lightOrangeColor">
    <td><xsl:value-of select="."/></td>
  </tr>
</xsl:when>
```

Refactoring Web Pages

Our XHTML document has been created with CSS and we've created a Web template that we can now go ahead and refactor. Although technically refactoring is referred to in the programming world (used to describe the process of rewriting source code so that it is more readable yet not changing its behavior) we can still use this term because the overall behavior does not change: output of XHTML Web pages. The XSLT style sheet referred to in this section is called kucingCMS.xslt and is located on the CD-ROM in the *CMS-project\src\templates* subfolder. The DTD file that is referenced (output-format.dtd), is located on the CD-ROM in the *CMS-project\src\CMS-dtds* subfolder.

ON THE CD

Whenever starting an XSLT style sheet, it helps to begin with a basic template file:

```
<?xml version="1.0" encoding="UTF-8"?>
<xsl:stylesheet version="1.0"
  xmlns:xsl="http://www.w3.org/1999/XSL/Transform">
  <xsl:output method="xml" indent="yes" encoding="UTF-8"/>
  <xsl:output method="xml"
    doctype-public="-//W3C//DTD XHTML 1.0 Strict//EN"
    doctype-system=
    "http://www.w3.org/TR/xhtml1/DTD/xhtml1-strict.dtd"/>
```

```
<xsl:template match="/">
  <!- content goes here ->
</xsl:template>
</xsl:stylesheet>
```

From here, we need to remember the structure of our XML tagset. Recall from Chapter 5, we created a DTD that represented our XML output format. This format is what we need to continue with our XHTML refactoring. Looking at the DTD, we know that we're starting with a `Page` element:

```
<!ELEMENT Page (Stamp, Keywords, Footer, (NewsSection)?, Menu,
  Sections)>
```

So our root template match now becomes:

```
<xsl:template match="/">
  <xsl:apply-templates select="Page"/>
</xsl:template>
```

We want to keep our style sheet highly modular, and so we should create separate templates for each element. This ideal cascades from the programming world because programs that are modular are easier to manage and easier to debug. Style sheets are no different in this respect. The page template is where most of the real action begins. The first time you perform this refactoring process, it may be difficult to think on both planes. On one hand, you are attempting to remember the XML tagset that you need to traverse through in order to retrieve nodes from it. On the other hand, you are trying to interleave XHTML content structure with the XML tagset. This can be tricky at times because the order in which you handle the XHTML is sometimes restricted based on the box model choices you make (e.g., the menu box is (not) inside of the title bar). The `Page` template with the handling of head content looks like:

```
<xsl:template match="Page">
  <html xml:lang="en" lang="en-CA">
    <head>
      <link rel="shortcut icon" href="{@icon}"
        type="image/x-icon" />
      <meta http-equiv="content-type"
        content="application/xhtml+xml; charset=UTF-8" />
      <meta name="author" content="{@author}" />
      <meta name="generator" content="{@generator}" />
      <xsl:apply-templates select="Keywords"/>
      <link rel="stylesheet" type="text/css"
        href="./css/kucingCMS.css" media="screen"
        title="Kucing CMS" />
      <title><xsl:value-of select="./@titleBar"/></title>
    </head>
```

```
      <body></body>
    </html>
  </xsl:template>
```

We've grabbed the Page element attributes and placed them inside of the meta elements of XHTML. We've also called a template for Keywords, which needs to be created somewhere in our style sheet:

```
<xsl:template match="Keywords">
  <xsl:if test="count(child::*) > 0">
    <xsl:element name="meta">
      <xsl:attribute name="name">keywords</xsl:attribute>
      <xsl:attribute name="content">
        <xsl:for-each select="./Keyword">
          <xsl:value-of select="./@text"/>
          <xsl:if test="position() != last()">, </xsl:if>
        </xsl:for-each>
      </xsl:attribute>
    </xsl:element>
  </xsl:if>
</xsl:template>
```

This traverses the Keywords element for Keyword children and if there are any, places them within the meta element inside of XHTML. Still within the Page template, we handle the body element in the XHTML that has been inserted into our style sheet. It contains several references to other templates (shown in bold):

```
<body>
  <div class="content">
    <div class="titlebar">
      <h1><xsl:value-of select="./@title"/></h1>
    </div>
    <xsl:apply-templates select="Menu"/>
    <div class="contentPane">
      <div class="sidebar">
        <xsl:if test="./@hasSearchLink='true'">
          <div class="floatBox">
            <h3>Search the Site</h3>
            <a href="./search.html"
               title="Go to customized search page">
               Go to search ...</a>
            <br/>
            <br/>
          </div>
        </xsl:if>
        <xsl:apply-templates select="NewsSection"/>
        <xsl:if test="./@hasForumLogin='true'">
          <div class="floatBox">
            <form action="./forum.html" method="post">
              <h3>Forum Login</h3>
```

```
                    Login name:
                    <input type="text" name="name"/>
                    <br/>
                    Password:
                    <input type="password" name="password"/>
                    <br/>
                    <br/>
                    <input type="submit" value="Submit"/>
                    <input type="hidden" name="action" value="login"/>
                  </form>
                </div>
              </xsl:if>
            </div>
            <xsl:apply-templates select="Sections"/>
          </div>
        </div>
        <xsl:apply-templates select="Footer"/>
      </body>
    </html>
```

We call templates based on the sequence that we want the XHTML to be displayed in. The first template uses the Menu element, which will call up the Menu template:

```
<xsl:template match="Menu">
  <div>
    <ul class="menu">
      <li><a href="index.html">Home</a></li>
      <xsl:for-each select="MenuItem">
        <xsl:sort select="./@text"/>
        <li class="menuItem">
          <a href="{./@url}"><xsl:value-of select="./@text"/></a>
        </li>
      </xsl:for-each>
    </ul>
  </div>
</xsl:template>
```

We have constructed a for loop that retrieves the values of MenuItem elements (the text and the url attributes). Notice we are using attribute value templates for this because we wish to place the attribute values of the MenuItem elements into anchor elements in our XHTML. The next template called handles the NewsSection element:

```
<xsl:template match="NewsSection">
  <xsl:if test="count(child::*) > 0">
    <div class="floatBox">
      <h3><xsl:value-of select="./@title"/></h3>
      <xsl:for-each select="NewsItem">
        <xsl:sort order="descending" select="./@date"/>
```

```
      <div>
        <h5><xsl:value-of select="./@date"/></h5>
        <p><xsl:value-of select="./Text/text()"/>
        <xsl:if test="./HyperLink">
          <a target="_blank" href="{HyperLink/@url}"
            title="Open link">
            <xsl:value-of select="HyperLink/@text"/> &#187;
          </a>
        </xsl:if>
        </p>
      </div>
    </xsl:for-each>
  </div>
  </xsl:if>
</xsl:template>
```

The `NewsSection` template first does a conditional check to see if there are any child elements (which is of type `NewsItem`). This check is performed because it makes no sense to display a news section box within the XHTML page when there are no news items to display. We're using the XSLT `sort` element to sort the news items in descending order (highest to lowest), which makes sense because we want to see the most recent news items before older ones. Once inside a news item, there is a check performed to see if the news item contains a link. If it does, the `HyperLink` element's attribute values are retrieved and placed into the XHTML anchor element. As we trace through the `kucingCMS.xslt` style sheet, we see another template which is for processing the `Sections` element:

```
<xsl:template match="Sections">
  <xsl:for-each select="Section">
    <a name="{./@id}"/><h3><xsl:value-of select="./@title"/></h3>
    <xsl:for-each select="./*">
      <xsl:if test="self::Paragraph">
        <xsl:apply-templates select="self::Paragraph"/>
      </xsl:if>
      <xsl:if test="self::List">
        <xsl:apply-templates select="self::List"/>
      </xsl:if>
        <!--See kucingCMS.xslt for full code listing -->
      <xsl:if test="self::SearchList">
        <xsl:apply-templates select="self::SearchList"/>
      </xsl:if>
    </xsl:for-each>
  </xsl:for-each>
</xsl:template>
```

Each if statement within this for loop is checking for the presence of a particular element. This is because our `output-format.dtd` DTD specifies that the following elements can be placed inside of the `Sections` element:

```
<!ELEMENT Sections (Section)*>
    <!ELEMENT Section (Stamp, ((ForumTopics | Forum) | (Table |
        Paragraph | Code | List | Image | ImageGallery)*) )>
```

Looking at the Table element, we find the following XSLT sprinkled with XHTML:

```
<xsl:template match="Table">
  <a name="{./@id}"/>
  <table class="text-table">
    <caption><xsl:value-of select="./@caption"/></caption>
    <tr>
      <xsl:for-each select="./TableHeader/Text">
        <th><xsl:value-of select="."/></th>
      </xsl:for-each>
    </tr>
    <xsl:for-each select="./TableRow">
      <xsl:sort select="."/>
        <xsl:choose>
          <xsl:when test="(position() mod 3) = 0">
            <tr class="table-row-alternate-color">
              <xsl:for-each select="./*">
                <xsl:if test="self::Text">
                  <td valign="top"><xsl:value-of select="."/></td>
                </xsl:if>
                <xsl:if test="self::HyperLink">
                  <td valign="top"><a href="{@url}"
                    target="_blank" title="{@url}">
                    <xsl:value-of select="@text"/></a>
                  </td>
                </xsl:if>
              </xsl:for-each>
            </tr>
          </xsl:when>
          <xsl:otherwise>
            <tr>
              <xsl:for-each select="./*">
                <xsl:if test="self::Text">
                  <td valign="top"><xsl:value-of select="."/></td>
                </xsl:if>
                <xsl:if test="self::HyperLink">
                  <td valign="top"><a href="{@url}"
                    target="_blank" title="{@url}">
                    <xsl:value-of select="@text"/></a>
                  </td>
                </xsl:if>
              </xsl:for-each>
            </tr>
          </xsl:otherwise>
        </xsl:choose>
    </xsl:for-each>
  </table>
  <br/>
</xsl:template>
```

At the top of this template, we notice that the XHTML `table` element is using the `text-table` class selector, which formats this XHTML table differently than, say, an image gallery table. The caption is retrieved from the XML format `Table` element. We then need to start handling all of the elements of the table, which start with the header. We extract the `TableHeader` element's `Text` element and place it into XHTML table header elements (`<th>`). Next, we handle each row by selecting `TableRow` elements within a for loop and sort each of the rows. Each row can either have straight text or `HyperLink` elements (mixed content model); so we must check for the presence of each, using the `choose` element in XSLT. We've made use of the `position()` function in XPath, so that we can set every third row to an alternate color for visual clarity. Recall from Chapter 5, that `Paragraph` elements require a `Stamp` element at the beginning, but mixed content afterwards:

```
<!ELEMENT Paragraph (Stamp, ParagraphContent)>
```

So in order to handle this, we actually have two templates for handling the `Paragraph` element:

```
<xsl:template match="Paragraph">
  <xsl:apply-templates select="./ParagraphContent"/>
</xsl:template>
```

which calls the paragraph content element template:

```
<xsl:template match="ParagraphContent">
  <p><a name="{../@id}"/>
    <xsl:for-each select="node()">
      <xsl:if test="self::text()">
        <xsl:value-of select="."/>
      </xsl:if>
      <xsl:if test="self::Hint">
        <acronym title="{self::Hint/@description}">
          <xsl:value-of select="self::Hint/@term"/>
        </acronym>
      </xsl:if>
      <xsl:if test="self::HyperLink">
        <a href="{self::HyperLink/@url}"
          title="{self::HyperLink/@url}">
          <xsl:value-of select="self::HyperLink/@text"/>
        </a>
      </xsl:if>
      <xsl:if test="self::B">
        <b><xsl:value-of select="self::B/text()"/></b>
      </xsl:if>
      <xsl:if test="self::I">
        <i><xsl:value-of select="self::I/text()"/></i>
      </xsl:if>
```

```
    </xsl:for-each>
  </p>
</xsl:template>
```

We've placed a series of if statements inside of a for loop, checking for the various types of content (straight text, Hint elements, HyperLink elements, bold, and italic elements). The for-each element is using the node function. This generalization is required because not all nodes in the source tree are elements—we do have straight text based on our mixed content model. Once inside of the for loop, we can use the self axis to reference each of the child nodes and retrieve the content either with value-of elements or with attribute value templates (for many of the attribute values). The List element is similar to the Paragraph element, in that it requires a Stamp element at the beginning, after which follows zero or more ListItem elements. Recall that we can have bulleted lists, numbered lists, and definition lists. Looking at the template that handles lists:

```
<xsl:template match="List">
  <p><a name="{./@id}"/>
    <xsl:if test="./@type='definitions'">
      <b><xsl:value-of select="./@heading"/></b>
      <dl>
        <xsl:for-each select="./ListItem">
          <dt><xsl:value-of select="./Term"/></dt>
          <dd><xsl:value-of select="./Text"/></dd>
        </xsl:for-each>
      </dl>
    </xsl:if>
    <xsl:if test="./@type='bulleted'">
      <b><xsl:value-of select="./@heading"/></b>
      <ul>
        <xsl:for-each select="./ListItem">
          <li><strong><xsl:value-of select="./Term"/></strong>
            <xsl:value-of select="./Text"/></li>
        </xsl:for-each>
      </ul>
    </xsl:if>
    <xsl:if test="./@type='numbered'">
      <b><xsl:value-of select="./@heading"/></b>
      <ol>
        <xsl:for-each select="./ListItem">
          <li><strong><xsl:value-of select="./Term"/></strong>
            <xsl:value-of select="./Text"/></li>
        </xsl:for-each>
      </ol>
    </xsl:if>
  </p>
</xsl:template>
```

We have three if statements, which check for the different types of list. Each of these allow us to call the different types of XHTML lists. This does cause a slight problem because bulleted lists (which map to unordered lists) and numbered lists do not contain terms such as how a definitions list does. This means that we have to add these ourselves to the unordered list and numbered list in XHTML. We do this by making use of the strong element in XHTML.

Refactoring Summary

It is important to isolate each of these steps that we've covered, so as to ensure that most or all inconsistencies and errors are caught in your templates. Always focus on each particular step of the Web page design process. The following steps can help make the process easier to implement your final design:

1. Start off with a design idea where you don't have to use a computer design tool to do this. A pen and paper is more than enough. Draw out your idea of the layout. Lay out all parts of design based on your data model. Possibly create several different layouts and place them on a table, look at each, and self-critique your own work. Decide which layout looks best. Also keep a mind for what the theme should be (if any) and who the audience is. Remember to make it easy for users to navigate through the pages.
2. Decide on a set of colors. Look around the house for physical objects that contain more than one color. Ties, comforters, furniture, even interior design choices can help you find a color theme that works.
3. Create the XHTML document that contains the content structure. Make use of the div and span elements for creating content structure. Remember to continually validate your XHTML documents against a validator (such as the one found at the W3C's Web site *http://validator.w3.org/*). Remember that if you're not using XHTML strict now, that in the future you probably will have to. Many Web browsers and the W3C itself is nudging the industry in that direction. At least, you should be ensuring that your XHTML is validating correctly against the transitional flavor of XHTML.
4. Implement your cascading style sheets (CSSs). Remember to use many class selectors and also create some default element selectors that can be used through the document for all elements (e.g., such as all paragraphs, anchors, and images). Be creative. Make use of flow in CSS because it helps you create interesting layouts without having to misuse the table element in XHTML. But also remember that there's nothing wrong with using the table element to display tabular data.

5. Test your XHTML Web page template against all elements of your XML data model. Ensure that all types of data display correctly and consistently.

6. Create your XSLT by ensuring you're using many different template calls, which makes for a modular style sheet. Ensuring your style sheet is modular aids in the debugging process, as well as future incremental alterations and improvements you may decide to do in your style sheet. Test the style sheet by running it through your software to ensure that it transforms all content from your XML data model correctly.

SUMMARY

In this chapter, we looked at the transforming process behind XSLT and transformers (including the source and result trees). We also looked at some of the more important XSLT elements such as `value-of`, `template`, `apply-templates`, `if`, `element`, `attribute`, `for-each`, and `sort` (to name a few). We looked at XPath and how to create queries, as well as how to use some of the more common functions that come with XPath. Finally, we structured our XSLT style sheet so that it addressed specific elements within our XML format and interwove those calls with XHTML. The finished style sheet gives us a consistent means of outputting our CMS Web pages. About the CD-ROM is next, and it offers a look into how the CMS we've been building throughout the book works, shows the features that we've talked about, and offers some interesting ideas as to how it can be improved upon by the reader.

ENDNOTE

1. A functional programming language is a programming language that focuses on evaluating expressions, rather than exposing fine details such as statements that change program state (e.g., showing the increment of a counter for a loop).

References

[Adler03] Adler, Jeff, et al., *Portable Network Graphics (PNG) Specification (Second Edition)*. Available online at: *http://www.w3.org/TR/PNG/*, The World Wide Web Consortium (W3C), November 10, 2003.

[Apple06] Apple Computer Inc., *Apple Human Interface Design Guidelines*, Available online at: *http://developer.apple.com/documentation/UserExperience/Conceptual/OSXHIGuidelines/OSXHIGuidelines.pdf.*

[Bray04] Bray, Paoli, et al., *Extensible Markup Language (XML) 1.1*. Available online at: *http://www.w3.org/TR/2004/REC-xml11-20040204/*, The World Wide Web Consortium (W3C), February 4, 2004.

[CMSMatrix06] Plain Black Corporation, *The CMS Matrix*. Available online at: *http://www.cmsmatrix.org/matrix.*

[Dürst03] Dürst, Freytag, *Unicode in XML and other Markup Languages*. Available online at: *http://www.w3.org/TR/2003/NOTE-unicode-xml-20030613/*, The World Wide Web Consortium (W3C), June 13, 2003.

[Fielding99] Fielding, Irvine, et al., *Hypertext Transfer Protocol—HTTP/1.1*, Available online at: *http://www.w3.org/Protocols/rfc2616/rfc2616.html*, The World Wide Web Consortium (W3C), June, 1999.

[FSF05] Free Software Foundation Inc. Available online at: *http://www.fsf.org/licensing/essays/free-sw.html*, Free Software Foundation Inc., February 12, 2005.

[Le Hégaret05] Philippe Le Hégaret, *Document Object Model (DOM)*, Available online at: *http://www.w3.org/DOM/*, The World Wide Web Consortium (W3C), January 19, 2005.

[Microsoft04] Microsoft Corporation, Official Guidelines for User Interface Developers and Designers, Available online at: *http://msdn.microsoft.com/library/default.asp?url=/library/en-us/dnwue/html/welcome.asp.*

[Perens97] Bruce Perens, *The Open Source Definition Version 1.9*. Available online at: *http://opensource.org/docs/definition.php*, The Open Source Initiative, 1997.

About the CD-ROM

In this appendix we will look at:

- Introduction to Kucing CMS
- What is on the CD-ROM
- Kucing CMS requirements
- Building Kucing CMS
- Using the Kucing CMS admin applet
- Adding further work to Kucing CMS

INTRODUCTION TO KUCING CMS 1.0

Kucing CMS 1.0 is the content management system software application that comes with the book *Creating Content Management Systems in Java,* by Arron Ferguson, published by Charles River Media. Kucing CMS is a Java Web application that runs within a Web server that supports Java servlet technology and uses XML as the data store for content persistence. XSLT is used as the transformation mechanism so that the entire site is skinnable (i.e., change the look-and-feel) of all presented content to the end user. The administration program is a Java applet that connects to the server using HTTP.

WHAT'S ON THE CD-ROM

The CD-ROM contains the following content:

- Chapter code listings for each chapter
- Kucing CMS 1.0 project folder
- Software folder containing software for the process of creating the Kucing CMS 1.0 project as well as for running Kucing CMS 1.0

Chapter Code Listings

For each chapter that contains code listings, there is a folder that contains the code samples which are meant to demonstrate a certain task. Chapters that do not have directories on the CD-ROM therefore do not have code listings in them. Figure A.1 shows graphical listing of the chapter folders on the CD-ROM as well as the project folder, the licenses folder (for open source software that is distributed with this book) and the open source software.

FIGURE A.1   Screen capture of chapter folders.

Kucing CMS 1.0

Since the book is all about creating content management systems in Java (this is the name of the book after all), the book comes with working CMS on the CD-ROM. The name of the CMS is called Kucing CMS (pronounced Koo-ching) 1.0 and offers many features including a search engine, a forum manager, an admin applet that allows users to update the CMS via the admin applet, storage of content using XML data stores, dynamic changing of the Web look-and-feel and many more features. The CMS-Project folder contains the actual project files which include everything required to build the CMS from scratch. Figure A.2 shows graphical listing of the Kucing CMS project folder on the CD-ROM.

Licenses And Software Folder

The licenses folder contains all software licenses for all software libraries required for Kucing CMS as well as all software applications that are included on the CD-ROM for use in creating Kucing CMS. The Books software license is also found in this directory. It is important for you to read these licenses and to understand the rules and restrictions that may be found in each of the licenses. Make sure that you

FIGURE A.2 Listing of Kucing CMS folder.

understand the licenses. The software folder contains development software for building the CMS project such as Apache's Ant build tool, JEdit, a source code editor, as well as software for running the CMS such as Apache's Tomcat 5.5 Web server. The libraries that Kucing CMS requires for runtime are also found in this folder, however, the specific Java Archive (JAR) files that Kucing CMS needs in order to run have already been extracted and placed into the CMS-project folder. Figure A.3 shows a graphical listing of the software folder on the CD-ROM.

FIGURE A.3 Screen capture of software folder.

KUCING CMS REQUIREMENTS

In order to run Kucing CMS you will need to have Apache Tomcat 5.5 installed (as mentioned in Chapter 2) as well as the Java J2SE™ Runtime Environment 5.0. You can use your choice of operating system such as Microsoft Windows 2000, Windows 2003 or Windows XP, Macintosh System 10 or Linux or any operating system that will run Apache Tomcat 5.5 and the Java J2SE™ Runtime Environment 5.0.

NOTE

You can use any servlet/JSP container that implements the Servlet 2.4 and JavaServer Pages 2.0 specifications. You should ensure that you have configured your Web container to auto-deploy as well as automatically unpack (Web Archives) WAR files. That way if the server is currently running, the Web app will automatically be extracted from its WAR file and run.

BUILDING KUCING CMS

As mentioned in Chapter 2, you will need to have Apache's Ant installed on your computer. Refer back to Chapter 2 on how to install and run Apache's Ant. Once you have Ant installed the Kucing CMS project can be built. However, as mentioned in Chapter 7, you will need to make one change to your Ant build file. Recall that there were several properties set up at the beginning of the Ant build file (`build.xml` in the root of your *CMS-project* directory).

There were two properties that we needed to change. The first property was the `deploy-dir` property which told Ant where to place the completed Web Archive (WAR). You can either choose a Web application folder that Tomcat 5.5 (or the Web container of your choosing) will use to launch Web applications or you can simply choose to store the WAR file for later use and not launch it immediately. The other property that you need to change the value of is the `servlet-api` property. The value to this property informs Ant as to where to find the `servlet-api.jar` library which is what is required for building applications that take advantage of the servlet API.

Building Kucing CMS as a Blank Template

The current build directory and supporting files and resources all build Kucing CMS with preexisting content. You may wish to start from scratch rather than having to delete content through the admin applet. For example, you can copy the entire contents of the CMS-project directory into a different directory and create a build project for creating template instances of Kucing CMS. This would allow you to have several different build projects. In order to create your own blank project, you will want to take the following steps (in addition to the ones we previously mentioned for changing properties in the `build.xml` file).

Clean out Media Directories

Currently Kucing CMS has some images that are stored in both the "CMS-project\src\media\images" folder and the "CMS-project\src\media\thumbs" folder. Unless you want these images for your own use, you can delete these since they'll just take up extra space.

Clean out XML Data Files

Since you'll want only your own content, you'll need to remove the content that is found in the XML files in the "CMS-project\src\xml" folder. The only XML documents that you won't need to edit are the `404-messages.xml` document and the `templates.xml` document. You may not even need to change the `users.xml` document unless you want different user accounts and different passwords.

It is very important that you follow these steps carefully so that Kucing CMS operates properly. Failing to follow the steps when creating a blank template will cause the CMS to fail to run.

CAUTION

Clearing XML Content

All XML files that contain content have a root element called `DataStore`. This element you must **not** delete. It is required for the data store for loading—it expects that element to be there. All of the child elements can be removed (**except** in the case of the `news-footer.xml` document which we will look at next). For example, if your `code-blocks.xml` document contains the following content:

```
<?xml version="1.0" encoding="UTF-8"?>
<DataStore>
  <Code author="Arron Ferguson" id="code_0" >
  <Stamp dateCreated="1141795155177" dateModified="1141795155177"/>
  <CodeContent>
    http://www.mydomain.net/kucingCMS-1.0/admin.jsp</CodeContent>
      </Code>
</DataStore>
```

you can remove the content so that all that is left is:

```
<?xml version="1.0" encoding="UTF-8"?>
<DataStore>
</DataStore>
```

Although it is useful to contain at least one page in the build, it is not necessary since you can create them in the admin applet. However, the first time you start Kucing CMS without any pages, the root of Kucing CMS as displayed in the Web browser will display the actual folders that are found inside of Kucing CMS. The first page you should create is the index.html page which is expected to be there.

The news-footer.xml document requires as a minimum the following content in it in order for Kucing CMS to work properly:

```
<?xml version="1.0" encoding="UTF-8"?>
<DataStore>
  <Footer>
  </Footer>
  <NewsSection title="">
  </NewsSection>
</DataStore>
```

Like the other types of XML documents you must **not** delete the DataStore element. However, you must also make sure that you do **not** delete the Footer or the NewsSection child elements either.

Do not change the names of the XML documents since Kucing CMS expects the file names that are found in this directory. Changing the names of the XML documents will result in runtime errors and a failure to load the content.

RUNNING KUCING CMS SERVER

Since Kucing CMS is a Web Archive (WAR) file, it can simply be placed into your Web application folder and run from there. As mentioned in Chapter 7, you should ensure that your server.xml file in Tomcat 5.5 contains the value true for both the unpackWARs attribute and the autoDeploy of the Host element that you wish Kucing CMS to be placed under. With these attributes set to true, the Kucing CMS WAR file will automatically be deployed and available on your Web server. You should ensure that you place it in the correct folder (e.g., webapps folder) based on your server.xml file for any virtual hosts you've created.

Any time you are trying out new software you should always test out the software on a development server that is private and not accessible on the Internet. That way if there are any problems with the software they will not affect any publicly available Web applications. As well, Kucing CMS installs with some default user accounts and passwords. Although it is unlikely that at the point in time you are installing Kucing CMS users are attempting to access it, it still could be a possibility. If someone were to know that you were installing Kucing CMS on a public

server and know the default user account names and passwords, they could log in and add new accounts before you have a chance to login yourself. Therefore, you should always test and configure a Web app (not just Kucing CMS) on a private development system that is not visible on the Internet.

Once this happens, you can attempt to access the Kucing CMS by typing:

```
http://www.myhost.com/kucing-CMS-1.0/
```

Assuming you are accessing it on the same computer that you installed the Web application and Tomcat server software on.

USING THE KUCING CMS ADMIN APPLET

This section covers how to use the admin applet in order to add, delete, and edit content within Kucing CMS. This section will cover the UI tools found within the applet and describe step-by-step how to perform all tasks found in Kucing CMS. The admin applet runs within a Web browser and so the requirement is that the Web browser has support for Sun's Java Runtime Platform Version 5.

Logging in

In order to access the applet the following URL is required:

```
http://www.mydomain.net/kucing-CMS-1.0/admin.jsp
```

Where `www.mydomain.net` is the name of your domain and `kucing-CMS` is the path of your Web application. The resource `admin.jsp` is the resource you need to connect to in order to access the admin applet. Figure A.4 shows the login form for the admin applet. As was mentioned previously, if you are accessing the Web application from the same local machine, then you would instead type:

```
http://localhost/kucing-CMS/admin.jsp
```

After typing your username and password (based on one of the three nonforum accounts already provided as defaults), you will be presented with the main menu form (shown in Figure A.5). The main menu form contains three buttons, each labeled: Manage Accounts, Manage Look-and-Feel, and Manage Content. Each of these options will take you to a different form but you can always navigate back to the main menu and from the main menu you can always log out by pressing the Logout button.

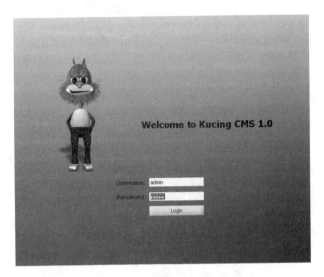

FIGURE A.4   Kucing CMS login form.

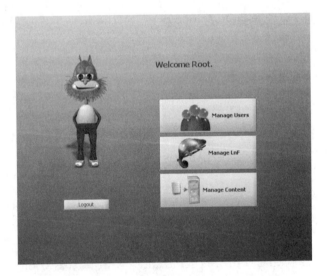

FIGURE A.5   Kucing CMS main menu.

Managing Users

The Manage Accounts button will allow you to navigate to the forms that offer account management capability such as adding and deleting other accounts and editing your own account.

The Manage Accounts button will be disabled for all author accounts. This feature will only be available to admin accounts.

Add User Tab

By default the Add User Tab will be the tab that is selected. Figure A.6 shows the Add User tab and the fields that are editable. User accounts can be given a first name, last name in addition to the login name and password. In order to ensure the desired password was entered, there is a Confirm Password field for consistency. The Account Type combo box allows the new account to be created to be of type administrator, author, or forum user. When finished, press the Add User button to save the newly created user account to the server. The server will respond with a dialog informing you of the status of the request either stating that the request proceeded correctly or that an error was encountered. As always, you can navigate back to the main menu from here by pressing the Main Menu button.

Kucing CMS is set to timeout after 15 minutes of inactivity (i.e., no requests to the server). If this happens, all changes that are in the client applet will be lost. It is therefore important to ensure that when you are working you do not wait more than 15 minutes between updates. If you wish to change (increase) the timeout quantum, you can do so by changing the session timeout element value in the deployment descriptor (in our project it is called kucingCMS.xml and is found in the CMS-project\src\deploydesc directory on the CD-ROM.

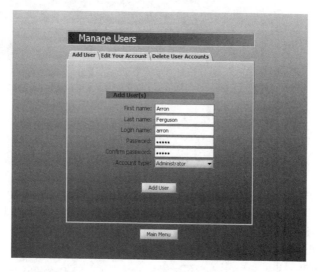

FIGURE A.6   Kucing CMS Add User Tab.

Edit Your Account Tab

The next Tab allows you to change certain aspects of your account such as the field containing your first name and last name. These fields are shown in the user interface and they are used to mark content sections as yours (the author attribute). In addition to these values you can also change your password. Again a Confirm Password field exists to ensure that you type the password correctly both times. The login name is not editable. This is a safety feature to ensure that no two account names can be the same—especially if one is already logged in. Figure A.7 displays the Edit Your Account Tab. When you've finished making changes, press the Update Account button. As always, you can navigate back to the main menu from here by pressing the Main Menu button.

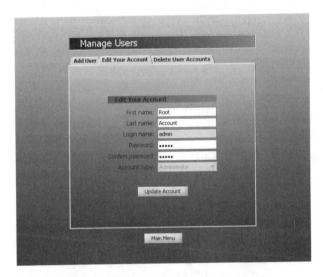

FIGURE A.7 Kucing CMS Edit Your Account Tab.

Delete User Accounts Tab

The Delete User Accounts Tab offers the feature of being able to delete user accounts. In order to delete user accounts you must first press the List Users button. This will contact the server which will return a list of users that are currently found on the system. Various pieces of information are listed in table format about each user including their first name, last name, login name, date created, date edited, and whether they are currently logged in or not. Figure A.8 shows the Delete User Accounts Tab.

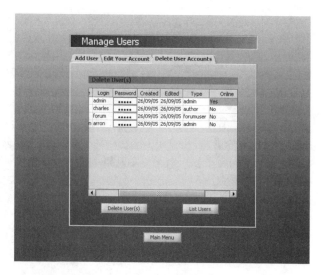

FIGURE A.8   Kucing CMS Delete Users Account Tab.

If a user is currently logged in then you will not be able to delete their account. This is a safety feature to ensure that content is not lost from the system. In order to delete a user account, you will most likely have to scroll the table view so that the rightmost column is shown (not visible in Figure A.8). This rightmost column contains check boxes which can be selected. Any user accounts that are selected will be deleted when you press the Delete User(s) button. As always, you can navigate back to the main menu from here by pressing the Main Menu button.

Managing the Look and Feel

Looking back on Figure A.5, the Manage LnF button offers us the feature of being able to change the look-and-feel of the entire CMS Web site instantly. Pressing this button takes us to the Manage Look and Feel form where we can view all of the installed look-and-feels that are currently installed on the server. Figure A.9 offers us a view of this form.

In order to view the names and descriptions of the look-and-feels, press the Get List button which will list all of the look-and-feels found on the server. In Figure A.9, the list on the left side of the form displays the look-and-feels installed and displays the current theme as a selected item. This is the look-and-feel that is presently being used by the server. On the right side of the form information is displayed about the selected look-and-feels as well as the look-and-feel that is applied to the CMS server (titled Current LnF). To change the CMS look-and-feel simply select a different list item in the LnF List and then press the Apply LnF button. A dialog box will be displayed after making this selection informing you of whether or not the

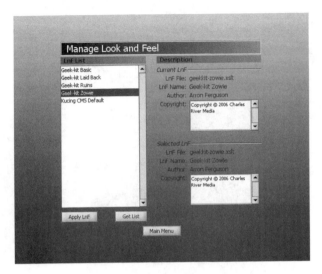

FIGURE A.9 Kucing CMS Manage Look and Feel form.

selection was successful. If your session has timed out you will have to log back in again. If the selection was successful then you can press the reload button in your Web browser to see the changes. You'll notice that the site now looks different but that the information presented has not changed.

Managing Content

The ability to add, update, and delete content within the CMS is the most important part of the admin applet since without this feature the CMS would be difficult to use. This next section presents the user interface for changing each type of content. Looking back on Figure A.5, we're presented with the Manage Content button. Pressing this button will take us to the Manage Content form which is displayed in Figure A.10.

On the lefthand side of the Manage Content Form there are three components: Site Tasks link items (top left), tree view of the site content (middle left), and Common Tasks link items (bottom left). Having just logged in, none of these options will be enabled except for the Get Site Content link item. This is because the admin applet has not downloaded content from the server. Click on the Get Site Content link item at the top left of the form. Depending on the speed of your connection to the server as well as the speed of your computer this operation may take a second or two in order to fulfill. Once the content from the server has been downloaded to the client, the Site Tasks link items, tree view of the site content, and Common Tasks link items will become enabled. Figure A.11 displays the update. You can now start creating content.

FIGURE A.10   Kucing CMS Manage Content form.

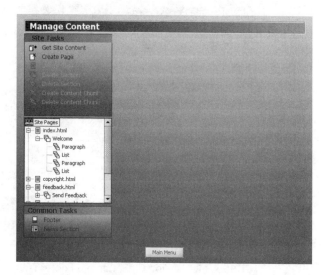

FIGURE A.11   Kucing CMS Manage Content form updated.

The left side of the screen contains components that can be selected by clicking on them. Each time you make a selection of one of these components a context sensitive subform will be displayed. For example, if you click the Footer link item in the Common Tasks component you will be presented with a subform in the bottom right of the main form that allows you to edit the footer. Selecting items in the tree view (left middle) will display subforms based on the type of component you selected.

Managing Footer Content

By clicking on the Footer link item in the Common Tasks (bottom left) component, the subform for editing the footer content is displayed in the right bottom of the Manage Content Form. This is shown in Figure A.12. In this subform you can list up to four different pages that will be linked to in each page that you create in the CMS. The four different pages are: the copyright page (for displaying copyright information), the contact page (for displaying contact information about you or your organization), the feedback page (if you wish to provide contacts that will accept feedback), and a privacy policy page (that displays a disclaimer informing users that the information collected will remain private. You do not have to include any of these if you do not wish to.

Each of these choices that you can make allow you to link to a page that already exists within your CMS. If you create a new CMS version from a template that you create (discussed earlier) then you should create these pages first in order for them to show up on the right column as combo box selections.

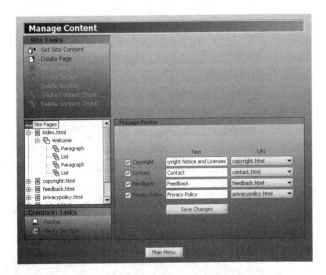

FIGURE A.12 Kucing CMS Manage Footer subform.

The Text fields allow you to provide the text that will show up in the footer and that link to a page. The combo box column on the right allows you to choose from a list of pages that already exist within the CMS. You can choose the page you wish without having to type in its name (thereby avoiding typing mistakes). If you do not want to have a link to any one of these pages simply remove the check from the check box in that row. This will remove any reference to that page in the footer (this will only remove the link to the page, not the page itself). When you are satisfied with your changes, press the Save Changes button to update the server with your content changes.

Managing News Section Content

By clicking on the News Section link item in the Common Tasks (bottom left) component, the subform for editing the news section is displayed. Figure A.13 shows the subform for editing the news section. News items provide a way to inform visitors to your site about new topics. You can (and should choose) a news section title (e.g., "News Flashes" or "What's New!"). You can add new news items by typing in a quick description in text using the News Item Text field. If you wish to add a URL to this news item, type the URL in the News Item URL field and the hyperlink text for that URL in the News Item URL text field. If you wish to create a new news item, you can press the Add News Item button which will add a new news item to the news item list (displayed to the right in this subform). Doing so will automatically insert the current date into the news item so you don't have to worry about typing in the date. News items will be displayed in ascending order in the CMS pages so that most recent news items are displayed to the user first.

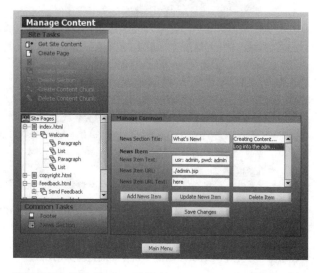

FIGURE A.13   Kucing CMS Manage News Section subform.

If you wish to edit a news item, simply select it in the news item list on the right. Doing so will display the contents of that news item in the News Item Text field, the News Item URL field, and the News Item URL Text field. After making the update to that news item, press the Update News Item button. If you wish to delete a news item, select the news item you wish to delete in the news item list (on the right) and press the Delete Item button. Doing so will delete the news item. When you are satisfied with your changes, press the Save Changes button to update the server with your content changes.

Managing Page Content

You can create pages as well as edit existing pages. Page editing subforms, like the rest of the types we'll be looking at, are context sensitive. That is, you need to make certain selections first before you can see the page editing subform. In order to view a page editing subform, click a page within the tree view. Pages look like elongated rectangles with horizontal lines through them. In Figure A.14 the tree view displays a page called index.html. Clicking on page nodes in the tree view will make visible the page editing subform. Figure A.14 shows this editor (top right of the Manage Content form).

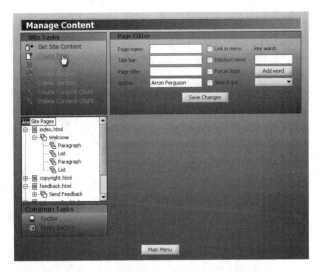

FIGURE A.14   Kucing CMS Manage Page subform.

There are several options that we can select with pages:

■ The page name, which is the name of the actual file placed in the filesystem of the CMS. If you provide a name with spaces in it, Kucing CMS will place underscores where the spaces are so that the page displays correctly.
■ The title bar (what is displayed in the Web browsers title bar).
■ The page title (displayed in the banner of the page).

■ The author (automatically inserted in the author text field based on the account first name and last name we logged in as).

■ Whether the page is in the menu that is displayed at the top of the page. You will want to leave this check box blank for when you create pages that will be linked in the footer.

■ Whether the page displays the news section. Typically you will only want the news section to be displayed on the main page of the site.

■ The forum login. This is a little form that will allow users to log into the forum. Usually you will want this link to be available at any point in your site.

■ A link to the search page. Usually you will want users to have access to the search page from any of the pages within the CMS.

■ Key words (metadata for the pages). Not necessarily required but helpful for search engines that may encounter your CMS site.

In order to edit an existing page, simply select that page in the tree view and the page editor subform will be displayed. If you want to delete that page, you can click on the Delete Page link item in the Site Tasks component (top left). You will be presented with a dialog asking you if you wish to continue with this operation since it will not be reversible. In order to create a new page, click on the Create Page link item found in the Site Tasks component (top left). Doing so will present you with the page editing subform. When you are satisfied with your changes, press the Save Changes button to update the server with your content changes.

Managing Section Content

The section editor subform is another context sensitive component. In order to bring it up you must be within the context of a page. That is, you must select a page in order to add, edit, or delete sections. The Site Tasks component will offer you the section editing options as you select the sections within the tree view component (left middle). Figure A.15 offers us a look at the section editing subform.

Sections are not directly visible. They are only containers of subchunks of content. The only content that we can put in a section is the author name and the section title. In order to edit an existing section, simply select that section in the tree view and the section editor subform will be displayed. If you want to delete that section, you can click on the Delete Section link item in the Site Tasks component (top left). You will be presented with a dialog asking you if you wish to continue with this operation since it will not be reversible. In order to create a new section, click on the Create Section link item found in the Site Tasks component (top left). Doing so will present you with the section editing subform. When you are satisfied with your changes, press the Save Changes button to update the server with your content changes.

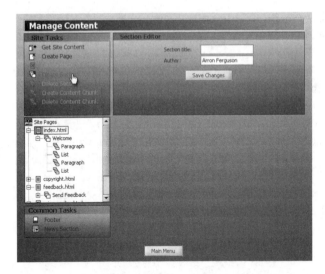

FIGURE A.15   Kucing CMS Manage Content subform.

Managing Subchunk Content

In order to make use of the limited amount of screen real estate (and to simplify the user interface), an intermediate component is displayed when you click a section in the tree view component and select the Create Content Chunk link item. In the top right of the Manage Content form a subform called the Content Chunk Selector is displayed with a list in it. Figure A.16 shows this subform.

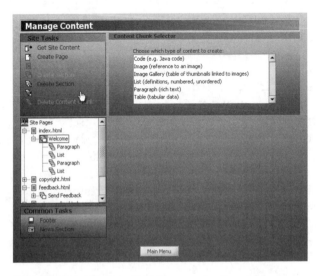

FIGURE A.16   Kucing CMS Manage Section subform.

The Content Chunk Selector list offers the types of content chunks that we can place within a section. In Figure A.16, we see the types Code, Image, Image Gallery, List, Paragraph, and Table. Selecting any one of these will bring up the appropriate editor subform for that type.

Managing Code Content

Code content is for when you wish to display snippets of code. This type of content, when rendered in XHTML, will keep its whitespace and therefore it's indenting. This is useful for when examples of how to write program code are needed. Figure A.17 shows the code subform editor. The code editing form is a non-styled text editor. You can type as much as you want in this field. As you add more, scroll bars will be displayed to you so that you can see what you are typing.

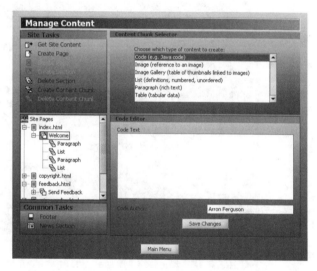

FIGURE A.17   Kucing CMS Manage Code subform.

In order to edit an existing code chunk, simply select that code chunk in the tree view and the code chunk editor subform will be displayed. If you want to delete that code chunk, you can click on the Delete Content Chunk link item in the Site Tasks component (top left). You will be presented with a dialog asking you if you wish to continue with this operation since it will not be reversible. In order to create a new code chunk, click on the Create Content Chunk link item found in the Site Tasks component (top left). Doing so will present you with the code chunk editing subform. When you are satisfied with your changes, press the Save Changes button to update the server with your content changes.

Managing Image Content

The image editor may be a bit of a misnomer since the editor subform doesn't actually allow you to edit images. What it does allow you to do is link to images that are already on the server. Figure A.18 displays this editor subform. As always, the author name is automatically populated with the name that you gave (or were given) for your account. The Image URL text field allows you to place the name of the file you wish to link to. You can type the name in manually or if you press the Get Image List button, you will be presented with a list of images that are available on the server. When you click on one of the image names (in the image list above the Get Image List button), the name of the image you selected is automatically inserted into the Image URL text field.

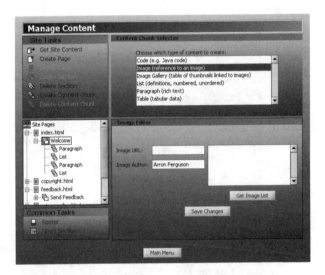

FIGURE A.18   Kucing CMS Manage Image subform.

In order to edit an existing image chunk, simply select that image chunk in the tree view and the image chunk editor subform will be displayed. If you want to delete that image chunk, you can click on the Delete Content Chunk link item in the Site Tasks component (top left). You will be presented with a dialog asking you if you wish to continue with this operation since it will not be reversible. In order to create a new image chunk, click on the Create Content Chunk link item found in the Site Tasks component (top left). Doing so will present you with the image chunk editing subform. When you are satisfied with your changes, press the Save Changes button to update the server with your content changes.

Managing Image Gallery Content

The image gallery editor allows for the creation of tables of images within a page. This editor makes the process of creating galleries incredibly easy. Figure A.19 shows us the image gallery editor subform.

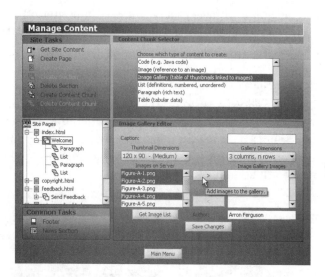

FIGURE A.19   Kucing CMS Manage Image Gallery subform.

An image gallery can have a caption by filling out the caption text field (right). As well you can choose the size of the thumbnails that will display in the image gallery. When a thumbnail is clicked on, a new window will be opened displaying the full-sized image. Kucing CMS actually generates the thumbnail images for you so you don't have to worry about this at all. You can also make several choices as to how many columns within your image gallery you wish to have. Kucing CMS limits your selection to two, three, or four columns since too many columns may not render properly in a page.

You'll notice in A.19 there are two lists. The one on the left contains images that are listed from the server. Simply click on the Get Image List button below this list to see a list of all images on the server. There are two arrow keys that allow you to move image names from one list to another. But selecting images in the lists you can select the images (and in the order you wish them to be in your gallery) by selecting images in the list and then pressing the arrow keys to move them. In order to edit an existing image gallery chunk, simply select that image gallery chunk in the tree view and the image gallery chunk editor subform will be displayed.

If you want to delete that image gallery chunk, you can click on the Delete Content Chunk link item in the Site Tasks component (top left). You will be presented with a dialog asking you if you wish to continue with this operation since it will not be reversible. In order to create a new image gallery chunk, click on the Create Content Chunk link item found in the Site Tasks component (top left). Doing so will present you with the image gallery chunk editing subform. When you are satisfied with your changes, press the Save Changes button to update the server with your content changes.

Managing List Content

The list editor allows you to create three different types of lists: unordered (also known as bulleted lists), ordered lists, and definitions lists. Each list can have a heading (or not) and each list item can have just a definition or a term and a definition. Figure A.20 shows the list editor subform. The combo box currently shows that the list will be a bulleted list.

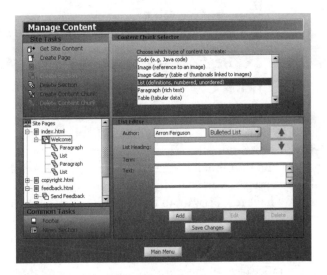

FIGURE A.20 Kucing CMS Manage List subform.

In order to add list items you simply type the term (if you choose to) and the definition. The definition is mandatory. You type these in the Term text field and the Text text field respectively. Once you've typed a term, press the Add button, which will add the list item to the temporary list within the admin applet (list at the bottom of the List editor subform). Selecting a list item in the temporary list in this subform brings up the term and the text for the list item selected as which point you can edit the list item. You can select a list item and delete it as well. You can also select a list item and move it up or down by pressing the arrow buttons within this form.

In order to edit an existing list chunk, simply select that list chunk in the tree view and the list chunk editor subform will be displayed. If you want to delete that list chunk, you can click on the Delete Content Chunk link item in the Site Tasks component (top left). You will be presented with a dialog asking you if you wish to continue with this operation since it will not be reversible. In order to create a new list chunk, click on the Create Content Chunk link item found in the Site Tasks component (top left). Doing so will present you with the list chunk editing subform. When you are satisfied with your changes, press the Save Changes button to update the server with your content changes.

Managing Paragraph Content

The paragraph editor is a rich text editor and will probably be the editor that you use the most since most content is usually in paragraph form. The editor itself offers undo and redo using the quick key CTRL-Z and CTRL-Y key combinations found in most text editors and word processors. A paragraph can contain plain text, bold text, italicized text, hyperlinks, and hints (which are translated into acronym elements in XHTML). Figure A.21 shows the paragraph editor.

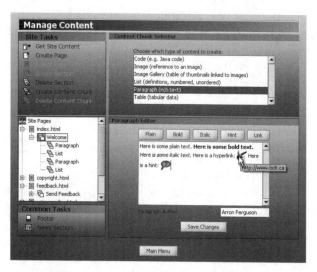

FIGURE A.21 Kucing CMS Manage Paragraph subform.

As you type text into the text area of this subform, you can choose to select text and change the style of the text by either pressing one of the buttons or using keyboard quick keys. For example, to make text bold, select the text and either press the

Bold button or press the quick keys CTRL-B. If you wish to make text italic, select the text and either press the Italic button or press the quick keys CTRL-I. If you wish to make the text plain, select the text and either press the Plain button or press the CTRL-P quick keys.

The editor ensures that users are not exposed to XML tags or elements and so in order to insert a hyperlink you can simply press the Link button which will insert a graphic within the text at the position where the caret sits. The graphic looks like a hand. To edit the hyperlink you must single click on the hand graphic. Doing so will bring up a dialog box which allows you to type both the URL and the text that is linked to the URL. If you wish to place a hint in the paragraph text, press the Hint button which will insert a graphic within the text at the position where the caret sits. If you wish to edit the hint you must single click on the hand graphic. Doing so will bring up a dialog box which allows you to type both the text and the description of what that text represents (e.g., an acronym and the words that make up the acronym).

In order to edit an existing paragraph chunk, simply select that paragraph chunk in the tree view and the paragraph chunk editor subform will be displayed. If you want to delete that paragraph chunk, you can click on the Delete Content Chunk link item in the Site Tasks component (top left). You will be presented with a dialog asking you if you wish to continue with this operation since it will not be reversible. In order to create a new paragraph chunk, click on the Create Content Chunk link item found in the Site Tasks component (top left). Doing so will present you with the paragraph chunk editing subform. When you are satisfied with your changes, press the Save Changes button to update the server with your content changes.

Managing Table Content

The table editor allows you to create tables easily without exposing you to messy XML tags or elements. The table editor offers a few choices such as a caption (like the image gallery), how many columns you wish to have (between two and size columns to ensure all content fits on the page) and as many rows as you wish (in theory). Figure A.22 shows the table editor subform.

In order to add rows simply click the up and down arrows within the Rows spinner. Use the combo box to choose your column count and enter in a caption. When you wish to edit cells in the table simply double-click on any cell. You can either type text in this cell or you can press the HyperLink button, which will bring up a dialog that allows you to enter a hyperlink. This is quite useful since you can place a hyperlink or plain text within a cell. If you create a hyperlink, the hyperlink text will be displayed once you finish editing the cell. Double clicking on the cell will display the actual XHTML code that makes up the hyperlink.

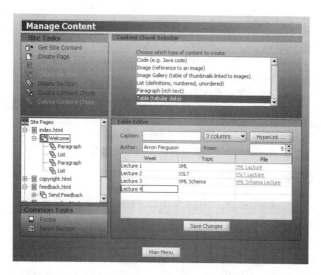

FIGURE A.22   Kucing CMS Manage Table subform.

In order to edit an existing table chunk, simply select that table chunk in the tree view and the table chunk editor subform will be displayed. If you want to delete that table chunk, you can click on the Delete Content Chunk link item in the Site Tasks component (top left). You will be presented with a dialog asking you if you wish to continue with this operation since it will not be reversible. In order to create a new table chunk, click on the Create Content Chunk link item found in the Site Tasks component (top left). Doing so will present you with the table chunk editing subform. When you are satisfied with your changes, press the Save Changes button to update the server with your content changes.

FURTHER WORK

Out of the box, Kucing CMS 1.0 is a fully functional content management system which can be used as a container for content for small- to medium-sized Web sites. There are, however, areas of improvement that you can add with your version of Kucing CMS 1.0 in order to make it a more powerful solution.

GUI Support For Many-to-Many Relationships

Currently the admin applet that comes with Kucing CMS 1.0 only supports a basic representation of the content model. For example, the tree view within the applet only shows a simple representation of the content where one page contains many sections and each section contains many content chunks. Recall that we designed back in Chapter 2, and in Chapter 6 we implemented a data model that allowed for many-to-many relationships between pages and sections and sections and content chunks. Currently the admin applet's GUI doesn't support this type of advanced *mode of editing* the content. This functionality could be added by creating an advanced mode form where the user could choose from existing pages, sections, or content chunks and draw references to them creating and using new associative nodes.

Shuffling of Content Chunks

Currently the GUI does not support the rearranging of content types such as sections and content chunks such as paragraphs, images, image galleries, tables, lists, and code chunks. Although this feature is not mandatory, it does mean that rearranging would require deleting elements created and then recreating them later on. Since the editing fields and areas allow for copy and paste, it is not impossible to do this. However, this approach is clumsy and isn't very forgiving. This support could be added either by offering up and down buttons that allow a selected component or group of selected components to be rearranged within the tree. However, the most convenient solution would be to offer the user drag-and-drop abilities using Java's drag-and-drop API. This would allow the user, for example, to drag a paragraph to another section or to drag a section to another page or to a different spot within the same page. This would give the user the most benefit.

Deletion of Certain Types of Content

At present time the Kucing CMS 1.0 admin applet does not allow key words within a page to be deleted nor does it allow news items to be deleted. Although this isn't entirely unworkable (assuming you know the XML format), it is an inconvenience. It would be more of a convenience if the user could delete key words from pages and be able to delete news items from the news section.

The admin applet also offers no support of deleting forum posts from the forum. This means that all forum posts will exist unless they are deleted on the server by going into the XML files (specifically the XXX.xml file). Editing the XML files requires shutting down the server so that the files can be updated. Without shutting down, the Kucing CMS 1.0 Web application still contains in-memory copies of the content.

Improved Memory Management

Kucing CMS 1.0 is quite fast since it loads the entire data model into memory. This allows for quick access, quick searches, and quick responses from the server. However, as the memory requirements grow from large amounts of content within the Web application, there will come a point where there exists no more memory to run the application. Further development could add a feature where certain chunks of content (elements or groups of elements) could be unloaded if they have not been accessed recently. This would be mandatory for using Kucing CMS 1.0 in an environment where large amounts of content are being saved, accessed, and modified.

Improved Protocol

The protocol that is used for communication could be improved by changing the string values with characters or byte values. This would improve efficiency. As well, the current protocol does not include delete cascade-like deletes. This means that there will be associative elements that still exist in the data model but that are not relevant since they contain references to elements (e.g., pages) that have been deleted). Although the admin applet will ignore these objects when it downloads them, they still exist within the data stores and over time if there are significant numbers of these associative nodes (i.e., thousands), this may cause the protocol to become sluggish as it will be sending nodes within the content model that are simply not being used.

Uploading of Content

Currently, Kucing CMS does not allow for content to be uploaded from the admin applet. Although this is not impossible, it would require the use of certificates and public key distribution since Java applets are restricted by a security manage and by default do not have access to the filesystem of the computer they are downloaded to. A future improvement could allow the user to upload files such as images and have the Kucing CMS server place the images in the appropriate folders on the server.

Advanced Search Capabilities

Currently, searching is only based on the content types (e.g., paragraph, image, image gallery, table, list, and content chunk). More search capabilities could be included, such as the ability to search based on content that was most recently modified (using the time stamp), content based on author (using the author attribute), or even search forum content as well.

Advanced Look-and-Feel Management

The current look-and-feel manager only allows for the setting of an existing look-and-feel. A useful feature would be to offer the user a set of steps for creating new look-and-feels based on a set of choices in color, layout, fonts, and styles. This would require quite a bit of effort since the admin tool GUI would have to allow for drag-and-drop or in the very least choosing several different options. The server would have to have the ability to create XSLT files dynamically based on choices from the admin applet and the protocol would have to be updated as well.

Looking Forward

Many of these changes are simply refinements rather than large upheavals in design. This makes Kucing CMS 1.0 a great starting place for aspiring content management developers who wish to get a head start in the field of content management. Hopefully you will have as much fun building this as it was to write from the beginning.

Index

ABOUT THE CD!

- ◆ Free open source software applications that are either required or useful in the process of developing the CMS included in this book
- ◆ Introductory JSP listing and XML examples
- ◆ XML documents and DTDs demonstrating data modeling with XML
- ◆ Custom document object model (DOM) examples using Java source code
- ◆ Java source code examples demonstrating servlets, Swing GUI design, custom UI components, and client and server code for dealing with HTTP
- ◆ XHTML and CSS examples
- ◆ XSLT examples that use XHTML and CSS

SYSTEM REQUIREMENTS

In order to run Kucing CMS (the CMS that comes with this book) you will need to have Apache Tomcat 5.5 installed as well as the Java J2SE™ Runtime Environment 5.0. You can use your choice of operating system: Microsoft Windows 2000, Windows 2003 or Windows XP, Macintosh OS X, Linux, or any operating system that will run Apache Tomcat 5.5 and the Java J2SE™ Runtime Environment 5.0. Although specifications for each named operating system will vary, you should typically have 40MB of free main memory (RAM) and 100MB of free disk space. NOTE: You can use any servlet/JSP container that implements the Servlet 2.4 and JavaServer Pages 2.0 specifications. You should ensure that you have configured your Web container to auto-deploy as well as automatically unpack (Web Archives) WAR files. That way if the server is currently running, the Web app will automatically be extracted from its WAR file and run. Otherwise, use the Tomcat software that comes with the CD-ROM.

CREATING CONTENT MANAGEMENT SYSTEMS IN JAV

Arron Ferguson

In today's fast-paced, information–packed world, it's critical for businesses to organize manipulate the data gathered from customers, sales, and product responses, etc. into us information. Content Management Systems (CMS) can do this for your business easily efficiently. There are several commercial systems available, but customizing one for specific needs is usually necessary based on your data. *Creating Content Management Sys in Java* teaches you how to develop an open source CMS from scratch using XML as storage mechanism, XSLT as the presentation layer, and Java and JSPs & Servlets to re the multi-tiered architecture. The book also covers data modeling in XML and the u XSLT as a presentation vehicle for custom XML formats.

Creating Content Management Systems in Java is written for Web and software develo (specifically Java developers) who wish to learn more about the field of content man ment. The book provides a practical, applied perspective with complete demonstra using code to show you how a solution or feature can be implemented. Throughou book you will work through the development of a complete, open source, working C example, beginning with the conceptual ideas of content management. From there y dive into the exploration of practical design solutions, and then move into the final im mentations in each tier of the software that becomes the CMS.

To benefit the most from this book, you should already know the Java programi language and have a basic understanding of the Web. You do not need to know X XSLT, CSS, or XHTML because these topics are covered thoroughly, although a understanding will be helpful. So, if you need to learn more about CMS developn this is the book for you.

HIGHLIGHTS

- ◆ Teaches the architecture, design, code, and creation of a CMS in Java
- ◆ Teaches how to perform data modeling in XML
- ◆ Demonstrates the use of XSLT as a presentation vehicle for custom XML formats and how the separation of content data from presentation data can allow for skinnable Web applications
- ◆ Covers design issues including interface design, multi-tiered architectures, and OOAD
- ◆ Teaches how to create custom document object models, something very rarely covered in other books
- ◆ Applies the topics covered to the sample CMS created throughout the book

ABOUT THE AUTHOR

Arron Ferguson Dipl. T. B. Tech. has been teaching various computer systems technology courses at the British Co Institute of Technology for nine years. Some of the topics he teaches include Java programming, XML techno games programming, multimedia authoring, 2D and 3D animation, and Web design.

| Shelving: | Software Development / Java Programming / Content Management |
| Level: | Beginning to Intermediate |

ISBN 1-58450
U.S. $49.95   Canada

CHARLES RIVER MEDIA
25 Thomson Place
Boston, MA 02210
(617) 757-7900
(617) 757-7969 FAX
crm.info@thomson.com
www.charlesriver.com

ISBN-13: 9781-58450-466-5
ISBN-10: 1-58450-466-8